SENTINELS
OF
HISTORY

SENTINELS
OF
HISTORY

Reflections on Arkansas Properties
on the National Register of Historic Places

Edited by
Mark K. Christ and Cathryn H. Slater

University of Arkansas Press
Fayetteville
2000

04   03   02   01   00   5   4   3   2   1

Designed by Liz Lester

♾ The paper used in this publication meets the minimum requirements of the American National
Standard for Permanence of Paper for Printed Library Materials Z39.48–1984.

LIBRARY OF CONGRESS CATALOGING-IN-PUBLICATION DATA

Sentinels of history : reflections on Arkansas properties on the National Register of Historic Places /
edited by Mark K. Christ amd Cathryn H. Slater.
p.   cm.
Includes index.
ISBN 1-55728-604-3 (alk. paper) —ISBN 1-55728-605-1 (pbk. : alk. paper)
1. Historic sites—Arkansas. 2. Historic preservation—Arkansas. 3. Arkansas, History, Local.
4. Arkansas—Antiquities. I. Christ, Mark K. II. Slater, Cathryn H., 1947–

F412.S46   2000
976.7—dc21   99-054979

ACKNOWLEDGMENTS

The origins of this book lie in a 1997 meeting with the University of Arkansas Press staff at which Beth Motherwell innocently asked what the Arkansas Historic Preservation Program staff planned to do to mark the millennium. What indeed?

Given the agency's mandate to identify, register, and preserve Arkansas's historic resources, it seemed natural to link a millennium project to our most visible and popular program, the National Register of Historic Places. Since the state is also blessed with talented writers, historians, and preservationists, we sought to involve these individuals with our project. Remarkably, only a handful of the men and women we contacted to provide essays—without compensation—declined to participate. We cannot adequately express our gratitude to those who told us "yes."

We attempted to select National Register properties that covered specific historic periods or broad themes in Arkansas history so as to cover everything from mound-building cultures to Fay Jones's architectural designs. A complete listing of every National Register–listed property in the state, as of June 4, 1999, is included as an appendix.

In some cases we tied the essays to specific periods in a building's history. Thus the essay on the Old State House, whose rich history could encompass a book in itself, is tied specifically to the Brooks-Baxter War, and the Rabbit's Foot Lodge, built in 1908, is connected to the 1936–41 period during which it was home to J. William Fulbright. In a few instances we included properties like Thorncrown Chapel and Titan II ICBM Launch Complex 374-7 that were nominated to the National Register by the AHPP's State Review Board but have yet to be listed. We continue to argue their merits with the National Park Service, seeking their official recognition as historically significant properties worthy of preservation.

The authors of the essays in this book were given broad guidelines in pursuing their topics. Each essay was to be linked to a specific property but not necessarily limited to it; the authors could use a property as a starting point to explore a related historic theme. We asked that the essays be at least five hundred to six hundred words but urged the authors to write as much as they needed to tell their stories. The resulting essays are as diverse as the historic places about which they are written.

We decided early on that we wanted to include a photograph of each historic property as it appears today but also wanted to include historic images. These images may not be connected to the property discussed in the essay but instead may be associated with the essay's general historic theme. So while Sequoyah may never have visited Cadron Settlement, he is linked to the Cherokee experience in Arkansas, and we have included his picture with Stan Hoig's essay. Similarly, the photograph of the Van Buren depot reflects the railroad prosperity associated with Carl Moneyhon's essay on the Fordyce depots.

This book would not have been possible without the assistance of many individuals who provided guidance, expertise, and materials. While trying to thank everyone who helped, we may unintentionally omit someone, for which we apologize.

Special thanks are due to Christie McLaren, special projects historian for the AHPP, who scoured photo archives throughout Arkansas and beyond for many of the images included in this book.

Thanks, too, to John Coghlan, Brian King, Kevin Brock, Liz Lester, and, of course, Beth Motherwell of the University of Arkansas Press; Dale Walters and Gail Moore of the Old State House Museum; Donna Perrin and Randy Roberson of the Arkansas State Parks; the staff of the Arkansas Historic Preservation Program, including Melissa Cloonan, Jeff Holder, Amy Bennett, Holly Hope, Ken Grunewald, Tammie Trippe Dillon, Rosemary McFarland, and Randy Jeffery; Muguette Dumont of the Musee de l'Homme, Paris; Swannee Bennett of the Arkansas Territorial Restoration; Bob Besom of the Shiloh Museum of Ozark History; Doug Keller and Bill Corcoran of the Pea Ridge National Military Park; Dr. John Slater; Storm Smith; Jama Best of Toltec Archeological State Park; Suzie Rogers of the Buffalo National River; Eull Dean Clark; the Prairie Grove Battlefield State Park; Don Hamilton; Richard Shrader and Tim Pyatt of the Wilson Library at the University of North Carolina at Chapel Hill; Sandra Taylor Smith; Ellen Shipley; Edith Bata; Andrea E. Cantrell, Michael Dabrishus, Cassandra McCraw, and Georgia Kunze of the Special Collections Division, University of Arkansas Libraries; Jane Ellen Murphy, John Jackson, and Linda Pine of the University of Arkansas at Little Rock Archives and Special Collections; Gail Sears of Hot Springs National Park; Lynn Ewbank of the Arkansas History Commission; Edwina Walls Mann of the University of Arkansas for Medical Sciences Library; Robin Tate of the *Batesville Guard;* Jimmy Bryant of the University of Central Arkansas Archives; John Sykes and Sonny Rhodes of the *Arkansas Democrat-Gazette*; Rosalie Gould; Juliet L. Galonska of the Fort Smith National Historic Site; Charles Blackburn; Jody Morris of the Parkin Archeological State Park; Joseph Hale Sr.; the Eureka Springs Historical Museum; the Quapaw Quarter Association; the Bill Clinton Birthplace Foundation, Inc.; Mrs. Lucille Smith and Dr. John C. Smith; and Ben Swadley and Randy Noah of the Plantation Agriculture Museum.

Mark K. Christ   Cathryn H. Slater
Arkansas Historic Preservation Program

CONTENTS

CONTRIBUTORS

MORRIS S. ARNOLD was born in Texarkana, Texas, in 1941 and was educated at Exeter, Yale, the University of Arkansas, Harvard Law School, and the University of London. He has taught at numerous American law schools, including Indiana, Stanford, Texas, Michigan, and the University of Pennsylvania, where he also served as vice-president of the university and was a professor of law and history. He is former president of the American Society for Legal History and former vice-president of the Selden Society. Judge Arnold has published eight books and numerous articles, mostly on the subject of legal history and the history of colonial Arkansas. The French government recently named him a Chevalier de l'Ordre des Palmes Académiques for his work on eighteenth-century Louisiana. A United States district judge for seven years, he was appointed to the United States Court of Appeals for the Eighth Circuit on May 26, 1992.

KENNETH C. BARNES is associate professor of history at the University of Central Arkansas, where he graduated with a B.A. in 1977. He completed his Ph.D. at Duke University and taught at universities in Illinois and Mississippi before returning to Arkansas in 1992. He is the author of several articles on German religious history and Arkansas history and of two books, *Nazism, Liberalism, and Christianity* (University Press of Kentucky, 1991) and *Who Killed John Clayton?: Political Violence and the Emergence of the New South, 1861–1893* (Duke University Press, 1998).

HELEN BARRY is a former survey historian, special projects historian, and National Register/survey coordinator at the Arkansas Historic Preservation Program. While at AHPP she conducted a statewide survey of Arkansas buildings designed by Fayetteville architect E. Fay Jones and nominated seven of them to the National Register of Historic Places. She is currently pursuing a Ph.D. in art history at New York University and working for the New York Landmarks Commission.

EDWIN C. BEARSS is chief historian emeritus of the National Park Service. He is the author and editor of fourteen books on the Civil War and western expansion and of more than two hundred historical monographs, including *Forrest at Brice's Cross Roads and in North Mississippi in 1864, Hardluck Ironclad: the Sinking and Salvage of the Cairo,* and *The Vicksburg Campaign.*

DIANE D. BLAIR of Fayetteville is a professor emeritus of political science at the University of Arkansas, where she taught for thirty years. She has published two books and numerous articles about Arkansas. From 1971 to 1973 she chaired the Arkansas Governor's Commission on the Status of Women. She is presently serving as chairman of the Corporation for Public Broadcasting.

S. CHARLES BOLTON grew up in Elmira, New York, and graduated from St. Lawrence University. He received a Ph.D. from the University of Wisconsin in 1973. He joined the faculty of the University of Arkansas at Little Rock that same year and has been teaching there ever since. His publications include *Southern Anglicanism: The Church of England in Colonial South Carolina* (1982); *Territorial Ambition: Land and Society in Arkansas, 1800–1840* (1993); and *Arkansas, 1800–1860: Remote and Restless* (1998).

MARIAN BOYD is state coordinator for the Main Street Arkansas downtown revitalization program, a position she has held since 1994. She was assistant state coordinator from 1988 to 1994. Prior to working with Main Street, Boyd was a partner in a marketing and advertising agency and was communications director for Diversified Financial Services. She holds a degree in marketing from the University of Central Arkansas. The daughter of the late Frank and Alberta Boyd, she lived in Harrison until 1972.

MARK K. CHRIST is community outreach director for the Arkansas Historic Preservation Program, an agency of the Department of Arkansas Heritage, where he works with the agency's National Register/Survey, Education, Special Projects, and Public Information programs. He joined the AHPP in 1990 after eight years as a professional journalist. Christ lives with his wife, Kim, and daughters, Emily and Cassie, in Little Rock. He served as editor of *Rugged and Sublime: The Civil War in Arkansas,* published by the University of Arkansas Press in 1994.

NEIL COMPTON was a lifelong resident of northwest Arkansas, a retired physician, a Navy veteran, and a nationally recognized conservationist and author. As a founder and officer of the Ozark Society Dr. Compton was instrumental in blocking projects to dam the Buffalo River and in seeing the Buffalo designated a National River. The recipient of numerous awards for his crusading conservation efforts, he was also the author of *The High Ozarks: A Vision of Eden* (1982), and *The Battle for the Buffalo River* (1992), among other books. Dr. Compton died in February 1999.

RICHARD W. DAVIES is the executive director of the Arkansas Department of Parks and Tourism, having served twenty-five years with the Department, including fourteen years as director of state parks. His grandfather was the project superintendent for the building of Petit Jean State Park and Mather Lodge and in 1937 was appointed to be the first director of state parks. His father, Samuel Ladd Davies, worked as a young engineer on the Petit Jean project and went on to become the director of the Arkansas Department of Pollution Control and Ecology. He still lives on Petit Jean Mountain. Richard Davies lives in North Little Rock with his wife, Betsy. They have two daughters, Katie and Sarah.

HESTER DAVIS is the former state archeologist with the Arkansas Archeological Survey and a professor of anthropology at the University of Arkansas. She was with the Survey since it was created by the Arkansas legislature in 1967 until her retirement in 1999. Prior to that she was assistant director of the University of Arkansas Museum. She has two M.A. degrees, one from Haverford College and one from the University of North Carolina, Chapel Hill, and received an honorary doctorate from Lyon College.

THOMAS A. DEBLACK is an assistant professor of history at Arkansas Tech University in Russellville. A 1969 graduate of Nashville (Arkansas) High School, he received a B.A. from Southern Methodist University in Dallas, Texas (1973), an M.S.E. from Ouachita Baptist University (1979), and a Ph.D. from the University of Arkansas (1995). DeBlack taught in the public schools in Arkansas for twelve years. He is a member of Phi Eta Sigma and Phi Beta Kappa academic honorary fraternities. He received the J. Hillman Yowell Award for Excellence in Teaching while a graduate teaching assistant at the University of Arkansas. Dr. DeBlack is a member of the Southern Historical Association, the Society of Civil War Historians, and the Arkansas Association of College History Teachers, and he sits on the Board of Trustees of the Arkansas Historical Association. He is a contributor to *Rugged and Sublime: The Civil War in Arkansas* (University of Arkansas

Press, 1994) and co-editor of *Civil Obedience: An Oral History of School Desegregation in Fayetteville, Arkansas, 1954–1965* (University of Arkansas Press, 1994). In August 1997 his article on "Plantation Arkansas" was published in the Sunday feature section of the *Arkansas Democrat-Gazette*. Dr. DeBlack lives in Conway with his wife, Susan.

MICHAEL DOUGAN is professor of history at Arkansas State University and the author or editor of several books on Arkansas history, including *Confederate Arkansas: The People and Policies of a Frontier State in Wartime* (1976) and *Arkansas Odyssey: The Saga of Arkansas from Prehistoric Times to Present* (1995).

ELIZABETH ECKFORD is the only one of the Little Rock Nine still living in Arkansas. She continues to foster her interest in education by sharing her story with school groups. A probation officer now, she has been a waitress, bank clerk, teacher and military journalist. Though she has been honored many times, the Army Good Conduct Medal is special to her. (It was "so-o-o hard being good," she says.) Ms. Eckford has received the Spingarn Medal, the NAACP's highest award, and has been honored by the ACLU. She received the congressional Gold Medal in November 1999.

WILLARD B. GATEWOOD, Alumni Distinguished Professor of History (Emeritus) at the University of Arkansas at Fayetteville, is the author or editor of a dozen books, including *The Governors of Arkansas; The Arkansas Delta;* and *Aristocrats of Color: The Black Elite, 1880–1920*. A former president of the Southern Historical Association, he was the co-founder of the University of Arkansas Press and is currently editor of the Press's Black Community Studies Series.

DONALD HARINGTON is a professor of art history at the University of Arkansas at Fayetteville and a novelist. A native of Little Rock who spent his childhood summers at his grandmother's house in the remote Ozarks, he has written nine novels about the mythical Ozark village of Stay More. The most recent, published in the autumn of 1998 by Counterpoint, is *When Angels Rest*. He is at work on a book about Arkansas painter Carroll Cloar. His forthcoming novel, *Falling Off the Mountain*, is about gubernatorial politics in Arkansas.

STAN HOIG is professor emeritus at the University of Central Oklahoma. He is the author of numerous books on Western history and Native American subjects, including *Sequoyah: The Cherokee Genius, Night of the Cruel Moon: Cherokee Removal and the Trail of Tears,* and *The Cherokees and Their Chiefs*.

DONALD HOLLEY is a professor of history at the University of Arkansas at Monticello. He holds a Ph.D. in American history from Louisiana State University and is the author of *Uncle Sam's Farmers: The New Deal Communities in the Lower Mississippi Valley* (1975) and *The Second Great Emancipation: The Mechanical Cotton Picker, Black Migration, and How They Shaped the Modern South* (University of Arkansas Press, 2000).

ROGER G. KENNEDY is a former director of the National Park Service and director emeritus of the National Museum of American History at the Smithsonian Institution. He is the author of nine books, including *Hidden Cities*, a volume on American archeology, and is the general editor of the thirteen-volume *Smithsonian Guide to Historic America*. He has created several television documentaries, served as White House correspondent for NBC, and has been a lawyer, banker, and investment adviser.

RUSTY LOGAN worked as a historian for the special projects division of the Arkansas Historic Preservation Program from 1995 to 1997 and participated in the project to nominate the state's Civil War commemorative sculpture to the National Register of Historic Places. Logan received a B.A. in American history from Connecticut College and an M.A. in American studies from New York University.

THOMAS F. "MACK" McLARTY III was born in Hope, Arkansas, in 1946 and has been a lifelong friend of President Clinton. After graduating summa cum laude from the University of Arkansas in 1969, he was elected to the state legislature at age twenty-three and served as chairman of the state Democratic party from 1974 to 1976. In 1983 he became chairman and chief executive officer of Arkla, Inc., a Fortune 500 company. He served as a member of the Saint Louis Federal Reserve Board from 1989 to 1992 and was appointed to the National Petroleum Council by President George Bush. McLarty served as chief of staff to President Clinton and as Special Envoy to the Americas. McLarty and his wife, Donna, have two sons and divide their time between their homes in Washington and Arkansas.

CARL MONEYHON is a professor of history at the University of Arkansas at Little Rock. He has written extensively about Arkansas history during the middle of the nineteenth century. His most recent book is *Arkansas in the New South,* published by the University of Arkansas Press.

DON MONTGOMERY has been a historian with Arkansas State Parks for more than twenty years. He started his career at Old Washington Historic State Park, where he remained for twelve years before transferring to Prairie Grove Battlefield State Park in 1990. He graduated from the University of Arkansas

with an M.A. in history and has won several awards for his articles about Arkansas history. He is an active member of several organizations, including the Prairie Grove Lions Club, the Arkansas Historical Association, the Civil War Trust, the Association for the Preservation of Civil War Sites, and the Civil War Roundtable of Northwest Arkansas, and is an elder in the First Presbyterian Church of Prairie Grove.

JAMES MORGAN is the author, most recently, of *The Distance to the Moon,* a book about the automobile and American restlessness that was published in 1999 by Riverhead. His other books include *If These Walls Had Ears* (Warner, 1996) and the critically-acclaimed *Leading With My Heart* (Simon & Schuster, 1994), a collaboration with Virginia Kelley.

LYNN MORROW has been director of the Missouri Local Records Preservation Program, Missouri State Archives, Office of the Missouri Secretary of State, since its beginning in 1990. He formerly served as research historian at the Center for Ozarks Studies, Southwest Missouri State University, Springfield, from 1977 to 1982 and managed his own historic preservation consulting firm, Kalen and Morrow, from 1983 to 1990. He has published widely in the *Missouri Historical Review, Gateway Heritage,* and *Missouri Folklore Journal.* He co-edited *A Connecticut Yankee in the Frontier Ozarks: The Writings of Theodore Pease Russell* (University of Missouri Press, 1988) and *The White River Chronicles of S. C. Turnbo: Man and Wildlife on the Ozarks Frontier* (University of Arkansas Press, 1994) and is co-author of *Shepherd of the Hills Country: Tourism Transforms the Ozarks, 1880s–1930s* (University of Arkansas Press, 1999).

CYNTHIA DEHAVEN PITCOCK is assistant professor in the division of medical humanities at the University of Arkansas for Medical Sciences, where she teaches history of medicine. She received a B.A. from Washington University; an M.A. from Vanderbilt University, where she studied on a Ford Foundation grant; and a Ph.D. in history from the University of Memphis. She has contributed papers to many historical and health-care journals, including the *American Journal of Obstetrics and Gynecology* and the *Journal of the History of Medicine and Allied Sciences*. She has made numerous presentations here and abroad on the history of medicine and is on the board of governors of the American Osler Society.

DAVID PRYOR comes by his love of his state and public service naturally. His father and grandfather both served as sheriffs of Ouachita County, and his mother was the first woman to run for public office in Arkansas after women gained the vote. In addition to being a newspaper publisher and an attorney, he has held many elected offices: Arkansas state representative, United States congressman, Arkansas governor, and United States senator. He served in the U.S. Senate from 1979 until his retirement in 1996. Since his retirement he has become a popular lecturer at Arkansas colleges and is presently a Resident Fellow at the Institute of Politics at Harvard University's John F. Kennedy School of Government. Pryor is married to the former Barbara Lundsford of Fayetteville. They have three sons—David Hampton Pryor Jr., Mark Pryor (Arkansas's present attorney general), and Scott Pryor—and three grandchildren.

BOBBY ROBERTS grew up in Helena, Arkansas, and graduated from Central High School there in 1962. He holds a master's degree in library science from the University of Oklahoma and a Ph.D. in American history from the University of Arkansas. He is currently director of the Central Arkansas Library System in Little Rock and an adjunct pro-

fessor of history at the University of Arkansas at Little Rock. His specialty is military history. He has a particular interest in the Civil War and has co-authored four books on that subject. In 1994 President Clinton appointed him to the National Commission on Libraries and Information Science, which advises the President and Congress on federal information policy. In 1997 *Library Journal* selected Roberts as Librarian of the Year.

CHARLOTTE TILLAR SCHEXNAYDER retired in 1998 after a newspaper career spanning fifty-three years in Desha County, eight at *The McGehee Times* and the remainder at *The Dumas Clarion*. A native of Tillar, a town founded by her family, she has served as president of the Arkansas Press Association; Arkansas Press Women; the Society of Professional Journalists, Little Rock Chapter; the National Federation of Press Women; and the National Newspaper Association. Her seven terms in the Arkansas House of Representatives ended because of term limits in 1998, but she continues her advocacy on behalf of southeast Arkansas from an office at the Dumas Chamber of Commerce and sits on the Main Street Arkansas Advisory Board.

GAYLE SEYMOUR, professor of art history, has taught at the University of Central Arkansas since 1986. A specialist in Victorian art, she has researched several Pre-Raphaelite artists, including Simeon Solomon and Edward Burne-Jones. She has lectured and written extensively on Solomon and is organizing the 2005 Solomon Centenary Exhibition, which will open in England and travel to other national and international venues. Her article about her discovery and research of a lost painting by Burne-Jones was published in the *Southeastern College Art Conference Review*. She has been active in efforts to identify and preserve outdoor sculpture and has received grants from the Science and Information

Liaison Office, the Arkansas Arts Council, and the Mid-America Arts Alliance. She received the 1993 UCA Teaching Excellence Award and was named the 1998 Carnegie U.S. Professor of the Year.

NED SHANK is currently the interim executive director of the new Writers' Colony at Dairy Hollow, a nonprofit organization scheduled to open as a retreat for working writers and song-writers in 2000 in the former bed and breakfast and restaurant at Dairy Hollow House. An active historic preservationist since moving to Arkansas in 1977, he writes and has made his home with his wife, writer Crescent Dragonwagon, in Eureka Springs, Arkansas, since 1979.

WILLIAM L. SHEA is professor of history at the University of Arkansas at Monticello and the author, co-author, or editor of numerous books and essays on American military history.

JEAN SIZEMORE grew up in Fort Smith and did her undergraduate work at the University of Arkansas at Fayetteville. Several years later, after becoming interested in art history, she received an M.A. and a Ph.D. in art history from the University of Iowa. She is currently an associate professor of art history at the University of Arkansas at Little Rock, where she has taught for thirteen years. Although art historians customarily deal exclusively with "high-style" architecture, she became enchanted with vernacular architecture through two graduate school projects: a study of Iowa farmhouses and the ways they changed in response to agricultural and cultural conditions and an intensive architectural survey of a remote, mountainous region of North Carolina. She is the author of *Ozark Vernacular Houses: A Study of Rural Homeplaces in the Arkansas Ozarks 1830–1930*, published by the University of Arkansas Press in 1994. She is currently researching buildings related to the plantation culture around Scott, Arkansas.

CATHRYN H. SLATER was born and raised in Forrest City, Arkansas, and received her under-graduate and graduate degrees from the University of Arkansas at Fayetteville. She is the deputy direc-tor for heritage resources at the Department of Arkansas Heritage and has served the state as its his-toric preservation officer since 1988. By Presidential appointment she is chairman of the Advisory Coun-cil on Historic Preservation, an independent federal agency and council whose mission is to advise the President and Congress regarding preservation issues and to oversee a federal review and compliance pro-cess for the nation's cultural resources.

KENNETH STORY is the preservation outreach coordinator for the Arkansas Historic Preservation Program, an agency of the Department of Arkansas Heritage. In this position he is responsible for iden-tifying, developing, and delivering public presenta-tions on a variety of preservation-related topics to both existing and new audiences. Previously he was the AHPP's National Register/Survey coordinator, a position he held after moving to Arkansas in 1988. He holds a B.A. in fine arts from Amherst College, Amherst, Massachusetts and an M.A. in fine arts from Tufts University, Medford, Massachusetts.

DAVID K. STUMPF graduated from the University of Wisconsin, Madison, in 1980 and has worked during the day as a plant biochemist for eighteen years. At night and on weekends he is one of the docent historians at the Titan Missile Museum National Historic Landmark in Arizona. Dr. Stumpf recently completed a comprehensive history of the Titan II ICBM program for the Air Force Legacy Program. The manuscript will be published in May of 2000 by the University of Arkansas Press.

CYRUS A. SUTHERLAND is a native of Rogers, Arkansas. He holds a Master of Architecture degree from Harvard Graduate School of Design. He joined the School of Architecture faculty at the University of Arkansas, Fayetteville, in 1958, teaching design, the history of ancient architecture, and historic preservation before retiring in 1990 as university professor emeritus. He served on the Arkansas State Review Board for Historic Preservation from 1971 to 1997, participating in the nomination of thousands of Arkansas buildings and sites to the National Register of Historic Places. Since 1991 he has served as state advisor to the National Trust for Historic Preservation. He is currently participating with the Society of Architectural Historians in its national publication project, *Buildings of the United States.* Sutherland is writing *Buildings of Arkansas,* with a publication date of 2001.

ELLIOTT WEST, professor of history at the University of Arkansas, Fayetteville, since 1979, is a specialist in the history of the American West and the American frontier. He has written books on saloons of the mining West and on frontier children. His most recent works concern environmental and Native American history: *The Way to the West: Essays on the Central Plains* (1995) and *The Contested Plains: Indians, Goldseekers and the Rush to Colorado* (1998). His books have twice received the Western Heritage Award as well as the Spur Award of the Western Writers of America.

JEANNIE M. WHAYNE received her Ph.D. at the University of California, San Diego, in 1989, then taught for one year at Western Washington University before joining the faculty of the University of Arkansas at Fayetteville. In addition to teaching, she has edited the *Arkansas Historical Quarterly* since 1990. She has published six articles, edited two books, co-edited two others, and published one book on her own. Her books have been recognized with the Virginia C. Ledbetter Prize,

two commendations from the Association for State and Local History, and the Arkansas Library Association's Arkansiana Award. She received fellowships at the Smithsonian Institution and the Carter Woodson Institution. She has served committee appointments in the Agricultural History Society, the Southern Historical Association, and the Southern Association of Women Historians. She currently serves as secretary-treasurer of the Conference of Historical Journals and as chair of the department of history at the University of Arkansas.

NUDIE WILLIAMS is associate professor of history at the University of Arkansas at Fayetteville, where he also serves as chair for African-American studies. He received his B.S. degree from Clark College in Atlanta and his M.A. and Ph.D. from Oklahoma State University, where he studied the experiences of blacks in the American West, a subject he has since written about extensively. He is a past chair of the AHPP's State Review Board and the State Black History Task Force.

RANDALL BENNETT WOODS is Cooper Distinguished Professor of History at the University of Arkansas, Fayetteville. He received his Ph.D. from the University of Texas in 1972 and has taught United States history at the Fayetteville campus ever since. Among his books are *Fulbright: A Biography* (Cambridge, 1995); *A Changing of the Guard: Anglo-American Relations, 1941–1946* (North Carolina, 1990); and *Dawning of the Cold War: America's Quest For Order* (Georgia, 1991). *Fulbright* won the Ferrell and Ledbetter Prizes. Woods has been the recipient of research awards from the National Endowment for the Humanities, the American Council of Learned Societies, and the American Philosophical Society.

WHAT IS THE NATIONAL REGISTER OF HISTORIC PLACES?

The National Register of Historic Places is the country's official list of historically significant sites worthy of preservation. Authorized under the National Historic Preservation Act of 1966, the National Register is part of a national program to coordinate and support public and private efforts to identify, evaluate, and protect our historic and archeological resources. The National Register is administered by the National Park Service under the Secretary of the Interior. Properties listed in the National Register include districts, sites, buildings, structures, and objects that are significant in American history, architecture, archeology, engineering, and culture. These properties contribute to an understanding of the historical and cultural foundations of the United States.

National Register properties are distinguished by having been documented and evaluated according to uniform standards. These standards were developed to recognize the accomplishments of all peoples who have made a contribution to our country's history and heritage. The criteria are designed to guide state and local governments, federal agencies, and others in evaluating potential entries in the National Register. Properties, whether sites, buildings, structures, objects, or districts, must possess integrity of location, design, setting, materials, workmanship, feeling, and association. They must also fit one or more of the following criteria:

A. Association with events that have made a significant contribution to the broad patterns of our history

B. Association with the lives of persons significant in our past

C. Embodiment of the distinctive characteristics of a type, period, or method of construction; representation of the work of a master; possession of high artistic values; or representation of a significant and distinguishable entity whose components may lack individual distinction

D. The potential to yield information important in prehistory or history.

Ordinarily, cemeteries, birthplaces or graves of historical figures, properties owned by religious institutions or used for religious purposes, structures that have been moved from their original locations, reconstructed historic buildings, properties primarily commemorative in nature, and properties that have achieved significance within the past fifty years are not considered eligible for the National Register. However, such properties will qualify if they are integral parts of districts that do meet the criteria or if they fall within the following categories:

A. A religious property deriving primary significance from architectural or artistic distinction or historical importance

B. A building or structure removed from its original location but significant primarily for architectural value, or which is the surviving structure most importantly associated with a historic person or event

C. A birthplace or grave of a historical figure of outstanding importance if there is no other appropriate site or building directly associated with his or her productive life

D. A cemetery that derives its primary significance from graves of persons of transcendent importance, from age, from distinctive design features, or from association with historic events

E. A reconstructed building when accurately executed in a suitable environment and presented in a dignified manner as part of a restoration master plan, and when no other building or structure with the same association has survived

F. A property primarily commemorative in intent if design, age, tradition, or symbolic value has invested it with its own historical significance

G. A property achieving significance within the past 50 years if it is of exceptional importance.

Listing in the National Register provides recognition that a property is of significance to the nation, the state, or the community; consideration in the planning for federal or federally-assisted projects; eligibility for federal tax benefits; and qualification for federal assistance for historic preservation when funds are available. Listing properties in the National Register also often changes the way communities perceive their historic resources and gives credibility to efforts of private citizens and public officials to preserve these resources as living parts of our communities. National Register status does not, however, interfere with a private property owner's right to alter, manage, or dispose of property. Historical commissions, design review committees, or special zoning ordinances are established by state legislation or local ordinances; they are not a part of the National Register program.

In Arkansas the National Register is administered by the Arkansas Historic Preservation Program (AHPP), which is the agency of the Department of Arkansas Heritage that is headed by the State Historic Preservation Officer. A constituent may receive an application from the agency. Upon completion and return to the agency, qualified staff members review the application. If determined eligible, the property is scheduled to be presented to the State Review Board, which must approve all staff nominations before they can be sent to the National Register office in Washington. The board meets three times each year and is composed of eleven governor-appointed professionals from various fields. In the process of nomination, the staff also conducts a site visit to the property to photograph and fill out an architectural resources survey form.

For more information on the National Register of Historic Places, write the AHPP at 1500 Tower Building, 323 Center Street, Little Rock, AR 72201; call the agency at (501) 324-9880, or send an e-mail message to info@dah.state.ar.us.

1. Toltec Mounds, Scott
2. Parkin Mounds, Parkin
3. Arkansas Post, Gillett
4. Louisiana Purchase Initial
   Survey Point Site, Blackton vic.
5. Lakeport Plantation, Lake Village vic.
6. Cadron Settlement site, Conway vic.
7. Pea Ridge and Prairie Grove
8. Poison Spring Battlefield
9. Pillow-Thompson House, Helena
10. Old State House, Little Rock
11. Eureka Springs Historic District
12. Harrison Courthouse Square
    Historic District

13. Boxley Valley Historic District
14. Smith Hospital, Paris
15. Cotter Bridge, Cotter
16. Conway County Library, Morrilton
17. Taborian Hall, Little Rock
18. Star City Confederate Monument
19. Crystal River Tourist Camp, Cave City
20. Ozmer House, Magnolia
21. Wortham Gymnasium, Oak Grove
22. Mather Lodge, Petit Jean State Park
23. Piggott Post Office
24. Rabbit's Foot Lodge, Springdale
25. Fordyce Depots
26. Marcella Church and School

27. Bill Clinton Birthplace, Hope
28. Thorncrown Chapel, Eureka Springs
29. Parnell-Sharpe House, McGehee
30. Wheel Store, Batesville
31. Little Rock Central High School
32. Fort Smith National Historic Site
33. Jacob Wolf House, Norfork
34. Bathhouse Row, Hot Springs
35. Tall Peak Fire Tower, Polk County
36. Washington Historic District
37. Joe T. Robinson House, Little Rock
38. Titan II ICBM Launch Complex 374-7,
    Southside vic
39. Rohwer Relocation Center Cemetery

Mound B at Toltec Archeological State Park. *Photo by Jama Best.*

TOLTEC

Roger G. Kennedy

Toltec Mounds
A.D. 700–1800
Scott vic., Lonoke County
Listed on the National Register of Historic Places on January 12, 1973
Designated a National Historic Landmark on June 2, 1978

" . . . [T]he Toltec Site is better preserved than many of the large sites in the Lower Mississippi Valley. As such, it has potential to yield much information about the intrinsic nature of the cultures of the area. The reasons for the rise of these complex cultural systems, for their dominance, and for the eventual abandonment of the large centers can be examined at the site. In addition, because of Toltec's location at the northern periphery of the large Coles Creek period sites, it has the potential to clarify relationships of Coles Creek culture within the developing Mississippian cultures of the central Mississippi Valley and with the Caddoan cultures to the west."

—*From the National Register nomination*

A ca. 1880 sketch by H. J. Lewis illustrates artifacts taken from Toltec, then known as the Knapp Mounds. *Courtesy of UALR Archives.*

ASSORTING THE B...

On Christmas Day in the year 800 of the Christian calendar, in the church of Saint Peter in Rome, Pope Leo III sought to bring order to a demoralized West by proclaiming as Carolus Magnus, Emperor of the Romans, a Frankish king who could not write his name. All the symbolic devices available to pope and king were deployed to make Charlemagne appear to be the heir to Augustus and thus to place him as emperor in the midst of an empire—which is to say an ordered space—and, through investiture, within an apostolic succession—which is to say an ordered sequence of time, as well.

While Leo and Charles were completing their liturgy across the Atlantic, at the north end of a series of bayous and rivers meandering southward out of Arkansas toward the Gulf, Native Americans were creating their own symbols of order in space and time, constructing the monumental architectural complex that we call "Toltec." This complex,

about fifteen miles southeast of Little Rock, was ordered in space in the following ways:

The builders cupped their complex within a mile-long, D-shaped ridge and ditch. In accordance with a pattern by then at least two thousand years old, they thus emulated by extension the form of the dominant natural feature of the area, the slow curve of the shore of the river. At Toltec this reinforcement and harmonization required a very long structure, sixty feet wide and at least ten feet high. It is still there, though eroded a little.

Within this hundred-acre precinct, Toltec's engineers laid out eighteen or more earthen buildings around two plazas, the larger of which is about the size of the square in front of Saint Peter's in Rome. In the traditionally signal position at the western center of the large plaza was placed the largest of these buildings, Mound A, a flattened cone fifty feet high, rising from a base of 150 by 280 feet. The second largest building, Mound B, is roughly ninety feet square and forty feet high. It was said to have contained many human bones admixed with the bones of animals.

With steadfast industry over several decades, the archeologist who knows Toltec best, Martha Ann Rolingson, has been able to determine how next its builders found means to order their buildings and, with their building, their lives: within their precinct, bounded by its wall and moat, they placed their structures on a grid composed upon a standard measurement of about 157 feet (47.5 meters). This same measurement was used in twenty-six architectural complexes in the lower Mississippi River Valley built within the same period as Toltec; 98 percent of these structures were deployed within 1/10th of 1 percent of the requirements of such a module.

So we have architecture laid out to harmonize a human artifact—a unit of measurement—with a natural terrain. This was done in a traditional way, with mound-bounded plazas within a D-shaped enclosure emulating a dominant physical feature, a riverbank. But Rolingson's other discovery is that this correlation of the ordering capacity of the human brain—quieting chaos by fitting buildings within a mathematical grid—was made at once even more sophisticated and reverent by fitting all such dispositions with a larger order of the universe. For the lines ordering the placement of these structures were drawn along the ground in accordance with the observed passage of the sun, moon, and stars overhead.

What Leo III was doing in Rome was achieved at the same time by the Native Americans at Toltec: ordering architecture and institutions in both space and time. A sacred space the Greeks would have called a *temenos* was created at Toltec, a space that was not arbitrary but carefully harmonized with the riverine environment. The Toltec builders made certain that all the structures within this enclosure conformed to a spatially ordered system of 47.5-meter modules. Then, as if to reiterate their point, they brought all this geometrizing into consonance with the repeated patterns described by the sun and the great stars moving across the heavens in regular, repeated patterns of location and time.

Toltec is a good place to begin an inquiry into the ways in which our species arranges things and tries to bring some order to life.

Effigy pot excavated at
Parkin Archeological
State Park. *Photo by
A. C. Haralson, courtesy
of Arkansas Department
of Parks and Tourism.*

PARKIN ARCHEOLOGICAL SITE, NATIONAL HISTORIC LANDMARK, CROSS COUNTY, ARKANSAS

Hester Davis

Parkin Archeological Site
A.D. 1300–1600
Parkin, Cross County
Listed on the National Register of Historic Places on October 15, 1966
Designated a National Historic Landmark on July 19, 1964

"The prehistoric Parkin site in Arkansas exemplifies the late Mississippian type culture in northeast Arkansas centering around the St. Francis River. It is an extremely 'rich' site in that many burials, usually accompanied by pottery vessels and other artifacts have been located there. There is a well-preserved temple mound overlooking the banks of the river. Although there has been a considerable amount of digging at the site over the past years, this digging has mainly been concentrated in the burial areas and all other material has been left alone. There are large middens, or refuse areas, of considerable depth, which contain a great deal of potential scientific information about these prehistoric inhabitants of Arkansas."

—*From the National Register nomination*

Have you ever held an arrowhead in your hand and wondered about the person who made it? What was life like a thousand years ago on the spot where you are standing? Images of cowboys and Indians go through your mind. Life must have been more tranquil, surely. How can you find out about the people who lost that arrowhead? Or built the mounds in that field nearby? You know so little about your own ancestors. How it is possible to learn of the people who lived in Arkansas five hundred years ago? Three thousand years ago? Archeological sites hold the answers to such questions.

Parkin Archeological State Park is representative of a period in Arkansas's history that bridges the time from prehistory to history. This site was a large town in prehistoric times, and it was recorded by de Soto and his army in the summer of 1541. The day the Spaniards arrived at the Parkin site was a fateful one. The Spaniards wrote about an encounter that brought a particular place into the historic record, but their visit changed the way of life of the Indians who lived in that place forever.

The evidence of this prehistoric town site is contained in about seventeen acres. The obvious physical remains are a large, double-leveled mound on the banks of the Saint Francis River in Cross County and portions of a ditch, which surrounded the site on three sides. Within the ditch the land is higher than the surrounding land, the result of hundreds of years of several thousand people living in the same place. The site is similar to several other contemporary villages scattered up and down the Saint Francis River, but it is especially significant to us today because it is the best preserved of these "protohistoric" sites and therefore can provide us with more information about the people who built the mound and lived in this town. Their lives were similar to those lived in the other contemporary sites, so we can interpret this whole area of the Saint Francis River from about 1400 to 1600 A.D. as a single "culture."

When information from the de Soto chronicles is combined with the information from scientific excavations at the site, it is possible to tell a story of a well-organized, rich life in the Mississippi Delta. The main source of food was cultivated crops, which included corn, beans, and squash, as well as other seed crops such as chenopodium and maygrass, which were used to make flour. Nuts, wild grapes, and berries were gathered in season; the Saint Francis River provided fish, turtles, and shellfish; and the forests surrounding the cleared fields were full of deer, turkey, bear, and the small mammals we find today in the woods. The ditch and a palisade mentioned by de Soto and recorded in archeological excavations indicate the need for protection of the community from enemies. Indeed, the *cacique,* or chief of this town, recruited de Soto and his army to help fight another tribe living along the Mississippi River. This chief, whose name de Soto recorded as Casqui, may have been a religious as well as a political and military leader. The organization of a large number of people (probably several thousand when de Soto arrived) for community projects such as mound-building and maintenance, ditch digging and maintenance, hunting forays, and religious ceremonies required a strong and respected leader.

Within the palisade, houses and probably granaries filled the area, with the chief and his relatives living on the mound. The houses were square, each with walls built of upright wooden poles covered by woven cane mats and a hipped roof covered in thatch. The dead were buried under the floor of a house, and then the house was probably burned, the area cleared, cleaned dirt brought in, and another house built. (In excavations, therefore, layers upon layers of house floors are encountered, each consisting of hard-packed earth covered with ash and charcoal.) The burial ceremony included placing in the grave two or three pottery vessels, tools probably used by the deceased in life, and perhaps food and other items of perishable material, which do not survive. These artifacts as well as others found by archeologists in the general trash of the village indicate a sophisticated technology and an understanding of the manipulation of raw materials available in the environment. Some of the pottery vessels are particularly beautiful artistic creations.

The Parkin site's protective moat *(foreground)* and mound *(background)*. *Courtesy of Arkansas Department of Parks and Tourism.*

What can the remains of this extinct way of life contribute to modern-day Americans? Why should the eroded mounds and broken artifacts be considered so significant as to lead the Arkansas legislature to make this a state park so that it can be protected and interpreted for the public?

The history of the use of the land on which we live is inherently interesting to most people, but there are also lessons to be learned from this site. Even though the people who lived here were not able to counteract the influence of the very foreign "culture" that visited them in 1541, their way of life was probably doomed to failure in any event. The fact that there was another organized tribe considered an enemy not more than thirty to forty miles to the east indicates there must have been competition for land and resources. Populations were large, living in confined spaces, and using great quantities of wood for fuel and housing. More land was needed for field crops as the population grew. As the forests were cut down, forest-dwelling mammals, particularly white-tailed deer, which provided the staple meat of their diet, could only be found further and further away. An increase in carbohydrates in the diet from consumption of large quantities of corn and a corresponding decrease in protein meant a less healthy population. Thousands of people living in a crowded space meant the quick spread of childhood diseases and a reduction in the

life span of the whole population. In fact, these "Mississippian" people, as archeologists call all the Indian groups living in the Mississippi River Valley between about A.D. 1000 and 1600, were so successful in their agriculturally based economy that they were outstripping the ability of the land and resources to provide them with the necessities of life. Does this sound familiar?

We know that after de Soto's army left Arkansas, no other Europeans appeared for 130 years. The Parkin site and many others in northeast Arkansas were abandoned, probably because the population contracted European diseases from which they had no immunity. The swift reduction in their numbers meant a profound change in their way of life. When the French came down the Mississippi from Canada in 1673 and found Quapaw Indians living in four villages near the mouth of the Arkansas River, there were few other remnants of the huge villages and towns that de Soto saw.

The Parkin site represents the story of a fascinating, productive way of life that was changed forever by circumstances over which the

HESTER DAVIS

Indians had some control—overuse of the natural environment—and by circumstances over which they had no control—invasion of a foreign army that left behind disease, took their stored food supply, told them that the Christian God was the only True God, and undermined the power of the *cacique*.

One particular episode recounted in the de Soto chronicles not only provides a clue to the identification of Parkin as the town of the leader Casqui but also gives us a vivid picture of the symbols that Europeans used in their efforts to influence and intimidate the Indians. A huge cross was built by de Soto's men and erected on top of the large mound, indicating, so de Soto must have thought, the power and supremacy of the Christian religion:

> Having arrived at the town, we found that the *caciques* there were accustomed to have, next to the houses where they live, some very high mounds, made by hand, and that others have their houses on the mounds themselves. On the summit of that mound we drove in the cross, and we all went with much devotion,

kneeling to kiss the foot of the cross. The Indians did as they saw us do, neither more nor less. (Hernández de Biedma 1993: 239)

Archeologists have uncovered the base of a large, bald cypress post in the top of the large mound at the Parkin site. Radiocarbon dating of the wood revealed a probable date for this post of between 1515 and 1663, at least within the range of the time of de Soto's visit. De Soto and his army wandered in Arkansas for two years, but at the present time the Parkin site is the only one in the state that can be identified with that first European invasion.

Reference cited:

Hernández de Biedma, L. 1993. "Relation of the Island of Florida by Luys Hernández de Biedma," newly translated and edited by John Worth. In *The De Soto Chronicles: The Expedition of Hernando de Soto to North American in 1539–1543,* edited by L. A. Clayton, V. J. Knight Jr., and E. C. Moore. Volume 1. University of Alabama Press.

A 1930s view of a mound at Parkin. *Courtesy of Arkansas Department of Parks and Tourism.*

Detail of *manteau aux trois villages,* a mid-eighteenth-century Quapaw tribe buffalo robe depicting the village of Arkansas Post. *Courtesy of Musee de L'Homme, Paris.*

ARKANSAS POST

Morris S. Arnold

Arkansas Post
1686–1865
Gillett, Arkansas County
Listed on the National Register of Historic Places on October 15, 1966
Designated a National Historic Landmark on October 9, 1960

"Arkansas Post served for almost two hundred years as a strategic outpost for three nations seeking control of America's interior: France, Spain, and the United States. Established first as a trading post and used successively as a military stronghold, a frontier settlement, and a territorial capital, Arkansas Post was primarily a frontier institution. It developed into an American town that played an important part in the early history of Arkansas."

—*From the National Register nomination*

Arkansas Post was founded in 1686 by Henri de Tonty, an associate of René Cavalier de La Salle, as an Indian trading post (hence its name) and a way station for travelers in the Mississippi region. The Post predated Saint Louis by eighty years, New Orleans by thirty-five, and Mobile by fifteen, and was thus the first European settlement in what would become Jefferson's Louisiana. Its population was always small and, by most accounts, inconsiderable, and the town changed locations three times, owing to floods and alterations in its strategic mission. Nevertheless, except for a short hiatus in the early eighteenth century, it enjoyed a continuous existence until its disappearance as a real town in the middle of the twentieth century. Indeed, there was a post office there until 1941. The tiny establishment survived two colonial wars, two all-out Indian wars, various Indian raids, the American Revolution, and the Civil War, despite its small size and precarious geographical setting.

The Post's first location was on a small, detached piece of Grand Prairie near what is now called Lake Dumond in Arkansas County. This is the first relatively high ground that one encounters traveling up the Arkansas River from the Mississippi and is therefore an obvious place for a settlement. Indeed, Indians had been occupying the site for centuries. In 1721 John Law, the most important financier in France at the time, planned to settle a large number of German colonists at the spot, but only about eighty people, probably all Frenchmen, established themselves there at that time. Six years later only thirty remained behind. In 1749 an English-inspired Chickasaw force razed the settlement at Arkansas Post, and it was relocated upriver about fifteen miles (six miles by land) to a place that the French called *Ecores Rouges* (Red Bluffs), the present site of the Arkansas Post National Memorial. In 1756, because of the French and Indian War, the Post relocated downriver to Desha County. There it remained until 1779, when it was moved (for the last time) back to *Ecores Rouges*.

The population of Arkansas Post never exceeded four hundred people, and in fact, in 1793, more than a century after it was founded, there were fewer than two hundred people resident there or thereabouts. The number of soldiers at the fort was always small. Sometimes there were as few as six, and there were never more than seventy-five permanently stationed there. There were twelve soldiers in the garrison that finally repelled the Chickasaw attack in 1749, and in 1783, in one of the two Revolutionary War engagements west of the Mississippi River, a force of about seventy soldiers and a few Quapaws routed a Chickasaw force of perhaps one hundred men.

The population of the Post during the colonial period was diverse. Among the whites there were representatives of all classes, from the true gentry to laborers and hunters. But the large number of vagabonds and bankrupts who operated in the area gave the Post an unsavory reputation. Most of the blacks (there were never more than sixty or so) were slaves, although there were a few free blacks, and the slaves' work varied considerably. Some, of course, were field hands, but many worked in the houses of the gentry, and others were skilled artisans and even clerks in their masters' mercantile businesses.

Probably the most interesting sociological aspect of life at the Post was the extent to which and the ways in which the French and the Quapaws depended on each other. The Quapaws were interested in acquiring European goods, especially guns for offensive and defensive use against the Chickasaws, and thus trade brought the two peoples together at an early date. The French (and later the Spanish) allied themselves with the Quapaws in their imperial struggle with the English for control of North America, and Europeans and Quapaws frequently fought side by side against various Indian

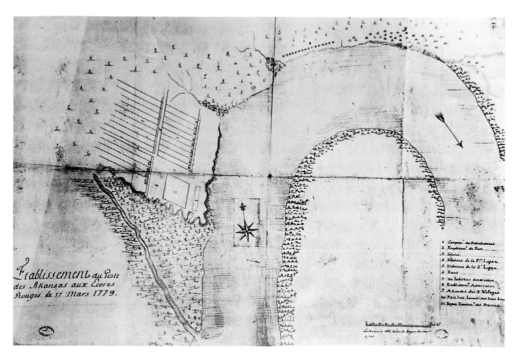

Historic map: Arkansas Post, March 17, 1779. *Courtesy of Archivo General de Indias, Seville/Morris S. Arnold.*

enemies. Since very few French women wanted to venture into the wilds of Arkansas to share the lives of the Frenchmen who lived there, there was considerable intermarriage between the Quapaws and their European visitors. All of this made for a complex skein of interconnections between two very disparate peoples.

With the American takeover in 1804 the Post changed very little at first. In 1819, however, it became the territorial capital, and its prospects were correspondingly lifted. But in 1821 the capital and the *Arkansas Gazette,* the state's first newspaper, were removed to Little Rock. The Post went into a kind of decline, although it did serve as a steamboat landing for many years. In 1863 a large earthen redoubt called Fort Hindman was located there, but it was taken in a furious, two-day battle that featured perhaps thirty thousand Union soldiers and a number of Union gunboats against a Confederate force that numbered about six thousand.

Today, except for a rather impressive nineteenth-century cistern, there is nothing on or near the ground to reveal to the visitor that there was ever a town called Arkansas Post. There is, however, a fine and well-maintained brick building that serves as the visitor's center for the Arkansas Post National Memorial and contains exhibits on the fur trade. It is well worth a visit, as is the town site itself, where a sidewalk and some occasional posted information help orient the visitor to what was once a village.

The story of Arkansas Post is in many ways inspirational and carries lessons that could well help Arkansas weather future social and political storms. There is evidence here of a society that struggled with poverty and a sense of difference from its neighbors and somehow made the best of it through sheer acts of will. There were numerous individuals here who led instructive and productive lives in the face of odds over which most people would never even have hoped to gain an ascendancy. Most relevant of all, perhaps, is the story of the interracial cooperation that sustained the tiny colonial settlement economically and emotionally for upwards of six generations.

MORRIS S. ARNOLD

The state park commemorating the Louisiana Purchase Initial Survey Point Site features this commemorative marker, placed in the swamp in 1926 by the Daughters of the American Revolution. *Arkansas Historic Preservation Program photo*.

LOUISIANA PURCHASE
INITIAL SURVEY POINT SITE

S. Charles Bolton

Louisiana Purchase Initial Survey Point Site
1815
Lee, Phillips, and Monroe Counties
Listed on the National Register of Historic Places on February 23, 1972
Designated a National Historic Landmark on April 19, 1993

"The Louisiana Purchase Marker denotes the point from which the lands acquired through the Louisiana Purchase of 1803 were subsequently surveyed. The land surveys for all or parts of the states of Arkansas, Louisiana, Oklahoma, Missouri, Kansas, Colorado, Nebraska, Iowa, Minnesota, North Dakota, South Dakota, Wyoming and Montana were measured from this point in the middle of an eastern Arkansas swamp. For more than 100 years the site lay forgotten in the marsh until it was rediscovered during a resurvey of the Phillips, Monroe, and Lee county lines in 1921. The

L'Anguille Chapter of the Daughters of the American Revolution of Marianna, Arkansas, erected a granite monument on the survey point on October 27, 1926. The site is currently managed by the Arkansas Department of Parks and Tourism and the Arkansas Natural Heritage Commission as a rare example of an intact headwater swamp."

—From the National Register nomination

The significance of the Louisiana Purchase Initial Survey Point Site grows out of two separate lines of historical development. The first of these is the Louisiana Purchase, which gave the United States all the land drained by rivers flowing east into the Mississippi River. After he had traveled down the Mississippi to its mouth in 1682, René Robert Cavalier, Sieur de La Salle, claimed this area for France and named it for Louis XIV. The French founded modest settlements along the west bank of the Mississippi River, among them Arkansas Post in what is now Arkansas and Sainte Genevieve and Saint Louis in Missouri, but were forced to give up almost all of their holdings in North America after being defeated in the Seven Years War. They ceded Louisiana to Spain in 1762, and the Spanish governed it until 1800, when Napoleon took it back in order to create a new American empire.

Fearful of powerful France controlling the Mississippi River, a waterway by then vital to American commerce, President Thomas Jefferson moved to purchase either New Orleans or some other potential port on the river. Napoleon, now "First Consul for Life," was by this time frustrated by a slave revolt on the island of Santo Domingo and facing the prospect of a new European war. He offered to sell all of Louisiana to the United States for fifteen million dollars, Jefferson happily accepted the deal, and on April 30, 1803, Louisiana became part of the United States. This massive windfall doubled the size of the new nation at a cost of about three cents an acre.

The other essential background for understanding the survey point monument is the history of pub-

lic land policy in the United States, particularly that related to survey and sale. As a result of the Treaty of Paris in 1783 the United States emerged from the War of Independence with a western boundary on the Mississippi River, and it became necessary to develop plans for administering territory belonging to the central government rather than to the states. To that end Congress passed the Land Ordinance of 1785, one of the few major accomplishments under the Articles of Confederation. The policy created by that law drew on the pattern followed in the New England colonies, whereby the surveying of land preceded its settlement, rather than that used in the South, in which settlement usually came before survey. Congress, however, rejected the New England policy of granting town-sized parcels of land to groups of settlers in favor of the southern policy of selling land to individuals who could choose the sites they wanted.

The new American system required that public land be surveyed into townships of thirty-six square miles and subdivided into sections of one square mile, each comprising 640 acres. The ordinance provided that the profits from section 16 in each township be used for public schools and that sections 8, 11, 26, and 29 be reserved for future disposition by Congress. The remaining land would be sold at public auction in amounts of at least one section. Almost immediately Congress made exceptions to the basic policy in order to satisfy special interests. The Ohio Company, made up of private investors, received 1.5 million acres (2,344 sections) along the Ohio River, paying for it in paper money worth about nine cents on the dollar.

S. CHARLES BOLTON

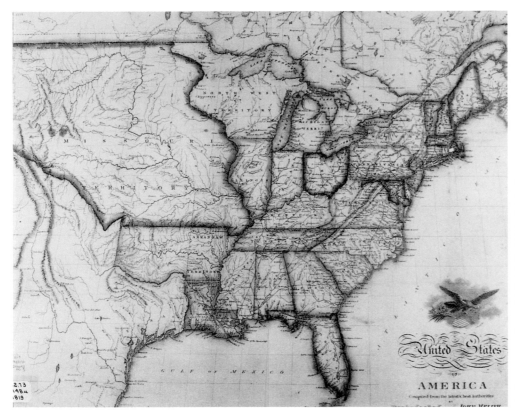

The Louisiana Purchase doubled the size of the young United States, as shown in this map compiled by John Melish and printed in Philadelphia in 1819. *Courtesy of Historical Map Collection, Special Collections Division, University of Arkansas Libraries, Fayetteville.*

Later changes in the basic law, of which there were hundreds by the mid-1830s, raised the price to two dollars per acre in 1796, allowed credit sales from 1800 to 1820, and dropped the minimum size of purchases to eighty acres in 1820 and to forty acres in 1832. In 1830 Congress recognized the popular idea of preemption, which gave squatters the right to purchase their holdings at a later date, and made it a general policy in 1841.

After the Louisiana Purchase it was inevitable that the public land system of the United States would expand across the Mississippi River, but the stimulus for the initial survey was the need to provide land to meet commitments made to veterans of the War of 1812. Congress set aside six million acres for these bounty lands, as they were called, two mil-

lion of which lay between the Arkansas and Saint Francis Rivers in what is now Arkansas, at that time the lower portion of Missouri Territory. Surveyors Prospect K. Robbins and Joseph C. Brown, working for the national government, arrived in Arkansas in the fall of 1812. Robbins began at the mouth of the Arkansas River, plotted a meridian, and followed it to the north. Meanwhile, Brown surveyed a baseline due west from the mouth of the Saint Francis River. At the intersection of the two lines Robbins and Brown established the starting point for all surveys in the Louisiana Purchase. This starting point is now known as the Louisiana Purchase Initial Survey Point Site. Designated on November 10, 1815, it is located approximately fifty-five miles north of the mouth of the Arkansas River and twenty-six miles west of the mouth of the Saint Francis River.

The survey and sale of government land had an important effect on Arkansas. The possibility of acquiring a well-defined tract and a clear title at a relatively low price encouraged settlement. In addition, there were a variety of associated state and federal programs that provided special bargains. The territorial assembly of Arkansas began to tax the military bounty lands in 1823, the first year they could legally do so; they then foreclosed on many non-resident, land-owning veterans, who probably did not know about the tax, and sold the land tracts at low prices that offered a fine opportunity for speculators. The federal government also made donations of land to settlers who were displaced by the New Madrid earthquake or by the northwest boundary between Arkansas and the Cherokee Nation. In both cases the administration of the laws was attended by widespread fraud that greatly enlarged the amount of land that made its way into private hands. The Swamp Lands Act of 1850 allowed Arkansas, by exaggeration of its eligible acreage, to acquire perhaps two million acres of federal land that also went to citizens at very low prices. The benefits of these measures often trickled down to small holders, but the greatest profits went to men able to buy much more acreage than the average settler.

In the early years of the territory, when paid positions were scarce, the land office business provided a few good patronage jobs—and often with them the first chance to buy choice land. Henry W. Conway, the territorial delegate to Congress, got his start as a supervisor of surveyors, and so did his brother, James S. Conway, who eventually became the first governor of the state of Arkansas. In 1825 James S. Conway surveyed the Choctaw Line, which defined the southwestern boundary of the state, slanting it toward the west in order to take a little more land from the Indians, and in 1832 he became Arkansas's first surveyor general. More jobs came with the creation of land offices: at Poke Bayou, which became Batesville, and Little Rock in 1822; at Washington and Fayetteville in 1832; and at Helena in 1834.

The land system of the United States has played a formative role in the development of the nation. It encouraged rapid settlement of the frontier all the way to California and created a distinctive rectilinear landscape that perhaps is best appreciated by looking out the window of an airplane on a clear day. The straight survey lines became boundaries for international treaties and for states and counties, and they sometimes defined the routes of local roads. The initial survey point, for example, forms an intersection point for Phillips, Lee, and Monroe Counties, and it marks the path of Baseline Road, which crosses southern Little Rock.

Critics of the system point out that various provisions of the land laws encouraged speculators and discouraged family farmers. Even the Homestead Act of 1862, which gave settlers 160 acres of free land, encouraged families to move on to the plains, where they needed much more land in order to be successful. The rigid, square townships and sections also ignored variations in terrain and often led to farming practices that were harmful to the environment.

For better or worse, it is clear that the pattern of public land-holding that began in 1785 and moved across the Mississippi River in 1815 made an indelible mark on the American landscape, agricultural economy, and body politic that will remain long into the future.

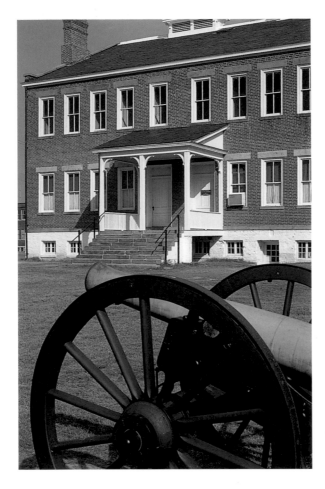

Fort Smith National Historic Site. *Photo by Joe David Rice, courtesy of Arkansas Department of Parks and Tourism.*

FORT SMITH

Elliott West

Fort Smith National Historic Site
1817–1917
Fort Smith, Sebastian County
Listed on the National Register of Historic Places on March 7, 1986
Designated a National Historic Landmark on December 19, 1960

"Fort Smith National Historic Site derives its significance from a long-standing, dynamic relationship with Indian Territory. The early fort was established to put down the inevitable conflicts that arose when many Indian tribes were congregated in an area that formerly accommodated a few nomadic populations. When other forts were established deeper in the Territory to continue that peacekeeping task, the Second Fort Smith supplied and provisioned them. Fort buildings served as courthouse, jail, and staff quarters for the District Court having jurisdiction in the Indian Territory and later as expanded prison facilities for the U.S. courts within the Territory. When Oklahoma acquired statehood in 1907, a prolonged frontier period was over, and not long afterwards Fort Smith's role as protector, peacekeeper and law enforcer for its unusual western neighbor came to an end."

—*From the National Register nomination*

Location is everything, as the real estate cliché reminds us. Certainly this cliché explains plenty about the origins and history of Fort Smith. In an age when rivers were the highways of personal and commercial travel, posts and settlements typically appeared close to the highest point on a stream that boats could regularly reach. On the Arkansas that was roughly at the mouth of the Poteau River, and it was there in 1817 that construction began on an army post first called Belle Point, then renamed Fort Smith in honor of General Thomas A. Smith. A crude settlement grew up around the post, feeding off the exchange that always occurs between the military and civilians. Gradually, it grew in size, if not always in respectability. A post office was established in 1829, and thirteen years later the settlement was incorporated.

By the mid-1820s the fort and the town found themselves along another sort of boundary, not between river traffic and the land beyond but between settlements of white pioneers and Indian peoples. The country west of Arkansas's territorial border had been designated Indian Territory. The federal government had negotiated with Native American peoples there, notably the Osages, to allow room for Indians being pushed out of the Gulf coastal frontier by the flood of white settlers after the War of 1812. The resulting rapid changes made this one of the most unstable parts of the frontier. Besides the usual conflicts and tensions between Indians and whites, there were plenty more among the Indian tribes and the factions within those tribes. Sitting near the heart of this turmoil, Fort Smith was expected to help maintain some sort of order.

Nonetheless, the post at first was a come-and-go enterprise. When Fort Gibson was established further up the Arkansas and within Indian Territory, Fort Smith languished and in 1834 was abandoned for four years. By the time it was reestablished in 1838 the federal government had established the "permanent Indian frontier." This line ran northward to and then along the Missouri River. It was meant to be part barrier, part protective wall. Whites on the east of the line could supposedly feel safe from the Indians to the west; on their side Indians supposedly would be free from white encroachments. The U.S. at this time reached only to Texas and to the continental divide. The newly reestablished Fort Smith, then, sat on the far western edge of the nation. It served partly as a supply center for the other posts in the region and also as one of the fortified gateways along a boundary between peoples and cultures.

Essential to U.S. strategy was the removal of Native American people from the southeastern states beyond the "Indian frontier." During the 1830s thousands of Choctaws, Chickasaws, Cherokees, Creeks, and Seminoles were taken from their homelands and resettled in Indian Territory. Some walked the entire way; many more traveled at least part of the way by boat. They moved by a variety of routes, but most converged on Fort Smith. Once more location made the post and town a focal point for the region's most important—and in this case most appalling—episodes. At this stage of their journey the

ELLIOTT WEST

Fort Smith, Arkansas, in 1821.
Courtesy of UALR Archives.

travelers were exhausted, demoralized, and often ill. An observer in late 1836 described Creeks approaching the post "with nothing more than a cotton garment thrown over them, their feet bare, . . . compelled to encounter cold, sleeting storms and to travel over hard frozen ground."

Positioned on the border of the "Nations," Fort Smith was also the natural spigot that sent illegal whiskey over the line. Merchants used "every act of cunning . . . to elude discovery" of the hundreds of gallons sent daily for sale among the tribes, an officer complained. Saloon owners and moonshiners also sold huge amounts of liquor to soldiers, further unsettling affairs. Disgruntled customers in uniform once shelled a tavern with the post cannon.

As the liquor trade showed, the supposed barrier between Indians and whites leaked badly, and, in any case, the "permanent" Indian frontier survived barely a few years. In 1845 Texas was annexed as a state. A year later the Oregon treaty with England added the Pacific Northwest to the nation, and in the Mexican War between 1846 and 1848 the U.S. seized California and the far southwest. The land west of Fort Smith in 1844 had been the republic's distant western fringe. Supposedly, it would be safe from outside pressures for the indefi-

nite future, some authorities said for a century or more. Four years later that territory stood squarely in the center of the nation. It would immediately feel the impact of a fiercely expansionist people.

Fort Smith now became another kind of transition point. At the moment the treaty was signed ending the Mexican War, astonishing news was trickling out of the California hills. Gold had been found on the American River. The discovery triggered a worldwide rush to the Pacific coast. Argonauts came from Chile, Peru, Hawaii, and Australia, then from Europe and China. From the U.S. thousands went by sea and across the Panamanian isthmus. Thousands more moved overland. Most of those chose the California Trail that followed the Platte River out of the middle Missouri River valley. Others chose the southern route along the Arkansas River, through New Mexico, and across the southwestern deserts via the Gila River. The prime departure point for this southern overland trail was Fort Smith.

About five thousand persons passed through Fort Smith along the southern, or Gila, trail in 1849. They formed quite a procession, moving through the town in overstuffed wagons and setting off down miry roads into Indian Territory. The

Fort Smith in 1865 at the time of the Fort Smith Council, when representatives of the federal government and thirteen tribes met to discuss the tribes' fates following the Civil War. *Courtesy of Fort Smith National Historic Site.*

gold rush helped establish the town as a mercantile depot and outfitting center for the westering surge of population at mid-century. Although the southern trail to California languished after 1849, with most emigrants favoring the overland route up the Platte River, travelers in considerable numbers passed through on their way to Texas, and traffic towards the far coast never entirely stopped. In 1857 a large overland party from Carroll and Benton counties left Fort Smith for California. A few months later all but a handful of children would be murdered by Indians and Mormons in the Mountain Meadows massacre. The next year the town was made the converging point of two routes —those from Saint Louis and Memphis—of the famous Overland Stage Line of John Butterfield. Out of Fort Smith stages rolled southwestward to begin a jostling, lurching, dust-choked journey many travelers would recall as the most grueling experience of their lives.

As a jump-off place Fort Smith resembled such border towns as Kansas City and Westport, Saint Joseph, Atchison, and Council Bluffs, bustling entrepots where emigrants bought oxen and mules from sprawling liveries, stocked wagons with supplies, and tossed down their last drinks in saloons before taking to the road. As always, however, there were regional differences. Westering travelers tended to move in parallel lines. So the crowds that passed through Fort Smith were mostly from the southern states. Visitors from the north commented, often unfavorably, on the drawling, tobacco-spitting, knife-carrying sorts they passed on the streets, and on the slaves at work in the growing town and in the country around it.

The tensions we can read from their descriptions erupted in 1861 in the deepest tragedy in the nation's history. During the Civil War Fort Smith's location made it a new boundary—that between Confederate and Union armies and sympathizers. One of the town's prominent politicians and attorneys, Albert Pike, shuttled from there into Indian Territory in a largely successful effort to win support for the Confederacy among tribes recently pushed out of the South, especially the Cherokees and Creeks. A minority among those tribes was loyal to the Union, however, and the region north and west of Fort Smith became a bloodily contested ground, with Unionist Indians driven into southeastern Kansas. Fort Smith was the launching place for Confederate campaigns, first the effort of Earl Van Dorn to invade Missouri and later that of Thomas Hindman to block Union control of western Arkansas. Both efforts failed, and in September 1863 the town was abandoned without a fight.

The war had taken a terrific toll. In the latter days of Confederate occupation troops were sent a hundred miles downriver to find scant forage for horses and rations for their riders. Fort Smith continued to languish, a neglected backwater as the conflict wound down. Five months after Appomattox the town was the site of a council between the government and tribes of the Indian Territory. In spite of the support among some Native Americans for the Union during the war, the government now insisted on reducing the holding of the tribes across the board so more Indians, these from Kansas, Nebraska, and elsewhere, could be moved into Indian Territory. Treaties signed later in Washington, D.C., did just that, and over the next decade many more tribes were crowded in the country west of Fort Smith.

By then the military presence in the town was dwindling fast. After hundreds of soldiers were mustered out from the post, a small garrison remained but, with the general military reduction after the war, played a limited role in the region's history. Two fires in 1870 inspired William T. Sherman to order the post closed and sold. A year later it was abandoned.

The town of Fort Smith, however, continued to play its part as a middle point between culture zones of the middle border. Its location on the eastern edge of Indian Territory made it the obvious headquarters for those charged with keeping minimum order west of the line. The cheapening of life during the Civil War, the vicious raids and counter-raids among guerrillas and militia, the endemic fuzziness of authority in this part of the frontier, the bad blood among families and factions among the Indians—all this made the two generations after 1865 particularly unsettled and violent. Outlaws and drifters found Indian Territory a fine refuge. By the time Fort Smith's military post was closed, the region had a reputation as one of the wildest and most dangerous in the nation.

In 1871 the town was designated the seat of the United States criminal court for the western district of Arkansas. In 1875, after its first judge, William Story, resigned amid rumors of graft, President Ulysses Grant appointed Isaac Parker, a native Ohioan then active in Missouri politics, as judge of the district. Parker presided over a judicial district that was both turbulent and, by some estimates, the largest in the world—all of Indian Territory, plus thirteen western Arkansas counties. His court, the

"Hanging judge" Isaac Parker. *Courtesy of J. N. Heiskell Collection, UALR Archives.*

offices of deputies and clerks, and the jail were on part of the old military post. Here Parker would hold court for twenty-one years.

There is a double injustice in Fort Smith's enduring reputation as headquarters of Parker, the "hanging judge." The grisly image of the gallows tends to blot out the town's larger, varied history. And the image itself is badly distorted. Parker, who looked a bit like Santa Claus, deplored capital punishment but considered it a weapon of last resort in dealing with an even more deplorable situation. More than thirteen thousand cases were handled by Parker's court. Of those more than nine thousand resulted in convictions or pleas of guilty. In his tenure of more than two decades Parker sentenced 151 men to be hanged; of those, eighty-three, or a bit more than half, were executed, most by the "Prince of Hangmen," George Maledon. It's hardly the record of a bloodthirsty sadist. Just how and why Parker's image took root is hard to say. A blood-and-thunder book by a disgruntled lawyer, S. W. Harman's *Hell on the Border,* is partly to blame, but partly the public was ready to associate Fort Smith with the frontier's rougher side. This impulse continues. Popular literature has played with the town's place on the line between worlds. In *True Grit* the feisty heroine, Mattie, and the hardshelled deputy, Rooster Cogburn, sally forth from Parker's court into Indian Territory in search of the murderer of Mattie's father. It's an Arkansas version of the classic myth—the courageous neophyte facing an ordeal of honor, helped by an older guide, in an alien land of monsters—with Fort Smith as the portal into the

Young members of the Buck Gang were among those who met their fates in Judge Parker's court. *Courtesy of UALR Archives.*

mysterious terrain of our hero's testing. In Larry McMurtry's *Lonesome Dove* Sheriff July Johnson sets off from the town on his own dutiful journey toward Texas. A "hanging judge" nicely fit Fort Smith's image as implied in stories like these. The Parker of the distorted legend combines the authority of a last outpost of order with the capricious, unbending violence of life on the far side of the line. Mythically, Fort Smith's location is still on a border, leaning a bit in both directions.

Visitors to the Fort Smith Historic Site might keep in mind this larger meaning of the legend of Parker and his gallows. Even in its distortions it reminds us of the many ways Fort Smith's true history has straddled the boundaries among the frontier's peoples and experiences. The legend invites us to explore the various meanings of a remarkable place.

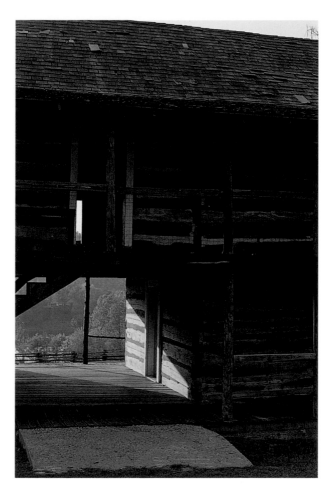

The two-story dogtrot Jacob
Wolf House at Norfork.
Photo by Cathryn H. Slater,
Arkansas Historic Preservation
Program.

THE JACOB WOLF HOUSE AT NORFORK

Donald Harington

Jacob Wolf House
Ca. 1825
Norfork, Baxter County
Listed on the National Register of Historic Places on April 13, 1973

"While local legend attributes the construction date of the Wolf House as being 1809–10, historical and architectural evidence obtained by the National Park Service leads to the conclusion that the Wolf House was constructed about 1825. Major Jacob Wolf was postmaster in Izard County and he represented its citizens in the Territorial Assembly and State Legislature. The claim that Major Wolf was an Indian Agent cannot be substantiated by published or unpublished documentation. If he were not an Indian Agent the story of his house being built by Indian labor is seriously in doubt. The most important event of historical significance associated with the Wolf House is its having been the seat of the first government of Izard County."

—From the National Register nomination

If we have a state flower, a state bird, a state tree, etc., why not a state house? Not a *statehouse*: we already have Gideon Shryock's splendid but faux-classique old capitol building (see page 50). If what is needed is a single building that, while atypical, could represent the spirit of the state, the Jacob Wolf House at Norfork would be the consensus choice of architectural historians, preservationists, and anybody who appreciates old houses . . . although if the legislature had to vote on a state house, politics might prevent the designation.

Of all the old buildings in the state of Arkansas, this imposing, two-story log house in the dogtrot style could come closest to serving as a visual symbol for the whole state. Arkansas began as a haven for adventurers from North Carolina, Tennessee, and Kentucky, with ties to Pennsylvania, who aspired to a better standard of living than they had in those crowded eastern states. Jacob Wolf came from North Carolina, with ties to Pennsylvania, and lived in Kentucky before searching out an ideal spot in the new territory of Arkansas.

The Wolf House is located on a symbolic rise, where the North Fork of the White River empties into the White, just as Arkansas itself straddles the lands where the river of that name flows toward the Mississippi. The house is built of massive logs hewn from the pine (the state tree). Tall chimneys rise at either end, and spacious brick fireplaces provide heat for each room.

It appears to be a log cabin with ambition, as the best Arkansawyers have always been overreachers. It incorporates most of the features of the typical log cabin but does them one better, and not simply by being two stories instead of one. Instead of mere puncheon, the floors are made from hewn planks. The logs meet at the corners with chamfer and notch joining. Each room, up and down, can be entered from the porches that run the full length of both front and rear of the house and provide platforms for looking out over (and lording over) the landscape and the neighbors.

Did Jacob Wolf's neighbors resent him for putting on airs? Probably. But his situation, and his house, were remarkably similar to those of Parson Capen of Topsfield, Massachusetts, who built in 1683 one of the loveliest still-standing Colonial houses in America on a rise above his townsfolk, in a place and attitude demanding their respect as well as their envy.

The dimensions of the warm, stately Parson Capen House are almost the same as those of the Jacob Wolf House, although the latter was of course built much later (ca. 1825). In color, texture, mien, and bearing, the two houses are much alike, and there is even a resemblance between the Capen House's overhang and the Wolf House's second-story porch.

Both buildings are truly vernacular: they speak an indigenous language of the people, free from European elegance or decoration. The size of the houses may have overshadowed their neighbors, but their language was the same: down-to-earth, homespun, friendly.

Parson Capen was sent to minister to the settlers of the new world and perhaps convert a few Indians into the bargain. Jacob Wolf wasn't a parson, but he was a good deacon of the Baptist church, and he cer-

　DONALD HARINGTON

Blacksmith, politician, and farmer Jacob Wolf. *Courtesy of Charles T. Blackburn.*

tainly had enough contacts with the Indians that we may suppose he tried to persuade a number of them that the Baptist version of Jesus Christ was truly God.

That Jacob Wolf was actually an official Indian agent is probably more a local legend than a fact, but he certainly dealt with the Indians as trader, storekeeper, and blacksmith. In *Let Us Build Us a City* I suggested that a major book remains to be written about Jacob Wolf, and I wrote of his dealings with both Indians and the white settlers who were beginning to take over the Ozarks, one of whom wrote to his parents back home in Massachusetts:

> I shall board with old Major Jacob Wolf, one of the oldest settlers in this country and bearing the name of a strictly honest and hon-

ourable man—he lived here for years when the country was inhabited by Indians and always retained their respect and good will. I have been down to see the old Major and he says if I will come down he will have the house put in good repair and send his ferry boat up after my things. . . .

Parson Capen is so commonly known by his title that his actual first name is forgotten, but Deacon Wolf was more commonly known as Major Wolf because of his commissioning in the Arkansas territorial militia soon after his arrival at Norfork. He never actually saw military service, but served in the territorial legislature, using that position to obtain the first road into his native county, Izard, just as years later, upon becoming governor, Orval Faubus would have the first paved road built into his native county, Madison.

The legislature of 1835, with its eye on statehood, proposed a bill "to encourage the killing of wolves in Arkansas." Jacob rose in his seat and suggested an amendment exempting "two-legged wolves" from the law.

When I set out to write the novel *The Architecture of the Arkansas Ozarks,* the only building I actually visited and researched, rather than inventing, was the Jacob Wolf House, and I probably used his name, Jacob, as the name for the patriarch and founder of Stay More, Jacob Ingledew, and I also used the idea that the Ingledew dogtrot (albeit only one story) serve temporarily as county courthouse. Jacob Wolf's house was not only the natural stopping place on any journey through northern Arkansas but it also served as the post office and courthouse for the new Izard County.

Most importantly, the double (or split) nature of the house probably inspired the concept of what I call "bigeminal" architecture: the building—whether house, church, school, store, whatever—which is divided into equal parts, doors, openings, rooms, divisions, perhaps, as I attempted to suggest, symbolic of the gender split between male and female. Parson Capen's house was divided between the two main rooms called parlor and hall (the huge central chimney precluded any dogtrot, even if they'd thought of it), and Jacob Wolf's was divided, upstairs and down, and it had twin chimneys.

All houses are occupied, usually, by both male and female, but only the bigeminal house can visually convey the idea that a house is a cohabitation of the sexes, a living day-to-day manifestation of how men and women relate to each other . . . and love each other.

Thus, as a "state house" the Wolf House at Norfork can not simply symbolize the mighty ambition of the settlers to carve a home place in the wilderness and watch it prosper, not simply speak volubly an earthy vernacular, not simply show the replacement of the Indian by the white newcomer, not simply embody the vantage view of the rest of the world from a place of outlook and even overlook, but also, and most importantly, express the eternal bond between male and female.

The Jacob Wolf House is the oldest house in Arkansas. Unlike the Parson Capen House, which is merely the handsomest of a number of seventeenth-century colonial houses in Massachusetts, the Wolf House is unique: the only two-story dogtrot in the state, possibly the only one in the country.

It is lonely in its grandeur.

The Trimble House at Old Washington Historic State Park. *Photo by A. C. Haralson, courtesy of Arkansas Department of Parks and Tourism.*

THE WASHINGTON HISTORIC DISTRICT

Don Montgomery

Washington Historic District
1830–1915
Washington, Hempstead County
Listed on the National Register of Historic Places on June 20, 1972

"Today, Washington exists as an outstanding example of an Arkansas city of the period 1824–1874. Washington grew and flourished in a fifty year period. During almost 100 years of decline, however, the town has managed to survive with most of its original fabric. There are gaps, where nature, man and time have destroyed or altered some of the original buildings. The same factors, though, that contributed to Washington's decline and decay have prevented new construction or radical alteration, and will permit the old fabric of the city to be rewoven and restored."

—*From the National Register nomination*

As the complexity and pace of life seems to increase, future visitors to the Washington Historic District in southwest Arkansas will have a great opportunity to take a deep breath, relax, and study several periods in Arkansas history from the pioneer days through Reconstruction at this unique historic village conserved and interpreted by Arkansas State Parks in conjunction with the Pioneer Washington Restoration Foundation. The variety of architectural styles in town includes both the simple vernacular of the Royston Log House and the sophistication of the Italianate 1874 Hempstead County Courthouse. A dozen or so Greek Revival structures dot the landscape marked with picket fences, boardwalks, and towering catalpa trees.

Needing a centrally located county seat, the citizens of Hempstead County established the town of Washington on a sand hill along the rugged Southwest Trail in 1824. This narrow wagon road was the main overland route from Little Rock to the Red River. Many immigrants passed through town on their way to Texas, including several famous individuals. Stephen F. Austin purchased land and lived in the area for a year before moving to Texas. Sam Houston stayed at a Washington tavern for several weeks in 1834. This stop was described by British traveler George W. Featherstonhaugh in his book, *Excursion Through the Slave States of North America* (1844). He wrote, " . . . [W]e made an agreeable excursion in the neighborhood, calling for a short time at the little insignificant village of Washington. . . . I was not desirous of remaining long at this place. General [Sam] Houston was here, leading a mysterious sort of life, shut up in a tavern, seeing nobody by day, and sitting up all night." The Englishman speculated that Houston was in Washington plotting revolution in Texas, which began soon after his departure. Davy Crockett and his men came through the community on their way to immortality at the Alamo. Other visitors included

the Bowie brothers, John and James, who spent many hours at the courthouse entering land transactions. James also visited local blacksmith James Black and had a knife made that was possibly the first "Bowie knife." Between 1831 and 1839 large numbers of Native Americans of the Choctaw and Chickasaw Nations passed through during their forced removal to present-day Oklahoma on the Trail of Tears.

Those earliest days are remembered at Old Washington Historic State Park with the Abraham Block House, the Royston Log House, the 1836 Hempstead County Courthouse, and the reproduction Blacksmith Shop and Tavern Inn, as well as at the Williams Tavern. An early merchant in town, Abraham Block was also one of the first Jewish settlers in Arkansas. His home, built in about 1832, is a unique Federal-style structure reflecting the family's wealth. The Hempstead County citizens constructed a new courthouse in 1836, the same year Arkansas entered the Union as the twenty-fifth state. Recently restored, this structure also served as the Confederate Capitol following the capture of Little Rock by Union troops in 1863. John W. Williams built a house seven miles from town on the Southwest Trail, which became a regular stop for weary travelers. Today the moved and restored structure contains the park's restaurant.

The community grew rapidly and prospered during the 1840s and 1850s, when "cotton was king" in the South. Professionals flooded into Washington to serve the wealthy plantation owners of the area. As the *Washington Telegraph* reported in 1854, "Our town is improving more rapidly at present, than it has done for a number of years. Several new buildings are going up, and others are being repaired and renovated." Four years later David French Boyd passed through the area and described it as "a pretty place. . . . Some evidence of wealth in the way of commodious and tastefully

DON MONTGOMERY

Washington blacksmith James Black made a knife for James Bowie *(pictured)*, which may have been the first "Bowie knife." *Courtesy of J. N. Heiskell Collection, UALR Archives.*

arranged buildings and grounds. . . . The town labors under one great disadvantage—the intolerable sand in the streets. . . ." According to the 1860 United States Census, Ozan Township, which included the Washington population, had seventeen lawyers, sixteen doctors, fifteen merchants, three hotel owners, and numerous small manufacturers, as well as fifteen carpenters, who constructed the many Greek Revival buildings in town.

William H. Etter arrived and published a weekly newspaper called the *Washington Telegraph* starting in 1840; it continued as a family-owned paper until its demise in 1946. It was the only Confederate newspaper in Arkansas to publish throughout the Civil War, although the press was moved across the Red River in 1864, when General Frederick Steele's Union Army advanced towards Washington during the Camden Expedition. The Etter family home still stands in town, although it went through a major renovation following tornado damage in 1907. There is also a printing museum, with several Etter printing presses and other artifacts.

Augustus M. Crouch came to Arkansas as a young man, settling at Washington in 1842. When the Mexican War started, he served as a bugler with the Arkansas Volunteers, fighting at the Battle of Buena Vista. Returning home, he went into the watchmaking and jewelry business. Built in 1857, the Crouch House displays examples of the quality work done by the town's carpenters and ornamental painters.

Dr. James Alexander Lafayette Purdom practiced medicine in Washington, while Dr. Robert Brunson did the same in the neighboring community of Columbus. The simple Greek Revival details of the small Purdom House are in sharp contrast to the elegant Italianate and Greek Revival trim of the massive Brunson House. While both were respected professionals, Dr. Brunson owned a plantation and fifty-eight slaves in 1860. The Civil War destroyed both men in different ways. Dr. Purdom volunteered as the surgeon of the First Arkansas Cavalry, but was forced to resign due to illness, which led to his death in 1866. The war bankrupted Dr. Brunson, who lost his property, but not his home in Columbus.

John Trimble owned one of the most successful mercantile businesses in Washington long before he was elected county judge, a position he held for four terms. Considered by many to be the finest Greek Revival restoration in Arkansas, the Trimble House contains the memories, heirlooms, and furnishings of several generations of this important Arkansas family.

Additional Greek Revival structures exemplifying Washington's peak years include the Stuart

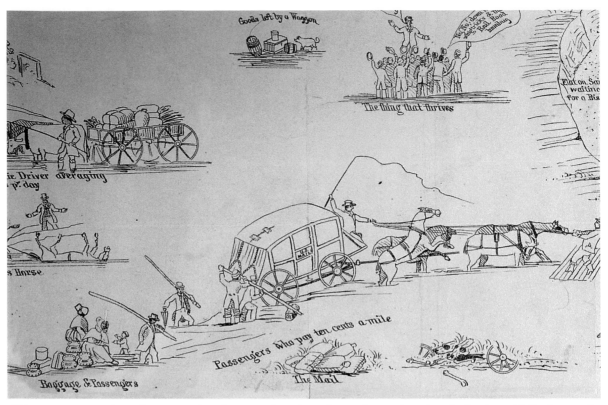

The labels within the cartoon read: "Goods left by a Waggon", "The thing that thrives", "Driver averaging ... pr. day", "Horse", "Baggage & Passengers", "Passengers who pay ten cents a mile", "The Mail".

This ca. 1855 cartoon by William Quesenbury lampooned travel in Arkansas along such roads as the Southwest Trail. *Courtesy of Arkansas History Commission.*

House, the Williamson House, the Monroe House, and the Woodlawn Plantation House. While constructed by Martin Moudy, a saddler by profession, in about 1842, the Stuart House was also home to Judge Thomas Hubbard, his wife, and his stepsons, Augustus and Rufus Garland. Mr. A. O. Stuart purchased it in 1868 and lived there for several years with his wife, Ruth McEnery Stuart, who was a popular American author of the late nineteenth century. Members of the Carrigan family built the Williamson House in about 1850, but the structure got its name from black owner John Williamson, who founded the Haygood Seminary in town to train black teachers and preachers. Lawyer John Field and his business partner Eli V. Collins con-

structed the Monroe House as a residence for the manager of their steam-powered circular saw mill in 1855. The family of James C. Monroe, a Confederate veteran and colonel of the First Arkansas Cavalry, C.S.A., acquired the structure in 1890, and they and their descendants lived there until 1978. The impressive, two-story Woodlawn Plantation House once sat amongst the cotton fields around Columbus, Arkansas. It now graces the site of Judge Abner B. Williams's home, which was very similar architecturally.

Religion played an important role in the social life of Washington in the nineteenth century. This is reflected in the town's historic and reconstructed houses of worship. Rev. William Stevenson, a circuit-riding preacher, established the first Methodist congregation in the area, which moved to a new Greek Revival structure in Washington upon its completion in 1861. The Methodists established the Washington Male and Female Seminaries to educate the young people of the area in 1845. The Presbyterians sponsored the Washington Male and Female Academies at about the same time, giving the community four private institutions of learning, two for the young ladies and two for the boys. The Presbyterians built the existing church structure in 1889 to replace the original church destroyed by fire. This unique building exhibits the Carpenter Gothic style with an impressive natural wood interior. The Mount Zion Baptist Church built in 1845 survived for 101 years before being destroyed by a tornado in 1946. The congregation built a reconstruction of the original Greek Revival structure in 1987. The faith of many Washington pioneers and later citizens can be attested to with a trip through the cemeteries on the west side of town. The Pioneer Cemetery is the last resting place of the earliest citizens, black or white, who passed away before the Civil War. The Presbyterian Cemetery contains the remains of many soldiers killed during the Civil War as well as other citizens of Washington.

The Greek Revival homes of Simon T. Sanders and Grandison D. Royston help visitors learn about the politics of the region. Simon T. Sanders served as the Hempstead county clerk for thirty consecutive years, then as postmaster. His home, built in about 1845, became the site of the wedding of his daughter, Sarah Virginia, to young lawyer Augustus Hill Garland, who became active in politics and represented Arkansas during the Civil War in both houses of the Confederate Congress. President Grover Cleveland chose Garland to serve as attorney general of the United States. As a lawyer and plantation owner, Grandison D. Royston was involved in Arkansas politics throughout his life. He was the youngest delegate at the Arkansas Constitutional Convention in 1836 and the oldest delegate and President of the 1874 Constitutional Convention. During the Civil War Royston served in the Confederate House of Representatives. Built in 1845 by carpenter John Brooks, the Royston House sits atop a hill overlooking the community.

When Arkansas seceded from the Union, the town of Washington and Hempstead County did their part for the cause, raising twenty companies of men for the Confederate Army as well as providing political and military leadership. In addition to Grandison D. Royston and Augustus Hill Garland, Arkansas chose Dr. Charles B. Mitchel as a Confederate senator and replaced Royston with veteran soldier Rufus K. Garland, brother of Augustus, in 1864. Among the military leaders was Col. Henry P. Johnson, a Washington merchant who died charging the Federal entrenchments during the Battle of Corinth, Mississippi, in 1862. Lt. Col. Daniel Webster Jones was shot through the breast during the same charge but survived to lead the Twentieth Arkansas Infantry through the rest of the war. Brig. Gen. Evander McNair, another Washington merchant before the war, commanded the Arkansas brigade that broke through the Union lines at the Battle of Chickamauga in 1863.

The town of Washington reached its zenith when it became the Confederate capital of Arkansas following the capture of Little Rock on September 10, 1863. Refugees and government officials flooded into the small community, filling it to capacity. Gov. Harris Flanagin called for a special session of the Arkansas legislature in 1864, which met at the old 1836 Hempstead County Courthouse.

When the Civil War ended, the Twelfth Michigan Infantry marched into the village and occupied the former capital for a year. The American Missionary Association opened a school for former slaves, many of whom became active in local politics.

Despite the hardships of war Washington recovered and built a new, two-story, red brick, Italianate courthouse in 1874. That same year the Cairo and Fulton Railroad bypassed the community and established the new town of Hope, which would quickly outgrow the old town. The decline of Washington began the next year, when a disastrous fire destroyed over four blocks in the business district. The *Arkansas Gazette* reported on another fire in 1883, stating, "The people are very much discouraged in consequence of their losses. This will cause a general depression in all branches of business." Washington would never be the same again.

During the 1920s a movement began to have the old Confederate Capitol building saved for future generations. The funds issued for the restoration of the 1836 Hempstead County Courthouse was the first state appropriation in Arkansas for historic preservation. Local citizens formed the Pioneer Washington Restoration Foundation in 1958 in order to restore other historic structures. The dedication of Old Washington Historic State Park took place on July 20, 1973. Today the citizens, the foundation, and the park work together to preserve more of this unique community. Alvin Toffler wrote in 1970 that the turbulence of the future will require a need for "enclaves of the past." The Washington Historic District will provide visitors in the new millennium with such a welcome place.

DON MONTGOMERY

The former location of Cadron Settlement now rests serenely by the banks of the Arkansas River. *Photo by Ken Story, Arkansas Historic Preservation Program.*

CADRON

Stan Hoig

Cadron Settlement
1834
Conway vic., Faulkner County
Listed on the National Register of Historic Places on May 17, 1974

"There are literally hundreds of questions that could be tested archeologically using the Cadron site as a model. This, added to its importance in the early history of Arkansas, makes it an especially significant site."

—*From the National Register nomination*

A ca. 1819 drawing of the humble Cadron Settlement. *Courtesy of Arkansas History Commission.*

The Cherokee Nation's struggle to maintain its homeland and its autonomy against the covetous aims of white citizens and their governments as well as the Cherokee removal over the Trail of Tears stand as tragic events in our national experience. The Trail of Tears casts a pall of shame upon many white Americans who were either personally or officially involved in the Cherokee removal. Obscured by this dark cloud, however, are a number of white Americans who stood forth bravely to support the Cherokees and their cause. No one event, perhaps, better illustrates the suffering of the Cherokees and courageous action in their behalf than what occurred at Cadron, Arkansas Territory, in 1834.

It was in mid-April of that year that a party of well over five hundred decimated and measles-stricken Cherokees bound for their new lands in the Indian Territory (present-day Oklahoma) arrived at Cadron Creek in three river boats under tow by the paddlewheeler, *Thomas Yeatman*. The Cherokee immigrants were under the charge of Lt. Joseph Harris, a West Pointer from New Hampshire.

Beset by severe drought, the river was too shallow for the travelers to proceed further by boat, and Harris was left with no choice but to put ashore and make camp near the small settlement of Cadron. A large number of the Cherokees were already ill when an epidemic of the dreaded cholera swept through the camp, causing death after death. In panic the Cherokees scattered through the woods, building their fires well away from one another in an attempt to escape infection. Harris's diary of April 16 described the scene:

> Notes of lamentation & of woe rose upon the morning air & the shrieks of the dying! Insatiate death stalks through our little camp & with a conspiring & awfully disfiguring hand, greedily gathers his victim to the garner. Every hope of yesterday has vanished— that all sweeping scourge the maliginant cholera is in our tents & has scattered dismay & horror around us.

Local physician Dr. Jesse C. Roberts, who had responded to Harris's plea for help, was also struck by the cholera. "I have devoted the day to my poor friend," Harris wrote in his diary. "He has none to help him! His poor weakly wife can scarcely crawl about." The country doctor could offer only opium and calomel before he, too, perished. Though deathly ill himself, Harris managed to secure wagons and teams for those Cherokees who were too weak to walk and carry their own effects.

He then struggled aboard a horse and rode ahead of the desperate entourage, scouring the drought-stricken countryside to find food for his charges. "There was great dignity in their grief which is sublime," Harris reflected, "and which, poor and destitute, ignorant and unbefriended as they were, made me respect them."

Eventually, on May 10, Harris and the Cherokees reached their destination at New Dwight Mission in the Indian Territory. Eighty-one of the immigrants had died en route, and more would perish later. Harris, his health ruined, would himself die in 1837. Few Americans would ever know of the disaster and the heroism that occurred at the Cadron settlement.

While this was possibly the most signal event in its history, Cadron is notable for other reasons as well. First established as a settlement in 1810 by John McElmurry, it soon became an important port for Arkansas River traffic. French fur traders stopped here prior to 1800, as did Lt. James Wilkinson of the Zebulon Pike expedition in 1806; Maj. Stephen H. Long in 1817; Thomas Nuttall, the English naturalist, in 1819; and many others who were seeking out the mysteries of the lands beyond the Mississippi River.

As early as 1810 a number of Cherokees had come to build homes and establish new communities along the Arkansas River above Little Rock. Cadron marked the eastern edge of their assigned lands in Arkansas Territory. The Cherokees drew to themselves an Indian agency, a government factory, and the Dwight Mission at Illinois Bayou. Still another noteworthy addition occurred when, in 1824, Sequoyah, the famed inventor of the

Cherokee scholar Sequoyah, who lived in Arkansas for a time. *Courtesy of Arkansas History Commission.*

Cherokee Syllabary, and his family arrived to take up residence above Cadron, near present-day Scottsville.

The Cherokees would maintain a prosperous society in Arkansas until 1828, when they signed a treaty with the United States exchanging their Arkansas lands for others in the Indian Territory. Cadron would eventually fade away as a settlement, but among its forested hills are the unmarked graves of Cherokees whose deaths connote a significant moment in American history when conspicuous acts of heroism occurred.

Lakeport Plantation, 1999. *Photo by Ken Story, Arkansas Historic Preservation Program.*

LAKEPORT: SHOWPLACE OF ARKANSAS'S "COTTON ARISTOCRACY"

Thomas A. DeBlack

Lakeport Plantation
Ca. 1850
Shives vic., Chicot County
Listed on the National Register of Historic Places on November 20, 1974

"Lakeport Plantation is a fine example of Arkansas's antebellum plantation architecture. Its classical features and spacious dimensions exemplify the residential tastes of a wealthy Southern planter in the years before the Civil War."

—*From the National Register nomination*

In 1831 forty-year-old Joel Johnson, the scion of a large and prestigious Kentucky family, sold his house and gristmill in Scott County, Kentucky, and, leaving behind a wife and five children, set off for Chicot County in the southeasternmost part of the Arkansas Territory. Johnson purchased a tract of land southeast of Old River Lake (present-day Lake Chicot), just above a large oxbow curve in the Mississippi River called American Bend. Over the course of the next fifteen years he established a large and prosperous cotton plantation there, which he called Lakeport after a nearby steamboat landing.

By the time of his death in 1846 Joel Johnson owned more than thirty-seven hundred acres of rich Delta land and ninety-six slaves. His estate was divided among his six surviving children, with his eldest son, Lycurgus Leonidas Johnson, receiving the largest share. Lycurgus Johnson expanded on his father's holdings, becoming by the late 1850s one of the wealthiest men in the state. Census records for 1860 indicate that he owned over forty-four hundred acres of land and 155 slaves. That same year Lakeport Plantation produced thirteen hundred bales of cotton and ten thousand bushels of corn.

In 1858 Johnson began construction of a plantation home worthy of his wealth and power. The Lakeport plantation house, built in a modified Greek Revival style, was an imposing, two-story, L-shaped structure containing seventeen rooms and measuring sixty-six feet long and forty-four feet wide. Constructed largely of the region's abundant cypress and situated in the midst of surrounding cotton fields, the mansion faced east toward the Mississippi. The front of the structure, along the base of the "L," was graced by a two-story portico with a triangular pediment gable and centered rose windows. Tapered, white columns supported both levels of the portico. From New Orleans came an ornate, wrought-iron, lacework grill. The grill, in an oak leaf and acorn design, surrounded a first-floor porch on the northeastern corner of the structure.

The house was built on a slight elevation in the terrain, and the first floor was set four feet above the grade as protection against flooding. Entry was gained through eleven-foot-high, wood-paneled doors, flanked by glass sidelights, into a large, central entry hall measuring over twenty-six feet long and almost sixteen feet wide. An elaborate ceiling rosette and chandelier adorned the fourteen-foot-high ceiling, and a decorative, painted cloth covered the floor. The hallway was large enough to accommodate parties and dancing.

In addition to this entrance hall the first floor contained ten rooms, including two parlors (one with a ceiling rosette), a formal dining room with adjoining servery, a music room, a drawing room, a sitting room, a kitchen, a cook's room, and a commissary. Back-to-back fireplaces with simple mantles provided warmth to all rooms in winter. Unlike many houses of the period, which had their kitchens separate from the main house as a protection against fire, the Lakeport house had an attached kitchen. Located on the rear ell, it featured a huge, cast-iron Dutch Oven encased in brick. The interior of the house was adorned with large portraits of Lycurgus and his wife, Lydia, painted by the noted portrait artist William F. Cogswell and encased in elaborate plaster frames.

The second story of the house consisted of three large bedrooms, a dressing room, a nursery, and a central hallway with a fourteen-foot-high ceiling and access to the second-floor porch. All doors were of rosewood grain finish and had adjustable overhead transoms for air circulation. The second floor was accessed by a two-level stairway with walnut handrails and spindles. The stair hall was offset from the entry hall, making the upstairs privately accessible to the rooms on the northern part of the first floor. This design made it possible for private family activities like sleeping, bathing, service, and child-care to go on without disturbing public functions on the south part of the first floor. It was a design well suited to a man like Lycurgus Johnson, who was engaged in various economic, political, and social activities.

Two brick accessory buildings, a smokehouse, a storage building, and an outhouse (said to have resembled the main house in detail and finish) were in close proximity to the big house, and undoubtedly slave cabins stood nearby. A brick walkway bordered the house on the front and sides and extended from the main entrance toward the river. Two large cedar trees flanked the front walkway, and magnolia and pecan trees also adorned the grounds. The walkways may have extended to formal gardens at the front and sides of the house. Two large live oaks near the levee indicate that an alley of oaks may once have led to the front entrance of the mansion. Southwest of the house was a small family cemetery.

The Lakeport plantation house was a showplace of the state's "cotton aristocracy," and Johnson staffed it accordingly. He purchased house servants to attend to the family's personal needs (including a well-trained dining room servant for whom Johnson paid $1,700) and hired a tutor for his children.

Like many wealthy planters, Lycurgus Johnson suffered major losses as a result of the Civil War, but unlike many of his contemporaries, Johnson quickly adjusted to the new realities of the postwar world and managed to regain some semblance of his prewar wealth and status. In 1870 Lakeport produced six hundred bales of cotton, making Johnson the largest cotton producer in Chicot County. A chronicler of the county in the postwar period referred to him as "a gentleman of superior education . . . noted for his hospitality, dignity and social culture." Even the local agent of the Freedmen's Bureau, an official generally not favorably disposed to the planters, referred to him as a "model man of Chicot County."

Ca. 1800–1850 etching of a slave picking cotton. *Courtesy of Arkansas History Commission.*

Lycurgus Johnson died in August 1876. Lakeport plantation remained in the Johnson family until 1930, when Lycurgus's son, Victor, sold it to Sam Epstein. Epstein was one of a number of poor Eastern European Jews who migrated to the United States and sought their fortunes in the Delta. Through hard work and skillful investments Epstein overcame poverty and religious bigotry to acquire a sizable fortune and become one of Chicot County's most respected citizens. Upon his death in 1944 his son-in-law, Ben Angel, took over management of the estate. Currently, Ben Angel's son, Sam Epstein

Angel, runs the Epstein Land Company, which encompasses some thirteen thousand acres, including Lakeport. Neither Sam Epstein nor any of his descendants ever lived in the great plantation house. In 1950 Alvin Ford and his family moved into the house and took over management of the farming operations at Lakeport. The Fords moved out in 1972, and the house has since been unoccupied.

Lakeport Plantation stands as a symbol of the people and the time that produced it—of the westward advance of "King Cotton" and the power and perseverance of that greatest of American staples, of the growing affluence of the enterprising antebellum planters who transformed a foreboding frontier wilderness into what one nineteenth-century traveler called "a continuous garden," and of the African-American slaves whose labor produced Lakeport's wealth (a wealth in which they did not share) and whose triumph over an immoral and unjust system created a unique American culture while enriching American culture as a whole.

Today Lycurgus Johnson's magnificent plantation house is empty and in decline. But it still stands at the center of a vast agricultural operation, towering over the surrounding cotton fields as it has for 140 years.

Acknowledgements:

The information for this essay was derived mainly from the survey and documentation performed for the Historic American Buildings Survey under the direction of Elam L. Denham, University of Arkansas, Fayetteville, 1984, and from "A Garden in the Wilderness: The Johnsons and the Making of Lakeport Plantation, 1831–1876," a doctoral dissertation by Thomas A. DeBlack, University of Arkansas, 1995.

African-American laborers were the mainstay of the "cotton aristocracy" before and after the Civil War. *Courtesy of UALR Archives.*

Pea Ridge National Military Park. *Photo by A. C. Haralson, courtesy of Arkansas Department of Parks and Tourism.*

PEA RIDGE AND PRAIRIE GROVE BATTLEFIELDS

William L. Shea

Pea Ridge National Military Park
1862
Pea Ridge, Benton County
Listed on the National Register of Historic Places on October 15, 1969

"Pea Ridge was the Civil War battle that saved the state of Missouri for the Union. The two-day engagement fought in the northwest corner of Arkansas was a Federal victory, despite the fact that Union forces were outnumbered and were fighting in Confederate Territory. The Battle of Pea Ridge was the final, dramatic stage in Federal General Curtis's campaign to drive pro-Confederate forces from Missouri. And it put an end to Confederate commander Earl Van Dorn's ambitions toward gaining control of the state and its nerve center, St. Louis."

—From the National Register nomination

Prairie Grove Battlefield State Park
1862
Prairie Grove, Washington County
Listed on the National Register of Historic Places on September 4, 1970

"Prairie Grove was the last major Civil War engagement in northwest Arkansas, and the Confederates never again tried to use the region as an avenue to invade Missouri. Although Prairie Grove may technically have been a draw, Hindman's retreat subsequently paved the way for Union occupation of northwest Arkansas; in effect, Prairie Grove represented a defeat for the Confederacy in the Trans-Mississippi west. Hindman's Cane Hill-Prairie Grove campaign to drive the enemy from Arkansas was an abject failure, and over the next year Van Buren, Fort Smith, and ultimately Little Rock were to fall as a result of the Confederate 'victory' at Prairie Grove."

—From the National Register nomination

During the Civil War more than seven hundred military engagements took place between organized bodies of Union and Confederate soldiers in Arkansas. At the close of the twentieth century all but two of those hundreds of battlefields have been paved over, plowed under, washed away, or simply forgotten. Pea Ridge and Prairie Grove are the sole survivors of nearly a century and a half of indifference and neglect.

Pea Ridge was the site of the largest, costliest, and most important Civil War engagement fought on Arkansas soil. Close to twenty-four thousand men clashed there on March 7 and 8, 1862, and well over three thousand were killed, crippled, or maimed. For nearly a century afterwards Pea Ridge remained a typical Ozark rural landscape, a mix of small fields, stunted timber, and rocky outcroppings. Local people harvested the battlefield and supplemented their income by selling bullets and cannonballs to visitors. In time the soil was depleted of this metallic crop, and the inhabitants returned to more traditional pursuits.

In 1957 Gov. Orval Faubus, a resident of nearby Huntsville, threw his not-inconsiderable weight behind the movement to preserve the site.

The state of Arkansas purchased forty-three hundred acres—the entire battlefield—and donated the land to the National Park Service. Perhaps it was a peace offering connected in some way to the uproar at Central High School. Whatever the motivation, the act was noble and unprecedented. No other state has made such an extraordinary gesture to preserve intact a historical site of national significance, and no other Civil War battlefield park in the nation is so perfectly preserved, so free of intrusive bronze and marble Victorian-era monuments. In 1962 Pea Ridge National Military Park was opened to the public. A long campaign, not yet fully realized, was launched to restore the battlefield to its appearance of a century earlier.

On December 7, 1862, another dreadful clash occurred at Prairie Grove. About twenty thousand men fought there, and another three thousand fell dead or wounded. After the war the community of Prairie Grove was established nearby, and farmers returned to cultivate the rich soil of Crawford's Prairie. For many years bumper crops of lead and iron were harvested along with wheat and corn. In 1908 the United Daughters of the Confederacy purchased a sliver of the battlefield for veterans' reunions

Prairie Grove Battlefield State Park. *Photo by Ken Story, Arkansas Historic Preservation Program.*

and other gatherings. After the last veterans faded from the scene, the hilltop preserve evolved into a de facto city park and became cluttered with swings, sand boxes, and picnic tables. It even served as a haven for pioneer Ozark homesteads rescued from oblivion elsewhere.

The former reunion site and city park became Prairie Grove Battlefield State Park in 1971, though evidence of its previous incarnations remains in place to this day. Unfortunately, no recent governor or legislature has seen fit to lavish funds on Prairie Grove. The park currently encompasses about four hundred acres, a fraction of the expansive battlefield. (Alas, much of the western half of the site has been paved over and built upon by the Prairie Grove

School District, a particularly dismal example of the impact of public education on Arkansas history.) But the modern pattern of woods and fields is suggestive of the historic landscape, and long-overdue efforts are underway to purchase as much of the battlefield as possible or at least protect it from the sprawl of the adjacent town.

The isolated national park in Benton County and the struggling state park in Washington County represent different approaches to battlefield preservation and interpretation. The parks as we see them today are the products of two distinct bureaucratic systems that reflect different philosophies, respond to different constituencies, and rely on different levels of funding and professional support. Visitors to

WILLIAM L. SHEA

Pea Ridge, for example, find a typical National Park Service visitor's center and museum, a tour road with turnouts and overlooks, riding and hiking trails, a slightly inaccurate reconstruction of Elkhorn Tavern, and a variety of static displays.

At Prairie Grove visitors encounter an eclectic mix of amateurish and professional interpretive efforts that reflects the site's complicated history: a visitor's center and museum donated by the son of the Confederate commander, an obelisk-like smoke-stack from a nearby historic steam mill, assorted original and reconstructed houses, and a driving tour (mostly outside the park) that wanders along narrow streets and over rolling hills. On the first weekend in December of even-numbered years, visitors can experience a smashing reenactment of the battle. With new interpretive schemes gradually replacing the old and additional acreage being acquired as funds permit, Prairie Grove is a work in progress.

Pea Ridge and Prairie Grove are bound together by more than proximity and alliteration. Hundreds of violent clashes occurred in Arkansas during the Civil War, and nearly every one destroyed lives and dreams, but only these two mar-velously bucolic battlefields tucked away in the northwest corner of the state have been preserved in any meaningful way. Perhaps two dozen other battlefields can be identified, but all are in private hands and subject to development.

Veterans of Pea Ridge continued to gather at Elkhorn Tavern well into the twentieth century. *Courtesy of Pea Ridge National Military Park.*

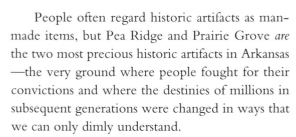

Eighteen-year-old Perry O'Kelly, 20th Wisconsin Infantry, killed at Prairie Grove. *Courtesy of Arkansas Department of Parks and Tourism.*

Confederate Gen. A. E. Steen, killed at Prairie Grove. *Courtesy of State Historical Society of Missouri, Columbia.*

People often regard historic artifacts as man-made items, but Pea Ridge and Prairie Grove *are* the two most precious historic artifacts in Arkansas—the very ground where people fought for their convictions and where the destinies of millions in subsequent generations were changed in ways that we can only dimly understand.

What should these battlefields—these unique, irreplaceable artifacts—mean to us today? A visit to Pea Ridge or Prairie Grove provides us with a tangible link to the past that allows us to glimpse what it must have been like on those fateful days, to gain a fleeting moment of empathy with our forebears.

But while these two battlefield parks *preserve* specific historic sites, they also *represent* all of the other blood-stained places that are lost, ignored, or forgotten. Interest in battlefield protection is at an all-time high in much of the rest of the United States, but as is often the case with national trends, Arkansas lags behind. And progress—which usually means bulldozers—presses ahead. Unless the state is caught up in an unprecedented frenzy of historic preservation in the very near future, Pea Ridge and Prairie Grove are likely to be all that we have left to remind us of another time.

WILLIAM L. SHEA

The appearance of the landscape at the Poison Spring battlefield remains largely unchanged from 1864. *Photo by Jeff Holder, Arkansas Historic Preservation Program.*

THE BATTLE OF POISON SPRING

Edwin C. Bearss

Poison Spring Battlefield
1864
Chidester vic., Ouachita County
Listed on the National Register of Historic Places on December 2, 1969
Designated a National Historic Landmark on April 19, 1994

"The ensuing battle was a complete victory for the Confederates. The Union force was shattered; the entire wagon train captured, as well as the accompanying artillery and a large number of prisoners. The victory served a two-fold purpose for the Confederacy in that it denied the Federals their much needed forage and rations, and effectively reduced the number of troops, animals and transport available to Steele."

—From the National Register nomination

The Lincoln Administration in mid-March 1864 undertook the Red River and Camden expeditions aimed at capturing Shreveport, Louisiana, and carrying the war deep into East Texas. The success of this campaign would result in huge benefits to the Union on the economic, diplomatic, military, and political fronts. It involved converging forces: Maj. Gen. N. P. Banks's army and Rear Adm. David D. Porter's squadron were to advance up the Red River Valley and meet Maj. Gen. Frederick Steele's columns coming south from the Arkansas Valley at Shreveport.

But events did not go as planned for the Federals, and by mid-April Banks and Porter had turned back. Steele's columns, harassed by Maj. Gen. Sterling Price and his Arkansas and Missouri Confederates and confronted by critical shortages of rations and provender, abandoned their march via Washington and headed for Camden on the Ouachita River.

It was Steele's Camden detour that led to the Battle of Poison Spring, a brief, savage, and decisive struggle in which racial animosities at their ugliest surfaced. The Arkansas battle took place six days after the Fort Pillow Massacre and three and one-half months before the Battle of the Crater, but even today it does not command the same attention as do those two battles in which African American soldiers received scant quarter. This is unfortunate, because the First Kansas Colored arguably has a more significant and heroic history than the Fifty-fourth Massachusetts of the movie *Glory* fame, and the Poison Spring battlefield possesses great integrity as to time and place.

Steele's army included thirteen thousand men, nine thousand horses and mules, eight hundred wagons, and thirty cannons. Supplying the army was a problem, and Steele later wrote that his supplies were nearly exhausted and so was the country. With men on half-rations for almost three weeks, it was almost impossible to enforce the commander's orders against unauthorized foraging and plundering. On April 17, 198 wagons left Camden under the command of Col. James M. Williams, traveling west on the Washington Road to collect corn seen on White Oak Creek farms during the army's advance on Camden. Williams's command included 193 cavalry from the Sixth Kansas, Second Kansas, and Fourteenth Kansas; two Second Indiana Battery guns manned by thirty-three artillerists; and 438 men of the First Kansas Colored.

The First Kansas Colored had been recruited and organized at Fort Scott, Kansas, from Missouri and Arkansas fugitive slaves who had fled to Kansas in 1861 and 1862. Kansas's reputation as a bastion of abolitionism generated hatred among many Southerners, especially at the thought of blacks in uniform. Many Northerners were uncomfortable with the notion of whites fighting alongside blacks, although the regiment's extraordinary conduct under fire soon tempered such concerns. Privates in the First Kansas were paid ten dollars a month, three dollars less than white privates received. As in most black combat units throughout the war, officers in the First Kansas were white, the noncommissioned officers black.

The Confederates had been enraged by news of the organization of the First Kansas Colored. Southern troops in Arkansas and Missouri spoke with loathing of the "First Nigger" Kansas regiment, and orders were issued that such "crimes and outrages" (the utilization of black soldiers) required "retaliation." Captured white officers commanding black troops were to be "executed as felons," while it was understood that Southern troops would take no black prisoners. Captured First Kansas soldiers would at best be returned to slavery. On one occasion, under a flag of truce in Indian Territory, Confederate forces exchanged a number of white prisoners with the First Kansas but refused to turn

EDWIN C. BEARSS

Hundreds of black soldiers died at Fort Pillow in Tennessee six days before the fighting at Poison Spring. The Tennessee battle has all but eclipsed the fate of the First Kansas Colored Infantry Regiment. *Etching from* Harper's Pictorial History of the Civil War, *1866. Courtesy of Don Hamilton.*

over any black prisoners. When Colonel Williams later received reports of the murder of one of the black prisoners, he ordered the execution of a Confederate prisoner. Williams's ruthlessness convinced the Confederates to stop murdering their black prisoners, at least for some time.

The First Kansas Colored had been the first black regiment to see combat in the war in a victorious skirmish at Island Mound near Butler, Missouri, on October 29, 1862. The following year, on July 1 and 2, the unit carried the day in the Battle of Cabin Creek, in modern-day Oklahoma, with only eight casualties, relieving Fort Gibson. Then on July 17, 1863, the First Kansas Colored played a key role in the Battle of Honey Springs

and in Maj. Gen. James G. Blunt's successful campaign to drive the Confederates out of northwest Arkansas. Blunt later remarked, "I never saw such fighting as was done by the Negro regiment . . . [T]hey make better soldiers in every respect than any troops I have ever had under my command." Their mettle would be tested again under ferocious conditions at Poison Spring.

General Steele had taken no measures to ascertain the whereabouts of the Confederate cavalry before the forage train's April 17 departure. Eighteen miles west of Camden the train dispersed to forage the countryside then returned to camp on White Oak Creek at midnight, loaded with corn. The next morning the train started back to Camden, and en route was reinforced by Capt. William Duncan and 383 men of the Eighteenth Iowa; ninety-six horse soldiers from the Sixth Kansas, Second Kansas, and Fourteenth Kansas; and twenty-five artillerists with two mountain howitzers. This reinforcement gave Colonel Williams one thousand men and four guns with which to guard the heavily loaded wagons.

Confederates, however, were well aware of the train's whereabouts and mission. On the morning of April 18 Missourian Brig. Gen. John S. Marmaduke rode northward from Woodlawn at the head of two thousand grim horse soldiers from Greene's, Cabell's, and Crawford's brigades. Turning into the Washington Road, the Rebels encountered Williams's train fourteen miles west of Camden at Poison Spring. As Marmaduke positioned his command to block the road, additional Confederates sent by General Price to bolster Marmaduke's command arrived. Numbering more that fifteen hundred, the newcomers included Brig. Gen. Samuel B. Maxey's division—Texans and Indians who had been previously bested by the First Kansas and gave the Confederates a decisive bulge: their thirty-one hundred officers and men, who outnumbered the Federals three to one.

Maxey was the senior Confederate officer present. But satisfied that Marmaduke, having arrived first, was familiar with the terrain, he gave Marmaduke tactical command of their combined forces. Marmaduke then formed Maxey's division—Tandy Walker's Choctaws and Chickasaws and Col. Charles De Morse's Texans—south of and parallel to the Washington Road. Crawford's and Cabell's brigades manned the roadblock, with Greene's Missourians in reserve. As soon as contact was made with the rebel roadblock, Colonel Williams had the teamsters close up and double park their wagons, and called to the head of the column the First Kansas Colored. The African Americans were posted in line by their officers, while Kansas horse soldiers

guarded the regiments' flanks. The Iowans protected the train's rear. Colonel Williams, aware that Maxey's Texans and Indians were south of the road, redeployed on the double a battalion of the First Kansas to counter this threat. What might have been a brief fight became a battle of attrition. Williams called on Duncan to rush reinforcements to the head of the column to assist in breaking the roadblock, but the messenger returned with grim news: the rear guard was so hard pressed it could spare no Iowans.

Marmaduke's artillery boomed, maintaining a destructive crossfire, while his horse soldiers, fighting dismounted, assailed the stalled train and its defenders front and rear. South of and parallel to Washington road, Maxey's people occupied a wooded ridge. Advancing, they swept down the ridge, jogged across an old field, and worked their way through a ravine. As they closed on the road, the Texans and Indians opened fire on the train's defenders.

Colonel Williams grimly determined to defend the wagons to the bitter end, in the hope that reinforcements might rush out from Camden. The Federals fought on and even counterattacked as the fight raged for the parked wagons. But there were too many Confederates. As Walker's Indian brigade advanced, Pvt. Dickson Wallace mounted a captured Union howitzer, from which he "gave a whoop, which was followed by such a succession of whoops from his comrades as made the woods reverberate for miles. . . ." Duncan's Iowans closed ranks as the Choctaw and Chickasaw assault forced him to pull his soldiers out of the field north of the road and place them along the edge of the woods. Assailed from the south as well as from the front and rear, the outnumbered Yanks, after a desperate close-range fight, gave way. One of Brig. Gen. William "Old Tige" Cabell's colonels recalled: "Away trotted the poor black men into the forest, clinging to their rifles but not using them, while the Confederates cut them down right and left." Confederate pursuit of the retreating Yanks continued for two and one-half miles, and although pockets of Union resistance on Lee's plantation north of the Washington Road slowed pursuit, all firing ceased by two o'clock P.M. Union losses might have been worse, as the bluecoats retreated through the hollows and swamps back to Camden, had General Maxey not pulled rank on Marmaduke. Marmaduke had ordered an all-out pursuit of the fleeing Federals, but Maxey countermanded this order, allowing fragments of Williams's force to escape.

The Confederates scored an overwhelming victory at Poison Spring, and Steele's Camden supply difficulties worsened. Union losses at Poison Spring totaled 301 killed, wounded, and missing. The First Kansas bore the brunt of the casualties, losing 42 percent of its strength, 182 killed and wounded out of 438 engaged. Union reports noted that the Confederates shot wounded black soldiers without mercy, and the Southerners reported only four black soldiers captured. Lending credence to a conscious Confederate massacre of African Americans is Cabell's report that "Morgan's regiment killed at least eight negros," although Morgan's unit did not participate in the battle but was stationed between Poison Spring and Camden to intercept fleeing Yanks.

The First Kansas had been savaged at Poison Spring, with nearly half of its personnel killed in four hours, at the hands of the same Texans and Indians they had defeated at Honey Springs nine months before. The Texans' revenge had been brutal. White soldiers taunted the wounded blacks with shouts of "Where is the First Nigger now?" answered by, "All cut to pieces and gone to hell by bad management," before they shot or bayoneted them. Black survivors vowed never again to take prisoners, and for the rest of the war "Remember Poison Spring" was a rallying cry for the First Kansas. By the war's end the First Kansas Colored had seen more combat than any other black Civil War regiment.

Confederate losses were almost a third less than those of the Federals: 114 killed, wounded, or missing. Almost two hundred wagons loaded with forage, as well as Union cannon, fell into the Southerners' hands. The Rebels had won their first victory of the Camden Expedition, and Price's troops' morale soared. Steele's supply difficulties deteriorated, and the bluecoats would remain on the defensive for the remainder of the ill-fated campaign.

The Old State House Museum, built in 1836. *Courtesy of the Old State House Museum.*

THE OLD STATE HOUSE
AND THE BROOKS-BAXTER WAR

Kenneth C. Barnes

Old State House
1836
Little Rock, Pulaski County
Listed on the National Register of Historic Places on December 3, 1969
Designated a National Historic Landmark on December 9, 1997

"The Old State House was the state capitol from 1836 until the new capitol was occupied in January 1911. The structure was the seat of Confederate State government from 1861–63. Early in 1864 it became the headquarters of the loyal Unionist government and remained so until Arkansas was readmitted as a state. It also housed the U.S. district court from 1842–69. After the General Assembly moved to the present state capitol in 1911, the Old State House was used at various times by the University of Arkansas Medical School, the American Legion, the state military department, and other state organizations."

—From the National Register nomination

The Old State House in Little Rock provided a gorgeous backdrop to Governor Bill Clinton's victory celebrations when he was elected president in 1992. A century earlier, when the building served as the state's Capitol, it was more than a backdrop as two rival claimants to the governor's office actually did battle there in the Brooks-Baxter War.

One of the most convoluted and confusing episodes in Arkansas history, the political quarrel known as the Brooks-Baxter War was played out largely on the grounds of the Old State House and the surrounding area. It brought an end to Reconstruction in 1874. The basic division during Reconstruction had pitted ex-Confederates against an alliance of local white Unionists, African Americans, and several Republican leaders who had come down from the North—so-called carpetbaggers—in the years following the Civil War. However, by 1872 this alliance crumbled as southern Unionists joined former Confederates (now Democrats) in support of the Republican candidate for governor, Joseph Brooks, ironically himself a carpetbagger. Brooks ran against the Arkansan Elisha Baxter, who was backed by the regular Republican Party apparatus under the control of former Gov. Powell Clayton. When Brooks lost, he cried foul, claiming fraud had cost him the election. However, when Governor Baxter began to pursue an independent line, acting contrary to Clayton's Republican positions on several key issues, both sides did an about-face. Clayton's faction shifted support to Brooks, claiming he had been illegally counted out of the election, and thus in effect admitting their own guilt in the election of 1872. Southern conservatives who had voted for Brooks now called Baxter the only honest man to come out of the Republican Party.

The courts, still dominated by members of Powell Clayton's Republican machine, declared on April 15, 1874, that Brooks, not Baxter, had actually won the 1872 election and was the rightful governor of Arkansas, and then swore Brooks into office.

Brooks and about twenty armed supporters proceeded immediately to the State House, where they stormed into the governor's office on the second floor of the building's west wing. Told by these men to vacate the office at once, Elisha Baxter complied as he looked into their muskets. He walked down Markham Street two blocks east to the Anthony House hotel, between Scott and Main Streets, where he established his headquarters for the debacle that would follow.

Both sides appealed to President Ulysses S. Grant and awaited federal intervention. Grant and Congress, however, preferred to let the matter be settled locally. For the following month the Brooks and Baxter factions dug in at their positions. Hundreds of supporters on each side flocked to Little Rock, and the whole state seemed to take sides. While on the one hand the affair seemed like a twisted conflict within the Republican Party, on the other hand it summed up the situation Arkansas faced during Reconstruction. The Brooks forces, largely made up of African Americans and Northern whites, represented the past policies of radical Reconstruction. The Baxter faction, mostly consisting of home-grown whites weary of Republican rule, was ready to settle old scores left over from the war and the violent Reconstruction days of 1868, when Governor Clayton's Republican militia had done battle with the Ku Klux Klan.

By nightfall on April 15 Brooks supporters had occupied the State House and armed themselves with guns from the state armory. They began erecting wooden barricades and digging earthworks on the lawns. Brooks's men took down the front and rear doors of the State House to place cannons in the doorways to protect against a Baxter attack. A plank mess hall was eventually erected on the Capitol's east side. Campfires on the lawn illuminated the white stucco walls at night. The noble Greek Revival structure had become an armed camp.

At the Anthony House a flag flying from the

"Political war in Arkansas: the Baxter-Brooks imbroglio. The capitol building in Little Rock defended by the troops of pseudo-Governor Brooks." *Quotation and illustration from* Leslie's, *May 2, 1874. Courtesy of UALR Archives.*

balcony signified that building's claim as the seat of state government. Hundreds of Baxter troops poured in from around the state and established pickets up and down Markham Street. Soldiers occupied the adjacent buildings, drilled in the streets, and did sentry duty at night. Baxter's men brought in "Lady Baxter," a large siege cannon resurrected from retirement at the Kramer schoolhouse on 2nd Street, where it had been used in the war. Later two Parrot guns, small artillery pieces, arrived from Texas and were positioned on Markham Street pointing west.

A company of U.S. Army troops tried to keep the two sides apart where they met at Markham and Main. The troops eventually placed a large fire truck in the middle of the street as a barrier between the two groups. The four weeks that followed were tense times as bugles blasted, troops drilled, and men jeered at each other in downtown Little Rock. Occasionally, trigger-happy soldiers let loose. Nearly all casualties resulted from indiscriminate shooting and the chaos that ensued. One guest at the Anthony House was shot and killed by a stray

bullet that came through the window. A chambermaid at the hotel fell from the second story and broke her leg during the confusion. Two black men were shot by stray gunfire, one in the wrist and the other in the buttocks. While troops were concentrated near one another in Little Rock, a couple of small-scale battles occurred in other parts of the state, particularly in Palarm and Jefferson County, with larger death tolls.

Despite the tension a carnival-like atmosphere prevailed most of the time. A brass band came up from Pine Bluff and entertained the Baxter crowd, while a black band played at the State House for Brooks's men. A popgun man showed up selling "so many shots for a dime." Drinking establishments did a thriving business, particularly Al Schwartz's saloon on Louisiana Street and Gennochio's, close to the action on Markham. On April 21 police arrested a woman, Alice Stanley, who showed up at the front line stone drunk, wearing men's clothing, carrying a substantial revolver, and declaring she wanted to join the army.

The conflict finally ended in mid-May when

President Grant directed the state legislature to vote on the disputed claims, and Baxter's supporters prevailed. On May 19, a month after he was forcibly removed from the State House, Elisha Baxter toured the premises and reclaimed his chair in the governor's office. The building had suffered tremendously from its occupation by as many as eight hundred men. The lawn was practically destroyed by barricades and earthworks, and piles of guns and munitions lay everywhere, inside and out. The whole building reeked of sour bacon and human body odor. The filthiest room was the state library, where books lay scattered through the room, trodden under foot. Soldiers had used bookshelves as dining tables and sheets of the state geological survey as table cloths. The cramped conditions at the State House had spawned an outbreak of measles and smallpox. Brooks's men responded by taking over Concordia Hall, a nearby building owned by Little Rock's Jewish Association, for use as a temporary hospital.

Despite the depressing appearances Baxter cheerfully proclaimed his victory. One hundred and one guns were fired in celebration. Glass windows in the vicinity shattered when the big gun, Lady Baxter, was fired. Misses Mollie Morton and Maggie Trigg assisted in pulling the lanyards to fire the smaller Parrot guns, with Miss Trigg receiving a slight wound on her face from the friction primer. The shot badly tore the hand and arm of one of the gunners. The Brooks-Baxter War retained a tragic-comical quality to its very end.

The war served as a fitting conclusion to Reconstruction, one last blowout before conservative white southerners resumed control over state government as the Democratic Party. The resulting settlement brought a new election and a new constitutional convention, which signified the end of Reconstruction and Republican rule. As a reminder Lady Baxter was positioned on the State House lawn and remains there today. The episode demonstrated

Reinforcements for Brooks cross the Arkansas River, 1874. *Illustration from* Leslie's, *1874. Courtesy of UALR Archives.*

Elisha Baxter. *Courtesy of UALR Archives.*

Joseph Brooks. *Courtesy of Arkansas History Commission.*

how control over the State House, the office of government, symbolized power.

As Arkansas approached the end of the next century, in July of 1996, at a larger, newer state house a mile away, a drama similar to the Brooks-Baxter War unfolded. Gov. Jim Guy Tucker resigned from office. Then, on the very day he was to turn over power to Mike Huckabee, the lieutenant governor, Tucker rescinded his resignation. For a moment it appeared that Arkansas had two men claiming to be governor. Huckabee, however, did not pull out the muskets. Instead, he threatened a special session of the general assembly to consider impeachment. There were echoes of Brooks-Baxter, nonetheless. Such events remind us that politics in Arkansas are sometimes violent, often rancorous, but always entertaining.

Bibliographical note:

This account has been drawn from the newspaper coverage in the Little Rock papers, the *Arkansas Gazette* and the *Daily Republican,* April 16–May 20, 1874, and the writings of two participants in the struggle: John Mortimer Harrell, *The Brooks and Baxter War: A History of the Reconstruction Period in Arkansas* (Saint Louis: Slawson, 1893); and Benjamin S. Johnson, "The Brooks-Baxter War," *Publications of the Arkansas Historical Association,* 2 (Fayetteville: Arkansas Historical Association, 1908):122–173.

The Brooks-Baxter War is discussed in all the surveys of Arkansas History. The most thorough account is Earl F. Woodward, "The Brooks and Baxter War in Arkansas, 1872–1874," *Arkansas Historical Quarterly* 30 (Winter 1971):315–336. For information about the Old State House, see Clara B. Kennan, "Arkansas's Old State House," *Arkansas Historical Quarterly* 9 (Spring 1950):33–42.

The board-and-batten, box-constructed, dogtrot Ozmer House. *Arkansas Historic Preservation Program photo.*

FRANK OZMER'S DOGTROT

Cyrus A. Sutherland

Ozmer House
1883
Magnolia vic., Columbia County
Listed on the National Register of Historic Places on November 20, 1986

"Architecturally significant for its excellent craftsmanship and as a representative of the homes built by farm families in south Arkansas, the Ozmer House was built in 1883 approximately two miles northeast of the courthouse square in Magnolia, Columbia County. Originally located in a rural farming area, the structure is a dogtrot with a kitchen ell. The one-story house is of box construction with board-and-battens both exterior and interior. The interior also possesses an unusual gambrel ceiling and handmade pine mantels. Typical in plan but exceptional in craftsmanship, the Ozmer House is a well-preserved representative of Columbia County's agricultural and architectural heritage."

—From the National Register nomination

John Bruce used locally available materials to build his Independence County home in 1854. *Courtesy of H. L. Miller Collection, Museum of Discovery.*

Small landowners in the state of Georgia, plantation owners, and tenant farmers who normally owned neither land nor slaves heard more and more tempting tales in the 1830s and 1840s that claimed that southern Arkansas and neighboring northern Louisiana were lands of plenty. Columbia County, Arkansas, seemed especially attractive to homesteading lumbermen, hunters, and farmers.

The county's pine and oak forests nurtured bears, wolves, and smaller game—an invitation to hunters who for two or three decades practiced "peltry." Hides of bear, wolf, beaver, raccoon, and deer provided a main medium of exchange. Peltry was welcomed by farmers. Carnivorous bears and wolves were a serious threat to livestock. Only

razorback hogs, descendants of swine imported in the mid-1500s by explorer Hernando de Soto, were well coached in self-defense and could take care of themselves.

Eight or ten powered gristmills and sawmills operated in the county by 1860. The Red River on the west and the easterly Ouachita River gave the area a practical, floating connection to the Mississippi and New Orleans markets. Columbia County made no promise of gold, silver, or coal mining, but early forest clearings had revealed the inviting, deep, rich soil of the gulf coastal plain.

How did word of the area's bounty get back to Georgia and Alabama? Through returned explorer scouts? Slow mail from relatives or friends? Probably

CYRUS A. SUTHERLAND

the most persuasive motivation for industrious but poor tenant farmers to emigrate westward was available free land. The Louisiana Purchase of 1803 extended the homesteading temptation for the land-hungry farmer who was able and willing to emigrate and meet the homesteading requirements. Of the lands washed by the Mississippi River, Kentucky and Tennessee were the earliest to receive statehood. Louisiana, Mississippi, and Missouri followed in that order. Arkansas was admitted to the Union in 1836.

The movement westward from Georgia had begun by the 1840s. Soon after Frank Ozmer's birth, ca. 1848, his parents loaded two ox-drawn wagons and moved to Alabama to try a new settlement, probably as tenant farmers. Here Ozmer watched more and more loaded Georgia wagons heading westward through Alabama and Louisiana. Frequently Ozmer's own 'Bama neighbors joined the trek from Georgia. By the late 1850s the Ozmers could no longer resist the pull of the west. They arrived in Columbia County, Arkansas, in 1860. Young Frank was twelve.

An 1860 census cited by historian Glen G. Mantel provides us with some information about Columbia County. At that time there were eighty-eight hundred free citizens living in Columbia County and thirty-five hundred slaves. Among the free citizens 429 families held slaves, and eleven hundred did not. An 1870 census indicated that only 50 percent of Columbia County residents were natives of Arkansas. Most of the rest came from Georgia and Alabama.

Mantel, who studied Columbia County extensively, found no information indicating that the Ozmers were slave owners in either Georgia or Arkansas. Frank Ozmer's father established his claim, estimated to be one hundred to two hundred acres, in the northwestern part of Columbia County, near present-day Magnolia. He joined neighboring farmers during the next decade in clearing woodland, first for small family gardens, and then in increasing annual increments, until the desired acreage was achieved. For the typical settler land clearing was an odious, time-consuming task. When possible it was best accomplished by contracting with an experienced lumbering team equipped with proper tools, log chains, and healthy oxen, supplemented no doubt by slave labor. Heavy timber removal contracts did not always include the tedious leftover labor of undergrowth clearing, rail splitting from selected logs, first and second site burnings, and stump removal. Mantel relates that under normal conditions three years or more were required to transform virgin forest to arable fields that could produce profitable crops of corn and the all-important cotton.

In 1873 Frank Ozmer, age 23, was married to Virginia Faulk of Athens, Louisiana. The early married years of Frank and Laura were spent in a log house of the commonest form, the dogtrot: two rooms separated by a wide breezeway, all three spaces sharing the same gabled roof. Many other types of log houses were built, and many still survive. The dogtrot was common throughout the early colonies, particularly in milder weather zones, where logs provided available shelter material. Dogtrots followed frontiersmen all the way to the Pacific coast.

This seems the appropriate point to reiterate the theory that early American vernacular building forms were rarely if ever committed to drawings on paper; they traveled through time and space in the memorized habits and experiences of builders. Formulae for room dimensions, door and window standards, ceiling heights, roof pitches, and chimney heights passed from father to son, master to apprentice, neighbor to neighbor. Vernacular forms were repeated year after year and in place after place, never precisely, and always with human variations, intentional or accidental. Vernacular forms change . . . but very slowly. Occasionally, near poetic perfection of an idealized image is achieved.

When Frank and Laura Ozmer were ready to build the house we admire today, they decided they were happy with the plan of the dogtrot they were moving from, except for two major considerations. They wanted their new house to be a frame structure, built largely of durable cypress. And they wanted it to be enlarged, expandable, and able to accommodate in the near future four additional rooms. Was this an Ozmer example of family planning?

My first reaction to this remarkably well-built vernacular farmhouse is to ask who built it? Was it Frank himself or an itinerant building crew? My proposed scenario is well within the realm of possibility for Frank and Laura Ozmer in 1883.

Frank was a serious farmer. He had spent all his youthful energies emulating his father and his father's success with the family agricultural enterprise. An important principle learned from his father was to allow major building projects—such as barns, smokehouses, and corn cribs—to be erected by skilled builders with experience.

So for his new house Frank made a building agreement with the reputable, (idealized) McPherson brothers—Zebulon, Joshua, and Ezekiel (Zeb, Josh and Zeke)—to build a new kind of two-room dogtrot, as described above. The McPherson brothers, as our story goes, had recently returned from several months working in the Little Rock vicinity. The McPherson brothers were already contracted with a team of brick masons to construct a dry goods store on the Magnolia Square, as well as a farmhouse and two outbuildings on land adjoining the Ozmer farm. The McPhersons assured Frank and Laura Ozmer that they were experienced in juggling two or three jobs at once and in scheduling the timing of their separate specialties. They took charge of the Ozmer house at once, with Zeb as team leader, project manager, building planner, and finish carpenter.

Josh managed materials, calculating quantities of cypress lumber of varying dimensions, structural timbers for use at foundation and roof level, floor joists and corner posts, milled rafters and other roofing members of pine, and sections of cypress logs to be riven at the building site with mallet and froe. Josh would order most of these products from Wilkins sawmill on Kendrick Creek near Waldo, four miles from the new house. By the early '80s the commercial properties around four sides of the courthouse square in Magnolia were almost all occupied. A few were two-story, brick commercial buildings, while others remained false-fronted frames. At one of the two general merchandise stores Josh ordered certain hardware, several pounds of cut nails, and a new hand saw, and placed orders for items not in stock. Three local blacksmiths could craft some hardware not available locally—hinges, special nails, spikes, bolts, latches, hasps, etc.

Zeke was the layout man and mason. The brothers had built a great number of dogtrots. They knew the dimensions of everything by heart—brick pier locations to receive floor structural members, sizes and locations of stone footings for the brick chimneys, proportions of lime, sand, and water for masonry mortar.

The McPhersons spent the greater part of the year coordinating their time on other projects and completing the house on a site not far from the Ozmers' former log house. Hand planing lumber is time consuming.

Several quality features of the structure deserve mention. Full-length porches spanned the dogtrot's front and rear façades. Shed roofs supported by chamfered posts sheltered the porches, greatly enlarging the shaded outdoor spaces already provided by the breezeway. Another notable feature of

CYRUS A. SUTHERLAND

The Heron Family gathers on the porch of their board-and-batten house on the Campbell Plantation at Scott, ca. 1948. *Courtesy of Arkansas Department of Parks and Tourism.*

the new house was its box construction, rarely used in northern climes. Structurally, box construction is an alternative to the modern stud frame. All walls, exterior and interior, are made of vertical boards one inch thick. These boards, with the help of sturdier corner posts, support the roof structure, a task performed in a modern frame building by stud frames. The butted vertical joints of the hand-planed cypress boards are covered on two sides by narrow, cypress battens. Wide baseboards on all interior surfaces add stability to the thin walls. The house's ceilings had a surprising, double-pitch, gambrel shape. Like the walls, the ceiling boards were hand-planed, and the gambrel shape resulted because they followed the special structural position of the roof rafters.

Not long after the Ozmers moved in to their new dogtrot, their first planned expansion was begun. The McPherson brothers added two rooms by enclosing opposite ends of the back porch. A

Logs, boards, shakes, and lattice work were combined in building the alfalfa barn at the Bonds Plantation in Saint Francis County, seen here in 1917. *Courtesy of Arkansas Department of Parks and Tourism.*

door from each room opened to the breezeway. A few years later the house was enlarged further by the addition of a two-room kitchen ell extending south from the southwest corner. A broad porch the length of the ell further enhanced the shaded outside space and simultaneously provided shelter to the separate doors of the two new rooms.

Frank Ozmer lived in the house until his death in 1941. The farmhouse's uncommon six-room spaciousness and its above-average materials and workmanship confirmed Ozmer's agricultural prosperity. Such prosperity was stimulated further throughout the region when the Cotton Belt Railroad came through Magnolia and Columbia County in the mid-1880s.

When the Ozmer house was threatened by encroaching commercialism, a quieter location for it was sought. The house was donated to the Southern

Arkansas University Farm, where it has enjoyed careful restoration and care. The new location is only a half mile from the dogtrot's original site. It now stands on its brick piers in a secluded grove, overlooking a placid pond. The cedar shingle roof installed at relocation time has deteriorated, but a new standing seam metal roof will provide protection almost indefinitely. Frank and Laura and the original construction crew (certainly skilled craftsmen like our McPhersons) would be pleased with the dogtrot's listing on the National Register of Historic Places.

Reference cited:
    Glen G. Mantel, "Early Days in Columbia County," Ph.D. dissertation, University of Arkansas, 1933.

CYRUS A. SUTHERLAND

The simple, unpretentious Wheel Store in Batesville has changed little in the century since its construction. *Photo by Amy Bennett, Arkansas Historic Preservation Program.*

THE WHEEL STORE

Donald Holley

The Wheel Store
1887
Batesville, Independence County
Listed on the National Register of Historic Places on December 8, 1988.

"The Wheel Store was built on land bought by the county cooperative arm of the Agricultural Wheel, a post–Civil War agrarian reform organization composed of farmers, sharecroppers and ordinary lower-class laborers from many trades. Built by this organization's local chapter, it originally housed a cooperative store on the first floor and a meeting hall above. It stands as a monument to the most active and significant farmer movement originating in Arkansas."

—*From the National Register nomination*

The Wheel Store in Batesville is one of the few remaining relics of the agrarian discontent that swept across Arkansas and the nation between 1870 and 1900. Farmers—who made up the bulk of the population—saw themselves increasingly beset by problems: low crop prices, high freight rates, and high mortgage rates. As the United States industrialized and urbanized, rural people were called hicks and hayseeds, but they maintained that they were the backbone of the country.

In the late nineteenth century farmers everywhere were caught up in complex international markets that they could neither understand nor control. They were suspicious of large corporations, which they called "trusts" or monopolies. They watched prices for their products decline from year to year, watched railroad rates for shipping increase, and saw their farms burdened by mortgages that threatened their hold on the land. Some of their grievances were valid; others were not. Agricultural prices did fall after 1880. For example, cotton plunged from ten cents to five cents a pound by the mid-1890s. Although farmers received less for their crops, however, their purchasing power actually increased.

Nor was their complaint about railroad rates entirely valid. Farmers believed that both major parties—Democratic and Republican—ignored rural needs while granting privileges to large industrial corporations. Railroads, for example, received huge grants of government-owned land, and these were the same railroads that, many believed, over-charged farmers to ship their produce to market. Yet railroad rates actually fell during the late nineteenth century.

Farmers signed mortgages because they hoped to expand their holdings or to purchase new machinery. These mortgages tended to be short-term, and they could be renegotiated at lower rates. But as commodity prices fell, many southern farmers became trapped in the crop lien system, which kept them in debt.

As usual, farm income was at the mercy of the weather and insect pests. Some farmers prospered while others suffered. Farm income generally tracked the national economy, falling in the 1870s, rising in the 1880s, and remaining steady in the 1890s. While Arkansas farmers did have justifiable complaints, they did not have a clear view of their main problem: too many farmers were trying to scratch out a living on too little land or on marginal land. Farmers and their families purchased more and more manufactured goods, and as a result they eroded their self-sufficiency.

Whatever the merit of their grievances, many farmers believed their condition had worsened, and the perception of injustice and hardship fueled their growing anger. They worked hard, but they believed they were being robbed of their wealth by greedy bankers, railroads, and merchants. They also suspected that they had suffered a loss of prestige, while cities and factories seemed to hold the nation's future. As described in Hamlin Garland's *Son of the Middle Border* (1890) and *Main-Travelled Roads* (1891), farm work was hard and rural life less exciting than the bright lights of big cities.

Increasingly on the defensive, farmers began to draw together in organizations that offered them a chance to address their grievances. After touring the South in 1867, Oliver H. Kelley, a clerk in the Department of Agriculture, founded the National Grange of the Patrons of Husbandry, better known simply as the Grange. This organization hoped to combat the monotony of rural life with social, cultural, and especially educational activities. During the 1870s depression the Grange grew rapidly in the South and Midwest. The Grangers set up cooperative stores, warehouses, and insurance companies. Grangers also made forays into politics by supporting railroad legislation.

As farm discontent continued to mount, additional organizations appeared. On February 15,

STRIKE -:- STRIKE -:- STRIKE

GENERAL STRIKE CALL!

Stop All Work – Stop Every Hoe – Stop Every Plow – Strike On Every Plantation and Farm!

SHARECROPPERS-TENANTS-DAYLABORERS

Every One Out of the Fields — Refuse to Do Another Day's Work
Force the Owners and Bosses to Deal With Your Union!

Do not return until your demands are won. By using the only power you have—the strength you show when all work stops—you can win a victory—that will never be forgotten. The Federal Government will be forced to act, in behalf of justice, when all work stops. Use your power, stop all work on every plantation and farm. Strike a blow that will be remembered forever.

STRIKE FOR:

The Right to Live Like Human Beings.
For a Fair Day's Wage for a Fair Day's Work.
For Decent Contracts for Sharecroppers and Tenants.
For the Right to Bargain Collectively with the Owners.
For Arbitration of Wage and Contract Disputes.

STRIKE AGAINST:

Forcing of Men to Work at the Point of Guns.
Against the Illegal and False Imprisonment of Honest Workers.
Concentration Camps or Stockades Erected to Force Strikers to Labor.
The Breaking Up of Meetings of Workers, and Jailing and Mistreatment of Leaders of Their Organizations.

By calling out every one from the fields and keeping them out we can force disarmament of plantation thugs. We can force resignation of brutal yellow curs who hold peace officers' commissions. We can put a stop to terrorism and intimidation. We can make Arkansas a fit place to live. Use your power—strike on every farm and plantation . . . shut down the works.

Pass This Leaflet On — Spread the Word — For Every One to Come Out

CENTRAL WAGE COMMITTEE
SOUTHERN TENANT FARMERS' UNION

The grievances that led to formation of the Agricultural Wheel extended beyond that organization's lifetime, as illustrated by this 1936 handbill from the Southern Tenant Farmers' Union. *Courtesy of Southern Tenant Farmers Union Papers, Southern Historical Collection, The Library of the University of North Carolina at Chapel Hill.*

1882, in a log schoolhouse near Des Arc, Prairie County, Arkansas, a small group of farmers formed the Wattensas Farmer's Club, later renamed the Agricultural Wheel. This latter name reflected both biblical passages and the belief that agriculture was the great controlling wheel of the world economy.

Though its initial purpose was vague, the Wheel stimulated a large response, indicating widespread discontent. Local chapters quickly appeared across Arkansas along with a State Agricultural Wheel organization. Unlike the Grange, which had admitted merchants and other urban people, the Wheel restricted its members to farmers and laborers engaged in farming. What had created this movement was summed up in one word: *monopoly*. One of the founders of the Wheel said:

> As we have assembled here tonight for the purpose of devising some plan by which to extricate ourselves from the grasp of monopoly, we believe it our duty first to take a view of the adverse circumstances which surround us, to-wit: Drouth, poverty and oppression by organizations whose avowed object is the reduction of laborers to financial and political slavery . . . We see, we know, that the products of our labor is [*sic*] being wrested from our hands at astonishingly low prices, and afterwards sold at prices so much greater as to seem almost incredible; yea, double price. We, who produced it by the sweat of our faces and that of our beloved wives and children, are publicly robbed in order that a few heartless and soulless middlemen may be made rich. . . . "

Monopolists included merchants, ginners, cotton buyers, railroads, and especially large out-of-state "trusts" that controlled the prices of farm commodities.

Like the Grangers, the Wheelers attempted to take control of their own production costs through the establishment of cooperative stores, whose chief purpose was to eliminate middlemen and their profit. These enterprises potentially enabled farmers to market their own crops instead of relying on local merchants and cotton factors. Wheelers also hoped to effect savings through the large-scale purchasing of farm tools and implements directly from manufacturers. The Wheel Store in Batesville, established in 1887, was typical of early cooperative stores. Unfortunately, such enterprises did not live up to expectations.

The Batesville store is a rectangular, two-story, sandstone commercial structure. The store itself

The logo of the Agricultural Wheel. *Courtesy of Special Collections Division, University of Arkansas Libraries, Fayetteville.*

occupied the first floor, while the second story served as a meeting hall. The exterior of the building, except for window replacements, has changed little over the past 110 years.

The Agricultural Wheel grew rapidly in the mid-1880s. While Arkansas remained its strongest area, the Wheel spread into Tennessee, Mississippi, and Missouri and then into other states. In 1885 the Wheel merged with another farmers' group called the Brothers of Freedom, which was centered in northwest Arkansas. Isaac McCracken, a leader of the Brothers, emerged as the new president of the Arkansas Wheel. Wheel candidates had already played a role in local politics but were not highly successful. It was clear, however, that farmers' organizations would have to get into politics to achieve their main objectives. They differed, however, on whether they should work through the existing parties or form an independent, third party. In any case, farmers made up a large potential voting block. By 1888, combined with the Brothers of Freedom and other groups, the Wheelers estimated their membership at five hundred thousand across the nation.

The Wheel's political platform quickly developed. In general Wheelers demanded that "the rights and privileges of the people shall no longer be trampled upon by monopoly." They issued a list of specific reforms: reserve public lands for actual settlers rather than railroads and speculators; abolish national banks and let the government issue its own money; pay off the national debt as rapidly as possible; lower tariffs; prohibit aliens from owning land; enact a graduated income tax; abolish free passes on railroads and discrimination in freight and passenger rates; and abolish convict labor that was in competition with legitimate labor. They also advocated the free and unlimited coinage of silver and gold, the prohibition of alcohol, a free public school system, an enforceable usury law, and property tax reform.

Given the organization's avowed political orientation, Wheelers sought to broaden their political base. They solicited the support of black farmers, who had formed their own organization. They also hoped to make alliances with laborers, who were beginning to form their own unions and to strike for higher wages.

In Arkansas the discontent of farmers and workers came together in the 1888 election. The Union Labor Party, a new third party, was a coalition of various groups, including influential Wheelers. This party nominated Charles M. Norwood, a one-legged Confederate veteran and a former state senator, for governor. The Republicans, deciding not to put up a candidate of their own, threw their support behind Norwood. The combined votes of Republicans as well as various farm groups posed the most serious challenge for Democrats in the late nineteenth century. In response Democrats selected James Phillip Eagle, a planter from Lonoke, as their candidate for governor. For most Wheelers the choice created a dilemma: they distrusted the Democrats, whom they identified with the monopolistic forces that had victimized them, but at the same time they were influenced by the Democrats' identification of the Union Labor Party with the shibboleths of Radical Republicanism, Reconstruction, and black rule. Though Norwood alleged election fraud, Eagle won by fifteen thousand votes. Voter turnout was heavy. Norwood polled 46 percent of the vote against the political establishment, the best showing of an opposition candidate in this period. The Union Labor Party claimed to have elected several candidates to the state legislature.

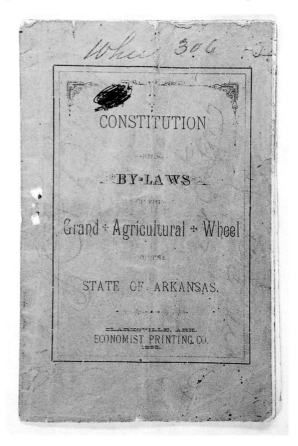

The constitution and by-laws of the Grand Agricultural Wheel in Arkansas. *Courtesy of Special Collections Division, University of Arkansas Libraries, Fayetteville.*

Since Democrats had been threatened by the specter of a biracial coalition, they began to explore the possibility of disfranchising black voters and crippling the farm movement. As late as 1890 black voters were still a viable political force, and twelve blacks served in the Arkansas legislature. In 1891, however, under the guise of election reform, the legislature enacted election laws that disfranchised black voters as well as many poor whites. Disfranchisement was soon coupled with segregation in public transportation and other facilities. These developments created the Jim Crow system that lasted until the 1960s.

By the end of the 1880s numerous farm societies across the Midwest and the South merged into two major organizations, the National Farmers' Alliance on the Midwestern plains, and the Farmers' Alliance and Industrial Union, based in the South. Southern Democrats promoted the Farmers' Alliance because it continued the radical rhetoric of the farmers' movement but favored the withdrawal of farmers from politics.

As the 1892 presidential election approached, the Northern Alliance formed a national third party, the People's Party or Populists. The Southern Alliance held back in the hope of capturing the Democratic Party. The Populists wanted to nominate Leonidas L. Polk for president, but after his sudden death they placed James B. Weaver of Iowa at the top of their ticket. Their platform was known as the Ocala Demands, formulated at Ocala, Florida, in 1890. Notably, the Ocala platform called for the creation of a "sub-treasury system," which would allow farmers to store their crops in government warehouses while borrowing up to 80 percent of their market value. In addition, farmers strongly supported the cause of free silver as opposed to the gold standard. With money backed by silver, they hoped to lower interest rates and infuse more money into the economy.

In a losing cause Weaver polled over a million votes, carrying Kansas, Idaho, Nevada, Colorado, and parts of other western states. Across the South Populists suffered intimidation and fraud. In defeat their influence declined. By 1896 Populists joined with the Democratic Party in supporting the orator William Jennings Bryan, who delivered the famous "Cross of Gold" speech in support of free silver. He, too, went down in defeat. After the turn of the century the farm economy not only improved but also entered its "golden" age of prosperity. Rural discontent was dead.

The Wheel Store in Batesville remains, then, a lonely symbol of a whole period of agrarian protest when farmers struggled with the new problems they faced in an industrializing and urbanizing America. In the short run the farm movements failed, but in the long run Progressive reformers in the early twentieth century and New Dealers in the 1930s implemented many of these movements' ideas.

The Pillow-Thompson House in Helena. *Photo by Holly Hope, Arkansas Historic Preservation Program.*

THE PILLOW-THOMPSON HOUSE

Bobby Roberts

Pillow-Thompson House
1897
Helena, Phillips County
Listed on the National Register of Historic Places on May 7, 1973

"The Pillow House is an outstanding example of High Victorian or Queen Anne Victorian architecture. It is significant, first because of its very ornate style executed completely in wood construction, with the exception of a brick foundation and chimneys. Secondly, the house is basically unaltered and in an excellent state of preservation complete with original roof and its enormous amount of elaborate trim. Lastly, the house embodies practically all of the Victorian period vernacular in terms of very irregular shape, multiple bays, towers, turrets and dormers and the whole accomplished in the ultimate eclectic manner of the late nineteenth century style in America."

—From the National Register nomination

In 1898 Jerome Bonaparte Pillow, a successful Phillips County farmer, moved into his new house in Helena on the corner of Beech and Perry Streets. The structure was a fine example of the High Victorian architectural style that was in vogue among prosperous merchants and planters across the South. Perhaps men like Pillow favored the new look because they understood that the South itself was changing and felt comfortable with the Victorian architects' disregard for the classical symmetry and formality of older building styles. Indeed, the dramatic towers, busy roof lines, and bright colors of Victorian residences such as the Pillow-Thompson home are metaphors for the profound changes that were gathering power as the old Confederate States continued to recover from the great Civil War.

Just thirty-three years before Pillow moved into his new home, this nation's only armed rebellion had been crushed, and much of the Old South had been destroyed. In human resources alone the

Helena's bustling river port brought prosperity to the town at the turn of the century. This photo shows the Main Street landing in Helena on March 25, 1897. *Photo courtesy of Arkansas History Commission, permission of Phillips County Museum.*

region had lost 260,000 soldiers, and among the civilian population disease, hunger, and neglect had added thousands more to the lists of the dead. The physical destruction was also staggering, and people who traveled anywhere in the South encountered burned-out buildings, ruined businesses, crippled railroads, and idle farms. In this human and physical wreckage lay the Old South's intertwined social, economic, and labor structure, which had rested on slavery. In the Arkansas Delta the immediate problem that people faced was how to reestablish a commercial farm economy that had primarily rested on unpaid labor. The ultimate solution was farm tenancy, which allowed landowners in cash-poor areas like Phillips County to acquire laborers by giving them a share of the crop. Sharecropping fell hard on both poor whites and blacks, creating hopeless debt and social stratification, but it did reengage the economic engine that had been destroyed by the Civil War.

As a modicum of economic growth returned to areas like Phillips County, towns such as Helena became centers of mercantile activity. Soon successful local landowners with money to invest joined outsiders who were looking for investment opportunities in such communities. The harbinger was the railroad, which came both to haul farm products to regional markets and to facilitate the exploitation of the abundant natural resources of Arkansas. Increasingly, men like Jerome Pillow crossed the line between farming and business by investing in the banks, factories, and railroads that were transforming the South.

In many small southern towns like Helena the merger of farming and business interests accelerated in the twentieth century, a trend that is personified in the career of Francis Thompson, who, for over fifty years, was involved in banking and farming in Phillips County. The Pillow-Thompson house is symbolic of the farming and mercantile interests that eventually dominated the South in the hundred years after the Civil War. Unfortunately, the prosperity that it represents seldom filtered down to the sharecroppers and workers whose toil fueled the South's economic recovery. Today the Pillow-Thompson home belongs to the Phillips Community College. Passers-by can enjoy this fine symbol of the rise of a New South that came from the ashes of the Civil War.

Eureka Springs is home to an eclectic blend of Victorian commercial and residential architecture. *Photo by Tim Schick, courtesy of Arkansas Department of Parks and Tourism.*

ALIVE IN A LIVING HISTORIC DISTRICT

Ned Shank

Eureka Springs Historic District
1880–1900
Eureka Springs, Carroll County
Listed on the National Register of Historic Places on December 18, 1970

"The significance of Eureka Springs as a historic district lies in the fact that here, preserved virtually intact, is a unique health resort community representative of the latter part of the nineteenth century."

—*From the National Register nomination*

On the first two weekends of the next-to-last December before the millennium, a group of about three dozen Eurekans put on six performances of Shakespeare's comedy *Twelfth Night* on the stage of the 1929 City Auditorium, proclaimed on bumper stickers and on T-shirts in the recent fundraising drive designed to save it as "THE auditorium." We ran our rehearsals in this and another Eureka Springs landmark building: the Basin Park Hotel.

The performances and dress rehearsals were held in the City Auditorium, an unprepossessing, three-story volume of cut limestone–enclosed space, designed by A. O. Clark, an architect from Rogers, Arkansas, who had just migrated down from the Midwest, somewhere around Saint Louis. (As a former marketing director for architectural firms, I wonder at his business acumen in moving to dirt-poor Arkansas right before the Great Depression.) Clark's overriding, programmatic, design criteria appears to have been, "Capture every square foot of the site for usable space! Who cares what it looks like!"

The Auditorium is famous locally for a number of reasons. Most recently it was itself the star in a movie titled *And Pass the Ammo,* doomed to failure when its controversial-at-the-start-of-filming, make-believe plot was outstripped in surreality by the unfolding revelations surrounding the downfall of evangelists Jim and Tammy Faye Bakker in the 1980s. The collapse of a part of the Auditorium, which served as the church headquarters of a corrupt television evangelist, was the climax of the film. The building had two fake, cathedral-like, stone towers added to the façade facing the 1905 Carroll County Western District Courthouse. The "towers" actually improved the appearance of the Auditorium tremendously, giving it some focus, verticality, and a visually sensible front door. In any case, the towers were dramatically demolished in controlled explosions when the National Guard stormed the church. (Six-foot-high gargoyles, made of a kind of rigid foam or plaster, which adorned the corners of the towers, can still be spotted lurking, outsized, from several second-floor porches of houses in the Victorian historic district.) And most Eurekans can tell you that when the Auditorium opened on a warm summer night in 1929, no less than John Phillips Sousa and his band performed to a full house. Boys who couldn't get in because of a lack of either space or financial means reportedly shimmied up trees to observe the band through the tall, rounded-arched windows in the sides of the hall. And of course the roller-skating rink in the basement of the Auditorium has always exerted a peculiar charm of its own as well.

But many of our earlier rehearsals were held in the U-shaped ballroom on the top floor of the Basin Park Hotel, slightly uphill on Spring Street from the Auditorium. From our aerie precipice we could look down on the twisting downtown streets of Eureka Springs, a town whose motto in the 1880s was "Where the Misfit, Fits," long home to many writers and artists. One evening, during a break in the acting exercises director Janet Alexander took us through—perhaps the exercise in which we each paired against another performer and simultaneously argued in a continuous stream for one minute, without pause or break, taking opposite sides of idiotically simple issues, such as whether chickens came before eggs, or whether Mac computers were better than IBMs—I found myself standing in front of one of the oversized, double-hung windows, framed outside on either side by sheet metal–formed round columns, looking out through the clear-glazed lower sash—the upper sash being divided into multiple small panes of colored glass—to the roofs of shop buildings nestled side by side seven floors below. Peering out next to me was an impossibly skinny and gifted high school senior named Ben Milam, playing the role of foppish Sir Andrew

This 1911 photograph shows a prosperous, expanding Eureka Springs. *Courtesy of UALR Archives.*

Aguecheek. He was easily twenty-five years my junior, and he was armed with a laser pointer. "What's the range on that thing?" I asked. "I don't know," he said, shining its red beam out the window. "Look!" he exclaimed, pointing it toward the parapet wall of a flat-roofed shop several hundred feet away, "There, can you see the red dot?"

Frequently, as we were working—reading our lines, warming up with acting exercises, blocking out movement on an improvised stage—we would be competing against the sound of the ballroom dancing club, their small boom box playing dance tunes for the four or five people dancing in the far reaches of the floor. The ballroom floor is reached by an elevator or by an interior staircase that wraps itself around the elevator shaft. Now-ancient Eureka painters Louis and Elsie Freund recently told my wife and me that it was down that spiraling staircase that their friend and Eureka writer Constance Wagner wanted to fly. "We saved her life!" intoned ninety-three-year-old Louis, his octogenarian and still-handsome wife Elsie nodding for emphasis. "We'd

been to a dance on the top floor, and she'd had a bit too much to drink. We had to hold her back at the top of the stairs. She said she wanted to fly down them!"

The hotel has recently been taken over by a couple who derived their money from computers in Connecticut and who have renovated and reinvigorated the 1905 structure. (A painful Eureka joke: How do you make a small fortune in Eureka Springs? Come here with a large one.) I first walked through the Basin Park Hotel in about 1979, when it was being run as the Basin Park Hotel Museum. For a couple dollars admission you could wander through the building and have the privilege of peering through window cutouts in various doors into plain rooms in poor repair, some with forties chenille bedspreads with the hotel name woven in a shaggy green script (I used to have the remnants of one, until it rotted away in the back of my Mazda pickup truck), inhaling the malodorous fumes of cooked cabbage, dead pigeons, and musty, closed-off building. On the second floor I passed an office

NED SHANK

door with a small metal plaque etched with the owner's name: "Reverend Paul Hansen, Hypno-Technician." Hansen, a ginger-haired, somewhat dissolute-looking version of Colonel Sanders, bought the hotel from Maryland-born, big-game-hunting, local banker John Cross, who had taken over his Grandpa Claude Albert Fuller's Bank of Eureka Springs—Fuller was mayor and responsible for getting the Auditorium built and later the roads paved in concrete—and once breathed out to me in a tone mixing both disbelief and respect, "That Paul Hansen could make money off a flat rock." On the top floor was Hansen's coup de grace: a car purported to be the late Elvis Presley's 1954 Cadillac convertible. Hansen, in a feat showing a shrewd understanding of the grand publicity stunt, had hired a large boom crane to hoist the car up to the ballroom level and roll it in through one of those large, double-hung, colored-glass windows (I'm not sure how or exactly when the car was removed). He confided to me that his other, thwarted, grand scheme was to run a ski lift–style gondola from the hotel roof across the historic district to the Christ of the Ozarks statue. He went on post-hotel-sale to buy a home created out of an inverted parabolic concrete bowl built by the man who wrote the script for the 1930s and 1940s rabble-rouser Gerald L. K. Smith's Passion Play, and who played the role of Jesus for many years, until ousted in internecine politics at the "Sacred Projects." Hansen dubbed his new home the Miracle Mansion and operates it as a wedding chapel. "Special Affordable Memories," the Yellow Pages ad reads. "1-888-2 MARRY U."

Another of the hotel's claims to fame was its frequent write-up by part-time Eureka resident Robert Ripley, who wrote "Ripley's Believe It or Not." This write-up, not unlike the promise of Hansen's Hotel Museum, was a come-on followed by an unsatisfying fulfillment: "The only hotel in the world with a street level entrance on all seven floors!" Backing up to a limestone bluff that was blasted out to accommodate the structure, the metal fire-escape catwalks on the back of the building meet the hair-splitting technicality of Ripley's claim, although in no way do they meet the image first conjured up in the reader's mind.

But architecturally the hotel inhabits an important place in the development of the town's built environment, for it straddles the past and the future of Eureka Springs. The eight-story, stone-faced hotel sits right next to the most historic site in Eureka: the Basin Park. Now built up twenty or thirty feet above the original spring, the Basin Park still allows one to peer down a circular shaft and see dark water rippling over the shallow depression of a flat stone. This is the basin that was reputedly hollowed out by hand by Native American Indians eons ago to hold the water they found to be healing, medicinal, and sacred. It was with the water from this basin that Dr. Alvah Jackson from nearby Berryville healed himself and his sons of various ailments, and healed the ailments of a judge friend. Those healed spread the word, and in 1879 Eureka Springs was founded around this very spring. The women of the CIA (Civic Improvement Association) spearheaded the creation of the current park, building it up with gracefully curving, cut limestone walls, a fountain, and a later bandshell. (This December the bandshell hosts yet another Christmas crèche despite the ACLU's efforts nationally to separate church and state on municipal property. This year, with Coca-Cola signs included in most Christmas displays as part of the company's underwriting the promotion of the holiday season's commercial benefit to the town, a small artistic cry of protest appeared halfway down the infrequently traveled side street on the steepest part of Mountain Street: a simple cross made of crushed Coke cans and a hand-lettered sign, reminiscent of "The End Is Near" cartoons, reading "The Anti-Coke Is Coming.")

The iron beams now hidden by the cut-stone exterior of the Basin Park Hotel are clearly visible during its ca. 1905 construction. *Courtesy of Eureka Springs Historical Museum.*

But the hotel also represents the modern age of architecture, despite its deceptive cut limestone exterior. Inside, hidden by its turn-of-the-century, antique-seeming interior finishes, is a structure of iron beams. This building, with its exterior curtain wall of stone, its internal metal skeleton, and its central-core elevator, welcomed the era of modern skyscraper construction to our town. All seated companionably next to the most venerable site in our tiny community.

To my eye this building, part of the revolution American architecture instigated on the world stage (for better and for worse), welcomed the millennium ninety-five years early to Eureka Springs. And yet by living in and growing in and actively using the buildings of our historic district, we bring alive through our constant engagement each advance of the millennial clock, whether through the advances of architecture and construction, or by revisiting a play written when the English language was young and just being invented in giant forward strides, in an age illuminated by the brilliance of a remarkable playwright. Ninety-three years after the Basin Park Hotel brought modern architecture to Eureka Springs's heart, seventy years after the Auditorium opened, and over three hundred years after Shakespeare wrote the comedy *Twelfth Night* for Queen Elizabeth to flatter Italy's visiting emissary, walking across the resilient wooden floor of the stage, delivering my lines as a dour, sick-with-self-love manservant aptly named Malvolio, I felt the living resonance of that aging floor and hall responding to our sound and action, I felt myself come alive to the character in my presentation, and I imagined—no, felt, sensed—that while the play itself quickened into life each night, the figure of a lanky, bareheaded, darkly garbed, and white-ruffed Elizabethan playwright came into existence, too, standing behind a curtain in the wings, his genius and passion infusing him with life again during the brief re-creation of his work. May our strange and twisty town so live on as well.

The Marcella Church and School in Stone County. *Arkansas Historic Preservation Program photo*.

THE MARCELLA CHURCH AND SCHOOL

Jean Sizemore

Marcella Church and School
Ca. 1900
Marcella, Stone County
Listed on the National Register of Historic Places on September 17, 1985

"At the turn of the century, Stone County was divided into 75 school districts. The people in each district were responsible for providing an educational facility. The Marcella Church and School, built around 1900, housed not only the district school, but also the local church. The frame rectangular building is covered in weatherboard and contains a single entry in the front gable façade. It is representative of the rural traditional church and school building."

—*From the National Register nomination*

The Marcella Church and School, constructed about 1898, sits remarkably unaltered at the edge of Highway 14 in Stone County. This winding, hilly road epitomizes the bucolic; serene pastures, woods, and brushy areas are interspersed with weathered, vernacular houses. Little of the raw newness of suburbia intrudes on this traditional landscape. Marcella is now the proverbial "wide spot in the road," and this building is the most tangible reminder that it once was a small but bustling trade center, with Highway 14 as its Main Street. Located near the White River, the village prospered as a receiver of goods from regularly scheduled steamboat traffic. As local historian Edwin Luther said, "[A]lmost anything could be bought in Marcella, from gunpowder to shot, to Springfield wagons to coffins."

The Marcella Church and School is one of the many one-room schoolhouses extant in Arkansas. Such structures were once so common that, as late as 1920, school officials regretfully observed that such schools were the norm throughout the state. In comparison to others, this is surely one of the most spacious, most soundly constructed, and best preserved, with a history of almost continual use by the community. It closed as a school in 1945, soon after state legislation ordered all schools with fewer than 350 pupils to be consolidated. But from the beginning the school building had been intended to serve a dual purpose and was owned both by the local school district and the Marcella Church of Christ, as it had been for almost forty years when the school closed in 1945.

I was privileged recently to receive an invitation to attend a Sunday service at the Marcella Church and School. I was deeply impressed with the reverent and alive spirit of this place; it was far from a dusty, antique relic of the past. From the five long windows on each side natural light streamed in, warmly reflected on the traditional, horizontal-board, flush paneling, which was painted white. At the top of the thirteen-foot-high ceiling, the boards curved instead of forming angles. Two flues in the ceiling marked the original positions of two wood stoves. Bare light bulbs still hang from long wires, but they weren't needed on this sunlit day. The teacher's platform now serves as the base for the lectern. Its spacious dimensions, twenty-six by fifty-two feet, exceed the twenty-four by thirty-five feet recommended by education officials when the structure was built, perhaps because it was intended to serve congregants as well as pupils. Set firmly upon its continuous fieldstone foundation, the Marcella Church and School is exceptionally pleasing in its proportions. At the rear a functioning outhouse remains.

Today there is a burgeoning interest in rural, one-room schools; photographs, documents and reminiscences are being collected and published. Such schools have become icons of nostalgia. But when contemporary education records are examined, the phenomenon at first appears puzzling, for they are stark reminders of an inadequate public school system. These one-room schools went from the first to the eighth grade, with, of course, one beleaguered teacher who doubled as janitor. Often the teacher was simply an eighth-grader who had attended a six-week session at a Normal Institute in order to pass the teacher's examination. There was no compulsory schooling, no compulsory taxes, and no standard school terms for many years. School districts could form without regard for their ability to maintain schools. In 1904 school officials lamented that only three other states had fewer school days in the term than Arkansas's average of 91.5 days.

Reading the reminiscences of former pupils, however, creates a happier impression. Children of all ages in the community formed close bonds over the years, and they had fun together—fun playing myriad games of their own devising at recess, fun playing pranks on the teacher, fun sharing lunches from their lard-bucket dinner pails. (Stoically enduring the often-meted-out corporal punishment was

The massive, wood-frame Methodist church was the heart of the Shark community, ca. 1900. *Courtesy of UALR Archives.*

less fun, but it doubtless fostered camaraderie.) These schools were truly community gathering places for many different occasions. The children themselves sometimes presented evening programs, in which they might put on plays, sing, have spelling and arithmetic contests, and invite local musicians to play. Sometimes neighboring schools would have contests between the pupils in their educational subjects. It seems that the Marcella School was somewhat "uptown," in that the pupil selected to draw water (who considered this task a privilege) did not have to walk a half-mile or so to the spring, as was sometimes the case, but obtained it from a well at a nearby house. The practice of everyone drinking out of the same dipper (and "thinking nothing of it," as one woman recalls) was, however, the same. It would seem, then, that these small buildings have become icons of nostalgia for a sense of community now lost.

The messages I see embodied in the Marcella Church and School revolve around two concepts: community and simplicity.

These schools were initiated by local people who constructed them on land donated by local individuals and who saw to it that the schools continued to operate on whatever meager resources were available. If we are to have communities in the future, however, beyond the privatized and gated ones from which those deemed "different" are locked out, we must be open to broader visions of community than Marcella's, where alliances were formed, of necessity, among people of shared backgrounds and values in insular locales. In our expanding world the enormous challenge of the next century will be to find ways of forming multicultural, multi-class communities, based on broader human values. While such a vision is still blurred, we can at least commit ourselves to public institutions that foster an inclusive sense of community in a multi-cultural world, as this little church and school did in its modest way in a simpler society.

Finally, the Shaker-like, simple beauty of this building is obvious to those who slow down enough to look. Less tangible is the Ozarks ethos that constructed and preserves it, and which is surely solid enough to remain with us even into a future of complexity and diversity. Build well and build to last when you can. Slow down your life to be able to sit on the porch and watch the sun set, to visit with friends and neighbors, to gather and play music. Know that newer does not mean better. Know that a sense of place is a treasure to the human heart and that simple human sharing may be the greatest gift of all.

Bathhouse Row, Hot Springs National Park. *Photo by Gail Sears, courtesy of Hot Springs National Park.*

THE HOT SPRINGS BATHHOUSE ROW
Michael Dougan

Bathhouse Row
1911–1935
Hot Springs, Garland County
Listed on the National Register of Historic Places on November 13, 1974
Designated a National Historic Landmark on May 28, 1987

"Because few of the great health spas of early twentieth century America are still in existence, Bathhouse Row in Hot Springs, Arkansas, is especially significant. The entire group comprises the finest row of historic bathhouses remaining in the nation. It remains today a picturesque reminder of America's early twentieth century interest in health spas."

—*From the National Register nomination*

Tucked away in the Ouachita Mountains and surrounded by rough but beautiful terrain, hot waters issued forth from the ground. In prehistoric times the lure of the hot water probably ranked second in importance to the area's rich sources of a rock called novaculite, from which some of the best stone points could be fashioned.

Trade with the Europeans ended the Stone Age, but reports that the hot waters possessed therapeutic value meant that in 1804, when President Thomas Jefferson sent Natchez amateur scientist William Dunbar and chemist Dr. George Hunter to report on the Ouachitas, the hot springs were on their list of sites to be explored. One abandoned log cabin and some hunter's huts constituted their development. Fourteen years later United States Army Maj. Stephen Long reported that sixty different springs contributed to forming the stream that came to be styled Hot Springs Creek. Already in that year some fifteen log cabins now dotted the creek. The uniqueness and reputedly therapeutic qualities of the waters led the federal government in 1832 to set aside the four sections on which the springs were located for permanent federal possession, thus anticipating the creation of a federal park system.

In time local promoters would construct elaborate stories of tribal usage and assert, on the very weakest of evidence, that Spanish explorer Hernado de Soto was rejuvenated by the healing waters. (This author remembers a local pageant where "Indians" mounted on horses [!] attacked the Spanish in a plot that involved true cross-cultural love!) Later in time, and with a bit more authenticity, Hot Springs could claim connections with Jesse James, Al Capone, Frank Nash, and Lucky Luciano among the criminal classes; big-name entertainers, starting with Joseph Jefferson (famous for his portrayal of Rip Van Winkle); several major league baseball teams, who trained there before Florida was developed; and

America's most exotic tourist attractions, the alligator and ostrich farms.

Hot Springs was famous in other ways as well. From the late nineteenth century up to the late 1960s Hot Springs was the gambling capital of America. Although every form of gambling except the horse racing at Oaklawn Park (after 1934) was illegal under Arkansas law, casino gambling had flourished in Hot Springs since the 1870s through an elaborate system of payoffs, until Gov. Winthrop Rockefeller shut it down for good in 1967.

Yet the center of Hot Springs from its creation up to the 1970s was Bathhouse Row, a series of buildings that epitomized the now-vanished culture the nineteenth century associated with the word "spa." Early Hot Springs could not compete with antebellum watering holes such as White Sulphur Springs in Virginia and Saratoga in New York, but with the coming of the railroad after the Civil War, visitors from Chicago and points south came to Arkansas in search of health and recreation. By the 1870s, in place of open bathing in the stream and log cabins for housing, elaborate hotels pretentiously modeled on Baden-Baden and other European resorts arose. Adjacent to a now enclosed and covered Hot Springs Creek and jammed in by mountains on either side, a series of bathhouses arose on one side of Central Avenue, eight of which survived fires and floods to be put on the National Register of Historic Places in 1974.

Spas flourished in the nineteenth century largely because they promised medical relief for sufferers as yet unserved by modern medicine. What sufferers of syphilis, the second most common disease recorded in 1885, received from the waters is unclear, but an immense industry arose to service those suffering from that malady.

Booster literature flooded the country, promising a combination of recreation and healing. In an age before government regulation, advertisements for the various springs were full of spurious claims for therapeutic qualities. Actually, Arsenic Springs had none of the chemical, and a claim for radio-activity for another spring backfired later in the twentieth century. As potential customers got closer to Hot Springs, they encountered drummers working the railroads and stations who were paid to steer customers to competing hotels and bathhouses. Central Avenue emerged regally as the area's social and economic center.

Opposite the bathhouses one could find a fully equipped opera house (torn down in the 1960s to make room for a parking lot), doctors' offices, hotels, casinos, and restaurants. During the town's heyday, from the 1920s to the 1950s, Mayor Leo Patrick Laughlin presided over one of the nation's most notoriously corrupt municipal governments, taxing illegal gambling, buying off state politicians, and defying federal laws. On the other side of the street, all by themselves in all their glory, were the bathhouses. Here, hot waters, physical therapy, and exercise were tailored to the needs of the patient. Both sides of the street complemented each other, so that it is impossible to say with certainty which was more important to the prosperity of Hot Springs.

In addition to competing with prices and services, the houses offered architectural variety as well. Beginning in 1878, fires, floods, and changing tastes altered the Row's appearance. For instance, the old-

The structures along Bathhouse Row displayed ornate Victorian architecture in 1884. *Courtesy of Hot Springs National Park.*

MICHAEL DOUGAN

est bathhouse, the Hale, began as a neo-classical building in 1892 but was converted to the Mission style in 1939. All the rest were constructed in the early twentieth century, with Renaissance Revival and Spanish Colonial Revival being the two most common styles.

By the early twentieth century medical claims for drinking waters were exploded. While many spas declined, Hot Springs emphasized water therapy, especially useful to polio sufferers. Only after World War II did this form of treatment go out of style. Meanwhile, all was not well across the street. The rise of legalized gambling, first in Nevada and then across the nation, lured away customers. The old Hot Springs was comatose by the time Governor Rockefeller ended the sleaze. The town declined over the next twenty years as one by one the bathhouses closed their doors, forcing the town to resort to other forms of tourism in order to survive.

Ironically, although this impressive row of buildings is in Arkansas, it reflects the world of middle- and upper-class people from the midwest. During the heyday of the Row, the average Arkansan did not make in a month what it cost to stay a day in one of these fancy resorts. Instead, for Arkansas's common people, work as attendants, waiters, cooks, and serving help constituted their part of the Bathhouse Row experience.

And tucked blocks away from Bathhouse Row were the bathhouses and hotels for blacks.

While Bathhouse Row in 1998 is undergoing restoration and some redevelopment, several blocks away on Malvern Avenue sits the hotel and bathhouse erected by the Woodman of Union, a black social club/union/fraternity. This building, whose facilities equaled those around the corner, is currently boarded up and for sale, a reminder of the racism that underlined Hot Springs history from the end of the Civil War to the present.

The Smith Hospital evolved over the years to accommodate the doctors' growing practice. *Photo by Tammie Trippe Dillon, Arkansas Historic Preservation Program.*

SIX COUNTRY DOCTORS:
THE SMITH HOSPITAL, PARIS, ARKANSAS

Cynthia DeHaven Pitcock

Smith Hospital
1913
Paris, Logan County
Listed on the National Register of Historic Places on April 11, 1994

"The Smith Hospital is being nominated under Criterion B with local significance for its association with Dr. John James (Jim) and Dr. Arthur McDanel Smith, who founded the first hospital in Logan County and initiated a pioneer hospitalization insurance plan. Under Criterion C, the hospital is also locally significant as a virtually unaltered example of an early twentieth century medical facility as well as an excellent example of the evolution of hospital architecture and scale."

—*From the National Register nomination*

From the beginning of settlement in the New World, medicine was a hit-or-miss affair. It became clear quite early that reputable, educated physicians did not wish to leave their European or British homelands to risk the six-week passage on overcrowded, stinking cargo ships that offered passengers every known disease and then to risk a perilous life in a wilderness where unknown diseases and terrifying savages stalked the unprotected righteous. Would-be physicians in the early colonies came in great variety: old ships' doctors, barbers, ministers, and tradesmen happily gave medical advice, raised blisters, bled clients copiously, or caused a "laudable puke" for a penny or two. Everyone watched the weather as the bringer of disease—wind direction, rainfall, thunderclaps, lightning, dry wells, hot spells, or ice too thick on the millpond.

At the close of the Revolution, when a few colonial towns had grown into cities, there were doctors in those places with degrees from Edinburgh or Lyden or from the American medical college in Philadelphia. These were "men of affairs," as Benjamin Rush put it, distinguished and successful. Their professional reputations were widely publicized; they were memorialized and revered and rewarded with wealth and opulence. The history of medicine in America had developed into two histories, parallel and yet quite different, fraternal rather than identical twins. There was the medicine practiced in Philadelphia, Boston, New York, Charleston, and New Orleans, available for a handsome price; this was city medicine.

But there was another medicine practiced in the wilderness, in wagon trains, in frontier outposts. Revolutionary veterans with their meager land grants had pushed settlement to the very cusp of the new republic. Into all these places, known and unknown, came the terrible fevers, the epidemic influenzas, the logging and farming injuries with which people simply coped. Old remedies were copied down; new remedies were borrowed and passed along; tonics

were brewed, poultices created, wounds cauterized, fractures splinted. This was country medicine, the second twin. Early rural practitioners were not memorialized or even remembered; they had not received medical training and were seldom paid. Life in rural America was brief and grim.

At no time in our history was the gap between city and country medicine wider than in the decades following the Civil War. This is a story of country medicine, of fathers and brothers and sons in a family named Smith who became doctors in a poor, rural state that had the bad luck to be on the losing side of the Civil War. The Smith doctors took care of people in Paris, Arkansas, beginning in the 1880s, and the youngest Smith doctor practices medicine there today.

The Smith Hospital, on the National Register of Historic Places, deserves study for several reasons. It represents a long struggle by inhabitants of the region to provide medical care for coal miners and farmers and townspeople who could not afford a trip to Fort Smith or Little Rock for treatment. Settlement in the Ouachitas had come later than settlement in the East; in the 1870s and 1880s, and at the turn of the twentieth century, it was still frontier. The Smith Hospital, built in 1913, operated for sixty-one years, seven days a week, twenty-four hours a day. During the 1920s the second generation of Smith doctors created a pre-paid medical plan for their patients. The plan was innovative, designed in direct response to the needs of the locale. It was in some respects an early HMO (Health Maintenance Organization), bearing a strong resemblance to those organizations in such wide use at the end of the twentieth century. The history of this family enterprise is the history of country medicine in an area defined and supported by the railroad, the coal mines, and the dreams of the people.

In 1874, when Arkansas counties were reshuffled, old Saber became Logan County. This county rides the ridges and shallow draws of the

Detail of brick buttresses, Smith Hospital, Paris, Arkansas. *Photo by Tammie Trippe Dillon, Arkansas Historic Preservation Program.*

Ouachita Mountains in the west-central part of the state, south of the Arkansas River. Named for a pioneer settler who was called Colonel and wore a stovepipe hat, Logan was given two county seats, one at Paris and one at Booneville, because in the center of the county is Mount Magazine, the tallest peak in Arkansas at 2,823 feet.

When the county was organized, named, and opened for settlement, scalawags and carpetbag Republicans controlled state government from the Old State House in Little Rock, and one of their primary projects was the building of railroads in the state. Deals were made, palms pressed, municipal bonds floated, and by 1872 Little Rock and Fort Smith were connected by a railroad, jauntily described by a Washington factotum as "that little stumptail of a railroad in a Southern state." But it was a major artery of commerce and settlers, many of whom were German immigrants who bought small plots of land at the railroad offices, the land on either side of the track having been given to the railroad companies as part of the deal. The town of

Paris, named for her ancient and more elegant ancestor in France, was incorporated five years after the railroad's completion. A one-story courthouse containing four civic offices was erected in the square, and the Paris railroad depot was built just off Elm Street.

The first Smith homesteaders had arrived in the region long before Paris was a town. Sometime before the Civil War, Arthur and Mary Jane Smith bought a plot of ground to make a farm in a place called Meg, Arkansas, not far from Chismville, in Franklin County. When the war came in 1860, Arthur joined up, leaving Mary Jane with seven children and a farm to run. He came home once on leave and then was captured. He subsequently died of fever in a military prison. He was forty-three years old. Mary Jane in due course gave birth to her eighth child.

Two boys of the fatherless Smith brood grew up to become doctors, John James and Arthur McDanel. John James, the older brother, earned the M.D. degree at Vanderbilt in 1879, when he was twenty-five years old. He and Arthur McDanel, who was also destined toward medicine, formed a business partnership with a third brother, Frank, who ran the family farm successfully and to considerable profit. The three brothers combined their earnings and bought additional land from time to time. Presumably from this financial base, John James was able to afford additional medical training at one of the nation's leading medical schools, Jefferson in Philadelphia, where he studied under Dr. Samuel Gross. Having availed himself of the best medical education city medicine of the day could offer, Dr. Jim came home to the area of Meg and Chismville and practiced medicine in a log cabin. He had an arrangement with the general store whereby patients could make payments on their medical bills when they came into town to trade. By 1899 Dr. Jim moved to Paris, a much bigger town than either Meg or Chismville, and he rented an office on the town square, above the pharmacy.

While Dr. Jim and country doctors everywhere made house calls in worn-out buggies in all kinds of weather, toting medical bags filled with surgical instruments and a few homemade remedies or patent tonics, city medicine was advancing apace. Private hospitals designed to treat specific ailments were springing up in Midwestern and Eastern cities and were advertised extravagantly in newspapers, popular magazines, and even in medical journals. An 1897 issue of the monthly *Bulletin of the Arkansas Medical Society* ran such an advertisement, one of several, occupying the entire back cover. An engraving showed a stately mansion, rather like a castle, complete with turrets and towers, in a pastoral setting. In block letters it was advertised as the "Oxford Retreat, A Private Hospital for the treatment of Insanity and Nervous Disorders. . . . G. F. Cook, M.D., owner and director, in Oxford, Ohio, 39 miles from Cincinnati, 84 miles from Indianapolis, ten trains daily." Pictured to rival Dr. Kellogg's fashionable health spa in Battle Creek, such physician-owned

private hospitals were popular in the post–Civil War decades in cities of the triumphant Union, which had been enriched by the war. Medical education in those northern cities was beginning to produce young doctors who had been trained in the basic sciences. Eastern and Midwestern medical schools reflected the nation's obsession with science and educational techniques learned in the newly created empire of Germany. City medicine in America approached the new century with the Progressive zeal for science, reform and modernization.

Meanwhile, in the country, Dr. Jim's younger brother, Arthur McDanel, who had graduated from the University of Arkansas and Tulane Medical School, joined him in practice in the office above the pharmacy. The doctors took turns with their horse (named "Old Ninety") and buggy. On designated days one would drive east on the road toward Subiaco to make calls; the other doctor, on his days, would drive west, toward Fort Smith. If anyone, black or white, along the road had sickness in the house, he hung a white bed sheet on a bush or tree limb, indicating that the doctor should stop. Likewise, families with sickness living down a farm road from the main road would hang a bed sheet at the corner, meaning that the doctor should turn off to make a house call further on. Payment for these services was often delayed until the crop came in or until payday at the coal mines. The two doctor-brothers just barely managed to make a living from their practice of medicine.

Everyone in Arkansas considered Little Rock to be the big city, because as the capital of the state, located almost exactly in the geographical center, it attracted business, cotton traders, legislators, and professional men from everywhere in the 1880s. It had hotels and saloons and newspapers, fine brick residences, a privately owned medical school, brick churches, and a splendid Greek Revival State House, but no hospital. As part of the recovering South even Little Rock, the biggest city in Arkansas, was leagues behind northern cities of the same size. It was still country.

The *Arkansas Medical Monthly,* attempting to appeal to the entrepreneurial spirit of doctors, ran this plea under "home news":

> Little Rock needs an infirmary. There is not a more inviting field for an enterprise of this kind in the union, than is presented here. A great number of invalids go from the southwest every year to St. Louis and other more northern cities to be treated for chronic diseases and to have surgical operations performed. A great many more suffer and die for want of means necessary to pay traveling expenses to these places, who might afford to come here. Our hotels and boarding houses very properly refuse to be converted into hospitals . . . we hope that some of our leading physicians and surgeons will soon undertake the establishment of such an institution.

Solo and office practices were going out of style as the new century approached, and every community, great and small, dreamed of a local hospital. The nation had become convinced that home was not the only place to receive medical care. Thousands of men returning from the Civil War in 1865 had received care in military hospitals and were not afraid to go to them. Everyone wished to progress beyond those amputations by lamplight in the doctor's office, with chloroform dripped through a cloth held over the patient's nose. In a hospital there could be extended care by nurses in stiffly starched white uniforms, trained to care for the sick. There might be more than one doctor attending. The place might be clean, and patients, like the wounded soldiers from Civil War battlefields, would be fed good food during their hospital stay. It would be a new age. Lives would be saved. The well-known array of Southern diseases might cease to sweep away children and whole families in dreaded annual epidemics of yellow fever, small pox, typhoid, and meningitis. There were also those chronic diseases that seemed to be ongoing, as if in permanent residence—tuberculosis, malaria, hookworm, and pellagra—feared by all, rich and poor alike.

In country medicine the great obstacle was always money. During the 1870s Arkansas doctors had attempted to form a statewide medical society in order to cope with epidemics, but when the governor signed a charter giving the medical society control of quarantine regulations throughout the state, he was unable to grant a penny of state funds to the effort. Instead, he made a plea for private donations from his economically depressed population, and the campaign was doomed. Volunteers in the countryside and in towns handled quarantine regulations. Boards of health were organized in a few counties, yet always the battle against disease in Arkansas was lost for want of funds.

The dawn of the new century brought American mania for reform to a fever pitch in the Progressive movement, and city medicine, only one of countless causes targeted by political and professional reformers for change, now included in its embrace medical education and state-of-the-art hospitals. Patient care in these gleaming, silent, tall buildings made available by 1900 everything new learned about disease since the Civil War. Tuberculosis victims were now removed from communities and treated in remote, fresh-air sanatoria. Isolation wards assured the general patient populations that contagious diseases would be safely contained within the hospital facilities. Doctors visited their patients in hospital, and their professional reputations were enhanced by elective hospital staff memberships. City medicine became the best in the world, and its future, in the optimistic rhetoric of the Progressives, was limitless. All the problems of mankind, especially poverty and disease, could be solved.

Dr. M. D. McClain Sr., *(seated at desk)*, speaks with C. C. Reed in a typical Little Rock physician's office, ca. 1909. *Photo courtesy of Historical Research Center, University of Arkansas for Medical Sciences Library.*

Arkansas did not share in the optimism of the Progressives, however. The election of 1900 gave the state a governor who called himself Jeff Davis and who styled himself as the redeemer of the "Lost Cause" and as the "Karl Marx for Hillbillies." He traded on racism, class envy, and old-fashioned bossism, and opposed any notion for change or reform that came from outside the state. Thus it was that Arkansas, urgently in need of the well-meaning ministrations of national reform projects, was held back in a distorted brand of agrarianism until the election of a governor who was a self-proclaimed Progressive and successful business man, George Donaghey, in 1909. During his political campaign he stumped the state by train, speaking from the rear platform along with William Jennings Bryan, champion of the common man, Populist, and hero of the Farmers' Alliance movement. Both Presidents Theodore Roosevelt and Woodrow Wilson would identify closely with Bryan in the hope that their own brand of Progressivism would be enhanced by his image.

In 1906 the town of Paris was proclaimed to be debt free. A new courthouse stood in the center of the square, and a brick jail had replaced the log building north of the square. The Doctors Smith dreamed of a hospital in Paris, but they continued with their office practice and their faithful house calls almost anywhere in the county. The power of their dream sent them out to look for a site for their hospital, but it was clear that there was nothing in town they could afford. Soon, however, the brothers learned that the old Theodore Potts homestead at the north end of Express Street was being sold in lots, and they made their investment, buying the lots one at a time until they had almost seven acres. They had become involved in the financial life of the region. John James was president of the German-American Bank, and Arthur McDanel was president of the Paris Cotton Seed Oil Mill. Also, the brothers owned part of two coal mines, and it was their coal-mining income that built the hospital.

The year 1910 was memorable for both city medicine and country medicine, because it was in

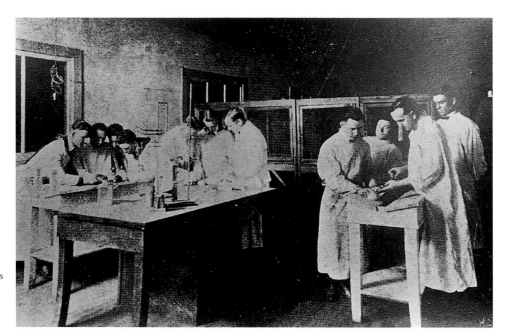

The pharmacology laboratory at the University of Arkansas Medical School, ca. 1924. *Courtesy of Old State House Museum.*

that year that the Carnegie Foundation published its explosive report on American medical education, compiled and written by Abraham Flexner. Under the sponsorship of the American Medical Association and the Carnegie Institute, Flexner and his committee had visited 155 medical schools and graded them according to a standard modeled after Johns Hopkins University, Medical School and Teaching Hospital, a standard that few medical schools in America could meet in 1910. The lower third of medical schools critiqued by Flexner closed relatively soon after the publication of the Flexner Report. The two competing medical schools in Little Rock fared badly in the report, and a political-medical furor arose as efforts were made to merge the two schools to create a single, university-affiliated medical school.

Up in Logan County, in 1910, the Smith brothers opened the Potts house as their temporary hospital while still keeping their office on the square. Plans for building a real hospital on the site were definitely in the works. Several major problems appeared at once, however. Since there were no municipal utilities as yet in Paris, there was neither water nor electricity on the Potts hill to supply the new hospital. Most residences in town had their own wells, so a water pipe was run from Dr. Mac's home three blocks away on Church Street. Electricity was somewhat more complicated, but at last a solution was agreed upon. Mr. August Bartsch's current generator downtown would supply electricity; a coal-powered steam furnace would heat the new building, with pipes to a radiator in each room. There was a third problem that gave everyone pause. A small cemetery was located beside the proposed entrance of the new hospital, and it was agreed that this would not be a welcome sight to patients arriving for treatment. The graves were swiftly relocated to a cemetery across town.

As American medical educators, principally in the South and Midwest, reeled from the impact of the Flexner Report, the nerve center of city medicine moved to the Baltimore Club in downtown Baltimore. There Abraham Flexner met with wealthy benefactors who wished to bestow portions of their wealth on deserving medical schools and hospitals. Flexner, now with the John D. Rockefeller Foundation, became the most powerful man in American medicine, for it was he who directed philanthropic monies to the "best" schools and hospitals for a time.

In 1911 the Rockefeller Foundation announced plans to form a sanitation commission to work in the South toward the eradication of endemic disease. In order to qualify for the Rockefeller funds, each state was required to have in place a functioning board of health and a bureau of vital statistics. Arkansas had neither. In a flurry of activity Governor Donaghey appointed a temporary board of health, based upon the unsuccessful medical society of 1870. As the new state capitol building had been finished after years of controversy and obstruction by Jeff Davis, the Old State House was to be vacated by state government, and the newly organized medical college was to be housed there. The board of health, still unfunded by state government, used the chemistry laboratories of the medical school for tests. Professors and students did the necessary laboratory work. The bureau of statistics was placed in a room on the first floor of the Old State House, attended by a lady named Miss Stella, who received no salary.

It took three full years of wrangling and debate to force the Arkansas state legislature to vote funding for a state board of health. During this interval the Rockefeller public health agents had begun their assault against hookworm disease in the state, and the director of the project had worked as long as he could with no salary. Women's clubs all over Arkansas petitioned their state representatives, begging for a fully funded board of health. The gap between city medicine and country medicine was narrowing.

In 1913 the fifteen-bed Smith Hospital opened its doors. It was a major event in the history of Logan County. People came on foot, on horseback, and in wagons and buggies from miles around. The building itself sat like a slightly elongated, two-story brick cube on the exact summit of the old Potts property, with a flat roof, trimmed around the parapet with a double row of brick dentils, giving the hospital almost the look of the Western Territorial style. A narrow porch supported by four white columns was in the center of the first floor, and the foundation, made of fieldstone, provided a full basement. Cement steps led up to the porch and to the wide front door. The building represented a triumph of function over form, and it was the only hospital in Logan, Franklin, Scott, and Johnson Counties. In the rush of new business the two Smiths took in a third physician, I. H. Jewell, for a time. He and his brother later built a competing hospital in Paris, but it lasted for only a few years.

A vital component of the Smith Hospital was the nurses' training program, which admitted unmarried girls who were high school graduates, eighteen years old. There was no formal contract, no official degree earned, no formal curriculum. The girls simply learned by doing, by assisting the doctors, and the program lasted for two years. The old Potts house, used in 1910 as the temporary Smith Hospital, became the Nurses' Home.

Dr. Jim and Dr. Mac had brought their professional training in city medicine to the country, where their people and their destinies were. They never sent a bill. Each doctor carried two wallets; one was his own, and the other belonged to the hospital. If a patient just released walked by the desk without stopping, that meant he was unable to pay. If he paused by the desk, he would discuss with one of the doctors how much he could pay that day. This tradition was carried on by the second generation of Smith doctors in the same way.

By the 1920s city medicine was creating medical centers in major cities which, in accordance with the Flexner model, contained a university and an affiliated medical school and teaching hospital, where "scientific medicine [could be] brought to the bedside of an enlightened public." Medical schools were in the process of standardizing curricula across the country, and a battle between full-time and part-time faculties was being waged. Many medical schools depended for their faculties upon physicians who practiced in the community and served as adjunct professors in medical faculties. When the advocates of a full-time faculty won the battle at Johns Hopkins, the nation's medical schools promptly followed suit and the enthronement of medical academia was complete.

In the 1920s Paris experienced a real boom in the coal-mining business. At one time there were over a thousand men employed in the Paris coalfields. In those days accidents in the mines were frequent, and since Saturday was payday, it was also the day of brawls and the settling of scores. All the injured were brought to the wide front door of the Smith Hospital for emergency treatment. One of the nurses, Miss Necey Bradshaw, had a room in the hospital, and when an injured person was brought to the front door, her buzzer sounded, and she admitted the patient. She then decided whether to call one of the Doctors Smith. They both took calls around the clock from Miss Bradshaw.

The community had outgrown the hospital, clearly, and the future seemed relatively secure to the Smiths because Dr. Mac's three sons were aspiring physicians. It was time to add on to Smith Hospital. Before launching this project, however, they devised their pre-paid medical plan, the Hospitalization Plan for Paris Hospital. The fee was one dollar per month per family, regardless of race, and it covered all hospital services from birth on. The coal-mining companies deducted the fee from the paychecks of miners who signed up for the plan. Townspeople and farmers joined as well, and although any form of

health insurance was anathema to the AMA (American Medical Association), this plan served well the people of Logan County and beyond.

In 1923 Smith Hospital was enlarged. An architect from Muskogee, Oklahoma, was engaged, and a three-story annex increased the capacity of the hospital to thirty beds. The first floor was devoted to private rooms and a four-bed ward that was used for emergencies or overflow. The second floor housed obstetrical patients and a nursery. The third floor of the new wing housed private patient rooms. An electric elevator, the first in the county, was installed in a tower connecting the new annex with the old building. In the old building were doctors' offices and a waiting room, the delivery room, the business office, the head nurse's office, a lab, an operating room, and a library. The Smith doctors were bringing, as best they could, "the scientific practice of medicine to the bedside of an enlightened public," in Flexner's phrase, but there were no turrets on their hospital. It did not look like a castle, and there were not "ten trains daily." Thousands of babies were born there instead of in farmhouses that were crowded and dimly lit. Thousands of surgical procedures were performed there, day and night.

In 1926 John Frank Smith, Dr. Mac's eldest son, joined the staff with his M.D degree from Tulane Medical School and a post-doctoral year in Pathology at Touro Infirmary in New Orleans. The fee for the hospitalization insurance plan was raised to two dollars per month per family, and the name was changed to the People's Hospital Association. At this point the hospital was open for regular hours to see patients on Sunday afternoons because families who had moved away from the area still paid their fees and returned to Smith Hospital for treatment on Sundays.

In 1929 Dr. Mac's second son, Charles McDanel Smith, joined the staff. He had completed the same training program as his older brother, at Tulane and

Dr. Jim *(left)* and Dr. Mac Smith, founders of the Smith Hospital in Paris, Arkansas. *Courtesy of Dr. John C. Smith and Lucille Smith.*

diseases, medical education and research had replaced patient care as the mission of the hospital. Patient care came in a slow third. Fields of medical specialization had arisen, with board members in each field examining candidates who had completed residency training in the teaching hospitals, lengthening medical training in some fields to a decade of post-doctoral work. Scientific medicine and city medicine were one.

As the country struggled out of the economic mire of the Great Depression, World War II interrupted whatever tentative progress had been achieved. The two younger Smiths, Dr. Charles and Dr. James, were drafted, and they were gone for four years. It was their older brother, Dr. John, who held the hospital together during the war. He became the administrator, the general surgeon, obstetrician, pathologist, and general practitioner. He had a cot in the basement of the old hospital building, where he could sleep for brief periods between emergencies.

The two younger brothers came home from the war and added equipment to the Smith Hospital. The staff was increased, and patients still crowded the waiting room and the porch, waiting to see their doctors. Dr. Charles had two sons, Arthur McDanel and John James, both of whom became physicians. Dr. James Turner had a daughter, Elaine, and a son, John Charles, who was graduated from the University of Arkansas for Medical Sciences in Little Rock. Of the three first cousins who became doctors, only John Charles came back to Logan County to practice. He was never permitted by his father, he said, to observe surgery when he was a young boy growing up in Paris, working summers and after school at Smith Hospital. His father always said, "Son, that is none of your business." When John Charles had applied to medical school and was waiting anxiously to hear from the admissions office, his acceptance was delivered to the hospital, and his father opened

Touro in New Orleans. The following year Dr. Mac died, and Dr. Jim retired. A new generation of Smiths ran the hospital, and not until a decade had passed did the youngest of Dr. Mac's sons, James Turner Smith, join his two brothers on the staff.

By the end of the thirties city medicine was dominated by huge teaching hospitals, presided over by a medical-academic elite who served as full-time professors in medical schools officially tied to the hospitals. Patient care was no longer the single purpose of the nation's hospitals. In the aftermath of Flexner and with the breakthroughs in infectious it. That night, when Dr. James came home very late, he walked as usual into John's room, then handed him the envelope and said, "Well, son, you've been accepted in medical school, and surgery is at seven o'clock in the morning. Now it is your business."

The Smith Hospital closed its doors and the Hospital Association ended on December 31, 1971, after sixty-one years of continuous operation. The end was commemorated by a mass of people who had been cared for there, who had been born there, who had received surgical procedures there. There was Mr. Whitecotton, a burn victim whom Dr. James had treated for months, and a little girl, now grown up, who had fractured her skull jumping off a roof on a dare. Dr. James had sat with her all night, waiting for her to regain consciousness. There was an elderly lady who had been treated for polio as a child at Smith Hospital, when the doctors made an isolation room for her on the third floor of the new building. They all came to say good-bye, to visit the rooms they had occupied, the nursery they had used, the waiting room they had paced.

A new Logan County Hospital, a branch of a Fort Smith hospital, opened to replace Smith Hospital. Dr. James went there to see patients, but he kept an office in his old hospital, and in time, his son, John Charles, joined him there, opening an office in the town of Ozark, thirty miles north of Paris, as well. Dr. James died in 1994, and his widow, Mrs. Lucille Smith, maintains their home on Church Street, three blocks away from Smith Hospital, where the water pipe was installed in 1910 to bring water to the old Potts hilltop.

And so there it stands, an oddly-shaped pair of brick buildings, connected by a curious sort of tower, surrounded by rangy shrubs and weeds, some windows boarded up, some with sagging window-unit air conditioners projecting at strange angles, with rust beginning to show. All the equipment is intact—the lab on the second floor, the X-ray machine, the operating table, and all the surgical equipment; the admitting station in the center of the downstairs hallway with all the hospital records in files; and a wicker wheelchair with a tall back and three steel wheels at the end of the corridor, beside an oak costumer with its curling brass hooks. It is all there, the story of country medicine, of country doctors who went away to cities to be educated and came back to Logan County to take care of people. Dr. James and Dr. Charles locked the wide front door in 1971 and left their hospital as it was, as the family had built it.

The fine old place stands there still on the hilltop, a time capsule, a story longing to be told, as the screen doors sag and the roof leaks, awaiting the redeeming hands of preservationists. And the sixth Smith doctor and his mother want their building to become a medical museum. They would gladly give it for that purpose. Meanwhile, caught in the impossible schedule of a late twentieth-century medical practice in Paris and Ozark, Dr. John Charles Smith says proudly, "I am a country doctor."

Acknowledgements:

The author acknowledges with gratitude the assistance of the Division of Medical Humanities Foundation Fund (UAMS); Basil Hicks III, research assistant; Edwina Walls Mann; and Judy Smith. Two members of the Smith Family in Paris, Arkansas, were especially patient during numerous interviews: Mrs. Lucille Smith (Mrs. James Turner) and her son, John Charles Smith, M.D. Arthur McDanel Smith, M.D., of Tacoma, Washington, was interviewed as well. The following individuals in Paris were generous and unstintingly helpful: Jackie Pollock Robinson at the Chamber of Commerce; Louanne Gilbert and Jane Ellen Young, Librarians; Geneva Morton, Curator of the Logan County Museum; Don Johnson; and Jim Maddox.

The Conway County Library still serves Morrilton readers more than eighty years after its construction. *Photo by Tammie Trippe Dillon, Arkansas Historic Preservation Program.*

GOOD WORKS BY ARKANSAS WOMEN

Diane D. Blair

Conway County Library
1916
Morrilton, Conway County
Listed on the National Register of Historic Places on April 15, 1978

"The Conway County Library is one of the most outstanding early buildings in Morrilton, Arkansas. It is representative of the early efforts of a group of dedicated women to establish library service for the city of Morrilton. Their efforts were recorded in the bricks that make a building that was meant to last."

—From the National Register nomination

Imagine an Arkansas without libraries or schools or hospitals, without pure water or parks or playgrounds, without a juvenile justice system or historic preservation programs. Such a civic wasteland is unthinkable now, of course, because today's citizens expect, and today's national and state and local governments provide, these and many other facilities and programs. It is no exaggeration to say, however, that these and many other services first appeared in Arkansas because determined women, working together, demanded, established, financed, and maintained them. The Morrilton Public Library is a splendid but by no means singular example of such endeavors.

The Morrilton Pathfinder Club, founded by twenty-five prominent community women in 1898, was one of many women's clubs established in Arkansas's growing small towns in the late nineteenth and early twentieth centuries. Like hundreds of other such literary and social clubs, the Pathfinder Club quickly moved from self-improvement and cultural appreciation to community betterment. Wanting to share their own love of reading and information with others, women who belonged to clubs first began pooling and sharing their own materials in makeshift libraries set up in everything from churches and town halls to stores and train stations.

Many clubs then took on the further task of raising funds for, and seeing to the construction and maintenance of, a permanent community library. The American Library Association once estimated that 75 percent of all public libraries in the United States were founded by women's clubs, and certainly that phenomenon is apparent in Arkansas: between 1880 and 1935 women's literary clubs had established twenty-eight libraries in such towns as Fort Smith, Helena, Malvern, Mena, Searcy, Van Buren, Camden, Stuttgart, Brinkley, and, of course, Morrilton (Martin 65, 67).

Urged on by the Arkansas Federation of Women's Clubs, to which most literary clubs belonged, energetic women raised private funds through a variety of imaginative mechanisms, successfully persuaded the state legislature to authorize local referenda on library millage, circulated petitions in their hometowns to place a library tax on the ballot, campaigned for that tax's passage, and then frequently served as volunteers to staff the resulting libraries.

This pattern—identifying a problem, rallying volunteers to address it, establishing a service widely recognized as essential or desirable, then making the solution permanent through governmental action—was followed repeatedly and successfully all over the state, in small matters and large, for decade after decade. And the civic uplift agenda taken on by these Arkansas clubwomen, both black and white, is an impressive one. It included education (universal and compulsory education, trained teachers, consolidated schools, free kindergartens, home economics education for poor rural women, more college scholarship opportunities for women), public health (a tuberculosis sanitarium, public sanitation systems, city beautification, traffic and railroad crossing lights, child labor restrictions, pure food and water, milk for undernourished schoolchildren), and a litany of other wrongs that needed righting.

Obviously, in the course of pursuing their library and other causes, women whose only previous activities outside the home had been church-related acquired a new array of skills for operating in the public arena: researching, writing, speaking, persuading, lobbying, campaigning, organizing, fundraising, collective action. Because, however, so much of what these women accomplished was done on a local, personal, and voluntary level, little of it, until very recently, was given the historical recognition it deserves. But as Anne Firor Scott has noted,

The members of the Mena Women's Literary Club dressed in costume to represent the countries of the League of Nations in this May 19, 1936, photograph. *Courtesy of Special Collections Division, University or Arkansas Libraries, Fayetteville.*

"Discussing 19th century social history without analyzing the effects of women's voluntary associations is somewhat akin to discussing plant growth without mentioning photosynthesis. . . . At a time when no government at any level took much responsibility for what we now call human services, women's groups set out to fill these needs" (Scott 281).

One of the few episodes in Arkansas history for which women are now given adequate credit is the creation in 1958 and subsequent influence of the Little Rock Women's Emergency Committee to Open Our Schools. Founder Adolphine Terry is quoted as having told the editor of the *Arkansas Gazette*, "The men have failed; it's time to call out the women." The courageous women involved in this enterprise exerted lasting and beneficial influence, but as the above brief narrative indicates, Arkansas women had been tackling tough problems ignored by the male establishment for many decades before the turbulent desegregation era (Murphy 67).

Some circumstances are dramatically changed as we enter a new millennium. Governments now provide not only essential services for our safety and survival but many amenities as well. Most women are now employed outside the home for most of their adult lives and therefore have less time for the kinds of club activities that once were a prominent part of middle-class women's lives. Furthermore, women are now free to participate openly in the public arena, not needing the respectable cloak of club membership to mask their interests and ambitions. Still, even in our own hectic times, many busy women manage to give generously of their time, individually and collectively, to address a variety of unmet human needs. Hopefully, this kind of creative altruism will always be a part of the Arkansas tradition.

After decades of neglect the significant contributions of women to Arkansas's history are at last being chronicled and celebrated. Among other important efforts, the Arkansas Women's History Institute organized an impressive exhibit in 1986 and published a handbook of Arkansas women's achievements entitled *Behold, Our Works Were Good*. One need only visit the Morrilton Public Library, still providing information, education, and pleasure to thousands of citizens in the building constructed through the efforts of the Morrilton Pathfinder Club, to know that Arkansas women's works have been not only good but indispensable.

Bibliographical note:
The records and scrapbooks of the Morrilton Pathfinder Club, 1897–1985, are housed in the Special Collections of Mullins Library, University of Arkansas, Fayetteville.
Other sources quoted from and relied upon in this essay include:
Karen J. Blair, *The Clubwoman as Feminist* (New York and London: Holmes and Meier Publishers, 1980).
Janie Synatzke Evins, "Arkansas Women: Their Contributions to Society, Politics, and Business, 1865–1900," *Arkansas Historical Quarterly* 44 (Summer 1985): 118–33.
Mrs. Frederick Hanger and Miss Clara B. Eno, *History of the Arkansas Federation of Women's Clubs, 1897–1934* (Van Buren: Press-Argus Printers, 1935).
Elizabeth Jacoway, ed., *Behold, Our Works Were Good* (Little Rock: August House, 1988).
Marilyn Martin, "From Altruism to Activism: The Contribution of Literary Clubs to Arkansas Public Libraries, 1885–1935," *Arkansas Historical Quarterly* 55 (Spring 1996): 64–94.
Sara Alderman Murphy, *Breaking the Silence* (Fayetteville: University of Arkansas Press, 1997).
Frances Mitchell Ross, "The New Woman as Club Woman and Social Activist in Turn of the Century Arkansas," *Arkansas Historical Quarterly* 50 (Winter 1991): 317–351.
Anne Firor Scott, *Making the Invisible Woman Visible* (Chicago and Urbana: University of Illinois Press, 1984).

Taborian Hall, partially restored in the early 1990s, stands as a reminder of the thriving commercial district that once lined Little Rock's Ninth Street. *Photo by Ken Story, Arkansas Historic Preservation Program.*

TABORIAN HALL: THE SILENT SENTINEL

Nudie Williams

Taborian Hall
1916
Little Rock, Pulaski County
Listed on the National Register of Historic Places on April 29, 1982

"Taborian Hall is one of the few remaining buildings that recall the era when West Ninth Street, between Izard and Broadway streets in downtown Little Rock, was the hub of black business activity. . . . Today, as a result of the 1960s urban renewal objectives and the contemporary construction of an adjacent freeway, very little original fabric of this once prosperous black commercial area survives, emphasizing the significance of preserving Taborian Hall as a valuable historic resource."

—From the National Register nomination

J. E. Henderson opened a jewelry store at 508 West Ninth Street in 1896, becoming Arkansas's first African-American jeweler. *Courtesy of Special Collections Division, University of Arkansas Libraries, Fayetteville.*

Standing like a majestic but lonely sentinel on the corner of Ninth and State Streets in Little Rock, Arkansas, Taborian Hall lends quiet testimony to its former status as one of the anchors of a thriving black business district. In its day the nine-block area from High Street to South Broadway was affectionately known as "the Line," and on any given day you could find many members of the black community "down on the Line." Most of the city's prominent black physicians, dentists, attorneys, and other black professionals, including leaders of the NAACP, had offices on "the Line." Two newspapers, the *Southern Mediator Journal* and the *State Press,* were published from there over the years. Visitors to the city had their choice of an overnight stay at the Savoy, the Miller, or the Tucker Hotels. Or they could visit the numerous cafes, cleaners, magazine stores, pool halls, barber and beauty shops, and men's and women's clothing stores and at the end of the day take in a movie at the Gem Theater. While the local pharmacy filled prescriptions for the community, one of three mortuaries—

Miller-Elston, Dubisson or United Friends—would be chosen to handle funeral arrangements for the deceased. Thus, "the Line" could possibly have rivaled Atlanta's Hunter Street or even challenged Tulsa's Greenwood Avenue for the title of "Negro's Wall Street." And Taborian Hall was always a mainstay in this district.

Presently, this architecturally sound, classical, three and one-half story masonry structure, with brick veneer, is in good repair and houses a business, Arkansas Flag and Banner, after suffering for many years in a serious state of decline. Unfortunately, there is little evidence left of this building's once-splendid interior; one can only speculate that it mirrored the exemplary details of the exterior.

The International Order of the Twelve Knights and Daughters of Tabor, Royal House of Media and Maids and Pages of Honor constructed this classical building on its present site in 1916. The Taborians were a mixed-gender, black fraternal order. The Order was established in 1871 by Moses Dickson, who also served as its first International Chief Grand

Mentor. Dickson, a Civil War veteran, a social activist, and an African Methodist Episcopal minister, wanted a fraternal organization that offered social advantages and financial protection to blacks. In 1907 the Order claimed a membership of one hundred thousand in thirty states and several foreign nations.

The organization provided each member with a three hundred dollar endowment, fifty dollars for funeral expenses, and an additional twenty dollars toward the purchase of a grave monument. Thus, its fraternal insurance society had more than enough capital to finance such a stately building. From its location at 800 West Ninth Street the structure served as the headquarters for the Order's state and international business.

The 1920 Little Rock City Directory provides an excellent glimpse of Taborian Hall serving as a social and civic center for the black community. Over the years it housed a long-term tenant, the Gem Pharmacy, and a number of health care professionals (physicians, surgeons, and one dentist), including W. B. Black, E. B. Boswell, Jesse B. Woods, and J. V. Jordan. Several restaurants and other businesses set up shop in the Taborian Temple, as well. Unfortunately, following the stock market crash of 1929, the Taborian Order was forced into foreclosure and lost the ownership of the building. Even under the new ownership occupancy remained high, and the Hall was still able to attract desirable clients. From the time it opened its doors in 1918 until well into the 1930s the Taborian landmark was a star attraction in the black business district.

From the early 1940s into the 1950s the pages of the *Arkansas State Press* chronicled the continuing prosperity of Taborian Hall in particular and the black business district in general. For example, in May 1941 there was a notice in the paper announcing the move of the Universal Life Insurance Agency branch office to the second floor of the Hall; Lloyd's new place, The Subway Café, featuring dining and dancing in air-conditioned comfort, took over the basement. However, the star attraction of Taborian Hall had to be the Dreamland Ballroom. The Ballroom was often in direct competition with acts booked at Little Rock's Robinson Memorial Auditorium downtown. It also had local competition from the Diplomatic, the Flamingo, and, later, the Morocco Clubs. Some district oldtimers interviewed by the *Arkansas Democrat* swore that all the legendary musicians of the time played in the Dreamland Ballroom.

The Dreamland's longevity could be attributed to its clever use of regular amateur contest nights, offering three dollars for first place, two dollars for second place, and one dollar for third place. S. W. Tucker, a local black promoter, developed this idea to keep loyal customers coming back to the Hall. He was able to organize local talent in amateur contests, coupled with a floor show and dance, between bookings of major, featured attractions. By scaling the price of admissions down to an affordable twenty-five to thirty-five cents, he was assured of a packed house. So when major attractions were booked, they included such traveling revues as the Brownskin Models, Ida Cox and her Darktown Scandals, Bartlett's "Vampin' Babies," and the Brown Derby Revue. However, all of these acts demanded an increase in admissions, to a charge of forty to fifty-five cents. Moreover, main attractions—such as Louis Jordan and His Orchestra, Benny Carter's Orchestra, Dizzy Gillespie's Orchestra Featuring Ella Fitzgerald, Andy Kirk and His Clouds of Joy, and Roy Milton and His Solid Senders—commanded $1.12 to $1.50 for advance tickets, $1.25 to $1.50 for door admission, and $1.50 to $2.00 for a table reservation.

Knowledgeable observers recall that the Ballroom and the entire business district began a serious decline. These observers are supported by the *Arkansas Democrat*. One reporter wrote, "Once the hub of black business activity, the four-block strip began declining in the late 1950s."

Other Arkansas communities contained black business districts, such as this one in Saint Francis County that was anchored by Scott Bond's store. *Courtesy of Special Collections Division, University of Arkansas Libraries, Fayetteville.*

Historically, there are many reasons that may explain why or how a whole vibrant black business community was displaced. Some reasons are more direct than others, but come, let us consider a few. First, when plans were announced to expand the Wilbur D. Mills Expressway eastward and build the Interstate 630 interchange in the 1960s, there were mixed emotions and discussions about how these plans would affect the district. More concretely, however, the conversion of Ninth Street to a three-lane, one-way thoroughfare, with no parking along the streets, proved to be a major contributing factor to the business district's failure. The *Arkansas Gazette's* 1977 story correctly pointed out "that the growing black patronage of the downtown Main Street also has led to the decline of Ninth Street businesses." Two years later the *Arkansas Democrat* wrote that "the Urban Renewal project apparently had some effect on area businesses as many more left in mass exodus to better and more modern facilities." Very few buildings survived the exodus.

Taborian Hall remains intact today largely through the efforts of the late Dr. Ruth Patterson, representing the Association for the Study of African-American Life and History, and Mike Shinn, a historian with the Arkansas Historic Preservation Program. Together they convinced the property's owner to consider placing the Hall on the National Register of Historic Places. On September 15, 1981, the property was nominated to the National Register and later accepted. A decade later it achieved new life after partial restoration by Kerry McCoy to house her business, Arkansas Flag and Banner.

But as we approach the new millennium, let us reflect and understand that brick and mortar do not tell the only story here. Long-time resident and Little Rock educator Leslie Rogers personalized the story best in a 1979 interview in the *Arkansas Democrat*. He described Ninth Street as "my school" and confirmed that his "high school prom was held in a pool hall in Taborian Hall." The gentleman pointed toward the Hall and said, "That's my heritage. That's where I built my self-concepts, and if I don't have my self-concepts I'm dead." Let the twenty-first century make at least a good-faith effort to remember the history embodied in the building known as Taborian Hall and keep this wonderful legacy alive as a symbol of a vibrant past.

Detail of the Cotton
Belt Railroad Depot
at Fordyce. Arkansas.
*Historic Preservation
Program photo.*

ARKANSAS AND THE RAILROADS

Carl Moneyhon

Cotton Belt Railroad Depot
Ca. 1925
Fordyce, Dallas County
Listed on the National Register of Historic Places on June 11, 1992

"This passenger and freight depot is associated with the *Railroad Growth and Development in Arkansas, 1870–1940* historic context as a structure financed and erected under the auspices of one of the larger early twentieth-century railroads in the state. As such, it is eligible under Criterion A by virtue of those associations; however, with its Craftsman cornice brackets and multi-pane windows, the Cotton Belt Railroad Depot in Fordyce is eligible not only under Criterion A, but also under Criterion C for its being a good example of the Mediterranean/Craftsman style."

—*From the National Register nomination*

Rock Island Depot
1925
Fordyce, Dallas County
Listed on the National Register of Historic Places on October 28, 1983

"The Rock Island Railway Depot was constructed around 1925. The construction of this brick depot in Fordyce reinforced the town's importance, as it became a center for rail connection and transportation in southern Arkansas. This company has through consolidation grown to be one of the major lines running through Dallas County. . . . The Rock Island Railway Depot is one of two brick depots remaining from an era that breathed new life into economically depressed Dallas County."

—*From the National Register nomination*

The Cotton Belt and Rock Island railroad stations at Fordyce are artifacts of the railroad boom that revolutionized the state's economic and social life in the years between the end of the Civil War and the 1920s. Both constructed in 1925, the two depots reflect the railroads at the height of their influence in Arkansas, particularly their critical role in providing local passenger transportation and merchandise service. Their current state, however, shows the changes that have taken place in the industry since its 1920s peak.

The construction of railroads in Arkansas in the years immediately following the Civil War solved a problem that had stood in the way of the state's development since statehood. An inhospitable terrain that hindered early efforts at building roads and treacherous rivers that limited the use of waterways restricted early efforts at integrating Arkansans and their economic goods into markets. Away from readily navigable waterways the economy languished. During the 1850s, however, the state's economic and political leaders planned for the construction of railroads to overcome these barriers. After fitful starts during that decade laying of track began in earnest in the post-war years. By 1900 railroad companies had built 2,383 miles of mainline track and 785 miles of branch and spur line. Steel tracks brought Arkansans into closer economic and social contact with each other and with the rest of the nation.

A combination of private entrepreneurship, outside capital, and local, state, and federal financial support produced the state's transportation revolution. At the turn of the century some thirty-nine different railroads ran trains in the state. However, three roads dominated the scene. The St. Louis & Iron Mountain (later the Missouri Pacific), the St. Louis Southwestern (the Cotton Belt), and the Choctaw, Oklahoma & Gulf (later the Rock Island) operated 75 percent of the track. The St. Louis & San Francisco (the Frisco), the Kansas City Southern, and the Missouri & North Arkansas (which brought rails into the Ozarks) joined the big three in the early twentieth century, when they carried out significant additional construction projects within the state.

The improved access these roads brought to economic markets throughout the nation generated major changes in agriculture. Farmers who had refrained from producing commercial crops because of limited access to markets suddenly found markets available. Almost everywhere in the state farmers shifted from self-sufficiency to cultivate more cot-

CARL MONEYHON

The Rock Island Railroad Depot, Fordyce, Arkansas. *Photo by A. C. Haralson, courtesy of Arkansas Department of Parks and Tourism.*

ton. A risky crop that often suffered from depressed prices, cotton nonetheless offered the farmer the one product with a sure market. In addition, the railroads took an active role in promoting the introduction of new crops to Arkansas farms. The Iron Mountain and the Missouri & North Arkansas encouraged farmers along their routes to diversify and even opened demonstration farms to show farmers how to cultivate truck crops and fruits. In the 1880s the Rock Island encouraged the immigration of farmers from Iowa, Kansas, and Nebraska to the Grand Prairie in order increase business along its route through eastern Arkansas. The result was the development of significant production of forage crops. By 1900 the state's agricultural produce was being sold throughout the nation and across the state. Arkansas farmers were engaged in more commercial agriculture than ever before.

The expansion of the railroads also made possible significant development of the state's timber and mineral resources. Timber companies and shortline railroad companies built tracks into the forests to help bring out cut timber, and the mainline roads facilitated the movement of processed timber to markets outside of the state. The Iron Mountain and the Rock Island played major roles in the development of coalfields in western Arkansas. By 1900 these mines shipped some two million tons of coal out on the railroads. The presence of the Missouri & North Arkansas, together with good prices during World War I, encouraged the development of zinc and lead mines in the northwest part of the state in the early twentieth century. As in agriculture the railroads helped to expand the state's economy.

The railroads not only made it possible for Arkansans to get their products to market more easily; they also gave people easier access to the goods being produced elsewhere in the country. By the turn of the century railroads made it possible for Arkansans to order goods from mail-order companies such as Sears, Roebuck and Co. Even rural stores offered their customers a greater variety of merchandise, as the railroads reduced the cost of transporting such goods to merchants.

All of the revolutionary impact of the railroads on Arkansas was not economic, however. The railroads changed the lives of Arkansans in other ways, as well. The improvement in transportation helped to break down the isolation of many rural peoples and helped connect more Arkansans to the surrounding world in a way not possible earlier. To be precise, the railroads made Arkansans more mobile. Specific changes in the time and cost involved in travel indicated the revolution taking place. In the 1870s an eighty-mile stage trip between Prescott and Little Rock took almost twenty-four hours and cost twelve dollars. When the Iron Mountain began operating passenger trains between the two towns in 1874, the distance was covered in three and one-half hours for $4.50. By 1937 the Missouri Pacific's trains covered the same distance in two hours. For decades the passenger trains provided the primary means of transporting people for both short- and long-distance travel. In addition, name trains such as the Missouri Pacific's "Eagles," "Southerner," "Texan," and "Sunshine Special"; the Rock Island's "Rockets" and

This early twentieth-century photograph of the Van Buren, Arkansas, depot shows a typical busy day during the heyday of the railroads in the state. *Courtesy of UALR Archives.*

CARL MONEYHON

"Californian"; the Cotton Belt's "Lone Star"; the Frisco's "Will Rogers" and "Meteor"; and the Kansas City Southern's "Southern Belle" provided first-class service from Arkansas to the rest of the nation.

The movement of trade and passengers along the railroads produced something of an urban revolution in Arkansas, as well. Towns into which the railroads moved experienced rapid population growth and an expansion of businesses providing services to support the increased economic activity that accompanied the roads. Some Arkansas towns even owed their existence to the railroads. Along with communities such as Brinkley, Paragould, and many others, Fordyce, named after a president of the Cotton Belt company, was developed by the railroad.

As early as the 1910s, however, the public construction of all-weather highways and the advent of the automobile and motor truck began to cut into the railroads' business. Most of the railroads tried a variety of innovations to hold on to their customers. The Frisco tried to regain passengers with its Southwestern Bus Line, gathering passengers in the countryside and feeding them to the railroad for long-distance traffic. The Frisco's Southwestern Transportation Company sought to pick up local merchandise and route it to the railroad for long-distance trade. Local traffic continued to decline, however, and the heyday of the railroads in the local economy ended.

The change in railroad operations produced by the automobile and truck did not, however, end the role of railroads in Arkansas. They have continued to perform a vital, if different, role in the life of the state and its people. Amtrak still maintains modest long-distance passenger service. The companies that have succeeded the turn-of-the-century railroads also provide the state with freight connections to the rest of the nation. Increasingly, the railroads also have offered access to the expanding Mexican market and should continue to play that role into the next century. In so doing, they should continue to play a vital role in the economic life of the state.

"guarded from false shame as to the political actions of their ancestors," as Mrs. Richard B. Willis, a historian for the Arkansas Division of the United Daughters of the Confederacy, said in 1904. For years the Arkansas UDC's "Endorsement of Books" committee exerted its influence on school textbooks in Arkansas, and in 1917 the Arkansas General Assembly agreed to a petition that the state UDC historian examine and pass on all U.S. histories before their adoption for use in the state's schools.

Histories approved by the state UDC no doubt had a profound effect on the consciousness of Arkansans, and they remained part of the curriculum until the so-called Second Reconstruction of the South, in which the events at Little Rock Central High School in 1957 played no small part. Yet, in the words of Gaines M. Foster, a historian of the Lost Cause movement, the Confederate patriotic organizations "preferred to speak in the language of monuments." As one turn-of-the-century memorialist observed, "Books are occasionally opened, monuments are seen every day . . . ." The groups—particularly the UDC, whose Arkansas division was responsible alone or in part for at least twenty-two Confederate monuments—worked with messianic zeal in an attempt to blanket the state with monuments that, through their symbolic power, helped convey certain historical and ideological assumptions. Mrs. Lizzie Pollard, president of the Southern Memorial Association in Fayetteville, a Confederate women's group independent of the UDC, gave the best explanation of the evocative nature of these monuments. In a 1904 book about the history of monument associations in the South, Mrs. Pollard wrote:

> These monuments we build will speak their message to generations. These voiceless marbles in their majesty will stand as vindicators of the Confederate soldier. They will

lift from these brave men the opprobrium of rebel, and stand them in the line of patriots. This is not alone a labor of love, it is a work of duty as well. We are correcting history.

The Southern Memorial Association created the Fayetteville Confederate Cemetery, where it reinterred the bodies of hundreds of Confederate soldiers, mostly casualties from the Pea Ridge and Prairie Grove battlefields. On June 10, 1897, the group unveiled a 26-foot-tall monument in the cemetery, topped by a bronze statue of a Confederate private in typical battle dress.

Starting immediately after the Civil War, women's monument associations began the process of interpreting defeat and attempting to extract meaning from the war. Throughout the South they built graveyards where they reinterred fallen Confederate soldiers, and, of course, they built monuments as the centerpieces of these cemeteries. In Arkansas the earliest Confederate monuments— such as the 25-foot-tall granite shaft dedicated in 1886 in the Confederate Section of Camden's Oakland Cemetery—are all the work of such associations. While the memorialists preferred the cemetery as the proper setting for commemoration of their martyred heroes, the more aggressive Confederate patriotic groups preferred locations with higher profiles. For example, in 1897 Colonel J. N. Smithee, editor of the *Arkansas Gazette,* launched a campaign to raise five thousand dollars for a monument in Little Rock "that the children of veterans can feel proud of." Smithee wanted the monument in a prominent place, not in a cemetery, so that "we can mourn our dead in the silent cemeteries and commemorate their deeds from the house tops." At the 1901 state encampment of the United Confederate Veterans a heated debate ensued when one veteran offered a resolution calling for the placement of the monument in a cem-

Thousands of people attended the 1911 unveiling of the Memorial to Company A, Capitol Guards, in what later became MacArthur Park in Little Rock. *Courtesy of Arkansas History Commission.*

etery. In response another veteran stated that memorialists in his home town of Helena consigned their two Confederate monuments—including one to General Patrick R. Cleburne, considered one of the Confederacy's best divisional commanders—to the Helena Confederate Cemetery, where they "went unnoticed by those whom [they were] intended to instruct." In the end the latter argument prevailed, and the Arkansas General Assembly kicked in more than five thousand dollars for the project. Frederick Wellington Ruckstuhl, a noted New York sculptor of the period, received the commission, and on June 3, 1905, Confederate veterans unveiled the finished product, an elaborate work featuring a bronze representation of "Fame" atop a stone pillar, with a

bronze likeness of a Confederate soldier on a tier below. Its location was on the front lawn of the yet-to-be-completed State Capitol building. All but one Confederate monument dedicated in Arkansas after the turn of the century was in front of a courthouse, in a public square, or in another suitably visible site. In fact, in 1906 the Sons of Confederate Veterans in Van Buren moved the town's 1899 Confederate monument from the Fairview Cemetery to the Crawford County Courthouse lawn.

Chapters of the Sons of Confederate Veterans and the United Daughters of the Confederacy still exist in Arkansas, but today the groups focus more on battlefield preservation, reenactments, and genealogy than on arguing the benevolent ends of

The 1907 Batesville Confederate Monument is the obvious centerpiece of this gathering at the Independence County Courthouse. *Courtesy of Arkansas History Commission.*

the Southern plantation system or apologizing for the "necessity" of the Ku Klux Klan. The ongoing reenactment phenomenon, which drew a record twenty thousand participants to Gettysburg in July 1998, along with a resurgence of interest in the Civil War in the 1990s, has increased the rolls of the Arkansas groups in recent years. But membership has not grown as significantly in this state as in the Deep South, where a neo-Confederate subculture is flourishing. This awakening of latter-day Confederates caught the attention of Tony Horowitz, a Pulitzer Prize–winning journalist, who after a decade of covering conflicts in Iraq, Bosnia, and Northern Ireland, returned to his home in Virginia only to be awakened early one Saturday morning by the musket fire of Confederate reenactors. His curiosity with the scene outside his bedroom window led him into almost three years of reenacting battles and "searching out the places and people who kept memory of the [Civil War] alive in the present day." His 1998 book about the experience, *Confederates in the Attic: Dispatches from the Unfinished Civil War,* features numerous interviews with unreconstructed Rebels who sport bumper stickers reading "If at First You Don't Secede, Try Try Again" and mouth the same platitudes promoted by Confederate patriotic organizations a century ago. Horowitz found one such group in Salisbury, North Carolina—the Children of the Confederacy, a UDC auxiliary for youngsters under age eighteen—who recite from a Confederate "Catechism." Asked about the "feeling of the slaves towards their masters," the Children responded by rote, "They were faithful and devoted and were always ready and willing to serve." Despite such incidents and the efforts of groups such as the South Carolina–based League of the South, whose goal, according to its website, is "the cultural, social, economic, and political independence and well-being of the Southern People," Confederate patriotic societies have but a modicum of the cultural and social cachet they possessed in the early part of the century, when they raised more monuments to Jefferson Davis than were erected to any other leader in U.S. history, other than George Washington and Abraham Lincoln.

History has dealt harshly with the ideas that animated the efforts of the Confederate patriotic groups, and few things today are as anachronistic as a monument that marks a town as Confederate territory. Yet, despite some weathering, the Confederate monuments endure, and it is their legacy and the issue of their preservation with which we must contend at the millennium. In an era saturated with the murky philosophy of political correctness, Confederate monuments would seem obvious targets for cultural cleansing. Despite the occasional scattered skirmish, these stone and bronze soldiers have engendered little of the overt acrimony that has suffused debates about the flying of the Confederate battle flag and its representation on the state banners of several Southern states. Today, in small towns throughout the South, Confederate monuments function less as symbols of defiance than as unofficial town mascots. In Star City, for example, many locals affectionately call their monument "Alex." This is not to say that Confederate monuments are innocuous; indeed, it is intellectually impossible to strip a Rebel monument moved from a cemetery to the courthouse lawn down to a mere memorial honoring fallen soldiers. Ideally, Confederate monuments would serve as cultural reference points for a discussion not only of the Civil War and its ramifications, which already receives its due, but of the eight decades after Reconstruction in which the South, with Federal acquiesence, decided the question of black equality. Clearly, this is a stretch, so surveys of American historical literacy inform us, in a society that doesn't know Shiloh from "shinola." Nevertheless, toppling every Confederate monument in the South will not expunge from the American "experience" the Peculiar Institution or the strange career of Jim Crow, to borrow a phrase from C. Vann Woodward, the iconic Southern historian. Nor will it serve as more than a stitch in the persistent wounds of racial and social injustice. The history is simply too complex and too much alive to be obliterated with a few passes of a wrecking ball.

The graceful arches of the Cotter Bridge traverse the White River in Baxter County. *Photo by A. C. Haralson, courtesy of Arkansas Department of Parks and Tourism.*

THE COTTER BRIDGE

Lynn Morrow

Cotter Bridge
1930
Cotter, Baxter County
Listed on the National Register of Historic Places on April 4, 1990

"Completed in 1930, the Cotter Bridge is significant as the only bridge in Arkansas known to be designed and engineered by the Marsh Engineering Company of Des Moines, Iowa. The Marsh Company is well known for its Rainbow Arch bridge, a design patented in 1912 by James Barney Marsh, the company's founder. The bridge is an excellent example of the Marsh Rainbow Arch construction technique, where the steel arches were assembled on the ground and then lifted into place on the piers. These steel arches supported their own formwork while the concrete was cast around them, thus eliminating the need for building costly and time-consuming falsework beneath the structure. Due to its strategic location on the only east-west route in northern Arkansas, the Cotter Bridge was instrumental in opening up a new region of the Ozarks, which was to become a major resort and recreation area in the United States."

—From the National Register nomination

The Cotter Rainbow Bridge is one of the great Arkansas landmarks of the twentieth century. It spans the White River on the only east-west highway through northern Arkansas. The construction of the bridge in 1930 was an important milestone in the Arkansas Highway and Transportation Department's plan for road modernization, and the bridge was essential to the expansion of the Ozarks tourism and recreation industry. The design and structural quality of the bridge achieved official recognition when it became Arkansas's first National Civil Engineering Landmark in 1986.

The bridge itself was a monumental project that signaled the influence of industrial changes on Arkansas, as similar projects did in the rest of the nation. It became part of the progressive social and economic transformation of early twentieth-century Arkansas, which brought the Ozarks into a larger marketing arena and national culture. The commerce brought by industry and recreation crossed its concrete supports and accelerated the value and pace of both. Just as the White River Railway, completed in 1905, replaced the movement of goods and services on steamboats, the Cotter Bridge of 1930, with its increased automobile and truck traffic, signaled an alternative to railroads. The bridge played a fundamental role in the regional economy by serving as a crucial link to tourism in the Ozarks interior and to corporate associations that promoted access to natural resources, marketable real estate, commodities, and other forms of entrepreneurship that required reliable transportation in order to expand.

Throughout its entire history the bridge has played an important role in the maturation of Ozarks tourism. Tourism was a product of modernization and, like good transportation—which was as essential to tourism's development in the Ozarks as it was elsewhere—evolved in each generation with increasing sophistication. The upper reaches of the White River had attracted investments in resorts and recreation for a long time. Such tourist meccas as Eureka Springs were known nationally in the late nineteenth century. So was Lake Taneycomo, completed in 1913 and located just across the Missouri state line. Coin Harvey's Monte Ne resort, founded in 1902, and his Ozark Trails Association of 1913 funneled promotional fervor to many who were interested in the marketable potential of recreation in the Ozarks. In the 1920s the Ozark Playgrounds Association (OPA) became the leading Ozarks promotional voice. Its slogan, "Land of a Million Smiles," helped fix the recreational opportunities of northwest Arkansas and southwest Missouri in the public mind. The OPA was a solid proponent of good roads and all-weather bridges for obvious reasons. The twenties witnessed a dramatic boom in Ozarks automobile tourism. For those seeking longer stays or permanent locations in the Ozarks playground, the real-estate developers promoted a variety of investments, including the new Bella Vista retirement community.

Regardless of whether development was long or short term, good roads and bridges were required to bring the automobile-traveling public into the region, and such improvements were not long in coming. Missouri's only concrete-arch Y-bridge

The new bridge at Cotter is packed with people on the day of its dedication, including the patriotic young man at right. *Arkansas Historic Preservation Program photo.*

was built in 1927 on the James Fork of the White River, while plans were simultaneously being made for the construction of the Lake of the Ozarks on the Osage River, and engineers were busy designing the future Table Rock Lake on the White River. This regional flood of public and private investment in new construction for tourism and commerce on the White River and its tributaries stimulated an acute awareness by Baxter County developers of the need for a new bridge across the White River. Such a new bridge would bring travelers to Baxter and Marion Counties and to emerging tourist destinations.

White River residents had witnessed traffic through their valley for generations. First there were keelboats, flatboats, and finally steamboats. Since 1905 the railroad hauled travelers and goods along the riverway. Sportsmen and tourists had floated the river on hunting and fishing trips since the 1890s, coming down from Forsyth, Missouri, and sometimes going past the future Cotter Bridge site all the way to Batesville. Locally, Lake's Ferry, a couple of

miles upriver from the future bridge site, was a summer resort for affluent city folks from the nearby county seats of Mountain Home and Yellville who wanted to pass a week or two in an Ozarks Arcadia. Once the White River Railway was completed and regular schedules were initiated to new railroad towns like Cotter, these sportsmen and their friends, families, and business associates could enjoy a float from Branson or Forsyth to Cotter and return with a trip on the train. Similar excursions went downriver from Cotter. Such adventures were part of packaged promotions to draw sportsmen to the Ozarks. River recreation gave rise to a modest infrastructure of guides, boat builders, outfitters, merchant suppliers, and innkeepers.

Mary Ann Messick, Sean O'Reilly, and Corinne Smith have recounted the history of Cotter and its famous bridge. Cotter was the speculative offspring of the Red Bud Realty Company and home to railroad and timber workers. In 1905 an instant town of six hundred souls appeared in the valley almost overnight. The town, dominated by timber industries, quickly assumed the typical look of American timber company towns, made up of numerous modern and quickly built pyramidal-roof houses.

In the early years a major obstacle to Cotter's growth and development was the problem of frequent flooding on the White River. The ford at Cotter was so frequently under water that anxious travelers in the twenties would detour as far north as Branson in order to cross the bridge over Lake Taneycomo. Relief, in the form of a bridge, was slow in coming. Locals had hoped that an authorizing legislative act of 1912 would attract an investor to build a bridge across the river at Cotter, but no such investor was forthcoming. Many travelers were compelled to wait for ferries in temporary riverside camps to negotiate the troublesome White River. Then in 1927 flooding of proportions never seen before struck the region. The catastrophe destroyed some 511 Arkansas bridges and devastated hundreds of miles of roads. In Baxter County the floods carried all the ferries away no less than four times, which caused major disruptions in travel. Worse still, several destroyed Cotter businesses decided not to rebuild after the benchmark flood.

These punishing floods paralleled and helped spur dramatic developments in the Good Roads Movement in Arkansas. In June 1930 the Arkoma Highway Association, after sustained promotion, succeeded in changing Highway 12, the east-west road through Cotter, to the federal designation of U.S. Highway 62. (The federal and state numerical identifications for public highways replaced all of the old regional road names like Ozark Trail, White River Trace, etc.) Thus, the completed bridge at Cotter became a key element in a national highway that ran from Maysville, Kentucky, to El Paso, Texas.

Federal bureaucracy in Arkansas road development was fairly new. In 1921 the Federal Highway Act introduced planning at the state level. Then in 1923 the Harrelson Road Law created an adminis-

trative bureaucracy in the Arkansas Highway Department for improving the roads. By 1927 the Martineau Road Law authorized fifty-two million dollars for implementation of an ambitious road-building program. Highway Commissioner Dwight Blackwood was responsible for overseeing the road construction. From the beginning of this effort the need for a bridge at Cotter was evident. Almost immediately, draftsmen in the highway department created plans for a toll bridge at Cotter. The proposed bridge became embroiled in legal disputes over toll bridge franchises and whether the state or the county courts held ultimate authority over highways and bridges. The judicial wrangling ultimately upheld the jurisdictional authority of the state's highway commission, but the lawsuit halted construction at Cotter for three years.

While the litigation dragged on, local newspapers lamented the fact that there was no bridge across White River above Batesville for over two hundred miles. Progressive citizens clamored for action. To appease these demands, the highway department commissioned traffic counts at several proposed bridge sites. In the Ozarks even this mundane bureaucratic duty passed into the regional folklore. When the highway commission met to review the survey, the Cotter study had "disappeared," but the authorities approved the bridge anyway, along with others under consideration. Although the report has never surfaced, a story has persisted that county judge R. M. Ruthven, a tireless promoter for Baxter County, suppressed the report out of fear that it revealed a traffic count that might have, if made public, halted state approval for the bridge.

With state approval of the bridge secured, in the spring of 1929 prospective contractors sent surveyors and engineers to study the geological and topographical characteristics of the site. The Cotter *Record* published a detailed accounting of all such activity surrounding the impending construction

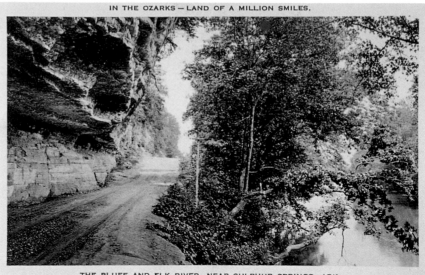

IN THE OZARKS — LAND OF A MILLION SMILES.

THE BLUFF AND ELK RIVER, NEAR SULPHUR SPRINGS, ARK.

Ozarks tourism boosters promoted the area's many attractions through the "Land of a Million Smiles" campaign, as on this postcard. *Courtesy of Shiloh Museum of Ozark History.*

project, the first major public work in Baxter County. The state awarded the bridge contract to the Marsh Engineering Company of Des Moines, Iowa, while companies in Saint Louis and Kansas City, Missouri, and Nashville and Chattanooga, Tennessee, secured additional contracts to provide lighting, steel, and cable. By November 1929 bridge materials had arrived, and dozens of local men began earning enviable wages at the largest project on the White River at the time. The Cotter Bridge symbolized what American big business could accomplish, and it also heralded the arrival of modernity to the Arkansas Ozarks.

The sight of machinery, men, temporary housing, and the extraordinary lighting system that hung over the rising structure, which allowed work to proceed around the clock, was a spectacle that impressed visitors and gratified locals. For once even the White River cooperated by not rising into flood stage during construction in the drought year of 1930. This enabled workers to mine sand and gravel from the riverside, utilizing natural resources from the site itself for construction material. Workers set bridge piers on limestone foundations and began

building the superstructure that would carry the five great, reinforced-concrete, steel arches of the bridge. The design was for a patented Marsh Rainbow Arch Bridge. The first fixed-arch bridge of this type in America had appeared in Philadelphia in 1909, and a generation later highway departments in Arkansas and Missouri were building concrete arch bridges throughout the greater Ozarks. Art historian David Quick has shown that American engineers chose conservative techniques for Cotter Bridge, much as they did in the rest of the country, while English builders created more progressive designs for their concrete bridges, built in Great Britain.

The magnificent Rainbow Arch Bridge required only a year to construct and was dedicated on November 11, 1930. It was an extraordinary engineering feat and it provided a delightfully pleasing image in a region famous for its natural beauty. The aesthetics of the Rainbow Bridge complemented the rippling, clear waters of the White River, which flowed underneath its huge spans; it was a scene that photographers loved. The Rainbow Arch Bridge and its sister concrete arch bridges in the Ozarks became promotional images that appeared in tourist brochures, magazines, Sunday features, and government reports. The bridge was a symbol of the new modern Ozarks.

The town of Cotter fully appreciated the enormous efforts required on many fronts to make the bridge a reality. City fathers staged a two-day celebration, which would be remembered for the rest of the century. Town leaders adorned the half-million dollar, 1,850-foot-long bridge with flags, while citizens decorated the town with colorful banners that waved in the breeze. To commemorate the event, invited guests from Springfield and West Plains, Missouri, joined Arkansas promoters and representatives from seven other states that were traversed by U.S. Highway 62.

This milestone in modernization called for a parade. Floats, bands, fireworks, music, local dignitaries, and Ozark maidens made a grand procession across the bridge. Political VIPs played their ceremonial roles, with U.S. senator Thaddeus Carraway crowning Elizabeth Ruthven queen of the event. At the crowning a plane overhead released a cascade of poppies, and Miss Ruthven christened the bridge with spring water and declared its name, "Progress."

For all the hoopla Ozarks progress was still defined by a restrained approach. Initially, conservative local tastes kept the bridge from being an economic success. Highway collections for use of the toll bridge were slow in coming because Marion County granted a license for a less expensive Cotter ferry, which the majority of thrift-minded people preferred to use. This lack of public patronage probably confirmed the fears of Judge Ruthven, who had worried over small traffic counts in the earlier feasibility study that was "lost." He knew that most Ozarkers did not have automobiles and that they instead still relied on horses, wagons, and their own ability to walk good distances in local travel. These residents did not need to hurry across the Rainbow Bridge but could choose instead a traditional ferry

crossing on the White River. The state was not going to tolerate this situation for long. In the summer of 1931 the Arkansas State Highway Commission bought out the ferry owner, destroyed the ferry, and prohibited any future ferries at that location. This action produced instant results. Within a very short time all travelers began to use the Cotter Bridge and made it a total success. Later, boosters touted it as a dramatic gateway of beautiful design to "The Trout Capital of the World."

The Cotter Bridge is representative of the long and uneven evolution of a process of modernization that took place in different regions at different times, as remote and difficult topography was brought into the mainstream of American economic life. The bridge demanded the capital and bureaucracy of central governments, with resources that extended beyond the ability and means of county courts. Its completion was crucial, providing an interlocking connection to the regional and national business that rolled on modern highways. The bridge brought expanded commerce, communication, education, health care, and tourism to a once-isolated region in rural Arkansas. In doing so it became a building block for social transformations and future development in the Ozarks. The process still continues.

Suggested readings:
Messick, Mary Ann. *History of Baxter County, Centennial Edition, 1873–1973*. Mountain Home, Ark.: Mountain Home Chamber of Commerce, 1973.
O'Reilly, Sean, and Corrine Smith. *Cotter Bridge.* National Register of Historic Places Nomination, Arkansas Historic Preservation Program, Little Rock. 1989.
Quick, David. "Early Twentieth Century Concrete Bridge Engineering and Aesthetics in the United States and the Y-Bridge at Galena, Missouri." *Pioneer America* 33 (1990): 27–35.

The Joseph Taylor Robinson House in Little Rock, built in 1904, was the senator's home from 1930 to 1937. *Photo by Ken Story, Arkansas Historic Preservation Program.*

A CENTURY OF ARKANSAS SENATORS

David Pryor

Joseph Taylor Robinson House
1930–1937
Little Rock, Pulaski County
Listed on the National Register of Historic Places on August 28, 1975
Designated a National Historic Landmark on October 12, 1994

"The Foster-Robinson House is a significant historical structure because of the statesman it housed. Robinson was politically powerful in a crucial period of American history and his contributions helped the country, among other things, to overcome the economic depression. He realized that Arkansas could not prosper until the nation prospered and he concluded that the nation would expand and progress just in proportion as the other nations prospered. Robinson was an unusual man in that he could hold the respect and esteem of even his adversary and through the force of this strong personality he managed to establish national as well as international prominence."

—*From the National Register nomination*

Situated on a tree-lined street in Little Rock is Hope Lodge, a respite for those whose treatment for cancer requires their presence in town. Hope Lodge, or the Foster-Robinson House, is the former home of Joe T. Robinson, one of the most notable of a long line of noteworthy United States senators from Arkansas. Such was Senator Robinson's stature that even President Franklin Delano Roosevelt visited him in this home.

As the twentieth century began and some three decades before Robinson moved into his home on Broadway, Arkansas was represented in the Senate by two Confederate Army veterans, James K. Jones and James H. Berry. Since that time Arkansas has sent fifteen men and two women to Washington to serve in the U.S. Senate. The first few were chosen by the state legislature, the remainder by popular election. All but three had held some other elected office, most having served as governor or congressman or both. And one of these senators was the first woman ever to be elected to the United States Senate.

James K. Jones, one of two Arkansas senators serving as the century turned, had been elected to the Senate from the U.S. House in 1885 and ultimately became the chairman of the Democratic National Committee. However, the state legislature, which chose senators prior to the adoption of the seventeenth amendment in 1912, denied Jones his bid for reelection in 1903, choosing instead James P. Clarke of Helena, a former Arkansas governor. Clarke served until his death in 1916 and was succeeded by William F. Kirby, who was chosen to fill Clarke's unexpired term.

Kirby, a former attorney general and state supreme court justice, was defeated in his reelection bid in 1920 for a full six-year term by Cong. Thaddeus Caraway of Jonesboro. Senator Caraway died in office in 1931. His wife, Hattie, was named by the governor to fill out her late husband's unexpired term of approximately one year.

Then a most unusual series of events took place. The entire Arkansas political establishment was shaken when, after only several months of service, Sen. Hattie Caraway abruptly announced in 1932 that she was seeking, in her own right, a full six-year Senate term. With the assistance of the former Louisiana governor and recently-elected U.S. senator Huey P. Long she became the first woman in America to be elected to the Senate. Long and Caraway barnstormed the state, making over thirty campaign appearances in an eight-day period, culminating in a huge victory for "the little lady."

Six years later Senator Caraway was reelected, successfully turning back a challenge for her seat from the current south Arkansas congressman, John L. McClellan. In 1944 Cong. J. W. Fulbright of Fayetteville challenged and ultimately defeated Mrs. Caraway, ending her career in elective office. Senator Fulbright held this seat until his defeat in 1974 at the hands of Dale Bumpers of Charleston, who had served four years as Arkansas's governor.

For twenty-four years Bumpers occupied his position in the Senate, until he retired in 1999. Former congresswoman Blanche Lincoln succeeded him. Senator Lincoln holds the seat as of this time.

As Sen. James Jones had at the beginning of this century, Sen. James Berry held elective office in Arkansas prior to his Senate tenure, serving two years as governor and serving in the Arkansas state legislature. And also like Senator Jones, his partner in the Senate, he served very little time in office after the twentieth century began. The wily governor Jeff Davis, who was our state's first chief executive to be elected for three consecutive terms, successfully challenged Berry in his reelection bid in 1906. However, Davis served only one term in the Senate before he died in January 1913, just days before Cong. Joe T. Robinson would be inaugurated governor of Arkansas.

Although Robinson was sworn in as governor, he remained in that position only long enough to push his programs through the legislative assembly

Two of Arkansas's twentieth-century senators: Joe T. Robinson and Hattie Caraway. *Courtesy of Arkansas History Commission.*

before the legislature chose him to become the new U.S. senator, succeeding Davis. A few months later the seventeenth amendment to the U.S. Constitution, requiring that all senators be elected by popular vote, would take effect. Among other distinctions Robinson has the one of being the last senator in Arkansas to be chosen by the general assembly. Joe T. Robinson became the Democratic leader of the Senate, a true Democratic loyalist, and a candidate on the national ticket for vice-president in 1928.

Following Robinson's death in 1937 Cong. John E. Miller was elevated to that seat in the Senate and served there until 1941, when he was appointed a U.S. district judge for the western district of Arkansas. Hope businessman Lloyd Spencer was appointed to serve out Miller's unexpired term in the Senate, but Spencer did not seek election for the next term.

Former congressman John McClellan then won the seat as a result of the 1942 elections. Senator McClellan served in the Senate for thirty-five years, until his death in 1977, thus becoming our state's longest-serving U.S. senator. The governor appointed Newport attorney Kaneaster Hodges Jr. to serve out the remaining year of McClellan's unexpired Senate term.

In the 1978 elections former congressman and current governor David Pryor of Camden was elected to fill McClellan's long-held Senate seat. He served until his retirement eighteen years later. Cong. Tim Hutchinson of Gravette, who became Arkansas's first Republican senator in this century, succeeded Pryor and is presently in his first term of Senate service.

A review of the seventeen men and women who have occupied Arkansas's two Senate seats yields a list of names very familiar in Arkansas politics. Many of these names are still imprinted on the Arkansas landscape: the McClellan-Kerr-McGee Navigation System on the Arkansas River, the J. W. Fulbright College of Arts and Sciences at the University of Arkansas, and the Foster-Robinson House and Robinson Auditorium in Little Rock. Our senators have wielded noted influence on the national scene as well: Caraway as the first woman ever elected to the Senate; Fulbright as chairman of the Senate Foreign Relations Committee; McClellan as chairman of the Senate Appropriations Committee; and Robinson, whose home we recognize in this book, as a leader of the Senate and a candidate for national office. Truly theirs is a legacy for the twenty-first century that deserves recognition at the turn of the millennium.

This cabin detail illustrates the intricate rockwork at the Crystal River Tourist Camp at Cave City. *Arkansas Historic Preservation Program photo.*

CRYSTAL RIVER TOURIST CAMP

James Morgan

Crystal River Tourist Camp
1934
Cave City, Sharp County
Listed on the National Register of Historic Places on June 6, 1991

"The Crystal River Tourist Camp is significant as the only known extant example of an intact twentieth-century automobile tourist camp designed in this 'Mannerist' interpretation of the organic Rustic style that was gaining currency during the 1930s. Built around the opening of a cave that shelters the largely underground Crystal River, this site has long been a popular recreational site for the surrounding community of Cave City."

—From the National Register nomination

Lonely travelers on the old Western trails would sometimes happen upon odd configurations of rocks, vaguely familiar shapes or patterns that made them feel that some hand or Hand had been at work there, that they weren't alone in a desolate universe. For travelers passing through Arkansas during the Great Depression, the Crystal River Tourist Camp on U.S. 167 in Cave City must have conveyed something of the same effect.

Here in the middle of practically nowhere was an exceedingly odd configuration of rocks—eleven stone buildings arranged in a semi-circle, each structure a mysterious assemblage of artifacts of both man and God: fieldstone, geodes, crystals, cave coral, seashells, petrified bone, petrified wood, petrified sponge, colored glass, iron ore, milky quartz, rose quartz, working tools, arrowheads. In this unlikely montage some materials were placed to form the shapes of crosses, others Indian fertility symbols, and along each roof line spikey stones jutted up like stalagmites.

In fact, the owner and proprietor of this tourist court, Hubert C. Carpenter, had instructed his stone mason, the magnificently named Prince Matlock, that he had three major themes in mind: Indians, caves, and religion. The Indian and cave motifs alluded to the bones found in the cavern around which this tourist court was built and which gave Carpenter's little town its name. Through this ancient Osage burial ground flowed a clear blue underground current—the Crystal River. Maybe these stellar examples of Nature's power and Man's timelessness inspired Carpenter, via Matlock, to the

kinds of religious musings that still show on the sides of these buildings.

But whether intentional or not, Hubert Carpenter's entire pile of rocks was itself an eloquent expression of a more secular religion loose in the land—the religion of constant movement, of relentless restlessness, of escape and search and self-reinvention. It was—is—a distinctly American liturgy. We built this nation by abandoning our known past for a chance to make ourselves anew. Once we reached these shores, we didn't stop. Instead, we began pushing ever westward, continually redefining ourselves, until finally we reached the end of our land. "The frontier is closed . . . ," said historian Frederick Jackson Turner at the end of the nineteenth century. He added that we were now a people frustrated because—and this is an interpretation of his words—we no longer could escape from ourselves.

Then the automobile was invented.

In 1900 there were only four thousand cars in the United States. By 1928 the number had zoomed to twenty-eight million. Had Wall Street not crashed in 1929, the thirties would surely have seen an exponential growth in the number of automobiles. As it was, people gave up their houses before they surrendered their cars, and the Great Depression gave those people ample reason to take to the road. In 1934, the same year Hubert Carpenter and his wife, Eunice, opened Crystal River Tourist Camp, James Agee wrote a piece in *Fortune Magazine* called "The Great American Roadside," in which he outlined what was even then a three billion dollar industry of

The Goodwin family of Cross County, Arkansas, prepares to hit the road, 1947. *Courtesy of Edith Bata.*

tourist courts and service stations and restaurants shaped like ice cream buckets.

Beyond Crystal River Tourist Camp's architectural significance (according to its National Register of Historic Places write-up, it is "unlike any other known extant automobile tourist court in the state, and is surprisingly intact"), it strikes me as having a poignant emotional significance as well. Though presented in three dimensions, its art is like a Grandma Moses painting—quaint, naive, almost childlike in its expression of the way we could see ourselves back then. For when the automobile came

along, it blinded us with its possibilities. It reopened our frontier. Once again we Americans could divert ourselves from our darker urge to keep moving and instead channel that drive toward the lighter and more acceptable notion of *adventure*. Delightfully off-beat roadside attractions like Crystal River and its cave allowed us to pretend that we were running toward something, instead of away from it.

The Carpenters operated their strange little tourist court for nearly four decades, through the boom years of the 1940s and 1950s and into the beginning of the trouble years. By 1956 there were some sixty million cars on America's roads, which were still mostly small two-lanes like the one that passed through Cave City. Those roads were becoming jammed. President Dwight Eisenhower and his board of experts decided that a system of wide interstate highways would fix the problem, and all through the sixties the nation built more and more roads. By 1970, though, the truth was out. A Little Rock newspaper published this shocking headline: "Volume of Traffic Is Much Higher Since Construction of Interstates."

Today most of the nearly two hundred million cars on this nation's highways bypass the Crystal River Tourist Camp. Instead, they whoosh along on the big four-lane some forty miles away. The people in those speeding cars have long since lost interest in authentic curiosities like Hubert Carpenter's odd little rock creation. They prefer chain motels with faux boulders in the atrium lobbies and theme parks where the mountains are magic, not real.

And yet it is part of the enduring wonder of this restless country that one man's rubble may be another man's fortress. Accordingly, the Crystal River Tourist Camp now has new owners, Dan and Irma Carrigan. They happened upon the place in 1995, when they were looking to reinvent themselves. The Carrigans and their children used to live in Little Rock, in an area where drive-by shootings were a common occurence. They wanted a quieter, safer life. In 1995, while ambling along U.S. 167, they spied this old motel complex boarded up behind a tangle of weeds and briars. The Cave City fire department had used the buildings for fire drills, so the soot was thick on the walls and windows. But the Carrigans are dreamers, and they fell in love with the idea of moving their family there. And not *just* moving, but reopening Crystal River Tourist Camp for business.

The place needs work, and they're tackling it as they're able. Meanwhile, prices at Crystal River are twenty-five dollars a night and one hundred dollars for a week. None of us, not even the Carrigans, can go home again. But I, for one, like knowing it's possible to visit.

The Wortham Gymnasium stands today as a symbol of the community tenacity that brought about its construction. *Arkansas Historic Preservation Program photo.*

WORTHAM GYMNASIUM

Willard B. Gatewood

Wortham Gymnasium
1939
Oak Grove, Nevada County
Listed on the National Register of Historic Places on April 19, 1990

"The Wortham Gymnasium, constructed during a period of great expansion of educational facilities in the black community of Oak Grove, is the only structure from that era to survive with sufficient integrity. It is also a locally significant example of a simple but handsomely balanced design that reveals the skill of the Works Progress Administration (WPA) workers."

—*From the National Register nomination*

Wortham Gymnasium, an imposing wood-frame structure on the grounds of the Oak Grove School in south central Nevada County, Arkansas, stands as a monument to the aspirations, perseverance, and resourcefulness of a rural African American community. That an all-black school district acquired such a facility in a time of severe economic depression and in a place that practiced rigid racial segregation attests to these attributes of the Oak Grove community as well as its ability to muster support among influential whites. The gymnasium was placed on the National Register of Historic Places in 1990 in recognition of its historic and symbolic significance.

The acquisition of education and land was a priority of blacks throughout the South in the decades following emancipation. Blacks in Oak Grove were no exception and succeeded against daunting odds in becoming landowners and in providing their children with access to education. The Oak Grove School that initially offered only the most rudimentary education and possessed only the most primitive facilities in time achieved an enviable reputation among African Americans both inside and outside Arkansas as an educational institution of high academic quality with an impressive physical plant. Because of its emphasis on vocational education, some visitors referred to Oak Grove as "a little Tuskegee," referring to the Alabama institution headed by Booker T. Washington. The construction of a facility of the size and quality of Wortham Gymnasium more than half a century after the school was organized was evidence of the persistent commitment of community leaders to provide their children with a school that, while separate from those attended by whites, came nearer to being equal to them than was the case in most black school districts in the rural south.

As with many black schools in the post–Civil War era, Oak Grove's school began in a church. In 1881 a white couple, Mr. and Mrs. E. J. Barksdale, gave the black residents of Oak Grove two and one-half acres of land "for school and church purposes." Shortly afterward the community organized a Missionary Baptist church and built a simple, rustic place of worship on the land donated by the Barksdales. To fulfill the conditions of the gift, the "church house" also served as a "school house" until a separate building could be constructed. While funding for all public schools in Arkansas during the late nineteenth century was limited, the paltry support of black schools in Nevada County and elsewhere in the state clearly bore the unmistakable stamp of racial discrimination in the distribution of educational funds. The decades after the 1880s witnessed a gradual movement toward a more equitable funding formula.

Despite a severely limited budget and all its consequences, such as short terms and inadequate facilities, Oak Grove School was a source of great pride in the black community. The school's administrators and faculty joined with community leaders in various endeavors that over the years improved and expanded educational opportunities for African American children. With the aid of county school superintendent J. W. Teeter and other influential whites, blacks persuaded the county school board in 1920 to create an all-black school district, known as Oak Grove District #4, with its own black superintendent and black school board. Through a process of gerrymandering the county board brought together several non-contiguous areas with predominantly black populations to create a consolidated black school district.

The Oak Grove school district had the good fortune to be guided by a succession of energetic and far-sighted superintendents and school board members, who not only rallied the black community to the cause of education but also gained the confidence and support of prominent whites. In

WILLARD B. GATEWOOD

1925, with the aid of the Rosenwald Fund, Oak Grove established a high school through grade ten. Previously, black students desiring to attend school beyond the elementary grades had to go elsewhere on their own. Building on the accomplishments of his predecessors, Superintendent L. W. Johnson (1935–1949) increased the size and quality of the faculty, extended the high school to twelve grades, and transformed the physical plant of Oak Grove school almost beyond recognition.

The idea of constructing a gymnasium at the school was the brainchild of Superintendent Johnson. The school produced first-rate basketball teams but had no indoor facility in which to practice or play games. Oak Grove's teams could on occasion schedule its games in the gymnasium at the white high school in Prescott, the county seat, but only if the facility was not in use by whites. There are indications that use of the gym by Oak Grove's team was granted grudgingly. When Johnson informed Basil Munn, the county school superintendent, of one particularly difficult situation that the Oak Grove players had encountered in Prescott, Munn agreed to assist him in searching for funds to construct a gymnasium at Oak Grove.

The funds were ultimately provided by the Works Progress Administration (WPA), an agency of Franklin D. Roosevelt's New Deal that had been created in 1935 by consolidating the functions of two earlier relief and recovery agencies. Few, if any, agencies of the New Deal directly affected as many African Americans during the Great Depression as did the WPA. Its director, Harry Hopkins, was especially sensitive to the condition and needs of blacks in the South. His assistant and "advisor on Negro affairs" was Alfred Edgar Smith, a native of Hot Springs and a member of Roosevelt's so-called "black cabinet," who possessed first-hand knowledge of Arkansas. Smith undoubtedly apprised Hopkins of the special needs of African Americans

in his home state. Whether Smith was involved in any way with the WPA grant to Oak Grove school is unclear, but what is certain is that he was an effective advocate of allocating WPA funds for African American projects.

There is some confusion about the date of the grant from the WPA for the construction of the gymnasium. The date usually cited is 1935, but this was actually the date of the WPA grant made to the Oak Grove School for the construction of a classroom-administration building to replace the Rosenwald Building that had been destroyed by fire. The WPA records in the National Archives clearly reveal that the proposal for the construction of a gymnasium at the school, signed by Superintendent Johnson and two members of his board, was submitted to the state office of the WPA on February 23, 1938, along with a proposal for funds to construct a home economics building.

The WPA consolidated the proposals and on March 3, 1938, approved a single grant of $13,655 in federal funds to construct the two buildings and to "perform work incidental and appurtenant unto," including landscaping and grading. The school district, as sponsor of the proposal, agreed "to assume responsibility for results and . . . for completion [of the projects] in the event that funds allotted to the project[s] are inadequate." The construction of the gymnasium provided Oak Grove School with a much-needed facility and created jobs for unemployed black residents in the area.

The WPA grant allocated a total of $8,954 in federal funds for construction of the gymnasium, and the school district was to provide $3,680, for a total of $12,634. WPA funds in the amount of $6,704 were earmarked for labor, $750 for superintendence, and $1,500 for material and supplies. The district's matching funds were to be expended for materials and supplies ($3,080) and equipment rentals ($600). Oak Grove blacks not only enlisted

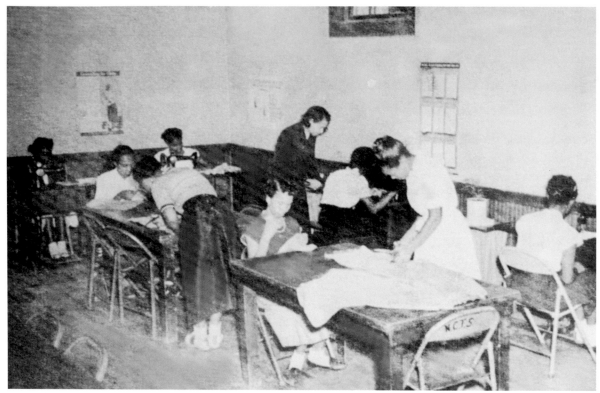

Mrs. Blanche W. Haynie's sewing class at Oak Grove. *Courtesy of Joseph Hale Sr.*

the support of locally prominent whites in securing the WPA grant, but they also secured contributions from white individuals and businessmen in raising the matching funds. But blacks themselves contributed their own resources. For example, C. C. Bazzelle, a highly respected black resident, who served as president of the district school board, had stands of timber that he called "school trees," from which came a portion of the lumber used in the gymnasium. The construction of the building got underway in May 1938 and was completed a little more than a year later. It was named the Wortham Gymnasium in honor of Roger Q. Wortham, Nevada County judge from 1929 to 1935, who was

viewed as a friend and supporter of the Oak Grove community and its efforts in behalf of education.

In justifying the need for the gymnasium, the application to the WPA stated simply: "The school does not have any building for recreational activities. Completion of this project would be of great benefit to the school from the standpoint of health as well as athletics." The gym did provide a place for the Oak Grove basketball team to practice and play games and for the school to host statewide basketball tournaments. It attracted much attention shortly after its completion when the famous New York Renaissance Big Five, popularly known as the RENS, the archrivals of the Harlem Globetrotters, played an exhibition game there. Actually, the structure served as more than a sports facility; it was a multi-purpose building in which physical education classes, plays, assemblies, graduation exercises, community gatherings, and other events also took place. The black community shared Superintendent Johnson's pride in the structure. Johnson never wearied of pointing out that Oak Grove had the first high school gymnasium for blacks in Arkansas. In fact, the only other gym for blacks in the state was at A.M. and N. College, the state-supported institution of higher education for blacks located in Pine Bluff. Johnson boasted that Oak Grove's facility was "larger than the college gym."

Wortham Gymnasium is a tall, single-story structure essentially without exterior ornamentation. Side sheds on both sides of the building extend the full length of the court or arena area. The building is well lighted by numerous windows grouped in such a manner as to give balance to the exterior. Described as "a remarkable specimen of WPA design and construction," the structure was extraordinarily impressive in scale and conveyed a sense of strength and permanence. It represented a major achievement for a black community that practiced the philosophy of self-help made famous by Booker T. Washington. Like Washington, Oak Grove residents sought and received assistance from individuals and agencies outside their community, notably the federal government, that enabled them to move beyond what they could accomplish with their own resources and tax monies for educational purposes .

Oak Grove School has undergone numerous changes since the construction of Wortham Gymnasium in 1938–1939. None of the changes were more significant than those that occurred in the wake of the *Brown Decision* (1954), which declared racially segregated schools unconstitutional. The post-1954 changes fundamentally altered the character of the school, so that the gymnasium in 1998 presents a picture of a forlorn, dilapidated building in desperate need of extensive repairs. Nevertheless, for residents of Oak Grove and school alumni, it is rich in memories and symbolism, so much so that they initiated efforts to find the means to restore the building. Their efforts were rewarded on August 28, 1998, when they received a grant of ten thousand dollars to rehabilitate the Wortham Gymnasium.

References cited:
Arkansas Gazette, 1935–1939.
Arthur R. Ashe Jr., *A Hard Road to Glory: A History of the African-American Athlete* (New York: Penguin, 1993).
Biennial Reports of the State Superintendent of Public Instruction in Arkansas, 1880–1940 (title varies).
W. L. Brazzelle, *A Developmental History of Oak Grove School District #4, Nevada County, Route 1, Rosston, Arkansas* (Hope, Ark.: W. L. Brazzelle, 1984).
Alfred Edgar Smith Papers, Special Collections, Mullins Library, University of Arkansas, Fayetteville.
"A Survey of Negro Education in Nevada County, Arkansas" (Mimeographed, Division of Negro Education of the State Department of Education, 1930).
John Teeter, information provided to author, Depot Museum, Prescott, Arkansas.
WPA Files, Division of Operations, Work Project #465-63-2-196, Microfilm, Reel #1577, National Archives, Washington, D.C.
Raymond Wolters, *Negroes and the Great Depression* (Westport, Conn.: Greenwood Press, 1970).
"Roger Q. Wortham," *Arkansas and Its People* (New York: American Historical Society, 1930), Vol. 3, 140–141.

The Rustic-style construction of Mather Lodge seems to erupt from the earth to blend with its environment. *Photo by Dr. John Slater.*

MATHER LODGE, PETIT JEAN STATE PARK

Richard W. Davies

Mather Lodge
1935
Winrock vic., Conway County
Listed on the National Register of Historic Places on May 28, 1992

"The original portion of this building was erected at Petit Jean State Park by the men of the Civilian Conservation Corps for the purpose of providing office space for park staff and social space for park visitors, and was intended to serve the visitors of the park as a reception/administration area and social center. Thus Mather Lodge is eligible under Criterion A for its associations with both the Civilian Conservation Corps' importance within Arkansas social history and in the development of outdoor parks dedicated to public leisure and recreational activities. It is also eligible under Criterion C due to its status as a representative and intact example of the Rustic style of architecture that was made popular nationwide by the CCC, and which has become virtually identified with it."

—*From the National Register nomination*

Upon first viewing the massive rock and timber construction of Mather Lodge, it's hard not to wonder about the story behind the building and how it came to be there. Who were the people who built it, how did they manage to gather and move all the massive stones and giant trees and assemble them into a thing of beauty, and why is it in this particular place in Arkansas? What were they trying to accomplish? Who decided this needed to be done? What's the story?

There are actually a number of stories, from all over the country, and they all came together on an Arkansas mountaintop called Petit Jean.

Early in the twentieth century a uniquely American idea was being developed: national parks. In the early days the parks were protected and cared for by the United States Army, until a National Park Service could be created. (That's where the traditional "campaign hat" for Park Rangers comes from: it was the U.S. Army hat of the World War I era.) This new park idea was popular, and a number of places around the country were nominated as possible national park sites. Petit Jean Mountain was among those suggested. The submittal was made by a long-time physician for the Fort Smith Lumber Company who had lived on the mountain, Dr. T. W. Hardison.

The first director of the National Park Service, who received the request concerning Petit Jean from Dr. Hardison and whose name would later adorn a lodge in Arkansas, was a fellow named Stephen Mather. It became apparent to Mather that all scenic places could not be national parks and that what the country needed was a number of state park systems to care for areas that were scenic or historic but not quite of national significance. In addition, he did not believe that providing recreation was a responsibility suited to national parks. To address the situation, he founded the National Conference on State Parks and traveled around the country promoting the idea of state park systems to provide for preservation, recreation, and, in some cases, tourism at the state level. In 1925 Mather's new organization met at Hot Springs National Park. (No matter what the National Park Service now claims, Hot Springs was the first national park, set aside some sixty years before Yellowstone. The problem was that no one knew what a park was back then!) Dr. Hardison invited Mather to Petit Jean to consider it for a national park, and that is where the idea of the Arkansas State Park System was born.

Arkansas had no state parks. In 1923, however, a law was passed to allow the State Land Commissioner to accept land for future state parks. The first donations were on Petit Jean Mountain from the Fort Smith Lumber Company and a number of citizens of nearby Morrilton. In 1927 the State Parks Commission was authorized by the legislature, with Dr. Hardison as its first chairman.

Act 172 of 1927, which created the State Parks Commission, charged its members "to protect and preserve in its original habitat and native beauty the flora, fauna, and wildlife therein and preserve the same for all future generations, thereby promoting health and pleasure through recreational places, resorts and scenic playgrounds for the people of the State and to attract visitors, home seekers and tourists to the State and to provide places of recreation and pleasure for them, and to increase the wealth and revenue of our State by means of such parks." That charge to the commission is still with us today.

The problem, however, was that in 1927 the state still had no parks, it had no staff to design and build them, and it had little, if any, money for the work.

Along came the Great Depression. If anything good came from that great national tragedy, it was the Civilian Conservation Corps (CCC) and what it accomplished. The CCC may be the only federal jobs program that ever really worked. Conceived of by President Franklin Roosevelt and Congress, it provided a way to put people to work, train them

Civilian Conservation Corps workers construct a bridge at Petit Jean State Park, 1935. *Courtesy of Arkansas Department of Parks and Tourism.*

in marketable skills, and get some badly needed conservation projects done—projects like state parks. As it turned out, the CCC also prepared a generation of American men for military-style living, which became very important in the 1940s, with the outbreak of World War II.

Here's how it worked. The United States Army fed, clothed, sheltered, and paid the "CCC boys" and then turned them over to a civilian authority, which would actually supervise construction. Arkansas's new State Parks Commission contracted with the National Park Service for design and supervision of the new state park projects, and the CCC members did the work. When the initial parks were completed in 1937, with no one to run them, the position of Director of State Parks was established, and so was a staff to operate the parks. What was established then continues to this day as the State Parks Division of the Department of Parks and Tourism.

Mather Lodge was originally built as part of this overall program. When Stephen Mather visited Petit Jean Mountain at Dr. Hardison's behest, he had deemed the mountain scenic but not up to National Park standards. He encouraged Dr. Hardison and the State of Arkansas to start a state parks system and to

begin at Petit Jean. Sadly, but fortunately for Arkansas's future, much of the land that would become Petit Jean State Park was property that had been forfeited to the state for back taxes during the Great Depression. This was also the case at other early state parks and CCC projects, such as Mount Nebo, Buffalo River, Devil's Den, and Crowley's Ridge.

The CCC crew at Petit Jean was a little unusual. Most "CCC boys" were just that: eighteen and nineteen years old. However, at Petit Jean the crew was made up of World War I veterans, who not only were older but also more skilled. I've heard it said that someone on the crew knew how to do almost anything that needed to be done. Mather Lodge provides a good example of the crew's skill. Imagine all that craftsmanship for five dollars a week, with four of those dollars mailed home to the family. It's hard for us today to imagine the abject poverty that existed at the time. On Petit Jean, during the tenure of the CCC camps, mountain residents would hang buckets on the mailboxes, and the CCC cooks would distribute leftover food to keep folks from starving. It was that bad.

To have a park at Petit Jean or anywhere else, resources and visitors are necessary. Many people throughout the years have said that park management and policy making are acts of perennial compromise between the conflicting purposes of use and preservation. Mather Lodge demonstrates this perennial compromise. It is a man-made addition to the landscape, yet its material came from the park itself. It was designed to blend into the park landscape rather than stand out. Even its color, "park brown," was chosen after an extensive study by the National Park Service designed to choose the least obtrusive shade within a forested environment. The rockwork surrounding the lodge does not come straight up with the walls but starts out from the ground and builds up like natural layers of stone to the actual structure, as if the whole thing grew from the earth. The exterior timbers still show the stubs of tree branches. These aesthetic touches did not happen by accident. The designers and builders knew exactly what they were trying to do. Mather Lodge was man-made, but it came from the earth.

The construction methods used to build the lodge were very old, even at the time. The exposed beams and rafters, the handmade light fixtures and furniture, and even the "king-pin" holding the whole thing together are reminiscent of an earlier time. The lodge reminds us of how things used to be, and so does the park. This was true in the 1930s, and it is even truer today. Again, this is no coincidence. This aspect of the park was an attraction then, and it's an attraction now. We'll never be able to replace the park or the lodge.

Mather Lodge has weathered all the ups and downs of the state parks system. In the past sixty years it has suffered its share of neglect, over-use, and lack of maintenance. It has also been an important feature during the good times. It has hosted four generations of visitors, family reunions, weddings, honeymoons, meetings, and conferences. It has seen the transformation from pot-bellied stoves, radio shows, and crank phones to central air-conditioning, televisions, and computers. Its visitors have come from all over Arkansas, the United States, and the world. It has had pieces of its original fabric rot away and replaced, and it has had two additions, one by the Works Progress Administration (WPA) in the 1930s and another in the 1960s. It has gone from being the only lodge in the only state park to being one of many in fifty-two Arkansas state parks. Mather Lodge is still there, doing its duty, reminding us of what parks are all about.

Unlike most CCC crews, the workers building this cabin at Petit Jean State Park consisted of older men, primarily World War I veterans. *Courtesy of Arkansas Department of Parks and Tourism.*

The French Eclectic–style design of the Parnell-Sharpe House in McGehee, Arkansas, is just one manifestation of the period revival designs that were popular in Arkansas in the early twentieth century. *Arkansas Historic Preservation Program photo.*

ARKANSAS'S ARCHITECTURE: THE PERIOD REVIVALS OF THE MID-TWENTIETH CENTURY

Kenneth Story

Parnell-Sharpe House
1936
McGehee, Desha County
Listed on the National Register of Historic Places on September 28, 1989

"Sharpe's concern for craftsmanship and quality is evidenced by the intact state of this house and the fact that its current owner has been required to devote minimal care to its upkeep. Though it encloses a relatively small amount of floor area, through its combination of a one-and-one-half story height and its rambling, picturesque elevations it is reminiscent of much larger farmhouses in France; as such it survives as a unique example of this particular style in rural Arkansas."

—*From the National Register nomination*

Located just a few blocks from the historic downtown of McGehee, Arkansas, the Parnell-Sharpe House raises its short, conical, circular-tower roof and sloping gables above the surrounding residential streets. Built in 1936 and designed in a style known as the French Eclectic, it remains one of the few known examples in the state of this particular architectural idiom and so might be thought of as unique. This, combined with its relatively small size and small, southeast Arkansas, cotton-town location, belie the national social and economic developments of which it is both part and representative.

The first two decades of the twentieth century was a period of enormous change in America, a period that was arguably the beginning of what is widely known as the modern era. Einstein's theory of relativity, which radically altered commonly held conceptions regarding the nature of time and space, was first published in 1904. By 1908 Frank Lloyd Wright was fundamentally altering our notions of architecture by breaking up the building's principal surfaces into large, unornamented planes. His designs would forever transform our notion of the architectural façade and the division between interior and exterior spaces (and, in so doing, prefigured what the European artists Pablo Picasso and Georges Braque would do in the field of painting three years later). By 1913 such artists as Marcel Duchamp were also transforming fundamental notions of what constitutes "art" through their use of "found objects" in such seminal exhibits as the 1913 Armory show in New York City. In 1907 the Italian Marchese Marconi developed the wireless telegraph, thereby allowing the first communication from ship to shore. And by 1913 American inventor and entrepreneur Henry Ford had not only developed a relatively dependable internal combustion engine designed to power "horseless carriages" but, much more importantly, had virtually invented the concept of mass production, which allowed him to build and sell his cars so inexpensively that most Americans could afford them.

To be sure, the automobile and its dramatic impact upon the growth and development patterns of the American cultural landscape only continued what the railroads had begun in the late nineteenth century. However, the gradual expansion of the American suburb that began with rail travel virtually exploded after World War I. The poor and unevenly maintained roads that hampered long-distance overland travel in America were not a problem within the larger cities, particularly within the smaller planned subdivisions that, usually as part of their marketing strategy, offered a high-quality and well-designed road system that provided smooth and dependable internal access. As city governments responded to the popularity of the new mode of transportation with wider, paved thoroughfares and residential streets, an interconnecting network of good roads developed in most American cities that virtually ensured the success of the suburb as a particularly American type of community.

The late nineteenth century—and its "streetcar suburbs"—had witnessed the coming and going of a number of national architectural styles. These styles were particularly popular when the large estates located within these new suburbs were designed. These estates took advantage of rambling, expansive lots, located upon previously rural land, which allowed room for such amenities as extensive flower gardens, rolling lawns, and canopies of spreading hardwoods. However, by definition the post–World War I American suburb consisted of smaller, regularly sized lots designed to lower lot price, increase density, and maximize profit. Thus, as Americans moved into the new, more affordable, automobile suburbs, they stubbornly clung to the idea that even their smaller homes could retain the architectural grandeur common to the streetcar suburbs. Toward this end period revivals served remarkably well.

Air Mail by Dan Rhodes adorns the lobby of the U.S. Post Office in Piggott, a relic of a Depression-era program to employ artists and bring art to the masses. *Arkansas Historic Preservation Program photo.*

THE PIGGOTT POST OFFICE MURAL

Gayle Seymour

Piggott Post Office
1937
Piggott, Clay County
Listed on the National Register of Historic Places on August 14, 1998

"The Piggott Post Office is associated with the historic context *Arkansas Post Offices with Section Art* as a U.S. Postal Service structure containing a mural financed through the U.S. Treasury Department's Section on Fine Arts. As such, it is eligible under Criterion A with statewide significance for its associations with the Section's efforts to employ Depression-era artists and place art in post offices around the country."

—From the National Register nomination

In 1937 the small town of Piggott, in the northeast corner of Arkansas, was just about like any other rural town in the state. There was Ingram's Used Cars, Perry's Shoe and Harness Shop, the Russell Mortuary, and Ralph Cole's Texaco service station, to name only a few of the local businesses. But life would be changed in 1937 by the construction of a Federal post office at the corner of North Third Street and West Main.[1] For the first time in Piggott's history the town would have an official post office building instead of a rented office space in the Trantham Building.[2] The Piggott post office, and thousands of others like it built across the United States during the Great Depression, was part of President Roosevelt's New Deal attempt to restore confidence throughout society at a time of national crisis.

The post office served as the most public of all public buildings. Here every citizen could post and receive mail, deposit or withdraw money from the Postal Savings System, and catch up on gossip or other news from around town. But the post office would also serve as America's art gallery. In 1934 the secretary of the treasury, Henry Morgenthau Jr., issued a directive requiring public buildings to be decorated with "suitable art" in order to raise the cultural taste of the citizens. Culture was recognized to be a strategically important terrain upon which people's sense of identity could be constructed. With over forty-five thousand post offices in the country and an estimated daily attendance of five hundred at each, the post office was the perfect public building to articulate the ideals of the New Deal social utopia, since it was seen by practically all of the residents of a town and visited repeatedly over the years.

Twenty-one mural commissions were executed in Arkansas post office lobbies between 1939 and 1942, with eighteen of them still remaining today.[3] The Piggott post office mural, by Daniel Rhodes (1911–1989),[4] entitled *Air Mail,* was executed in 1941 and installed in February of that year over the postmaster's office door. Unlike more traditional murals painted directly on the wall, this mural was painted in the artist's studio using oil on canvas, then brought to the site and adhered to the wall with white lead and varnish.[5] The Piggott mural, along with approximately twelve hundred other murals and three hundred relief sculptures, was commissioned by the Treasury Department's Section of Painting and Sculpture (later the Section of Fine Arts). The Section commissioned hundreds of America's best artists during the nine years of its existence, from 1934 to 1943, to decorate Federal buildings on the basis of regional and national open, anonymous competitions. For the first time in American history the Federal government found itself in the business of funding public art on a massive scale. But as an official patron of the arts, the New Deal government exercised constant supervision and bureaucratic control, requiring artists to work within a certain safely net, depicting images and scenes of local significance and using a representational style. It would be art, in the words of President Roosevelt, that "was painted for the people of this country by their own kind in their own country, and painted about things they know and look at often and have touched and loved."

Because these murals were to be on walls in specific locations, frequented by a specific clientele, Section artists were required to work with the local postmaster and townspeople to elicit possible themes of local history or interest and, whenever economically possible, to visit the town before developing the mural. In the case of the Piggott mural, it does not appear that Rhodes felt it necessary to visit the site in advance. He wrote to Section Superintendent Ed Rowan on August 21, 1940, that because he was accepting a teaching position in New Concord, Ohio, in the fall, he would not be able to "inspect

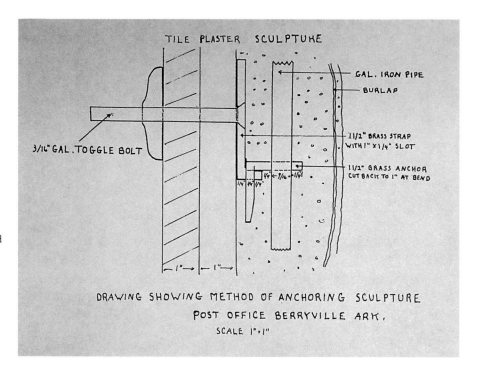

TILE PLASTER SCULPTURE

GAL. IRON PIPE

BURLAP

3/16" GAL. TOGGLE BOLT

1 1/2" BRASS STRAP WITH 1" X 1/4" SLOT

1 1/2" BRASS ANCHOR CUT BACK TO 1" AT BEND

DRAWING SHOWING METHOD OF ANCHORING SCULPTURE POST OFFICE BERRYVILLE ARK. SCALE 1"=1"

Artist Daniel Olney provided detailed instructions on how to install his sculpture *Man and Woman, Arkansas* in the Berryville, Arkansas, Post Office. *Courtesy of National Archives and Records Administration.*

the building and the local scene."[6] Rhodes's claim that since he had already decorated three post offices of the same type and felt confident he could complete another one is, in fact, instructive. One of the major controversies of the mural program was that it rewarded artists who would conform to "safe" themes—often depicting covered wagons arriving in the wilderness or scenes lauding the delivery of the mail—to boost their chances of being awarded a commission. Indeed, Rhodes had already depicted the theme of mail delivery—the train and workers moving the mail from country to city—in his 1939 mural, *Communication by Mail,* for the Marion, Iowa, post office and no doubt assumed a similar theme would be just as appropriate for Piggott.

Air Mail continues the theme of communication Rhodes had earlier investigated. The mural depicts a local citizen, at the left, handing his letter to the post-master who, at the center, personally assists the pilots loading mailbags onto a waiting aircraft. "I feel the

Air Mail is of unusual significance to the smaller and more isolated community," Rhodes explained in a letter to Rowan, "linking them as it does with the most distant centers. I have tried to convey the sense of stream-lined power which is behind the mail service." Rhodes's reference to "stream-lined power" is characteristic of a new emphasis on vehicular technology that was popularized in 1939 at the New York World's Fair. The didactic message of this theme is clear; this well-oiled action—of both men and machine—signals that through national cooperation and technology, modern society might move from the dilemma of Depression stagnation to the dynamic future of prosperity.

But how appropriate was an image of air mail delivery to a town not only without air mail but also without an airport? If the success of these murals was rooted in the fact that they depicted "things [people] know and look at often and have touched and loved," then how may we explain the success of the

Piggott mural? In 1941 mail in Piggott was still moved by train—the St. Louis Southwestern Railroad (the Cotton Belt). But airplanes, like the DC-3 depicted in the mural, were regularly seen by the local population not in the skies but in the local news press. By 1941 the specter of war in Europe had begun to replace America's preoccupation with the Depression. Even in small rural newspapers like *The Piggott Banner,* photographs of the war in Europe— planes, bombs, Hitler—were regularly published. Ironically, the success of the Piggott mural may be due to the fact that it was misunderstood. One contemporary citizen of Piggott, who was around at the time the mural was installed, told the author that she had always thought it was a war mural. Perhaps the image of a gleaming plane and strong heroic men—

an image which was already familiar from the press and the movies—created a kind of popular culture billboard, reassuring the citizens of Piggott of American might and stability.

Regardless of what people thought of the Piggott mural in 1941, the work lives on today as it has for fifty-seven years, bringing art to a culturally and geographically isolated town in Arkansas. As we approach the millennium, it seems appropriate to look back at programs like the Section of Fine Arts and at regional murals like the one in Piggott in order to ensure that the memory of these achievements persists. But instead of simply representing a unique chapter in American cultural history, the Piggott mural presents us with lessons for today and the future. Just as it was during the

Louis Freund touches up a mural for the Heber Springs, Arkansas, Post Office. *Courtesy of Shiloh Museum of Ozark History.*

Depression, Federal patronage for the arts remains problematic. While the correspondence files now in the National Archives reveal the massive bureaucracy and control that artists like Daniel Rhodes were faced with, today's struggling artists also understand the perils of control. However, programs like the Section of Fine Arts or the National Endowment for the Arts have led the way for greater public acceptance of the arts in American society. The Section murals also promoted a sense of national identity during difficult times. In many ways they were intended as a celebration of the strength and dignity of common men and women. At the end of the century, in a post-modern age, perhaps it is time to return public art to its traditional function—portraying important stories of the towns and townspeople of the American scene and thereby celebrating common cultural aspirations and enriching the lives of ordinary people.

Notes:

1. The total budget for the Piggott post office project was $61,922, of which $700 (or approximately 1 percent of total costs) was reserved for mural production. Archival information about the Piggott mural is contained in the correspondence files, now in the National Archives in Washington, D.C. My grateful thanks to Bob Besom for sharing these materials with me.

2. The first post office in Piggott opened in 1881. See Russell Pierce Baker, *From Memdag to Norsk: A Historical Directory of Arkansas Post Offices 1832–1971* (Hot Springs: Arkansas Genealogical Society, 1988), 175. According to Robert Webb, this first post office was the home of Dick Throgmorton until it moved to Brown's store. See *History and Traditions of Clay County* [n.d.], 43.

3. Post office murals and relief sculptures can be seen in Benton (moved to Saline County Courthouse), Berryville (sculpture), Clarksville, Dardanelle, De Queen, De Witt, Heber Springs, Lake Village, Magnolia, Monticello (sculpture), Morrilton, Nashville, Paris, Piggott, Siloam Springs, Springdale (moved to Shiloh Museum), Van Buren, and Wynne. Murals were also produced for Clarendon, Pocahontas, and Osceola but are now destroyed.

4. Before accepting the commission for the Piggott mural, Daniel Rhodes was already an accomplished muralist, having received numerous awards and commissions for murals in Washington, D.C.; Glen Ellyn, Illinois; Clayton, Missouri; Marion, Iowa; and Storm Lake, Iowa. Rhodes later distinguished himself as ceramicist, teacher, and author. See Robert McDonald, "Daniel Rhodes," *American Craft* 46 (1985), 18–21.

5. The Section murals were carefully documented throughout the process. Artists were required to submit detailed information about the brands of paints used, the canvas used, and even the exact colors used on their palettes. While this nit-picking attention to detail may seem excessive and even adverse to creativity, these documents provide invaluable insights into the working methods of artists as well as a wellspring for contemporary conservators.

6. Information in a letter to Edward Rowan from Daniel Rhodes, August 21, 1940, National Archives, Washington, D.C.

7. Karal Ann Marling has already shown that Rhodes's *Communication by Mail* (1939, USPO, Marion, Iowa) is based on Charles Sheeler's *Rolling Power* (1939, Smith College Museum of Art), calling Rhodes a "thief or sincere flatterer." See Karal Ann Marling, *Wall-To-Wall America* (Minneapolis: University of Minnesota Press, 1982), 145.

8. Information in a letter to Edward Rowan from Daniel Rhodes, November 4, 1940, National Archives, Washington, D.C.

The Tall Peak Fire Tower stands sentinel in a morning fog in the Ouachita National Forest. *Photo by Todd Ferguson, courtesy of Arkansas Historic Preservation Program.*

TALL PEAK FIRE TOWER, POLK COUNTY

Jeannie M. Whayne

Tall Peak Fire Tower
Ca. 1938
Athens vic., Polk County
Listed on the National Register of Historic Places on October 20, 1993

"The Tall Peak Fire Tower was constructed ca. 1938 by members of the 742nd Company of the Arkansas CCC District stationed at the Mena Camp that was located approximately eight miles to the northwest, near the small town of Shady. It was constructed to function as a fire and observation tower to help prevent the forest fires that heretofore had ravaged the forest with devastating effect."

—*From the National Register nomination*

The lumber industry has been a major employer in Arkansas since the nineteenth century. These logs are being hauled from the Cold Springs Ranger District of the Ouachita National Forest. *Courtesy of the Arkansas History Commission.*

The Tall Peak Fire Tower, built by the Civilian Conservation Corps in about 1938, stands within the Ouachita National Forest in Polk County. It was one of a series of observation towers located within the National Forest to protect against the devastating forest fires that had threatened the area. A unique structure epitomizing the best of traditional buildings utilizing native materials, the two-story building, constructed on a continuous stone foundation, is made up of both fieldstone and wood. Both materials were locally available in great abundance, and the tower also rises as a monument to the lumber industry's impact on the state of Arkansas and to the federal government's determination to protect natural resources.

The lumber industry in Arkansas grew to importance in the late nineteenth century, largely as a result of the building of railroads that opened up the state's forests to the national marketplace. Significant railroad construction began in the 1880s and was funded by a combination of local, national, and international capital. Polk County followed the pattern established elsewhere in Arkansas when in 1896 the Kansas City Southern completed its line into the county with the help of Dutch capitalists as well as local entrepreneurs. By 1899 there were five railroads transiting the Ouachita Forest. The Kansas City Southern set up a division shop a few miles north of Dallas, which was then the county seat of Polk County, and, as happened wherever railroads estab-

JEANNIE M. WHAYNE

lished headquarters, a boom town emerged. The new town, named Mena, attracted settlers and by the turn of the century became a center of lumbering, with sawmills, stave mills, and hoop factories operating feverishly. By 1909 the five railroads served the purposes of eleven lumber companies in the Ouachitas, which produced millions of board feet of lumber. That year marked the high point of lumber production in the state. The 2.1 billion board feet produced in its mills ranked Arkansas number five in the nation in lumber production.

The decision of railroad officials to move the division shop elsewhere in 1910 ended the boom in Mena but did not destroy the town. The lumber industry continued to thrive, and the town also surfaced as a commercial center servicing an agricultural community. But two additional important facts ensured that Polk County's forest industry would deviate from the typical scenario established elsewhere in Arkansas. First, the incentive to remove all timber from the area was lacking because, unlike the Delta in eastern Arkansas, the land in the southwestern section of the state was not as appropriate

for agricultural production. In the Delta lumber companies and speculators realized enormous profits from selling cut-over land to farmers and planters. Thus today eastern Arkansas is almost entirely bereft of the abundant forests that literally blanketed the area one hundred years ago.

Southwestern Arkansas's deviation from the Delta's forest history was additionally ensured by the creation of the Arkansas National Forest in 1907, the first national forest to be established east of the Great Plains and the first to be established in the South. Created by order of President Theodore Roosevelt, who was determined to guarantee conservation of the nation's natural resources, it was renamed the Ouachita National Forest in 1926. It consists of nearly one million acres with abundant stands of short-leaf yellow pine and various hardwoods. Selective lumbering continues, but it continues in the context of a conservatory program. The Tall Peak Fire Tower has played an important role in protecting the Ouachita National Forest from fires and thus maintaining its integrity.

The Fulbrights transformed the rustic Rabbit's Foot Lodge into a country showplace. *Arkansas Historic Preservation Program photo.*

RABBIT'S FOOT LODGE

Randall Bennett Woods

Rabbit's Foot Lodge
1936–41
Springdale, Washington County
Listed on the National Register of Historic Places on September 11, 1986

"Rabbit's Foot Lodge was built in 1908 for Dr. and Mrs. Charles F. Perkins. Little did Dr. Perkins know that in decades that would follow, this structure would gain notoriety throughout the state of Arkansas for its unusual design and for the far-reaching impact one of its owners would have on both state and national policies. While log structures are commonplace in Arkansas's history, the size and sophistication of details found in Rabbit's Foot Lodge elevated this type of construction to a new prestige. J. William Fulbright, president of the University of Arkansas and later United States congressman and senator, owned Rabbit's Foot Lodge from 1936 to 1941 and remarked in a recent letter, 'I spent some of the finest days of my life in that beautiful and interesting house.'"

—*From the National Register nomination*

Rabbit's Foot Lodge was home to J. William Fulbright, his wife, Elizabeth (Betty), and their daughters, Elizabeth (Betsy) and Roberta (Bosey), from 1936 to 1941. Author of the Fulbright-Connally resolution, which committed the United States to participating in the United Nations, and creator of the exchange program that bears his name, Bill Fulbright was the longest-serving and most powerful chair of the Senate Foreign Relations Committee. Both an intellectual and an internationalist, Fulbright exerted great influence over the course of American foreign relations in the 1960s and 1970s.

Fulbright was also the most prominent and most effective congressional critic of the Vietnam War. His dissent was particularly galling and damning to Lyndon Johnson because Fulbright was, like George Kennan, a pragmatic cold-war liberal who could not be dismissed as an ideologue. He and his staff used hearings by the Foreign Relations Committee as a forum in which to advance their penetrating criticism of the war.

During his tenure as chair Fulbright not only opposed the war in Vietnam but also championed détente with the Soviet Union and pressed for a U.N.-guaranteed, land-for-peace solution to the Arab-Israeli conflict. His books—which constitute an ongoing, comprehensive critique of American foreign policy—sold hundreds of thousands of copies and, together with the exchange program, made him one of the best-known Americans of his time both at home and abroad.

But back in 1935 Bill Fulbright was teaching law at George Washington University in Washington, D.C. His mother, Roberta, was having some difficulty running the Fulbright family businesses in Fayetteville, Arkansas. Roberta asked Bill and Betty to come back to Northwest Arkansas and give her a hand. Bill loved and—what was more important, given his makeup—respected his mother. It would

be very difficult for him to reject her request for help. Moreover, Betty was anxious to get away from the East Coast, at least for a time. Her mother, Mrs. Elizabeth Williams of Philadelphia, could be dictatorial, even suffocating. Betty was a strong-willed person in her own right, and she longed for the freedom to develop her own life and friends. A daughter, Elizabeth (Betsy) Fulbright, had been born in February, and Fayetteville sounded to Betty like a congenial place to raise children. As coincidence would have it, Robert Leflar, an old acquaintance of Fulbright's who taught law at the university, wrote saying that he would be on leave for the 1936–1937 term at the University of Missouri. He had talked the matter over with Julian Waterman, dean of the law school, and they had decided that Fulbright was just the man to fill in for him.

Bill Fulbright was thirty-one years old when he returned to Fayetteville. The next two years were to be among the most carefree in his life. Aside from knees that occasionally ached from old football and rugby injuries, he was in good health and blessed with a devoted wife and a brand-new baby girl. He was free of debt (as he would remain for the rest of his life) and back in the bosom of his family.

Every Anglophile—and the Fulbrights were certainly that—dreams of owning a country estate, and Bill Fulbright was no exception. A couple of months after returning to Fayetteville, he and Betty purchased a 150-acre farm several miles northwest of Fayetteville and west of Springdale. In the middle of the spread sat a three-story, chinked-log house. Originally built by a local architect who was enchanted with the region's frontier history, Rabbit's Foot Lodge featured a natural stone fireplace, wooden shutters, and a wraparound porch. It had been named for a Cherokee Indian chief alleged to have ruled the area in bygone days. The structure sat atop the crest of a hill overlooking a tree-filled

Sen. J. William Fulbright receives the Senate Foreign Relations Committee gavel as President John F. Kennedy and Vice-President Lyndon B. Johnson look on. *Courtesy of J. William Fulbright Papers, Special Collections Division, University of Arkansas Libraries, Fayetteville.*

pasture that more closely resembled a park than an area for grazing the fifty white-faced Herefords that Bill bought. The house was surrounded by white oaks, magnolias, and catalpa trees. A natural, low stone wall bordered Rabbit's Foot Lodge, and the yard was crisscrossed with flagstone walks. At the bottom of the hill, across the dirt road that divided the house from the main pasture, was a natural spring.

At the time Fulbright purchased Rabbit's Foot Lodge, the farm had been neglected for several years. Moreover, it possessed neither heating nor indoor plumbing. Betty was attracted to the notion of farm life, but bare wooden-plank floors, smoke-stained timber walls, and outhouses were a bit much. For three months she devoted herself completely to bringing her new home into the twentieth century.

The living room remained dark paneled, but Betty painted the rest of the interior colonial white to brighten it up. "She decorated in chintz," Bill's niece, Suzie Zorn, recalled. The house may have been rustic, but Betty had meals served on the best china—an English country pattern, of course. The spring-fed stream was dammed up and a small swimming pool built for the family and its visitors. Additional trees were planted, the ground landscaped, and soon Rabbit's Foot Lodge was transformed into a country showplace. In addition to the cattle, Bill bought hogs and chickens. He was not, however, a "hands-on" farmer; a tenant family lived on the place and performed most of the chores.

Rabbit's Foot Lodge still stands as a monument to frontier architecture and a symbol of life for the Fulbrights before Bill entered public life.

A concrete monument erected by Rohwer internees looms over the graves of Japanese Americans who died while held in the Desha County internment center. *Photo by Mark Christ, Arkansas Historic Preservation Program.*

ROHWER RELOCATION CENTER

Charlotte Tillar Schexnayder

Rohwer Relocation Center Site
1942–1945
Rohwer, Desha County
Listed on the National Register of Historic Places on July 30, 1974
Cemetery designated a National Historic Landmark on July 6, 1992

"The Rohwer Relocation Camp Memorial Cemetery features exquisitely detailed and distinctive funerary monuments, which were designed and erected by the evacuees themselves during their internment; of the three relocation camp cemeteries that survive, Rohwer is singularly significant as the most elaborately detailed, and the most unique."

—*From the National Register nomination*

From her front porch swing at Rohwer twelve-year-old Frances Edgin watched a tragic chapter in American history unfold in 1942 and today wonders how American citizens could have been treated so shabbily.

This is the view of someone who was there, who can best describe how it happened, how hysteria and fear overcame fairness and constitutional rights.

In the beginning Frances, her brother, Bill, and their mother, Mrs. Sam Edgin, watched the construction of the wooden barracks, "with big old windows from floor to ceiling," and communal halls on a ten thousand-acre swampy farm site, which became the Rohwer Relocation Center. They knew the site was to house Japanese Americans and their families being moved from the West Coast, where World War II jitters prevailed and an invasion seemed imminent since the Japanese bombing of Pearl Harbor.

Remembers Frances, "We stood on our porch and watched as they unloaded the people from the trains and were really frightened to think they were Japanese. Mother had said, 'If you see any of them, just run. They are our enemy.'"

Now Mrs. Clarence Hopman of Dumas, Frances continues: "Those Japanese Americans came with their belongings in their hands. You could tell they were worn out. . . . And there were the guards standing with their guns. They frightened us, too."

The "sneak Jap attack on Pearl Harbor," as many said, and the national government's move to bring people of Japanese descent inland created an atmosphere of distrust, sometimes hatred, and often suspicion. No such grudge existed against Italian or German Americans, because they looked like the rest of us.

The detainees had been required to divest themselves of property in just two weeks before leaving California, and some had been wealthy.

Watercolor painting of Rohwer Relocation Center by Edward Inouye, ca. 1944. *Courtesy of Rosalie Gould.*

Living in starkness, with each family assigned one or two barrack rooms with a cot for each family member and no privacy, the detainees had no running water except in communal bathrooms and mess halls. However, food trains arrived daily at the camp, leading some local citizens to complain, "They eat better than we do."

Even the Japanese customs and music coming from the camp added to that time of fear. "It was eerie music like we hadn't heard coming from loud speaker in the camp. Somehow, we all felt like they were plotting against us. I look back today and think how utterly ridiculous," Frances adds.

At a time when we depended solely upon government information amid the peril of World War

II, few of us questioned the national policy. It was contact with the relocated Japanese Americans that changed local attitudes.

Frances explains: "The Japanese would slip out the back of the camp and go to our little stores in the community. They were friendly, very courteous. They spoke English. One day a woman asked Mother if she would sell eggs. Mother was excited to make any kind of money, as Daddy was working away as a dragline operator. Our fear abated. We discovered they were people like we are. Nice, friendly people."

Further breaking the prejudice against the detainees, Frances's brother Bill, 15, met a new friend, Joshua, 17, when invited to a service club in the camp. "They had similar likes or dislikes," recalls Frances. "Joshua was really upset about being treated like a foreigner in his own country. So our attitude began to change. Their families were like our families."

"No one in our community had really understood the situation until then. We felt like they were prisoners of war. That was the real tragedy," she adds. Truly a tragedy, as sons of those in the Rohwer Center were fighting heroically with the U.S. Army in Italy at a time of much prejudice against their families.

Far from their once prominent status, many of the relocated returned home three years after their internment with no money. Shattered lives had to be rebuilt.

Most of us, like Frances, look back on that period with shame at our ignorance and fear-induced prejudice. As a young newspaperwoman in Desha County, I had no opportunity to go inside Rohwer Center, and objectivity was not within my reach.

For descendants of the Japanese Americans at Rohwer, whom we've contacted in later years, there is both a lingering resentment and a move-ahead attitude.

Could this tragedy happen again?

In a world of instant communication, which combats misinformation, it is doubtful. But even the remembrance causes a shudder.

In 1943 Rohwer Relocation Center interns watch as a train takes segregants to the Tule Lake camp in California, reserved for "all those in the other centers who indicated that their ties with Japan were stronger than to the United States." *Photo by Fred Yamaguchi, courtesy of National Archives and Record Administration.*

A jeering mob taunts
Elizabeth Eckford
after she is turned
away from Central
High School in 1957.
*Courtesy of Arkansas
History Commission.*

Its decorative elements are a blend of Collegiate Gothic and historic eclecticism, reminiscent of an old European college. The two-block-wide building is also Art Deco. Visitors climb the ziggurat stair steps in the middle, leading to the second floor. The band room used to be way up in the fifth-floor tower.

Some things change. Some remain the same. An old man from the class of '28 or '29 stopped the art teacher and asked if the north wing still leaks. It does. And sophomores are still being sold tickets to the non-existent elevator.

Traffic between classes moves briskly. One must hustle to get from the third floor of the main building to the ground-level gym or library out back. We (the Nine) race-walked to class as fast-moving targets. Back then my guard seemed to be way across the hall while I was being body-slammed into lockers. Now one side does not seem so very far from the other side.

During a tour in 1987 we walked slowly down the halls while students were inside their classrooms. Students stamping their feet on the concrete floor of the auditorium while applauding no longer make me wonder when they will break out in a frenzy. Being in a hallway crush of students is not scary anymore. Nobody is being knocked down or kicked anymore.

I went back to the ground floor, where the police car sped through a tunnel, carrying us to safety. It is really a quiet, brightly lit hallway. The print shop is gone, and students are not passing out hate messages. Fifty-five students effectively silenced most other students. Most turned their backs, studiously ignoring us.

Many students from our time in the fifties come back with memories different from ours. In their reunion stories they say they didn't see anything, didn't hear anything, and didn't know anything of the attacks on us. I call this the plague of the three monkeys: hear no evil, see no evil, and do no evil.

In looking back, each finds their own place in time. Some can avoid the question, "How did you respond to what you saw?" But photographs, FBI interviews, and records of school disciplinary reports prevent the denial of some history.

Central is famous architecturally as one of America's most beautiful high schools. It is infamous internationally because of pictures of the howling mob in front of it in 1957. That image is repeated in textbooks, news stories and documentaries.

How one sees Central depends on one's point of view. The first graduates, from 1927, are as proud of their education as are contemporary graduates bound for the competitive colleges that recruit from Central High. Today all five of Little Rock's public senior highs offer college preparatory and general education courses. Until twelve years ago a classical education was available at Central alone.

After a boycott in 1957 the school lost two hundred students, dropping down to nineteen hundred. Over the years about sixteen hundred was Central's average population. But the Black and Gold has rebounded in popularity. The two-block-long building now has 1,880 students. It will continue to operate as a school even though it is now part of the Park Service as a National Historic Site.

For forty-two years visitors from around the world have come to see Central High. Public memory has been shaped by the images of 1957. This was a time of constitutional challenge. Here television was first effectively used to show the context in which dramatic events occurred.

Previously, in Clinton, Tennessee, and in Marshall, Texas, mob rule had been allowed to overturn court-ordered desegregation efforts.

In Little Rock the governor called out the National Guard to keep away nine black children. He later removed the Guard, and local police were unable to control the mob. A reluctant President Eisenhower federalized the Guard and sent in paratroopers from the 101st Airborne Division. On September 25, 1957, the desegregation of Central began, and the standoff between state and federal power ended.

Central High is an icon of the constitutional challenge resolved in 1957. Its students are emblematic of the cultural transformation of the South.

The vernacular buildings of the Parker-Hickman Farm in the Big Buffalo Valley Historic District are typical of the structures traditionally found in this area of the Ozark Mountains. *Photo by Storm Smith.*

THE BOXLEY VALLEY HISTORIC DISTRICT

Neil Compton

Big Buffalo Valley Historic District
1850–1930
Ponca vic., Newton County
Listed on the National Register of Historic Places on July 29, 1987.

"Boxley Valley provides the most significant cultural landscape found along the Buffalo River. It is a well-preserved example of a rural Ozark Mountain Valley representing a time span of over 150 years. The valley's collection of tangible and intangible cultural features exemplifies the traditional regional settlement pattern. The landscape includes a collection of agricultural fields and significant vernacular features. The valley represents a collection of single-family operated farms, whose occupants continually adapted to an ever-changing agricultural economy and the forces of nature, especially flooding from the river. Descendants of the original settlers remain today in the valley."

—*From the National Register nomination*

I am a once-busy physician, now long since retired, who after a stint in the U.S. Navy in World War II became involved with the conservation of some of the natural world here in the Arkansas Ozarks.

I have been presented with the question of why a small-town physician from Bentonville, Arkansas, would ever become so entangled in a contest to stop the Corps of Engineers from building two high dams on the Buffalo River and to place that river instead in the hands of the National Park Service. To begin with I answer that it may have been due to an inborn behavior pattern. Some of us, when becoming aware of the earth's marvels, are overcome by the urge to monkey with them: "Let's make a reservoir out of this river." Others, like me, feel urges just as strong to leave them alone.

My action as an environmentalist had not been significant before the Second World War. I was the county health officer for Washington County, Arkansas. I was not a determined outdoorsman but a sightseer and modest naturalist. There were astonishing places in southern Washington County, and with friends and family we toured that region to see Devil's Den, White Rock Mountain, and Weedy Rough, places that I would dream about during those many months on duty out on Guadalcanal, Fiji, and Espiritu Santo. The first thing I did when the war was over was see what I had missed in the pre-war days. I made a trip north on Arkansas 21 through Ozone, Fayetteville, and Mossville, and down into Boxley Valley. There was no pavement on that route then, and I for one preferred the intimacy of the old, steep, winding way through that charming hill country to the relatively straight, paved speedways that our highway department would one day inflict upon the Boxley Valley.

At the time of that trip, in April 1946, something was going on in Boxley Valley at a place called Cob Cave, which was a part of what was later to be named Lost Valley. Interesting news items appeared in the *Arkansas Gazette,* the *Arkansas Democrat,* and the *St. Louis Globe-Democrat.* The reports about Cob Cave were submitted by Avantus Green (who also went by the name Glenn Green), publicity director for the Arkansas Publicity and Parks Commission. Green's first trip up into Lost Valley, as he named it, included people from the National Geographic Society. Soon thereafter Green came up with the idea that some of the scenery in Newton County was good enough to be included in the National Park System. All of that inspired me to make numerous trips to Lost Valley, which proved to be more beautiful than Green had been able to describe. But Green could not find backers for his National Park proposal, and he, unfortunately, left the state.

But there were others who, like me, were concerned about Lost Valley. One was a young student from the University of Arkansas at Fayetteville named Ken Smith, who was in a hiking club that made many trips to Lost Valley. He made an intensive study of the area and arranged for the Nature Conservancy to purchase it, but the owner would not sell. Ken then decided to move to California, but before he left, he and a Nature Conservancy agent came to me, asking that I take over the effort to protect Lost Valley. It was a challenge that I accepted with misgivings but as something that needed to be done. Local loggers had bulldozed a road into the heart of Lost Valley, leaving it in chaos. But it wasn't too long before we became aware of a much greater problem.

In Little Rock Harold Alexander, an employee of the Arkansas Game and Fish Commission, kept up with developments along Arkansas's streams. Harold called my attention to the disturbing fact that the Army Corps of Engineers was now in a good position to build two high dams, one at Lone Rock and one at Gilbert, on the Buffalo River. Thus, that beautiful stream would be wiped out as a river and transformed into a fluctuating reservoir, something that we had too many of already. The

A 1950s baptism on the Buffalo River. *Courtesy of Eul Dean Clark.*

bill to accomplish this had been presented to Congress three times already by our congressman, Jim Trimble, but economy-minded President Eisenhower vetoed the legislation each time. However, Eisenhower was on his way out, and a pro-dam successor was waiting in the wings. Only a handful of concerned citizens around Fayetteville and a few in Little Rock knew of the marvels of the Buffalo River and wanted to save it.

After much discussion we finally arrived at a grand conclusion: why not adopt Glenn Green's idea of a national park? A park not limited to Newton County but encompassing the entire Buffalo River and its better tributaries, all the way to the White River. It would then be a National River, out of bounds for any kind of dams or other man-made abuses. To do this, on May 24, 1962, we put together a shaky organization that we called the Ozark Society to Save the Buffalo. None of the several possible

leaders of the new group was willing to take charge of the organization, and it fell to my lot to do so. This would be temporary, I thought, but in the end the term proved to be for ten years. As for time, it soon developed that I might have some extra hours. I did not play golf or spend any time hunting and fishing or working in a shop. There were hours in the evenings for photography, letter writing, and trying to figure out what to do next.

By taking advantage of the breaks, we were able to keep the Ozark Society to Save the Buffalo River on top of most developments.

The first of these developments we did not initiate, but it soon had a nationwide audience. On July 14, 1961, *Time* magazine published an outdoor recreation issue. It had a full-page color photograph of the Ozark Wilderness Waterways Club (OWWC), under the leadership of Harold and Margaret Hedges of Kansas City, camped under the five-hundred-foot

Big Bluff on the Buffalo River. This picture was seen by Supreme Court Justice William O. Douglas, a well-known outdoor enthusiast, who asked those campers to take him down the river to see Big Bluff. In order to get in on this event, the Ozark Society wasted no time in contacting OWWC, asking for an invitation to go along. Thus we met at the low-water bridge in Ponca on May 1, 1962, with Justice Douglas and all those Kansas City canoe paddlers, who knew our Buffalo River better than we did. News coverage of that expedition was nationwide, with even the *New York Times* giving it some space. After that our train was on the track, its engine running, ready to go. Important personalities—mostly from the field of politics, where decisions of environmental import are made—became interested, and we did not fail to reap the advantage.

At our urging Sen. J. William Fulbright was an early convert. He obtained a small grant to pay for a survey of the Buffalo River by a National Park inspection team to see if it was feasible to include the river as a unit in the park system. I was able to go along with the inspectors for a couple of days and hear their decision firsthand. "We had no idea that there was anything as wonderful as this in Arkansas!" they said. The Buffalo was their baby from then on.

On December 10, 1965, the much-maligned Orval Faubus, governor of Arkansas, exercised his power and put the axe to the Gilbert and Lone Rock Dams. The big dam supporters and the Army Corps of Engineers pulled in their horns and waited for the voters to send them a favorable governor, but such a man they were never able to see.

Arkansas's Sen. John McClellan was a great dam builder (the Arkansas River Seaway), but we approached him in a friendly manner, and he joined Senator Fulbright in espousing the Buffalo National River. After that our congressional delegation, except for Congressman Trimble, fell into line.

The year 1966 was critical for the proposed Buffalo National River. Congressman Trimble had been in Congress for twenty-two years. He was running for another term, and his reelection might well cause his plan for Gilbert Dam to be realized. Even if not, we would still have two to four more years of conflict between the Ozark Society and the Buffalo River Improvement Association (BRIA). Congressman Trimble was a Democrat, and in Arkansas that was tantamount to election. But he was to have a Republican opponent, John Paul Hammerschmidt, whom we sought out to support the river if he was elected. He was receptive to that.

Never was the state of Arkansas so surprised as it was the morning after the general election in 1966. Hammerschmidt had defeated Trimble by ten thousand votes. The BRIA then tried mightily to embarrass or delay legislation for the Buffalo National River, but now they were without a program or anywhere to go.

As for the legislation, due to the simple inertia of Congress we had to fitfully hold the line for five more years. But the day finally came. President Richard Nixon signed the bill for America's first National River, the Buffalo, on March 1, 1972, one hundred years to the day after President U. S. Grant signed the bill for Yellowstone National Park.

After that stroke of the pen those of us who had weathered the storm for the free-flowing river could feel nothing but satisfaction—tempered, however, I hope, with modesty. We were nothing more than an ordinary group of citizens with a good idea, in the right place at the right time. Had we not been there we would now have another drowned valley to leave to posterity.

In retrospect let us now walk the trail in the mind's eye, into Lost Valley, as we did in 1946. Let us stand amid the big, square limestone blocks at the barrier bluff from which they had tumbled and consider the short tunnel cave through which Clark Creek falls to form a wide, clear pool in a limestone

The businesses on the Harrison County Courthouse Square still command a share of the trade in the Boone County seat. *Photo by Ken Story, Arkansas Historic Preservation Program.*

SQUARE ROOTS

Marian Boyd

Harrison Courthouse Square Historic District
Ca. 1895–1947
Harrison, Boone County
Listed on the National Register of Historic Places on May 6, 1999

"The buildings in the Harrison Courthouse Square Historic District represent a continuum of the city's development. The Harrison Courthouse Square Historic District is also significant in its parallel representation of the formation and development of Boone County, Arkansas. The buildings are indicative of the events which have shaped the county and the city of Harrison."

—*From the National Register nomination*

Having spent the last ten years in the downtown revitalization profession, I have worked closely with twenty-three particular downtowns and toured and worked with about fifty or sixty others around the state. I view historic downtowns in a different way since signing on with Main Street Arkansas.

I feel a connection with the square, in both its physical and historical aspects. The connection is not just to these historic downtowns but to the people who recognize the importance of restoring their community cores. And surely I am connected to no group or no downtown square as much as I am to the Boone County Courthouse Square in Harrison, Arkansas.

When I was a child, in the 1960s, downtown was my destination. My sister Virginia and I were latchkey kids well before that term was coined. On Saturdays, or on just about any summer day, our parents went off to work, and Virginia and I could find plenty to do within walking distance of our house. You see, everything revolved around the courthouse square, and our house was just two blocks away, at 208 North Pine. We could walk to church, to the city pool, to school, and, of course, to all the stores on the square. We would often spend the afternoon on the square together or, more likely, with our respective friends, in an effort to get away from each other.

We might have lunch, a bowl of chili at Kleppers, and then go to a matinee at the Lyric Theater. My friends and I would spend afternoons at the soda fountains both at Coffman's and Sim's Drug Stores. A grilled cheese sandwich and a Dr. Pepper were certainly under a buck, and then we could shop, try out the perfume samples, and read the magazines and comic books. They loved us there. I'm sure I remember that.

In the fall we'd get our new shoes at Heuer-Wilson's or the Style Spot and buy new school clothes at Crooms, Walters, or Guys and Dolls, on the east side of the square. We ordered our senior class rings from W. T. Harrison or Shipman's Jewelry, both on the west side of the square.

School supplies—brand new paper, notebooks, and pens—were all bought on the square, either at the Ben Franklin or at Wellworth's (not Woolworth's) Five and Dime. For birthdays we would shop for toys at Crest Variety, and as we got a little older, we'd choose just the right gift at the Party House.

Before the discounters, the big box retailers, the strip centers, the malls, catalog shopping, and the internet, you could pretty much get anything you needed in the downtown district. You could get your photo taken, your shoes repaired, your teeth fixed, and your taxes prepared. Early on you could even buy groceries on the square at Hudson's Grocery. For a time you could get a haircut on the south side of the square, at the Franklin James Studio, predecessor to Coiffures Et Cetera.

One of my very favorite things to do after school was to go to Ashley's Music Store and buy a new 45 or splurge four dollars on an album. And if Gus, the guitar teacher, had been a non-smoker, I might today be a great musician. (It was a very small room with no circulation, in the back of the store.)

Downtown Harrison was complete, and it was safe. There were seasonal festivals and carnivals that magically took shape around the square. I participated in many parades downtown—either as a Girl Scout in Bina Williams's Troop Twenty-Eight, as a First United Methodist church member, or as a Harrison Junior High School Goblin band member. I played the flute very badly, but I marched along with the best of them. (It was a family flute, passed down from my sister Joan, to Jeanie, to Virginia, and then to me.)

Of course all my downtown memories weren't so great. Our family doctor was located just off the square. There were many agonizing visits to his

The Boone County Courthouse, designed by Charles Thompson, is the focal point of the downtown Harrison historic district. *Arkansas Historic Preservation Program Photo.*

office, including the time I had to get five stitches in my left knee after a fall on Rush Street. They were making street improvements, and I had, of course, been on my way downtown. I still have the scar.

Also there were the dreaded piano lessons at Drena O'Brien's studio and house. She taught piano to all five Boyd children, starting with my brother in 1943. By the time she got around to me, she was older—I mean better. After leaving the junior high school, I had a stop at Thompson's Grocery Store for a sugar fix, thirty grueling minutes at the piano, and a quick walk home in time for Wally and the Beaver.

There is nothing particularly unique about these memories. They are probably similar to your own childhood memories.

That is, unless you're under forty.

Oh sure, the downtown is still there and in pretty good shape, and you have some of your own memories, but they've probably been diluted by the memories of afternoons at the shopping mall or driving out to the discount stores. (I'm not naming names.)

Aside from being the setting for my simple memories of the sixties, that courthouse square was the setting for much of Boone County's history, long before my time. Winston Churchill said, "We shape our buildings, and then our buildings shape us." The buildings in the Boone County Courthouse Square Historic District are indicative of the events that have shaped Boone County and the city of Harrison.

Looking at the construction dates of some of the anchor buildings downtown, you start to realize that there was a lot of new construction going on in the first three decades of this century. In fact, the greatest period of growth in the city of Harrison was during these first thirty years. Many of the buildings have survived natural disasters and urban renewal. Some have not.

The federal courthouse building, which anchors the square on the northeast corner, was built in 1905. This building, which housed the post office for many years, is one of the most historically significant buildings in the downtown. Today the building is used for county offices.

The county courthouse was built in 1909, after a fire destroyed the original building three years earlier. Charles Thompson, Arkansas's most popular architect during the first half of the century, designed the new courthouse. The three-story, Classical Revival–style building sets an imposing, formal tone, while the courthouse square provides an informal, park-like setting.

Three years later, in 1912, the high school was built on Cherry Street. Today it still serves to educate by housing the Ozark Heritage Museum and a classroom for beginning computer whiz kids. While I'm trying to focus on only the first three decades of the century, I want to mention Central Elementary School next door. Central was built by the WPA (Works Progress Administration) in 1940 and still functions as a middle school. The building has twelve-foot ceilings, a hardwood stage, and the original, theater-style box office. In the sixties these two buildings housed Harrison Junior High School, where I learned math from Mr. Hefley, American history from Mr. Cooper, and English from Mrs.

McCorkindale, and I *tried* to learn Spanish from Mrs. Nickels.

The county jail was built in 1914. Charles Thompson also designed this building, which sat with its back to the south side of the square. Had they had a window, these criminals would have had a perfect view of Crooked Creek, which strongly influenced the development and appearance of downtown Harrison. I never went to jail in Harrison. Well, not officially, but it seems like Mrs. Mae Brown's second-grade class might have toured the county jail as an incentive to be better behaved.

The Midway Hotel, just east of the courthouse square, was built in 1915. By the time I was growing up, it was some kind of a long-term residential hotel. Men would sit on the porch and whittle all day long. They would leave three-foot-high whittle piles on the lawn. At least that's the way I remember them. Today I'm told that the fraternity of whittlers operates on the courthouse square. Inclement weather moves them to the courthouse boiler room.

The Methodist church was also built in 1914. I was baptized there, and my family, sans my dad, spent many hours each week in that wonderful old building, which served as a western anchor for the square. In 1979 an explosion across the street at the telephone company destroyed the building's beautiful, Tiffany stained-glass windows. The building was finally razed. Today it is an empty lot.

Just across the street the Holt Building stood from 1926 until 1998. This two-story building survived the 1979 blast but was destroyed by fire in 1998. John W. Bass, a nationally known builder who also built Harrison's Montgomery Ward Building and Lyric Theatre, designed the building. The building originally housed the Missouri and North Arkansas Railroad offices, but in my days it housed Holt Sporting Goods.

The Montgomery Ward Building, with the exception of the two courthouse buildings, is

Little Rock's downtown commercial district, like its cousin in Harrison, was a thriving business center in 1911. *Courtesy of Quapaw Quarter Association.*

undoubtedly the most impressive structure still standing on the square today. The 1927 structure is an adaptation of the Spanish Revival style. For years it was the Old Town Mall and housed several retail outlets. Today it is a furniture store. (By the way, the Montgomery Ward in Harrison wasn't the only department store that Bass designed; he also designed the original Macy's Department Store in New York City.)

Two years after he built the Montgomery Ward, Bass built the Lyric Theatre. If I had a nickel for every time I went to the Lyric Theater—well, it turns out I'd only have about thirty dollars. There I saw Tarzan, the Three Stooges, Elvis, Frankie Avalon, and James Bond. I even saw the Beatles in *A Hard Days Night* with free tickets I had won at

Rowland's Department Store on the west side of the square.

The Hotel Seville was built in 1930. Its architect, Eugene Johnson, also incorporated the Spanish Revival style in many aspects of the building. In the winter my neighborhood friends and I would ride our sleds down four steep blocks on Ridge Street and veer into the driveway of the Hotel Seville to avoid landing in the path of cars on U.S. Highway 65 North. Of course, I didn't get this at the time, but the Hotel Seville, when it was first built, was *the* community gathering place. Today it is has been restored for reuse and is listed on the National Register of Historic Places.

In the spring of 1961 water poured from Crooked Creek, and the entire downtown square was under water. News of the flood made the front page of the newspaper in Los Angeles, where my brother Roy was stationed in the Navy. Many downtown merchants were caught off-guard and stranded in their stores. Hugh Cotton, or "Uncle Hugh" as I call him, drove his bass boat downtown and saved two people standing on the roof of Sim's Drug Store on the south side of the square. I remember hearing about the owners of Bergman's Grocery Store downtown holding on to pipes at ceiling level, waiting for rescue. Buildings were actually moved off their foundations and carried two blocks away. According to the *Harrison Daily Times,* 80 percent of the business district was destroyed.

Uncle Hugh remembers many stories about the history of Harrison and loves to tell them. He has probably played a part in many more that I don't even know about. Now he helps document and educate people about Harrison's history by being a part of the Boone County Historical and Railroad Society.

It's my job to work with downtowns and revitalization. But it is people like Uncle Hugh and his cohorts at the historical societies all around the state who understand the importance of a community's heritage and are truly making a difference around our state. As our state and country become more and more homogenized, it is gratifying to see more and more people join this preservation and heritage movement.

When our forefathers began to build these historic buildings, they took so much pride in their construction that they etched their names on the buildings for prosperity—Milburn, Capps-Paul, Kirby and Wood. How forward-thinking they were in those early days.

As the millennium approaches, I'd like to think that some of these buildings might be around for another hundred years. I hope so. As new trends in shopping change the structure of our downtowns, and as Mother Nature continues to take her toll, it seems like a tough battle. The National Trust for Historic Preservation has a new motto for the millennium—"Protecting the Irreplaceable." It's a motto every community can embrace and employ as a mission for the next century. I hope Harrison will.

A hardened concrete pad and an earthen mound marking the launch duct's location are among the remains of Titan II ICBM Launch Complex 374-7, a site that commanded the world's attention in 1980. *Photo by Ken Grunewald, Arkansas Historic Preservation Program.*

WE CAN NEITHER CONFIRM NOR DENY

David K. Stumpf

Titan II ICBM Launch Complex 374-7
1980
Southside vic., Van Buren County
Nominated to the National Register of Historic Places on September 2, 1998

"The missile silo complexes of the 308th Strategic Missile Wing served in many ways as the front lines of the Cold War, and their deactivation under President Ronald Reagan's strategic arms modernization program is a key part of their history. The deactivated silos, as they appear today with their earthen mounds and concrete pads, reflect their entire history, which ultimately culminated in their demobilization and abandonment. Titan II ICBM Complex 374-7 remains a silent and moving reminder of the days when the 308th SMW stood at the forefront of the nation's nuclear deterrent."

—*From the National Register nomination*

On September 18, 1980, a sequence of events began at the Titan II ICBM Launch Complex 374-7, located near the town of Damascus, that spelled the beginning of the end of the Titan II ICBM program. The surface of this site twenty years later gives not even the faintest clues as to the event that took place early in the morning of the next day, September 19, 1980. A Titan II missile, fully loaded with propellant and armed with the single largest thermonuclear warhead used in the strategic missile forces, was destroyed by an explosion. Twisted piles of reinforcing steel bars, two inches in diameter and stripped of tons of concrete, lay curled at the top of the 145-foot-deep launch duct. Massive girders weighing hundreds of tons had been hurled clear of the silo. The devastation, while for the most part confined to the launch duct, was overwhelming to those who searched for survivors. In its present state the site serves as an illustration of the success of a sometimes-controversial major weapons system of the Cold War.

The sequence of events was initiated when a propellant transfer system team member dropped a nine-pound wrench socket off a work platform on Level Two of the launch duct, approximately ninety feet from the thrust mount that held the missile in a vertical position. The socket bounced off the thrust mount and punctured the Stage I fuel tank. Fuel, under pressure, began to spray out of the estimated one-quarter-inch square hole and the rest, as the saying goes, is history.

But before further discussion of the Damascus accident, a brief reprise of the history of the Titan II program up to this point is necessary. Titan II was born out of the necessity to make our strategic missile forces capable of nearly instantaneous response. The first generation missiles, Atlas and Titan I, required fifteen to twenty minutes to prepare for launch. The second generation, Titan II and Minuteman, required less than a minute to

launch. The Titan II program came to Arkansas on October 5, 1960, when the Little Rock Area Office of the U.S. Army Corps of Engineers Ballistic Missile Construction Office was established at Little Rock Air Force Base. Construction began on January 3, 1961, and by December 1963 all eighteen launch complexes were completed for the 308th Strategic Missile Wing, joining identical deployments at the 309th Strategic Missile Wing, Davis-Monthan AFB, Arizona, and the 381st Strategic Missile Wing, McConnell AFB, Kansas.

The safety of the Titan II program had always been a concern for the people who inhabited the farms and towns near the launch complexes. The very features that made Titan II capable of launch at a moment's notice made it extremely hazardous. The fuel and oxidizer were hypergolic, i.e., ignited on contact. Oddly enough, however, if the populace had thought about the relative dangers of filling their cars every day with a highly flammable, carcinogen-containing liquid called gasoline, the dangers of the Titan II propellants would have been placed in appropriate perspective.

Titan II was also controversial, for some people, because of the complexity of the system. Up until 1978 the accidents that had occurred in the Titan II wing at Little Rock AFB had been "contained" within the grounds of the launch complex. The major accident before 1978 had been in August 1965, when a flash fire caused by a welding operation near high-pressure hydraulic lines at Launch Complex 373-4, near Pangburn, killed fifty-three construction workers. Then in January 1968 an enlisted man fell to his death after slipping on a hydraulic fluid–soaked, work-platform surface at Launch Complex 373-5 near Center Hill. In September 1976 a cleaning operation using freon caused the asphyxiation of an enlisted man at Launch Complex 373-4. And in January 1978 the first accident that affected the surrounding populace

Huge pieces of reinforced concrete and twisted metal were thrown hundreds of feet by the explosion. *Courtesy of the* Arkansas Democrat-Gazette.

took place when an oxidizer-holding trailer heater went out of control at Launch Complex 374-7 and caused the tank to vent oxidizer fumes that injured several nearby farmers.

After a massive oxidizer spill in August 1978 at one of the 381st Strategic Missile Wing sites, Launch Complex 533-7, near Rock, Kansas, the call to retire the Titan II missiles began. A congressional review committee was formed and a thorough review of the program initiated. In May 1980 their report was published. While critical of the need for updating training procedures and the need to retain experienced personnel within the program, the report considered Titan II to be as safe, if not safer, than a comparable industrial activity. The missile itself, as well as the launch complexes, had been modified and upgraded

during the previous seventeen years. Many of the maintenance personnel at the time felt that the missile and its support systems were in better condition than they had been when originally installed.

Back to September 18, 1980. The tank puncture occurred at approximately six thirty P.M. Within twenty minutes the wing commander had formed a missile potential hazard team. In conjunction with higher headquarters the problem of saving the missile and complex was addressed. The missile combat crew and the propellant transfer system personnel evacuated the site at approximately nine o'clock P.M. Approximately one hour later security police began evacuating nearby residents. Efforts to assess the condition of the missile and estimate the amount of fuel spilled continued through the night.

DAVID K. STUMPF

At three o'clock A.M., just as a two-man propellant transfer team sent to evaluate the condition of the silo reached the top of the access portal stairs and were preparing to sit down to await further orders, it is believed that fuel vapors in the launch duct ignited, causing a low-order explosion, not a detonation, that blew the 740-ton silo closure door an estimated two hundred feet into the air and nearly six hundred feet to the northeast of the silo. Stage II of the missile, carrying the reentry vehicle that housed the W-53 thermonuclear warhead, was jettisoned from the launch duct and exploded in mid-air, shattering the reentry vehicle shell.

The explosion destroyed the launch duct and silo. The W-53 warhead was found intact, lying in a ditch near the access road, perhaps one hundred feet from the site entry point. No radiation was found to be leaking from the weapon; its fail-safe features had worked correctly. One member of the two-man team was killed and the other seriously injured. A number of support personnel were also seriously injured. Interestingly enough, and of comfort to many combat crew members at Little Rock AFB and the other Titan II wings, a half-filled glass of Coca-Cola was found in the launch control center, 250 feet from the explosion, without a drop spilled.

Another congressional inquiry was launched,

The shattered remnants of the launch duct are clearly visible in this overhead view of Titan II ICBM Launch Complex 374-7. *Official Air Force photograph courtesy of the Titan Missile Museum National Historic Landmark Archives*

which reached much the same conclusions as the similar study conducted six months earlier. The need for improved communications between the Titan II wings and local communities in case of accidents was clear. The need to clearly state the condition of the nuclear weapon, if present, was prominently pointed out and Air Force policy modified. The inquiry findings did not suggest that Titan II should be deactivated but that the program should be continued until a system replacement was in hand. In October 1981, as part of the Reagan administration's strategic forces modernization program, the decision to retire Titan II was made. The process had begun.

Does the historical significance of Launch Complex 374-7 rest solely on the fact that it was the site of one of the two most famous missile accidents at the time? Will historians of the future dwell on what could have or might have happened? Or will they see the final condition of the site, representative of fifty-three of the fifty-four operational Titan II complexes, as indicative of the powerful forces of the Cold War that were never unleashed?

The legacy of Launch Complex 374-7 for the children and young adults of the new millennium, who will have only the faintest recollections of the Cold War, is a lesson about tenacity. These young people will learn, should they carefully research the subject in order to form their own opinions, that our leaders and our populace spent the necessary time and money to deter what would most likely have truly been the war to end all wars. Using the best technology of the time and working hard to modify and upgrade the program systems, the Air Force fielded a weapons system that the Soviet Union was forced to respect. That the Titan II system is now retired having never been fired in anger is testimony to the dedication of civilian and military personnel alike. This dedication made the Titan II program work.

Thorncrown Chapel at Eureka Springs is a masterpiece of E. Fay Jones's organic architecture. *Photo by Helen Barry, courtesy of Arkansas Historic Preservation Program.*

E. FAY JONES AND THORNCROWN CHAPEL

Helen Barry

Thorncrown Chapel
1980
Eureka Springs, Carroll County
Nominated to the National Register of Historic Places on June 5, 1996

"Designed by E. Fay Jones and completed in July of 1980, Thorncrown Chapel was awarded the American Institute of Architects (AIA) Honor Award in 1981, and this recognition led, in part, to Jones's presentation with the AIA Gold Medal in 1990. Thorncrown Chapel is being submitted as part of the multiple-property submission *The Arkansas Designs of E. Fay Jones, Architect* and is being considered under Criterion C and Criterion Consideration G with national significance as an exceptional example of the work of the architect, an example that has led to national and international acclaim."

—From the National Register nomination

Thorncrown Chapel, located a few miles outside of Eureka Springs, Arkansas, is recognized as architect E. Fay Jones's most significant architectural achievement. Completed in July of 1980, Thorncrown Chapel received the renown of the architectural community with the American Institute of Architects (AIA) Honor Award in 1981. This recognition led, in part, to Jones's being presented the AIA Gold Medal in 1990.

Thorncrown Chapel is located on a hillside at an elevation of twenty-five hundred feet in a wooded, rather secluded site. Built of humble materials with a simple plan and of a modest size, the chapel is the most recognized and lauded of Jones's works. The popularity of Thorncrown Chapel has been greater than many ever dreamt, and thousands of people visit the chapel each year. Commissioned by James Reed, an Arkansas native who retired in Eureka Springs, the building was constructed at a cost of $250,000. The chapel was inspired during Mr. Reed's daily walks down the hill from his house to the mailbox, when he noticed that a number of people enjoyed visiting his property to take advantage of its panoramic view of the Ozarks. Rather than enclose his property to keep visitors out, he decided to build a glass meditation chapel where anyone could come enjoy the beauty of nature. A stranger in a restaurant who was eavesdropping on Reed's conversation directed him to consult with the architect Fay Jones. Architect and client soon developed an empathetic collaboration: Reed's notion that "we have something here that is very fragile . . . we don't want it destroyed" harmonized with Jones's belief in an "organic" architecture that could nourish the site.

Indeed, it was Reed's mandate that the building preserve "the spirituality of the place."[1]

An expression in glass and wood, Thorncrown Chapel was constructed out of two-by-four pieces of southern pine, as well as two-by-six and two-by-twelve pieces and large sheets of glass. While walking around the site during the design process, Jones realized that preservation of the woodland was essential. In order to ensure minimal disturbance of the wooded site, Jones decided that "no structural member, for example, could be larger than two men could carry through the woods." With this in mind the trusses were assembled on site, tilted into place, and then in-filled with glass. Using only standard-size lumber also helped to avoid the high cost of using premium wood. The constraints the site presented directly influenced the evolution of the simplicity of the structure. For instance, it was through the consideration of economic necessity that Jones discovered the use of the welded, x-shaped connectors for the two-by-fours, which create the diamond voids at the intersections of the cross-bracing.

Visitors approach the chapel from the southwest, winding along a tree-lined path. Blending in with the setting, the wood and glass chapel was hand-rubbed with stain until Jones thought the color matched the bark of the surrounding trees. One notices that the high, vertical nature of the chapel, which rises forty-eight feet, seems to respond to and reflect the surrounding wooded environment. The chapel is rectangular in form, only twenty-four feet wide and sixty feet long. The verticality of the structure is emphasized by the diamond-shaped voids between the hollow, metal joints. The repetitive pat-

PEACE FOUNTAIN

Architect Jones sketched this preliminary design for the Fulbright Peace Fountain at the University of Arkansas, Fayetteville, on the back of an envelope. *Courtesy of E. Fay Jones Papers, Special Collections Division, University of Arkansas Libraries, Fayetteville.*

tern leads the eye upward and further in, creating a play of pattern and light.

When one views Thorncrown Chapel from the side, the simplicity of the structure is even more apparent. Eighteen simple, wooden, structural members support the straight gable roof, which is crowned by a large skylight at the center of the ridge, visually opening the chapel roof to the sky above. To preserve the appearance of simplicity, low field-stone foundation walls house the heating and cooling ductwork for the structure, and air is distributed through holes in the mortar joints with the air return through floor grilles in the dais. This system of air-flow creates a "comfort zone" at the lower level of the chapel. The materials that Jones chose for the chapel interior are simple: flagstone floors, fieldstone walls, oak pews, blue cloth, and sculptural metal

pieces. The organic simplicity of his material selections allows the focus of the visitor to be uncluttered by a forced aesthetic and enables the contemplative mood that the chapel evokes. The choice of materials and site was something that Jones felt very strongly about, given his interest in the organic principles of Frank Lloyd Wright and his architectural and academic training.

A native Arkansan, Euine Fay Jones was born in 1921 and enrolled in the first class of the University of Arkansas architecture program in 1945. After graduating, Jones moved to Houston to accept a graduate teaching assistantship and fellowship at Rice University. While a student at Rice, Jones began closely following the career of architect Bruce Goff and made a special trip to meet him, which led him to accept the offer of a teaching position working under Goff at the University of Oklahoma, where he remained for three years until moving back to Arkansas to teach in 1953. It was during this time that Frank Lloyd Wright invited Jones to Taliesin West during an Easter break and followed the invitation with another to bring his wife, Gus, and their two daughters to spend the summer of 1953 at Taliesin in Wisconsin. Jones was to return for nine Easter visits and for Wright's birthday celebrations. Jones visited Wright at Taliesin West just a few days before his death in 1959.

Wright's work certainly had an influence on Jones's design scheme, and this is especially evident when one examines the "principles" of design that Jones aspires to manifest in his architecture—principles that are often associated with Wright. Very simply put, the first principle is the importance of the building-site relationship, the second is the idea that "the part is to the whole as the whole is to the part," and the third is the concept that the nature of the materials should be fully expressed in the structure. These three generative ideas have been a part of the design philosophy of "organic" architects throughout the late nineteenth and twentieth centuries. Thorncrown Chapel is an excellent example of a building that expresses these three design tenets. However, what makes Thorncrown exceptional is that Jones has brilliantly expressed a fourth, very personal notion: the idea of the power of the "operative opposite." To illustrate, the inspiration for the design of Thorncrown was traditional, European ecclesiastical Gothic architecture, yet Jones creates a Gothic building through employing quite opposite means. Traditionally, a Gothic building is supported by the compression created by the exterior buttress system. At Thorncrown, however, the walls are load bearing, and the intricate repetition of the crossed timber braces above the nave is the primary structural framing mechanism for the chapel. The buttress system in the Gothic manner of construction usually creates a heavy interior space, with the areas of light and penetration into the space further exaggerating the sense of mass and density. At Thorncrown the wood framing is so minimal that the visitor is enveloped in light, and the structure becomes an ornament for the natural environment around the chapel. Its light becomes dappled, with the rhythm and texture of the surroundings expressed in the layered quality of the structure and the cross-bracing forcing the eye upward. This layered quality is also evident in the attention that Jones devotes to every element of a building he designs. At Thorncrown the total esthetic experience is key, and every square inch is architect-designed, including the light fixtures, the door pulls, the lecterns, and benches. In Jones's words, "[E]very part, every piece has a part to play, and they join together to the benefit of all."[2]

While many of Jones's other buildings are more readily compared to the work of other "organic" architects, his chapels are unique and personal expressions, evolving far beyond their original inspiration. Although they take historic styles as their models, they are in no way "postmodern." They reflect a new way of expressing the tenets of organic architecture. Robert Twombly, a noted architectural scholar, writes that Jones's "chapels are among the century's most beautiful . . . [and] may be the most sensitive, elegant, and original interpretations of the Gothic in this nation's history."[3]

Notes:

1. Charles K. Gandee. "A Wayfarer's Chapel by Fay Jones." *Architectural Record* (March, 1981): 90.

2. ibid., 90–2.

3. Robert Twombly. *Power and Style*. (Canada: HarperCollins, 1995): 111.

◆ indicates County Seat

APPENDIX

Arkansas Listings on the National Register of Historic Places
(June 1999)

Note: Most houses listed on the National Register are private residences and are not open to the public.

ARKANSAS COUNTY

DEWITT

Arkansas County Courthouse, Southern District, Courthouse Square. 1931 Art Deco structure. 11/20/92.

DeWitt Post Office, 221 W. Cross St. 1939 structure featuring Depression-era mural. 08/14/98.

First United Methodist Church, Jefferson and Cross Sts. 1923 Classical Revival design by architect Charles L. Thompson. 09/04/92.

Halliburton House, 300 W. Halliburton. Circa-1850 home of prominent local politician. 11/05/74.

GILLETT

Arkansas Post National Memorial, eight miles southeast of Gillett via Hwys. 1 and 169. Site, between 1686 and 1865, of Spanish and French outposts and of battles during American Revolution and Civil War. Arkansas Post is a National Historic Landmark. NHL: 10/09/60. NR: 10/15/66.

SAINT CHARLES

Saint Charles Battle Monument, junction of Arkansas St. and Broadway. 1919 commemorative monument. 05/03/96.

Saint Charles Battle Site, junction of Hwy. 1 and White River. Site of June 17, 1862, naval and land battle. 12/02/74.

STUTTGART

Arkansas County Courthouse, Northern District, E. 3rd and S. College Sts. 1928 Classical Revival design. 11/20/92.

Riceland Hotel, 3rd and Main Sts. Designed in 1923 by Mann and Stern architectural firm in Neoclassical style. 05/21/86.

Standard Ice Company Building, 517 S. Main St. 1926 Spanish Colonial Revival structure. 07/02/79.

ADDRESS RESTRICTED

Menard-Hodges Mounds. Late prehistoric–1680s site containing Baytown and Mississippian components and evidence of early contact with Europeans. The Menard-Hodges Mounds are a National Historic Landmark. NHL: 04/11/89. NR: 10/31/85.

Roland Mound Site. 600–1500 A.D. site. 05/02/75.

ASHLEY COUNTY

CROSSETT

Crossett Experimental Forest Building Number Two, Hwy. 133 south of Crossett. Circa-1939 log structure built by Civilian Conservation Corps. 10/20/93.

Crossett Experimental Forest Building Number Six, Hwy. 133 south of Crossett. Circa-1940 novelty siding-clad structure erected by CCC. 10/20/93.

Crossett Experimental Forest Building Number Eight, Hwy. 133 south of Crossett. Circa-1940 wood-frame building constructed by CCC. 10/20/93.

Wiggins Cabin, city park. Circa-1845 double-pen log cabin. 09/04/84.

Naff House, Portland, Ashley County.

HAMBURG

First United Methodist Church, 204 S. Main St. 1910 church designed in Moorish variant of Gothic Revival style. 04/27/92.

Hamburg Presbyterian Church, Lincoln and Cherry Sts. 1871 Stick-style church adapted to Craftsman appearance around 1920. 05/14/91.

Watson House, 300 N. Cherry St. 1918 Classical Revival home of pioneer Hamburg family. 12/06/75.

Watson-Sawyer House, 502 E. Parker St. 1870 Greek Revival I-house with Italianate details. 12/06/75.

W. R. Bunckley House, 509 E. Parker St. 1903 Folk Victorian–style residence. 03/17/94.

PARKDALE

Dr. M. C. Hawkins House, 4684 Hwy. 8. 1912 Prairie-style design by architect Frank Gibb. 03/28/96.

Dr. Robert George Williams House, corner of Hwys. 8 and 209. 1903 home of prominent doctor. 10/04/84.

PORTLAND

Dean House, off Hwy. 165. Circa-1910 Charles L. Thompson Louisiana Raised Cottage design. 12/22/82.

John P. Fisher House, west of County Rd. 50 and north of Hwy. 278. Circa-1850 I-house. 09/29/95.

Naff House, 3rd Ave. and 1st St. Circa-1919 Prairie-style structure. 07/24/92.

Pugh House, off Hwy. 165. 1905–7 Thompson Classical Revival design. 12/22/82.

BAXTER COUNTY

BIG FLAT

Big Flat School Gymnasium, County Rd. 121 south of Hwy. 17. 1938 structure built by National Youth Administration. 11/19/93.

BUFORD

Buford School Building, Hwy. 126. 1936 Works Progress Administration–built educational structure. 09/04/92.

COTTER

Cotter Bridge, U.S. Hwy. 62 over White River. 1930 Marsh rainbow-arch bridge. The Cotter Bridge is a National Historic Civil Engineering Landmark. 04/04/90.

Old Cotter High School Gymnasium, 412 Powell St. 1936–38 structure built by WPA. 09/29/95.

MOUNTAIN HOME

Baxter County Courthouse, Courthouse Square. 1941–43 WPA-built structure. 05/26/95.

Case-Shiras-Dearmore House, 351 E. 4th St. 1880 Plain/Traditional–style home linked to prominent local families. 02/03/92.

Casey House, fairgrounds. Circa-1858 dogtrot structure built by pioneer, soldier, and politician. 12/04/75.

NORFORK

Davis House, southeast corner of Wolf St. and Hwy. 5. 1928 pyramid-roof cottage 03/23/95.

Jacob Wolf House, off Hwy. 5. Circa-1825 two-story, dogtrot log home of pioneer leader; oldest known standing structure in state. 04/13/73.

North Fork Bridge, Hwy. 5 over White River. 1927 steel-deck Warren-truss bridge. 04/09/90.

ADDRESS RESTRICTED

Old Joe Site. Circa-1500 rock art site. 05/04/82.

BENTON COUNTY

BELLA VISTA

Bella Vista Water Tank, Suits Us Dr. and Pumpkin Hollow Rd. Circa-1927 circular water-storage structure faced with field stone. 08/14/92.

Blackwell-Paisley Cabin, Suits Us Dr. 1924 vacation cabin. 01/28/88.

Bogan Cabin, Cedarcrest Mountain. Circa-1925 vacation cabin. 01/28/88.

Deaton Cabin, Suits Us Dr. Circa-1924 vacation cabin. 01/28/88.

Hagler-Cole Cabin, Mount Pisqua Dr. Circa-1920 vacation cabin. 01/28/88.

Lamberton Cabin, 8 N. Mountain. Circa-1920 vacation cabin with decorative board-and-batten band. 01/28/88.

New Home School and Church, McKisic Creek Rd. south of Bella Vista. Circa-1900 vernacular frame public building. 01/28/88.

Pharr Cabin, 2 N. Mountain. Circa-1920 vacation cabin. 01/28/88.

Princedom Cabin, Lookout Dr. Circa-1923 cabin later adapted as two-part residence. 01/28/88.

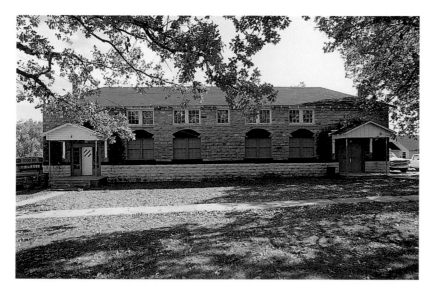

Big Flat School Gymnasium, Big Flat, Baxter County.

Sunset Hotel, off Hwy. 71. 1929 resort hotel. 08/14/92.

Sutherlin Cabin, 4 N. Mountain. Simple circa-1924 vacation cabin. 01/28/88.

Wonderland Cave, Dertmoor Rd. Natural cave adapted circa 1925 as nightclub. 01/28/88.

BENTONVILLE

Alden House, Rt. 1. Circa-1900 farmhouse with Eastlake and Colonial Revival details. 01/28/88.

Benton County Courthouse, 106 S.E. "A" St. Designed by Rogers architect A. O. Clark in Neoclassical style in 1928. 01/28/88.

Benton County Jail, 212 N. Main. Clark-designed 1911 Neoclassical structure. 01/28/88.

Benton County National Bank, 115 W. Central Ave. Designed by A. O. Clark in 1906 in Classical Revival style. 09/01/83.

Bentonville Confederate Monument, Public Square Park. 1908 commemorative sculpture. 04/26/96.

Bentonville High School, 410 N.W. 2nd St. 1928 design by architect John Parks Almand melds Spanish Colonial, Mission, and Mediterranean styles. 01/28/88.

Bentonville Third Street Historic District, first two blocks of S.E. 3rd St. Structures built between 1885 and 1926, including Craftsman, Italianate, Folk Victorian, and Stick-style architecture. 11/12/93.

Bentonville Train Station, 414 S. Main. Circa-1925 Frisco Line depot. 01/28/88.

Bentonville West Central Avenue Historic District, between S.W. "A" St. and S.W. "G" St. Forty-one structures built from 1885 to 1935. 10/22/92.

Bertschy House, 507 N.W. 5th St. Circa-1925 Craftsman bungalow. 01/28/88.

Blake House, 211 S.E. "A" St. Circa-1885 vernacular residence. 01/28/88.

Bogart Hardware Building, 112 E. Central Ave. Circa-1885 commercial structure. 01/28/88.

Braithewaite House, Old Bella Vista Hwy. Circa-1855 brick house; may be the oldest in county. 01/28/88.

Col. Samuel W. Peel House, Bentonville, Benton County.

Breedlove House and Water Tower, Rt. 4 east of Bentonville. Circa-1887 house with Italianate and Eastlake-style details; altered in 1907 to include Neoclassical porch; brick water tower added around 1920. 01/28/88.

Col. Samuel W. Peel House, 400 S. Walton Blvd. 1875 Italianate-style structure. 05/04/95.

Col. Young House, 1007 S.E. 5th St. Circa-1873 Italianate house. 01/28/88.

Craig-Bryan House, 307 W. Central Ave. Circa-1875 Italianate brick house. 01/28/88.

Daniels House, 902 E. Central Ave. Circa-1855 vernacular Greek Revival cottage. 01/28/88.

Elliott House, 303 S.E. 3rd St. 1887 Italianate structure. 01/20/78.

Henry-Thompson House, 302 S.E. 2nd St. Circa-1890 Italianate house. 01/28/88.

Jackson House, 207 W. Central Ave. Circa-1902 structure showing transition of Victorian styles to Neoclassical. 01/28/88.

James A. Rice House, 204 S.E. 3rd St. Circa-1879 Italianate house. 11/01/84.

Koons House, 409 N.W. 5th St. Circa-1908 vernacular house. 01/28/88.

Linebarger House, 606 W. Central Ave. Circa-1920 Craftsman bungalow. 01/28/88.

Macon-Harrison House, 309 N.E. 2nd St. 1910 home of applejack distiller. 01/28/88.

Massey Hotel, Hwy. 71 Business Rt. 1910 vernacular Neoclassical structure. 12/01/78.

Maxwell-Hinman House, 902 N.W. 2nd St. Circa-1881 Italianate house. 01/28/88.

Morris House, 407 S.W. 4th St. Circa-1855 central-hall cottage. 01/28/88.

Rice House, 501 N.W. "A" St. Circa-1890 house in Eastlake-style design. 01/28/88.

Roy's Office Supply Building, 110 E. Central Ave. Circa-1885 Italianate commercial building. 01/28/88.

Smith House, 806 N.W. "A" St. Circa-1925 rubble-stone-faced Tudor Revival design. 11/07/96.

Stroud House, southeast corner of S.E. "F" St. and E. Central Ave. 1903 structure with Colonial Revival and Queen Anne Revival elements. 05/10/96.

Terry Block Building, 101–103 N. Main. 1888 Italianate commercial structure. 05/13/82.

BETHEL HEIGHTS

Beasley Homestead, Hwy. 71. Circa-1927 Craftsman bungalow with Craftsman-influenced outbuildings. 01/28/88.

CAVE SPRINGS

Methodist Church, Hwys. 112 and 264. Circa-1895 vernacular church building. 01/28/88.

Shores Warehouse, Hwy. 112. Circa-1911 commercial building. 01/28/88.

DECATUR

Kansas City–Southern Depot, Hwy. 59. Circa-1920 Plain Traditional–style concrete-block building. 06/11/92.

GARFIELD

Garfield Elementary School, Hwy. 62. 1941 Rustic Revival–style stone building. 06/28/96.

Markey House, Rt. 1 near Garfield. Circa-1880 log house. 01/28/88.

GENTRY

Bank of Gentry, Main St. Richly detailed 1904 commercial structure. 01/28/88.

Carl House, 70 Main St. 1913 Craftsman bungalow with Prairie influences. 01/28/88.

Mitchell House, 115 N. Nelson. 1927 Craftsman bungalow. 01/28/88.

GRAVETTE

Bolin Barn & Smokehouse, southeast of Gravette on Spavinaw Creek Rd. Circa-1890 board-and-batten smokehouse. 01/28/88.

Kindley House, 503 Charlotte St. Circa-1873 Italianate brick house. 01/28/88.

HIWASSE

Banks House, west of Hiwasse on Hwy. 72. Circa-1900 double-pen frame house. 01/28/88.

Hiwasse Bank Building, Hwy. 279. Circa-1890 small-town commercial structure. 01/28/88.

LARUE

Coal Gap School, County Rd. 920. 1928 Plain Traditional–style building. 09/04/92.

LOGAN

Gailey Hollow Homestead, 1/4 mile east of Logan intersection. Circa-1910 double-pen house with six outbuildings. 01/28/88.

McIntyre House, Logan Rd. near Logan Community. Circa-1910 farmhouse with Queen Anne ornamentation. 01/28/88.

Lane Hotel, Rogers Commercial Historic District, Rogers, Benton County.

LOWELL

Green Barn, McClure St. Unusual circa-1910 barn. 01/28/88.

Pinkston-Mays Store Building, 107–109 Lackson St. Circa-1902 commercial building. 01/28/88.

MAYSVILLE

Coats School, Spavinaw Creek Rd. near Maysville. Circa-1905 one-room schoolhouse. 01/28/88.

Sellers Farm, Old Hwy. 43 on Oklahoma state line. Circa-1910 I-house with outbuildings. 01/28/88.

MONTE NE

Monte Ne, mostly beneath Beaver Lake. Remains of resort complex linked to W. H. "Coin" Harvey, idealist and reformer; site dates from 1890 to 1936. 02/17/78.

Oklahoma Row Hotel Site, Hwy. 94 spur near Monte Ne. Remains of circa-1909 hotel building linked to W. H. Harvey. 05/20/92.

Stack Barn, Hwy. 94 spur near Monte Ne. 1901 gable-roof livestock barn. 01/28/88.

NORWOOD

Norwood School, Norwood Rd. and Hwy. 16. Circa-1937 cut-stone school built by Works Progress Administration. 01/28/88.

OSAGE MILLS

Council Grove Methodist Church, Osage Mills Rd. Circa-1890 vernacular church. 01/28/88.

Osage Mills Dam, north of Osage Mills on Little Osage Creek. Circa-1890 stone dam; formerly site of grist mill. 01/28/88.

Piercy Farmstead, Osage Mills Rd. Vernacular Colonial Revival farmhouse built circa 1909; farmstead includes ten outbuildings. 01/28/88.

Rife Farmstead, Osage Mills Rd. 1920 Craftsman bungalow with two circa-1910 barns. 01/28/88.

PEA RIDGE

Miller Homestead, one-half mile east of Pea Ridge on Hwy. 94. Circa-1907 farmhouse with Classical details. 01/28/88.

Pea Ridge National Military Park, Hwy. 62. Site of March 7–8, 1862, Civil War battle. 10/15/66.

Shady Grove School, Hwy. 94 near Pea Ridge. Circa-1922 two-story frame school. 01/28/88.

PRAIRIE CREEK

Rocky Branch School, 200 N. Hwy. 303. Circa-1914 country school. 03/25/88.

ROGERS

Applegate Drugstore, 116 S. 1st St. 1905 structure designed by Rogers architect A. O. Clark; features intact commercial interior. 06/23/82.

Bank of Rogers Building, 114 S. 1st St. Designed by Clark in 1906 in Classical Revival style. 06/23/80.

Blackburn House, 220 N. 4th St. 1907 Neoclassical home of lumberman, philanthropist, and U.S. senator from Arkansas. 01/28/88.

Bryan House Number Two, 321 E. Locust St. Circa-1900 double-pen residence. 01/28/88.

Campbell House, 714 W. 3rd St. Circa-1893 Eastlake-style residence. 01/28/88.

Charles Juhre House, 406 N. 4th St. 1908 Colonial Revival/Classical Revival design by A. O. Clark. 02/25/93.

Drane House, 1004 S. 1st St. Circa-1890 I-house. 01/28/88.

Freeman-Felker House, 318 W. Elm St. Circa-1903 residence designed by Clark. 01/28/88.

James House, Rt. 2 south of Hwy. 71 between Rogers and Bentonville. Circa-1903 vernacular prow house. 01/28/88.

Kefauver House, 224 W. Cherry St. Circa-1920 Craftsman bungalow. 01/28/88.

Lane Hotel, 121 Poplar St. 1929 Spanish Colonial Revival structure. 01/28/88.

Lillard-Sprague House, Pleasant Grove Rd. 1907 frame prow house. 01/28/88.

Merrill House, 617 S. 6th St. Circa-1918 Prairie-style influenced house. 01/28/88.

Mutual Aid Union Building, 2nd and Poplar Sts. Designed by A. O. Clark and William E. Matthews around 1913 in Neoclassical style. 10/14/76.

Myler House, 315 N. 3rd St. Circa-1895 home of master mason. 01/28/88.

Parks-Reagan House, 420 W. Poplar St. 1898 Colonial Revival house. 01/28/88.

Raney House, 1331 Monte Ne. 1912 concrete block residence. 01/28/88.

Rife House, 1515 S. 8th St. Circa-1920 cast-concrete house. 01/28/88.

Rogers City Hall, 202 W. Elm St. Colonial Revival structure designed in 1929 by A. O. Clark. 01/28/88.

Rogers Commercial Historic District (as amended), bounded roughly by Walnut St., 1st St., Poplar St., and 2nd St. Structures built circa 1895 to circa 1938 and featuring styles ranging from Italianate to Art Moderne. Originally listed: 01/28/88. Amended: 09/30/93.

Rogers Post Office Building, 120 W. Poplar St. 1917 Colonial Revival building. 01/28/88.

Stroud House, 204 S. 3rd St. Clark-designed Colonial Revival adaptation of Eastlake-style house, circa 1912. 01/28/88.

Vinson House, 1016 S. 4th St. 1896 Eastlake cottage. 01/28/88.

SILOAM SPRINGS

Alfrey-Brown House, 1001 S. Washington. 1905 Colonial Revival residence of Methodist evangelist John E. Brown. 10/04/84.

Bratt-Smiley House, University and Broadway. Circa-1900 residence with Queen Anne and Colonial Revival details. 01/28/88.

Carl's Addition Historic District, S. College, W. Alpine and S. Wright, between Sager Creek and W. Twin Springs Ave. Structures from 1895 to 1946 in Queen Anne Revival, Craftsman, Colonial Revival, Folk Victorian, Tudor Revival and Mediterranean styles. 07/17/97.

Connelly-Harrington House, 115 E. University. Circa-1913 house with elements of Prairie, Craftsman, and Classical styles. 01/28/88.

Duckworth-Williams House, 103 S. College. Circa-1910 English Tudor Revival residence. 01/28/88.

First National Bank, 109 E. University. Circa-1890 Romanesque Revival structure. 01/28/88.

Fred Bartell House, 324 E. Twin Springs St. Circa-1900 Queen Anne house with Neoclassical details. 01/28/88.

German Builder's House, 315 E. Central. Circa-1880 I-house. 01/28/88.

Grand Army of the Republic Memorial, south end of Twin Springs Park. 1928 commemorative monument. 05/03/96.

Gypsy Camp Historic District, off Hwy. 59. Eight structures and associated landscape features in campground dating from 1921 to 1928. 01/28/88.

Henry Furniture Store Building, 107 W. University. Circa-1900 Classically influenced commercial structure. 07/15/94.

House at 305 East Ashley, 305 E. Ashley. Circa-1900 structure with Queen Anne and Classical elements. 01/28/88.

Illinois River Bridge, six miles east of Siloam Springs on County Rd. 3. 1922 solid-filled concrete bridge. 01/28/88.

Lakeside Hotel, 119 W. University St. 1881 commercial building. 11/15/79.

Maxwell-Sweet House, 114 S. College. 1921 Craftsman house. 01/28/88.

Oak Hill Mausoleum, west of junction of Benton St. and Hwy. 43. 1916 Neoclassical funerary structure. 12/06/96.

Pyeatte House, 311 S. Mount Olive St. 1932–34 English Revival design. 11/29/95.

Quell House, 222 S. Wright St. Circa-1920 bungalow. 01/28/88.

Reeves House, 321 S. Wright St. 1895 Queen Anne Revival–style residence. 09/07/95.

Siloam Springs City Park, W. University and Mount Olive. Circa-1890 city park. 01/28/88.

Siloam Springs Downtown Historic District, bounded by Sager Creek on the west, Ashley St. to the north, Madison Ave. to the east, and Twin Springs St. to the south. Containing sixty-five commercial and institutional structures built between 1890 and the mid-1940s. 05/26/95.

Simon Sager Cabin, John Brown University campus. Circa-1830 log home. 01/30/76.

Stockton Building, 113 N. Broadway. Vernacular 1894 commercial building. 01/28/88.

Thurmond House, 407 Britt. Circa-1910 American Foursquare house. 01/28/88.

SPRINGDALE

McCleod House, Rt. 1. north of Springdale. Circa-1866 I-house. 01/28/88.

SPRINGTOWN

Wasson House, Main St. Circa-1890 I-house. 01/28/88.

SULPHUR SPRINGS

Adar House, off Hwy. 59 near Sulphur Springs. 1897 house with Neoclassical details. 03/25/88.

Jones House, 220 Bush St. Circa-1896 Eastlake-style residence. 01/28/88.

Shiloh House, off Kibler St. 1927 Craftsman bungalow. 01/28/88.

Wee Pine Knot, 319 Spring St. 1918–19 Craftsman-style house with Rustic details. 01/21/99

TONTITOWN

Osage Creek Bridge, four and one-half miles north of Tontitown on County Rd. 71. 1911 Pratt through-truss bridge. 01/28/88.

VAUGHN

Douglas House, eight miles off Hwy. 12. Circa-1890 double-pen cottage. 01/28/88.

WAR EAGLE

War Eagle Bridge, County Rd. 98 over War Eagle River. 1907 Parker steel through-truss bridge, 10/19/85.

ADDRESS RESTRICTED

Goforth-Saindon Mound Group. 950–1550 A.D. Mississippian site. 01/23/86.

Haggard Ford Swinging Bridge, Harrison vicinity, Boone County.

BOONE COUNTY

BELLEFONTE

Missouri and North Arkansas Depot, Center St. and Keeter Dr. 1901 Plain Traditional–style depot. 06/11/92.

BERGMAN

Bergman High School, County Rd. 48. 1930 Craftsman-style educational structure. 09/10/92.

EVERTON

Everton School, Main St. 1939 Works Progress Administration–built structure. 09/10/92.

HARRISON

Boone County Courthouse, Courthouse Square. 1909 Classical Revival design by architect Charles L. Thompson. 07/21/76.

Boone County Jail, Central and Willow. 1914 Mediterranean Revival design by Thompson. 12/12/76.

Grubb Springs School, northeast corner of Hwys. 43 and 397 near Harrison. Vernacular stone school built between 1892 and 1896. 03/29/96.

Haggard Ford Swinging Bridge, over Bear Creek eight miles north of Harrison at Cottonwood Rd. 1938–41 suspension bridge built by WPA. 06/30/95.

Harrison Courthouse Square Historic District, bordered by N. Walnut, W. Ridge, N. Willow, and W. Stephenson. Featuring examples of late nineteenth- and early twentieth-century commercial architecture. 05/06/99.

Hotel Seville, northwest corner of Vine and Ridge. 1929 Spanish Revival structure. 05/19/94.

VALLEY SPRINGS

Valley Springs School, 1 School St. 1940 WPA-built structure. 09/10/92.

Ederington House, Warren, Bradley County.

BRADLEY COUNTY

WARREN

Adams-Leslie House, Rt. 1 south of Warren. 1903–4 Folk Victorian–style house. 08/09/79.

Bailey House, 302 Chestnut St. Circa-1900 home of local druggist and Confederate veteran. 08/28/75.

Bradley County Courthouse and County Clerk's Office, Courthouse Square. 1903 structure with Classical styling. 12/12/76.

Davis-Adams House, 509 N. Myrtle St. Circa-1860 I-house with 1890s Folk Victorian embellishments. 02/18/99.

Dr. John Wilson Martin House, 200 Ash St. Built between 1860 and 1868 in vernacular interpretation of Greek Revival style. 12/27/90.

Ederington House, 326 S. Main. 1926–27 H. Ray Burks Craftsman design. 06/21/84.

Saint Luke's Catholic Church, 508 W. Pine St. 1907 Gothic Revival–style building. 05/29/98.

Warren and Ouachita Valley Railway Station, 325 W. Cedar St. 1909 frame depot; rebuilt after 1911 fire. 08/03/77.

CALHOUN COUNTY

HAMPTON

Calhoun County Courthouse, Courthouse Square. 1909 building with Classical and Colonial Revival details. 12/12/76.

Dunn House, Hwy. 4. 1909 Colonial Revival home of pioneer family. 05/04/76.

THORNTON

State Highway 274 Bridge, Hwy. 274 over Little Cypress Creek. 1940 timber-trestle bridge. 05/18/95.

ADDRESS RESTRICTED

Boone's Mounds. 600–1700 A.D. mound site. 04/14/80.

Keller Site. 600–1200 A.D. Coles Creek and Caddoan site. 10/29/79.

CARROLL COUNTY

BEAVER

Beaver Bridge, Hwy. 187 over White River. Wire-cable suspension bridge built in 1943 by Pioneer Construction Co. of Malvern. 09/06/90.

BERRYVILLE

Berryville Agricultural Building, off Freeman Ave. 1940 stone-veneer structure. 09/10/92.

Berryville Gymnasium, off Freeman Ave. 1936–37 Works Progress Administration–built educational building. 09/10/92.

Berryville Post Office, 101 E. Madison Ave. 1938 structure featuring Depression-era mural. 08/14/98.

Carroll County Courthouse, Eastern District, Public Square. 1880 public structure enlarged to present appearance in 1904 and 1905. 08/27/76.

BLUE EYE

Mo-Ark Baptist Academy, south of west end of Park St. 1918 educational structure. 09/27/96.

CARROLLTON

Yell Masonic Lodge, off Hwy. 68. 1876 vernacular meeting house. 11/01/84.

CISCO

W. D. Crawford House, County Rd. 27 one mile north of County Rd. 98. Circa-1900 stone building linked to important area educator. 11/20/92.

EUREKA SPRINGS

Eureka Springs Historic District (as amended), most of the area in Eureka Springs. Virtually intact late nineteenth- and early twentieth-century health resort community. Originally listed: 12/18/70. Amended: 01/29/79.

Lake Leatherwood Dam, end of County Rd. 61. 630-foot-long cut-stone dam built between 1938 and 1940 by WPA and CCC. 08/12/92.

Lake Leatherwood Park Historic District, County Rd. 61. Circa-1938 ensemble of recreational and construction structures. 11/24/98.

Lake Leatherwood Recreational Structures, end of County Rd. 61. 1938–40 Civilian Conservation Corps–built bathhouse and barbecue pit. 08/12/92.

Yell Masonic Lodge, Carrollton, Carroll County.

Sam Epstein House, Lake Village, Chicot County.

Mulladay Hollow Bridge, County Rd. 61 over Mulladay Hollow Creek. Two-span masonry-arch bridge built in mid-1930s. 04/06/90.

Tall Pines Motor Inn, Hwy. 62 and Pivot Rock Rd. Rustic-style 1947 tourist court. 01/15/99.

OSAGE

Dog Branch School, off Hwy. 412. 1898 stone building with Italianate and Romanesque Revival details. 09/08/92.

Stamps Store, Hwy. 103 and Old Hwy. 68. 1899–1902 vernacular stone Romanesque Revival commercial building. 09/05/90.

WINONA SPRINGS

Winona Church/School, Rockhouse Rd. south of Hwy. 62. Circa-1886 vernacular Greek Revival church. 06/05/91.

CHICOT COUNTY

DERMOTT

Dermott Bank and Trust Co. Building, northwest corner of N. Arkansas and E. Iowa. 1910 Classical Revival structure. 05/19/94.

Walker House, 606 Main St. 1918 Charles L. Thompson Craftsman design. 12/22/82.

EUDORA

American Legion Post Number 127 Building, Cherry and Armstrong Sts. 1934 Rustic-style structure built by Works Progress Administration. 10/08/92.

Dr. A. G. Anderson House, Duncan and Main Sts. Circa-1901 central-hall board-and-batten house. 07/24/92.

First Baptist Church, Hwy. 159 S. 1900 church of black congregation; rebuilt after 1946 storm damage. 06/03/98.

P & J Liberto-Rosa Portera Building, Main St. 1921 commercial building linked to Italian community. 10/08/92.

GRAND LAKE

A. Landi General Merchandise Building, Hwy. 8. Circa-1920 wood-frame commercial building owned by Italian immigrants. 10/08/92.

LAKE VILLAGE

Carlton House, 434 S. Lakeshore Dr. Circa-1906 vernacular Colonial Revival house. 06/05/91.

John Tushek Building, 108 Main St. 1906 vernacular Beaux Arts–style commercial building. 08/05/93.

Lake Village Confederate Monument, Lakeshore Dr. median between Main and Jackson. 1910 commemorative sculpture. 05/03/96.

Lake Village Post Office, 206 S. Cokley St. 1938 structure featuring Depression-era mural. 08/14/98.

New Hope Baptist Church Cemetery, Historic Section, Saint Mary's St. Early twentieth-century graves are oldest historic resource associated with town's black community. 09/21/92.

Sam Epstein House, 488 Lakeshore Dr. Circa-1910 home of prominent Jewish citizen. 09/21/92.

SHIVES

Lakeport Plantation, three miles southwest of Shives off Hwy. 142. Circa-1850 plantation house. 11/20/74.

CLARK COUNTY

AMITY

Old Bank of Amity, northwest corner of square. Circa-1906 commercial structure with Italianate influences. 06/05/91.

ARKADELPHIA

Arkadelphia Confederate Monument, courthouse lawn. 1911 commemorative sculpture. 05/03/96.

Bozeman House, Hollywood Rd. at Hwys. 26 and 51. Circa-1847 Greek Revival structure. 11/14/78.

Capt. Charles C. Henderson House, 10th and Henderson. 1906 Queen Anne–style home with circa-1920 Craftsman and Neoclassical additions. 08/24/98.

Clark County Courthouse, 4th and Crittenden. 1899 structure designed by Charles L. Thompson in Romanesque style. 12/01/78.

Clark County Library, 609 Caddo St. 1903 Classical Thompson design. 11/05/74.

Domestic Science Building, 11th and Haddock. 1917 Thompson Colonial Revival design. 12/22/82.

Flanagin Law Office, 320 Clay St. 1855 office of Confederate governor of Arkansas. 12/22/77.

Hudson-Jones House, ten miles east of Arkadelphia on State Rd. 2. Circa-1840 Greek Revival I-house with associated outbuildings. 09/30/82.

James E. M. Barkman House, 406 N. 10th St. Circa-1860 house combines Greek and Gothic Revival styles. 07/30/74.

Magnolia Manor, six-tenths of a mile southwest of I-30 and Hwy. 51. 1857 house with Greek Revival and Italianate characteristics. 09/27/72.

Missouri-Pacific Depot, S. 5th St. Circa-1917 Mediterranean-style depot. 06/11/92.

Rose Hill Cemetery, 1200 block of Main St. Historic burial ground. 02/01/99.

Dr. Boaz House, Clear Spring, Clark County.

Sheeks House, Corning, Clay County.

CLEAR SPRING

Dr. Boaz House, State Rd. 26 near Clear Spring. Circa-1891 dogtrot residence. 01/28/92.

FENDLEY

Loy Kirksey House, County Rd. 59 near Fendley. Circa-1895 dogtrot residence. 02/03/92.

GURDON

Gurdon Jail, corner of W. Joslyn and Front Sts. 1907 lumber-town jail. 11/24/89.

Horace Estes House, 614 E. Main St. 1934 Tudor Revival–style residence. 09/21/93.

June Sandidge House, 811 Cherry St. 1935 English Revival–style structure. 02/25/93.

Missouri-Pacific Depot, near junction of N. 1st and E. Walnut Sts. Circa-1917 Mediterranean-style structure. 06/11/92.

OKOLONA

Clear Springs Tabernacle, State Rd. 36 and Bobo Rd. near Okolona. Circa-1887 religious meeting shelter. 02/13/92.

PRESCOTT VICINITY

Little Missouri River Bridge, County Rd. 179 across Little Missouri River. Camelback Pratt through-truss bridge from early twentieth century. 04/09/90.

ADDRESS RESTRICTED

Bayou Sel. Prehistoric Native American site; location of historic salt refinery. 09/10/74.

Habicht-Cohn-Crow House. 1870 Greek Revival structure. 10/03/85.

Ross Site. 1200–1400 A.D. Caddoan site. 10/10/85.

CLAY COUNTY

CORNING

Oliver House, 203 W. Front St. Circa-1880 structure altered in 1901 and 1909 to include Classical details. 12/08/78.

Sheeks House, 502 Market St. 1879 home of prominent local lawyer and businessman. 08/22/75.

KNOB

Knob School and Masonic Lodge, Hwy. 145. 1923 Craftsman school shared since construction with Masonic lodge. 05/30/91.

PIGGOTT

Pfeiffer House and Carriage House, 10th and Cherry Sts. Family home of novelist Ernest Hemingway's wife from 1927 through 1940; site where he wrote much of *A Farewell to Arms.* 06/10/82.

Piggott Post Office, 119 N. 3rd St. 1937 structure featuring Depression-era mural. 08/14/98.

RECTOR

Scatterville Cemetery, County Rd. 404 west of Hwy. 90 near Rector. Last vestige of antebellum community; contains graves dated from 1857 through 1931. 03/31/95.

SAINT FRANCIS

Chalk Bluff, two miles north of Saint Francis on Saint Francis River. Site of antebellum river community and of May 1 and 2, 1863, Civil War battle. 10/29/71.

SUCCESS

Baynham House, Stephens St. 1911 frame house from town's hey-day as lumbering community. 08/31/78.

Waddle House, west side of S. Erwin. 1909 home of pioneer doctor. 03/28/77.

CLEBURNE COUNTY

HEBER SPRINGS

Clarence Frauenthal House, 210 N. Broadway. 1914 Craftsman-style residence, 11/19/93.

Cleburne County Courthouse, Courthouse Square. 1914 Classical Revival courthouse. 07/12/76.

Dr. Cyrus F. Crosby House, 202 N. Broadway. 1912 structure featuring Prairie and Craftsman influences. 11/19/93.

Hugh L. King House, 110 W. Spring St. 1893–94 Queen Anne house built onto circa-1882 structure. 09/08/92.

T. E. Olmstead & Son Funeral Home, 108 S. 4th St. 1910 cut-stone mortuary building. 12/13/95.

Women's Community Club Band Shell, northeast corner of Spring Park. 1933 structure of native stone and concrete. 08/16/94.

IDA

Dill School, State Hwy. 5/25 west side, north of Ida. 1938 one-story, stone-constructed building. 08/16/94.

Women's Community Club Band Shell, Heber Springs, Cleburne County.

QUITMAN

Quitman High School Building, Hwy. 25. 1938 National Youth Administration–built structure. 09/04/92.

Quitman Home Economics Building, 2nd Ave. 1938 NYA-built educational building. 09/04/92.

CLEVELAND COUNTY

NEW EDINBURG

Attwood-Hopson House, State Hwy. 8, north side. Circa-1890 one-and-one-half story Queen Anne–style residence; redesigned in 1917 to reflect Craftsman-style architecture. 08/16/94.

Barnett-Attwood House, northeast of New Edinburg. 1835–36 log dogtrot house. 07/29/77.

Marks' Mills Battlefield Park, junction of Hwys. 8 and 97. Commemorates April 25, 1864, Civil War battle. The Marks' Mills Battlefield is part of the Camden Expedition National Historic Landmark. NHL: 04/19/94. NR: 01/21/70.

RISON

Cleveland County Clerk's Building, fairgrounds. 1902 frame office of county clerk. 01/31/76.

Cleveland County Courthouse, Main and Magnolia. 1911 Beaux Arts structure. 04/11/77.

Mount Olivet Methodist Church, fairgrounds. 1867 vernacular Greek Revival church. 12/01/75.

WOODLAWN

Wesley Chapel, Hwy. 15. 1872 structure with restrained Greek Revival design. 12/07/95.

COLUMBIA COUNTY

ATLANTA

William H. Smith House, north of junction of Hwy. 98 and County Rd. 85. Circa-1857 Greek Revival residence. 11/27/92.

Cleveland County Courthouse interior, Rison, Cleveland County.

BUSSEY

Frog Level, near Bussey. 1854 plantation house. 09/22/72.

CALHOUN

Harvey C. Couch School, northeast of intersection of Calhoun Rd. and County Rd. 25. 1928 Craftsman-style structure. 06/08/93.

MAGNOLIA

Columbia County Courthouse, Court Square. 1905 Renaissance Revival structure. 04/15/78.

Columbia County Jail, Calhoun and Jefferson. Circa-1920 Charles L. Thompson Second Renaissance Revival design. 12/22/82.

Couch-Marshall House, 505 W. Monroe St. Circa-1840 house expanded to Plain Traditional/Queen Anne Revival appearance circa 1890. 07/24/92.

Dr. H. A. Longino House, 317 W. Main St. Early Craftsman structure built in 1910. 06/14/82.

Kate Turner House, 709 W. Main St. 1904 house with Queen Anne and Colonial Revival details. 08/26/82.

Old Alexander House, northeast of Magnolia. 1855 raised dogtrot house. 01/09/79.

Ozmer House, Hwy. 82 bypass at Southern Arkansas University Farm. 1883 dogtrot cabin. 11/20/86.

RICHLAND

Mount Prospect Methodist Church, intersection of County Rds. 446 and 61. 1886 vernacular Greek Revival church. 03/22/90.

SPOTVILLE

W. H. Allen House, northwest of Spotville off Hwy. 98. 1873 dogtrot house; later enclosed and expanded. 10/14/76.

CONWAY COUNTY

CLEVELAND

Cleveland School Cafeteria Building, County Rd. 511. Circa-1930 Craftsman-style structure. 09/10/92.

MORRILTON

Aycock House, 401 W. Church. 1904 house with Queen Anne and Colonial Revival details. 05/13/76.

Coca-Cola Building, 211 N. Moose. 1929 Colonial Revival/Art Deco Charles L. Thompson design. 12/22/82.

Conway County Library, 101 W. Church. 1916 structure with Mediterranean details. 04/15/78.

County Courthouse, Moose and Church Sts.. 1929–30 late Classical Revival structure. 11/13/89.

Cox House, Bridge St. 1871 house with Greek Revival and Italianate influences. 10/22/74.

First National Bank of Morrilton, Main at Moose. Circa-1925 Classical Revival and Craftsman design by Charles L. Thompson. 12/22/82.

Moose House, 711 Green St. Circa-1868 frame house of prominent Morrilton family. 10/22/74.

Kate Turner House, Magnolia, Columbia County.

Morrilton Post Office, 117 N. Division St. 1936 structure featuring Depression-era mural. 08/14/98.

Morrilton Railroad Station, Railroad Ave. Circa-1915 depot. 09/13/77.

Saint Anthony's Hospital, 202 E. Green St. 1937 Art Deco hospital designed by Little Rock architect A. N. McAninch. 03/28/86.

PETIT JEAN MOUNTAIN

Cedar Creek Bridge, Hwy. 154 over Cedar Creek. 1934 masonry deck-arch bridge. 04/09/90.

Trinity Lutheran Church, approximately seven miles south of Atkins off Hwy. 154. 1887 frame church. 12/13/76.

PLUMERVILLE

Plumerville School, Arnold St. Circa-1925 church made into school in 1939 by Works Progress Administration. 09/10/92.

Plummer's Station, south of Plumerville on Gap Creek. Home of pioneer that began as 1830s log cabin; altered over years to present appearance. 08/11/75.

WINROCK

Administrative Office, Hwy. 154 at Petit Jean State Park. Circa-1935 Civilian Conservation Corps–built Rustic-style structure. 05/28/92.

Blue Hole Road Historic District, Blue Hole Rd. at Petit Jean State Park. Circa-1935 set of eleven CCC-built culverts, a guard rail, and a retaining wall. 05/28/92.

Cabins One, Six, Nine, and Sixteen, campground access road at Petit Jean State Park. Circa-1935 Rustic-style, CCC-built structures. 05/28/92.

Cedar Falls Trail Historic District, adjacent to main access road at Petit Jean State Park. Three footbridges and nine sets of stone steps built by the CCC around 1935. 05/28/92.

Concrete Log Bridge, Hwy. 154 at Petit Jean State Park. Circa-1935 CCC-built concrete bridge. 05/28/92.

Culvert Number One, Hwy. 154 at Petit Jean State Park. Circa-1935 stone-box culvert surrounded by stone work. 05/28/92.

First National Bank of Morrilton, Morrilton, Conway County.

Lake Bailey–Lake Roosevelt Historic District, east and north of Hwy. 154 at Petit Jean State Park. Circa-1935 CCC-built lakes, waterfall, structures, walls, and steps. 05/28/92.

Mather Lodge, main access road at Petit Jean State Park. Circa-1935 stone-and-log building constructed by CCC. 05/28/92.

Office Headquarters, Hwy. 154 at Petit Jean State Park. Circa-1935 Rustic-style structure. 05/28/92.

Water Treatment Building, off Hwy. 154 at Petit Jean State Park. Circa-1935 building designed in Rustic style. 05/28/92.

ADDRESS RESTRICTED

Eleven Rock Art Sites. Dating from around 1500. 05/04/82.

CRAIGHEAD COUNTY

DIXIE

Craighead County Road 513C Bridge, County Rd. 513C over unnamed ditch one and one-half miles east of Dixie, east of County Rd. 669 junction. 1942 steel-truss deck bridge. 05/18/95.

JONESBORO

Bell House, 303 W. Cherry. 1895 Queen Anne residence. 11/07/76.

Berger-Graham House, 1327 S. Hampton St. 1904 house joining Classical Revival and Richardsonian Romanesque styles. 10/10/85.

Berger House, 1120 S. Main St. 1896 residence of early Jonesboro businessman. 11/07/96.

Craighead County Courthouse, Western District, 511 N. Main St. 1934 Art Deco–style public building. 09/11/98.

Frierson House, 1112 S. Main St. Circa-1885 house linked to Francis Cherry's successful run for governor. 04/24/73.

Nash-Reid-Hill House, 418 W. Matthews Ave. Ornate Queen Anne–style structure built circa 1898-1902; renovated around 1934 to present appearance. 08/16/94.

West Washington Avenue Historic District, 500–626 Washington Ave. Structures built from 1890 to 1930 include American Foursquare, Queen Anne, Classical Revival, Tudor Revival, and Spanish Revival styles. 10/22/82.

LAKE CITY

Saint Francis River Bridge, Hwy. 18 over Saint Francis River. 1934 I-beam, vertical-lift span bridge. 04/09/90.

ADDRESS RESTRICTED

Bay Mounds. 1200–1400 A.D. site. 02/14/78.

CRAWFORD COUNTY

CEDARVILLE

Cedarville School Building, County Rd. 523. 1931 educational structure. 09/10/92.

West Washington Avenue Historic District, Jonesboro, Craighead County.

Bob Burns House, Van Buren, Crawford County.

CHESTER

Col. Jacob Yoes Building, Front St. 1887 structure from railroad boom days. 06/05/75.

Number Twelve School, east of County Rd. 402 six miles west of Chester. Circa-1895 one-room schoolhouse. 01/04/96.

COVE CITY

Lee Creek Bridge, Hwy. 220 over Lee Creek. Late nineteenth-century Pennsylvania through-truss bridge. 04/09/90.

MOUNTAINBURG

Frog Bayou Bridge, Hwy. 282 over Frog Bayou. 1942 Parker steel through-truss bridge. 05/26/95.

MULBERRY

Mulberry Home Economics Building, Church St. 1939 National Youth Administration–built structure. 09/10/92.

NATURAL DAM

Crawford County Road 32D Bridge, County Rd. 32D over Cove Creek. 1937 open-masonry substructure bridge. 05/26/95.

Lee Creek Bridge, Hwy. 59 over Lee Creek. 1930s Pennsylvania steel-truss bridge. 04/06/90.

RUDY

Cedar Creek Bridge, Hwy. 348 over Cedar Creek. 1938 steel Pratt through-truss bridge. 05/26/95.

UNIONTOWN

Slack-Comstock-Marshall Farm, north of Hwy. 220. Plain Traditional–style farmhouse built between 1885 and 1918 and related historic outbuildings. 06/09/95.

VAN BUREN

Bob Burns House, 821 Jefferson. 1885 frame house; home of 1930s radio and movie star. 04/30/76.

Bryan House, 105 Fayetteville St. 1886 Queen Anne Revival structure. 01/09/78.

Clarke-Harrell-Burson House, Parkview St. behind City Heights Methodist Church on Fayetteville Rd. 1841–42 Greek Revival home of early newspaper publisher. 05/14/91.

Dr. Charles Fox Brown House, 420 Drennan St. 1867 house joining Greek Revival and Italianate styles. 09/06/78.

Drennan-Scott House, Drennan Reserve, N. 3rd St. 1836 home of town founder. 09/10/71.

Fairview Cemetery, Confederate Section, southwest of junction of McKibben and 10th Sts. Civil

War–era burial ground for dead southern troops. 12/06/96.

Henry Clay Mills House, 425 N. 15th St. Circa-1892 home of former slave who later became successful entrepreneur. 12/16/77.

Joseph Starr Dunham House, 418 Broadway. Circa-1870 "carpenter Gothic" house. 05/03/76.

Mount Olive United Methodist Church, Lafayette and Knox Sts. 1889 vernacular Gothic Revival church of black congregation. 07/30/76.

Van Buren Confederate Monument, 3rd and Main Sts. 1899 commemorative sculpture. 04/26/96.

Van Buren Historic District, six blocks of Main St. Commercial structures from 1880 through 1900. 04/30/76.

Van Buren Post Office, 22 S. 7th St. 1936 structure featuring Depression-era mural. 08/14/98.

Wilhauf House, 109 N. 3rd St., rear. Circa-1838 Greek Revival house. 08/27/74.

ADDRESS RESTRICTED

High Rock Petroglyph Shelter. Circa-1500 rock art site. 05/04/82.

CRITTENDEN COUNTY

EARLE

George Berry Washington Memorial, Hwy. 149 north of Earle. Sculpted funerary memorial atop 1928 grave of prominent African-American landowner and preacher. 08/11/94.

Missouri-Pacific Depot, Main and Commerce Sts. 1922 passenger and freight depot. 03/06/86.

MARION

Crittenden County Bank and Trust, south side of Military Rd. 1919 Neoclassical building. 04/19/84.

Crittenden County Courthouse, 85 Jackson St. 1910–11 structure with Classical Revival influences. 08/03/77.

SUNSET

Marion Colored High School, west of Hwy. 77. 1924 African-American high school erected through Julius Rosenwald Fund support. 03/23/95.

WEST MEMPHIS

Dabbs Store, 1320 S: Avalon. 1912 commercial structure. 05/20/82.

Hamilton Apartments, 113 W. Danner St. 1936 structure with Craftsman and English Revival details. 06/03/98.

George Berry Washington Memorial, Earle vicinity, Crittenden County.

Giboney-Robertson-Stewart House, Wynne, Cross County.

Lawrie House, 600 N. 7th St. 1939 Colonial Revival–style residence. 03/28/96.

CROSS COUNTY

LEVESQUE

Capt. Isaac N. Deadrick House, northwest of junction of Hwys. 64 and 163. Circa-1850 home of Confederate cavalry officer. 09/16/93.

PARKIN

Parkin Archeological State Park, off Hwy. 64. Mississippian site from 1300 to 1600; believed to have been visited by Hernando DeSoto expedition in 1541. The Parkin Site is a National Historic Landmark. NHL: 07/19/64. NR: 10/15/66.

WYNNE

Giboney-Robertson-Stewart House, 734 Hamilton Ave. Circa-1895 Queen Anne–style residence. 06/05/98.

Grace Episcopal Church, corner of Garland and Poplar. 1917–18 English Parish–style church with Colonial Revival and Craftsman elements. 03/03/92.

Isaac Block House, 404 E. Hamilton St. 1885 Queen Anne–style structure moved from Wittsburg around 1900. 07/15/98.

Woman's Progressive Club, Rowena St. and Merriman Ave. 1937 civic-club building erected by Works Progress Administration. 03/27/90.

Wynne Post Office, 402 E. Merriman Ave. 1936 structure featuring Depression-era mural. 08/14/98.

DALLAS COUNTY

CARTHAGE

Bank of Carthage, Hwy. 229. 1907 Charles L. Thompson Classical Revival design. 12/22/82.

Garrison House, south of Hwy. 48. Circa-1861 braced-frame structure. 10/28/83.

Hampton Springs Cemetery, off Hwy. 48. Black section contains graves dating to at least 1916. 10/28/83.

Mount Zion Methodist Church, northeast of Carthage. 1910 vernacular Greek Revival church. 10/28/83.

DALARK

Henry Atchley House, off Hwy. 8. 1908 Plain/Traditional design. 10/28/83.

FAIRVIEW

Thomas Homestead, off Hwy. 7 between Dalark and Sparkman. 1910 wood-frame dogtrot and eight historic outbuildings. 03/27/84.

FORDYCE

Amis House, 2nd St. Circa-1900 frame I-house. 10/28/83.

Charlotte Street Historic District, four blocks of Charlotte St. Houses built from 1910 to 1930, including many Craftsman Bungalows. 09/14/87.

Cotton Belt Railroad Depot, Main and 1st Sts. 1925 Mediterranean/Craftsman structure. 06/11/92.

Dallas County Courthouse, 3rd and Oak Sts. 1911 Classical Revival structure. 03/27/84.

Dr. Waters House, 515 Oak St. 1907 Thompson Colonial Revival design. 12/22/82.

Elliott House, 309 Pine St. 1925 Craftsman Bungalow. 03/27/84.

Fielder House, Hwy. 79B. 1875 dogtrot that evolved into present structure; novelist Harold Bell Wright wrote part of *Trail of the Lonesome Pine,* the first outdoor technicolor feature film, in this house. 10/28/83.

First Presbyterian Church, 212 W. 4th St. 1912 Collegiate Gothic structure. 10/28/83.

First United Methodist Church, E. 4th and Spring Sts. 1925 church designed by architect John Parks Almand. 10/28/83.

Fordyce Home Accident Insurance Co., 300 Main St. 1908 Romanesque/Classical Revival design by Charles L. Thompson. 12/22/82.

Jessie B. Smith House, 200 Charlotte St. Circa-1890 central-hall-plan structure. 10/28/83.

John Russell House, 904 Charlotte St. 1925 Craftsman structure with elaborate porch detailing. 10/28/83.

Old Fordyce Post Office, north side of E. 2nd St. 1890 brick commercial structure. 10/28/83.

Rock Island Depot, 3rd St. Circa-1925 railroad depot. 10/28/83.

Wynne House, 4th and Pine Sts. Circa-1914 Classical Revival design. 10/28/83.

Welch Pottery Works, Address Restricted, Dallas County.

HOLLY SPRINGS

Captain Goodgame House, Hwy. 128. 1918 structure is only historic building remaining in town. 10/28/83.

JACINTO

Mount Carmel Methodist Church, Hwy. 9. Circa-1900 Greek and Gothic Revival church. 10/28/83.

PINE GROVE

Brazeale Homestead, southeast of Hwy. 128. Complex of eleven structures dating from 1850 to 1900. 10/28/83.

Ed Knight House, off Hwy. 128. Circa-1861 dogtrot structure that evolved to current appearance. 10/28/83.

PRINCETON

George W. Mallett House, off Hwy. 8. Circa-1853 dogtrot cabin that evolved to present appearance. 10/28/83.

Princeton Cemetery, off Hwy. 9. Graves date to 1849. 03/27/84.

Princeton Methodist Church, Hwy. 9. Circa-1905 church with cross-gable roofline. 10/28/83.

SPARKMAN

Sardis Methodist Church, northeast of Pine Grove off Hwy. 128. Circa-1895 wood-frame church. 10/28/83.

TULIP

Butler-Matthews Homestead, southwest of Tulip off Hwy. 9. Sixteen structures dating from 1850s to 1930s. 10/28/83.

Tulip Cemetery, off Hwy. 9. Contains graves dating to 1842. 10/28/83.

ADDRESS RESTRICTED

Bird Kiln. 1843 pottery kiln site. 05/29/75.

Culbertson Kiln. 1858 pottery kiln site. 05/29/75.

Welch Pottery Works. 1851 pottery kiln site. 05/12/75.

Womack Kilns. 1891 pottery kiln site. 06/10/75.

Temple Meir Chayim, McGehee, Desha County.

DESHA COUNTY

ARKANSAS CITY

Arkansas City Commercial Historic District, DeSoto Ave. and Sprague St. Commercial buildings from 1900 to 1910. 02/18/99.

Arkansas City High School, Robert S. Moore Ave. and President St. 1910 Renaissance Revival school. 10/04/84.

Desha County Courthouse, Robert S. Moore Ave. 1900 Romanesque Revival structure. 07/12/76.

Thane House, Levy and 1st Sts. 1919 Charles L. Thompson Craftsman design. 12/22/82.

Xenophon Overton Pindall Law Office, corner of Capitol and Kate Adams. Circa-1882 Italianate-style law office of Arkansas governor. 05/10/99.

DUMAS

Dr. J. D. Watts House, 205 W. Choctaw St. Circa-1909 structure with Queen Anne and Colonial Revival elements. 12/04/94.

McKennon–Shea House, 206 Waterman St. Circa-1910 home of early Dumas entrepreneur, cotton planter, and landowner. 06/08/93.

Merchants and Farmers Bank, Waterman and Main Sts. 1912 Charles L. Thompson Classical Revival design. 12/22/82.

MCGEHEE

Missouri-Pacific Depot, Railroad St. Circa-1910 Mediterranean/Craftsman–style structure. 06/11/92.

Parnell-Sharpe House, 302 N. 2nd St. 1936 French Eclectic–style house. 09/28/89.

Temple Meir Chayim, 4th and Holly. 1947 synagogue with Romanesque/Mission–style design. 04/22/99.

ROHWER

Rohwer Relocation Center Site, off Hwy. 1. Location of Japanese-American relocation camp from 1942 to 1945. The Rohwer Relocation Center Memorial Cemetery is a National Historic Landmark. NHL: 07/06/92. NR: 07/30/74.

DREW COUNTY

LACEY

Veasey-DeArmond House, fifteen miles south of Monticello on Hwy. 81. Circa-1850 vernacular Greek Revival farmhouse. 09/14/89.

MONTICELLO

Drew County Courthouse, 201 S. Main St. 1932 Classical Moderne–style building. 10/17/97.

Garvin Cavaness House, 404 S. Main St. 1906 Classical Revival residence. 05/23/80.

Hotchkiss House, 577 N. Boyd. Circa-1895 house designed by architect S. C. Hotchkiss to reflect a variety of styles. 12/12/76.

Lambert House, 204 W. Jackson. 1905 Colonial Revival structure. 12/22/83.

Veasey-DeArmond House, Lacey, Drew County.

First United Methodist Church, Conway, Faulkner County.

Monticello Confederate Monument, Oakland Cemetery. 1915 commemorative monument. 04/26/96.

Monticello North Main Historic District, N. Main St. area. Twenty structures dating from 1845 to 1925 and reflecting several styles. 02/02/79.

Monticello Post Office, 221 W. Gaines St. 1937 structure featuring Depression-era sculpture. 08/14/98.

Robert Lee Hardy House, 207 S. Main St. 1908–9 Colonial Revival residence. 04/26/82.

Saint Mary's Episcopal Church, 115 S. Main St. 1906 Gothic Revival–style church building. 04/04/96.

NEW HOPE

Champ Grubbs House, Hwy. 172 west of New Hope. 1859 log dogtrot structure. 11/20/92.

SELMA

Selma Methodist Church, north of Hwy. 4. Circa-1874 vernacular Gothic Revival church. 09/22/72.

TILLAR

Frank Tillar Memorial Methodist Episcopal Church, South, W. Railroad St. north of Hwy. 277. 1913 Classical Revival–style structure. 06/04/97.

WINCHESTER

Taylor Log House and Site, Hwy. 138. Features circa-1846 cypress-log dogtrot house, historic cemetery, and plantation farmstead site. 10/16/95.

FAULKNER COUNTY

BARNEY

Blessing Farmstead, east of Hwy. 107 on east fork of Cadron Creek. Circa-1900 log-and-frame dogtrot with outbuildings. 09/05/90.

CONWAY

Brown House, 1604 Caldwell St. 1900 Charles L. Thompson Colonial Revival style. 12/22/82.

Cadron Settlement, five miles west of Conway on Arkansas River. Site of prehistoric Indian activity, French fur trade in late 1700s, and first permanent white settlement in central Arkansas. 05/17/74.

Conway Confederate Monument, Robinson Ave. and Center St. 1925 commemorative sculpture. 04/26/96.

D. O. Harton Jr. House, 607 Davis St. 1913 American Foursquare structure with Colonial Revival influences. 07/19/96.

Farmers State Bank, 1001 Front St. 1918 Classical Revival Thompson design. 12/22/82.

Faulkner County Courthouse, 801 Locust St. 1936 structure combining Colonial Revival and Art Deco styles of architecture. 11/27/95.

Faulkner County Jail, Courthouse Square. 1896 jail converted to library circa 1938. 07/20/78.

First United Methodist Church, Prince and Clifton Sts. 1913–15 Classical Revival–style building. 11/20/92.

Frank E. Robins House, 567 Locust. 1922 Colonial Revival–style home of newspaper publisher. 05/20/94.

Frank U. Halter House, 1355 College Ave. 1905 Colonial Revival home of major contractor. 08/29/80.

Frauenthal & Schwarz Building, 824 Front St. 1879 commercial structure altered to present appearance around 1925. 10/23/92.

Fraunthal House, 631 Western. 1913 Colonial Revival Charles L. Thompson design. 12/22/82.

Galloway Hall, Hendrix College Campus. 1912 Tudor Revival Thompson design. 12/22/82.

Greeson–Cone House, 928 Center St. 1920–21 Craftsman bungalow. 09/07/95.

Harton House, 1821 Robinson. 1890 home of leading local merchant blending Queen Anne and Classical Revival styles. 05/25/79.

J. E. Little House, 427 Western Ave. Circa-1919 Neoclassical-style home of plantation owner. 01/26/99.

Martin Hall, Hendrix College Campus. 1918 Collegiate Gothic Charles L. Thompson design. 12/22/82.

Michael M. Hiegel House, 504 2nd St. Circa-1911 Tudor Revival–style home of prominent businessman. 08/14/98.

O. L. Dunaway House, 920 Center St. 1923 Prairie-style residence. 07/19/96.

President's House, Hendrix College Campus. 1913 Craftsman design by Charles L. Thompson. 12/22/82.

S. G. Smith House, 1837 Caldwell St. 1924 Colonial Revival Thompson design. 12/22/82.

Young Memorial, north of Reynolds Science Hall on Hendrix College campus. 1920 monument honoring World War I casualties from Hendrix. 07/19/96.

GUY

Guy High School Gymnasium, Hwy. 25. 1938 Works Progress Administration–built structure. 09/10/92.

Guy Home Economics Building, Hwy. 25. 1936 building erected with WPA labor. 09/10/92.

HAMLET

Liberty School Cafeteria, Hwy. 36. 1935 Plain Traditional–style school building. 09/10/92.

SPRINGFIELD

Springfield Bridge, County Rd. 222 at Cadron Creek. 1871 iron bowstring-arch bridge; oldest bridge in Arkansas. 07/21/88.

TWIN GROVES

Solomon Grove Smith-Hughes Building, south of County Rd. 29. 1938–39 school building of local African-American community. 12/09/94.

WOOSTER

Patton House, Hwy. 25. 1918 Craftsman-style residence. 09/30/93.

FRANKLIN COUNTY

ALTUS

Altus Well Shed/Gazebo, northwest corner of N. Franklin and E. Main. Circa-1920 octagonal gazebo built atop railroad well. 09/12/96.

Center Cross School, County Rd. 95. 1930 wood-frame school. 10/08/92.

Church of Our Lady of Perpetual Help, north of Saint Mary's Mountain. 1902 basilica-style church. 05/03/76.

Wiederkehr Wine Cellar,
Altus, Franklin County.

German-American Bank, Main and N. Franklin.
1905 vernacular Italianate structure. 09/13/90.

Missouri-Pacific Depot, 118 Hwy. 64. Circa-1920
Plain Traditional–style depot. 07/08/92.

O'Kane-Jacobs House, Rossville Rd. 1881 farmhouse with unusual lattice-porch detailing. 05/14/91.

Wiederkehr Wine Cellar, Saint Mary's Mountain.
Circa-1880 wine cellar with circa-1900 addition.
05/02/77.

CASS

**Gray Spring Recreation Area/Forest Service
Road 1003 Historic District,** Forest Service Rd.
1003. Picnic area, culverts, and road built in 1934 and
1935 by Civilian Conservation Corps. 09/11/95.

CHARLESTON

Franklin County Courthouse, Southern District,
Hwy. 22. 1923 design by Frank W. Gibb features
Classical details. 10/18/76.

OZARK

Bristow Hotel, 112 S. 2nd St. 1909 vernacular commercial building. 02/18/99.

The Cabins, Manitou Mountain. Circa-1904 vacation
structure with four log cabins sharing common floor
and roof. 04/13/77.

First Methodist Episcopal Church, South, 503
W. Commercial. 1909 Gothic Revival structure.
09/04/92.

Franklin County Courthouse, 211 W. Commercial.
1904 structure remodeled to current appearance in
1944. 09/22/95.

Franklin County Jail, 3rd and River Sts. 1914 vernacular native-stone building. 06/23/82.

Missouri-Pacific Depot, River St. 1910 stone-
masonry depot. 06/11/92.

WEBB CITY

Shelton-Rich Farmstead, Rt. 3 off Hwy. 23
between Caulksville and Ozark. Circa-1880 Midland
Tradition two-story log house with outbuilding and
well. 11/20/89.

FULTON COUNTY

CAMP

Camp Methodist Church, Hwy. 9 six miles east of
Salem. Single-story, wood-frame structure built around
1878. 05/09/97.

GEPP

County Line School and Lodge, northwest of
Gepp, west of Baxter-Fulton county line, and two
miles south of Arkansas-Missouri line. Circa-1879 two-
story frame school. 03/27/75.

MAMMOTH SPRING

Kansas City, Fort Scott and Memphis Railroad Depot, Mammoth Spring State Park. 1885 Queen Anne–style structure. 06/11/92.

Saint Andrew's Episcopal Church, Hwy. 9. 1888 Gothic Revival church. 11/26/86.

T. H. Morris House, 6th and Bethel Sts. 1908 American Foursquare house. 09/13/90.

GARLAND COUNTY

BEAR CITY

Harley E. Green House, north of Bear City. 1885 vernacular Eastlake-style cottage. 07/19/79.

CRYSTAL SPRINGS

Camp Clearfork Historic District, south of Hwy. 270 west of Crystal Springs. Featuring a dam, cabins, buildings, and a lake constructed circa 1935 by the Civilian Conservation Corps. 10/21/93.

Charlton Bathhouse, north of Hwy. 270 west of Crystal Springs. Circa-1938 CCC-built stone structure. 10/20/93.

Kansas City, Fort Scott and Memphis Railroad Depot detail, Mammoth Spring, Fulton County.

Charlton Spillway/Dam, north of Hwy. 270 west of Crystal Springs. Circa-1938 dam built by CCC. 10/21/93.

Mayberry Springs, south of Hwy. 270 west of Crystal Springs. Circa-1895 vernacular residence on site of early Garland County resort and stagecoach inn. 09/05/90.

FOUNTAIN LAKE

South Fork Bridge, next to Hwy. 128 near intersection with Hwy. 5, spanning Saline River. 1928 concrete closed-spandrel arch bridge. 04/09/90.

HOT SPRINGS

Bathhouse Row, north side of Central Ave. between Reserve and Fountain Sts. Eight bathhouses dating from 1911 to 1935. Bathhouse Row is a National Historic Landmark. NHL: 05/28/87. NR: 11/13/74.

Belding-Gaines Cemetery, Hwy. 270 east of Hot Springs. Burial place of Hot Springs pioneers Ludovicus Belding and William H. Gaines. 02/25/93.

Bill Clinton Boyhood Home, 1011 Park Ave. 1896–1900 Queen Anne house remodeled to Tudor Revival appearance in 1938; Clinton's home from 1954 to 1961. 05/18/95.

Carpenter Dam, 1398 Carpenter Dam Rd. 1929–31 concrete gravity dam that created Lake Hamilton. 09/04/92.

Charles N. Rix House, 628 Quapaw Ave. 1907 structure linked to prominent local banker. 10/15/92.

Citizens Building, 723 Central Ave. 1911–12 office building. 08/09/79.

Confederate Section, Hollywood Cemetery, near junction of Hollywood Ave. and Mote Rd. 1900 burial plot featuring 1919 fieldstone monument. 12/06/96.

Doherty House, 705 Malvern Ave. 1907 house with Queen Anne details. 11/14/78.

Dr. Williams Mansion, 420 Quapaw Ave. 1891 structure with Colonial and Gothic Revival details. 11/30/78.

First Presbyterian Church, 213 Whittington. 1907 Charles L. Thompson Gothic Revival design. 12/22/82.

Carpenter Dam, Hot Springs, Garland County.

Fordyce House, 746 Park Ave. Circa-1910 Thompson Colonial Revival design. 12/22/82.

Forest Service Headquarters Historic District, south of intersection of Winona and Indiana Sts. Six Plain Traditional–style structures built circa 1933 by CCC. 10/20/93.

Garland County Courthouse, Ouachita and Hawthorne. 1909 Renaissance Revival structure with 1930 jail addition in rear. 12/06/79.

George Klein Tourist Court Historic District, 501 Morrison St. Collection of nine circa-1940 Craftsman-style structures. 06/08/93.

Hot Springs Central Avenue Historic District, Park to Prospect on Central Ave. Historic hotels, stores, restaurants, and office buildings erected between 1886 and 1930. 06/25/85.

Hot Springs Confederate Memorial, Landmark Plaza. 1934 commemorative sculpture. 04/26/96.

Hot Springs High School, Oak St. between Orange and Olive. 1914 Late Gothic Revival building with 1925 addition. 01/28/88.

Hot Springs Railroad Warehouse Historic District, 401–439 Broadway. Collection of two 1900 to 1920 brick warehouse structures. 05/27/96.

Interstate Orphanage, 339 Combs. 1928 Charles L. Thompson Craftsman design. 12/22/82.

Jones School, Linwood and Hobson Aves. 1913 Neoclassical structure. 05/05/88.

Medical Arts Building, 236 Central. 1929 Art Deco skyscraper; tallest in Arkansas until 1960s. 12/01/78.

Missouri-Pacific Railroad Depot, Broadway and Market Sts. Circa-1917 Italianate/Mediterranean–style structure. 06/11/92.

Old Post Office, Convention Blvd. 1901 Renaissance Revival building. 04/12/90.

Park Hotel, 210 Fountain. 1930 Charles L. Thompson Spanish Colonial Revival design. 12/22/82.

Passmore House, 846 Park Ave. 1873 Second Empire–style house. 10/08/76.

Riviera Hotel, 719 Central. Circa-1930 Chicago School Thompson design. 10/08/76.

Saint Luke's Episcopal Church, Spring and Cottage Sts. 1925 Thompson Gothic Revival design. 12/22/82.

Short-Dodson House, 755 Park Ave. Circa-1902 Queen Anne residence. 05/03/76.

Stitt-Patterson House, 824 Park Ave. 1877 house with Queen Anne and Italianate details. 05/03/76.

Visitors Chapel A.M.E., 319 Church St. 1913 structure mixing Gothic Revival and Classical Revival styles. 06/02/95.

Wade Building, 231 Central. 1927 Thompson Classical Revival design. 12/22/82.

Walter Beauchamp House, 492 Prospect Ave. 1905 "double-decker" style residence. 05/19/94.

W. H. Moore House, 906 Malvern St. Circa-1895 house synthesizing Queen Anne and Colonial Revival styles. 03/27/90.

Wildwood, 808 Park Ave. 1884 Queen Anne house. 10/08/76.

William H. Martin House, 815 Quapaw Ave. 1904 Colonial and Classical Revival home of prominent lawyer; designed by Little Rock architect Frank Gibb. 06/11/86.

Woodman of Union Building, 501 Malvern Ave. 1923 structure erected by African-American social club/union/fraternity. 06/27/97.

JESSIEVILLE

Iron Springs Dam, Hwy. 7 north of Jessieville. Circa-1933 fieldstone structure built by Civilian Conservation Corps. 10/21/93.

Iron Springs Shelter Number One, Hwy. 7 north of Jessieville. Circa-1933 CCC-built log structure. 10/20/93.

Iron Springs Shelter Number Three, Hwy. 7 north of Jessieville. Circa-1933 CCC-built log structure. 10/20/93.

ROYAL

Gillham House, County Rd. 584 north of junction with Hwy. 270. Circa-1866 log dogtrot residence. 03/17/94.

ADDRESS RESTRICTED

Couchwood. Circa-1939 concrete sculptures by Dionicio Rodriguez. 12/04/86.

Little Switzerland. Circa-1939 concrete sculptures by Rodriguez. 12/04/86.

W. C. Brown House. Queen Anne house remodeled in 1919 into Neoclassical style. 10/16/86.

GRANT COUNTY

LEOLA

Jenkins' Ferry Battleground, northeast of Leola on Hwy. 46. Site of April 30, 1864, battle as Union troops retreated to Little Rock during Red River Campaign. The Jenkins' Ferry battlefield is part of the Camden Expedition National Historic Landmark. NHL: 04/19/94. NR: 01/21/70.

Jenkins' Ferry Battleground, Leola vicinity, Grant County.

Gulf Oil Company Service Station, Paragould, Greene County.

OAK GROVE

Oak Grove School, south of Hwy. 270. 1938 frame Craftsman school built by Works Progress Administration. 06/14/91.

SHERIDAN

Dr. John L. Butler House, 313 Oak St. 1914 Colonial Revival structure. 10/09/86.

Glaser-Kelly House, 310 N. Oak St. Circa-1920 Craftsman bungalow linked to local merchant and doctor. 01/23/92.

GREENE COUNTY

PARAGOULD

Beisel-Mitchell House, 420 W. Court St. 1930 Spanish Colonial Revival–style structure. 09/27/96.

Eight Mile Creek Bridge, Hwy. 135 over Eight Mile Creek. 1929 Pratt pony-truss bridge. 04/06/90.

Greene County Courthouse, Courthouse Square. 1888 Beaux Arts–style structure. 08/11/76.

Gulf Oil Company Service Station, junction of Main and S. Third Sts. 1927 gas station designed in Craftsman style of architecture with Mediterranean-style influences. 08/16/94.

Jackson-Herget House, 206 S. 4th St. Queen Anne–style home of prominent businessman. 07/24/92.

National Bank of Commerce Building, 200 S. Pruett St. 1923 Classical Revival design. 05/14/93.

Old Bethel Methodist Church, west of Paragould off Hwy. 141. 1901 frame church structure. 04/19/78.

Paragould War Memorial, 3rd and Court Sts. 1924 memorial honoring World War I veterans. 06/20/97.

WALCOTT

Bathhouse, main service center area access road at Crowley's Ridge State Park. Log-and-frame building erected circa 1935 by the Civilian Conservation Corps. 05/28/92.

Bridge, main service area access road at Crowley's Ridge State Park. Circa-1935 native-stone masonry-arch vehicular and pedestrian bridge built by CCC. 05/28/92.

Comfort Station, campground and cabin area access road at Crowley's Ridge State Park. CCC-built circa-1935 single-story log structure. 05/28/92.

Dining Hall, employee housing area access road at Crowley's Ridge State Park. Circa-1935 CCC-built structure. 05/28/92.

HEMPSTEAD COUNTY

COLUMBUS

Columbus Presbyterian Church, Hwy. 73. Circa-1875 vernacular Greek Revival church. 11/17/82.

HOPE

Bill Clinton Birthplace, 117 S. Hervey St. Circa-1915 house where President Clinton lived for first four years of his life. 05/19/94.

Brundidge Building, W. 2nd St. Circa-1893 Romanesque Revival commercial building. 03/27/90.

Carrigan House, 704 W. Ave. "B." Circa-1893 frame home of noted local lawyer. 07/20/78.

E. S. Greening House, 707 E. Division St. 1903 house with Queen Anne influences and elaborate interior. 07/09/87.

Ethridge House, 511 N. Main St. 1894 house, remodeled in 1912; home of veteran Hope educator Mabel Ethridge. 12/01/93.

Foster House, 303 N. Hervey St. Circa-1912 Charles L. Thompson Craftsman design. 12/22/82.

Foster House, 420 S. Spruce St. 1918 American Foursquare house with Prairie and Craftsman influences. 06/05/91.

Hempstead County Courthouse, northwest corner of 5th and Washington. 1939 Art Deco–style building. 05/19/94.

Hope Historic Commercial District, bounded by Union-Pacific tracks, Louisiana St., 3rd St., and Walnut St. Contains commercial structures built between 1880 and 1945. 07/28/95.

McRae House, 1113 E. 3rd St. Circa-1917 Charles L. Thompson Prairie-style design. 12/22/82.

Missouri-Pacific Railroad Depot, E. Division and Main Sts. Circa-1917 Mediterranean-style structure. 06/11/92.

North Elm Street Historic District, bounded by Union-Pacific tracks, Hervey St., Ave. "G,"and Hazel St. Structures from 1890 to 1945 designed in Queen Anne Revival/Folk Victorian, Colonial Revival, Prairie, English Revival, Craftsman, and traditional building styles. 07/28/95.

North Washington Street Historic District, eastern half of western blocks along N. Washington between "B"and "E" Sts. Features Folk Victorian, Craftsman, Colonial Revival, and Prairie-style structures built between 1900 and 1945. 07/28/95.

Saint Mark's Episcopal Church, 3rd and Elm Sts. 1904 church in simplified Gothic Revival style. 05/06/76.

Nesburt T. Ruggles House, Shover Springs, Hempstead County.

Gatewood House, Malvern,
Hot Spring County.

Ward-Jackson House, 122 N. Louisiana. Circa-1903 Folk Victorian structure. 09/14/89.

MCCASKILL

Dr. Thomas S. Jacques House, County Rd. 339 near McCaskill. Circa-1875 vernacular Greek Revival farmhouse. 11/10/89.

OZAN

Goodlett Gin, three miles west of Ozan on Hwy. 4. 1883 steam-powered cotton gin. 01/17/75.

SHOVER SPRINGS

Nesburt T. Ruggles House, east side of Hwy. 32. Unusual 1912–14 bungalow design. 12/09/94.

WASHINGTON

Confederate State Capitol, Main St. 1840 wood-frame courthouse that housed Confederate state government from 1863 to 1865. The Confederate State Capitol is part of the Camden Expedition National Historic Landmark. NHL: 04/19/94. NR: 05/19/72.

Grandison D. Royston House, Alexander St. Circa-1830 Greek Revival house. 06/21/71.

Washington Confederate Monument, Presbyterian Cemetery off Hwy. 4 on west side of Washington. 1888 commemorative memorial. 12/06/96.

Washington Historic District, city limits of Old Washington. Structures built from 1830 to 1915 in Greek Revival and various Victorian-era styles. 06/20/72.

HOT SPRING COUNTY

BISMARCK

Hodges House, Hwy. 7. 1907 Folk Victorian–style home of local historians and archeologists. 06/02/95.

JONES MILL

Remmel Dam, Remmel Dam Rd. 1923–24 flat-slab buttress dam that created Lake Catherine. 09/04/92.

MALVERN

Alderson-Coston House, 204 Pine Bluff St. 1923 Craftsman bungalow with extensive landscape features. 05/26/95.

Bank of Malvern, 212 S. Main St. 1889 Richardsonian Romanesque structure partially rebuilt in more modern style after 1896 fire. 03/13/87.

Clark House, 1324 S. Main St. 1916 Charles L. Thompson Craftsman design. 12/22/82.

Gatewood House, 235 Pine Bluff St. 1905 vernacular interpretation of Shingle style. 07/24/92.

Hot Spring County Courthouse, 210 Locust. 1936 Art Deco–style building. 11/07/96.

Missouri-Pacific Depot, 1st St. Circa-1918 Mediterranean-style structure. 06/11/92.

Pine Bluff Street Historic District, between Bois D'Arc and McNeal Sts. Residences built between 1890s and 1940s. 02/16/99.

Strauss House, 528 E. Page. 1919 Charles L. Thompson Dutch Colonial design. 12/22/82.

SAGINAW

Morrison Plantation Smokehouse, off I-30 at Donaldson. Circa-1854 hexagonal rock smokehouse from antebellum plantation complex. 12/28/77.

SHOREWOOD HILLS

Bridge Number Two, Hwy. 171 west of Slunger Creek at Lake Catherine State Park. Circa-1935 single-span bridge built by Civilian Conservation Corps. 05/28/92.

Cabin Number One, cabin area access road at Lake Catherine State Park. 1941 Rustic-style CCC-built structure. 04/20/95.

Cabins Numbers Two and Three, cabin area access road at Lake Catherine State Park. Circa-1935 structures built by CCC. 05/28/92.

Nature Cabin, camping area access road at Lake Catherine State Park. Circa-1935 log building erected by CCC. 05/28/92.

SOCIAL HILL

Blakely House, west of Social Hill on Hwy. 84. 1874 dogtrot house. 05/03/76.

ADDRESS RESTRICTED

Jones Mill Site. Site features evidence of Archaic, Fourche Maline, and Caddo culture periods; dates from 6000 B.C. to 1200 A.D. 09/12/88.

Lake Catherine Quarry. Site of aboriginal mining of black novaculite. 09/11/75.

HOWARD COUNTY

CENTER POINT

Adam Boyd House, east of Center Point on Hwy. 26. Circa-1848 dogtrot house altered to present appearance circa 1926. 05/13/76.

Nashville American Legion Building, Nashville, Howard County.

Clardy-Lee House, Hwy. 26. Circa-1873 vernacular Greek Revival residence. 11/10/77.

Ebenezer Campground, north of Center Point off Hwy. 4. Circa-1854 Methodist campground. 03/26/76.

Russey-Murray House, south of Center Point on Hwy. 4. Circa-1851 brick house. 05/04/76.

MINERAL SPRINGS

Memphis, Paris and Gulf Depot, City Park. 1908 wood-frame railroad structure. 12/04/78.

NASHVILLE

Elbert W. Holt House, 902 N. Main St. 1910 Colonial Revival structure. 09/20/84.

First Christian Church, N. Main St. 1911 Gothic Revival structure. 11/04/82.

First Presbyterian Church, 2nd and Hempstead Sts. 1912 building with Gothic and Stick-style elements. 05/04/76.

Flavius Holt House, Kohler St. Pre-1877 vernacular Greek Revival building used as inn. 12/01/78.

Garrett Whiteside Hall, junction of N. Third Ave. and Lockesburg St. 1940 single-story frame gymnasium designed in Plain Traditional style with minimal Colonial Revival–style influences. 11/21/94.

Howard County Courthouse, Main St. 1939 Art Moderne courthouse built by Public Works Administration. 06/14/90.

Nashville American Legion Building, Hwy. 27. 1933–34 stone Civil Works Administration structure. 09/13/90.

Nashville Post Office, 220 N. Main St. 1937 structure featuring Depression-era mural. 08/14/98.

Womack-Parker House, 903 N. Main St. Circa-1878 central-hall structure with historic outbuildings. 12/01/78.

INDEPENDENCE COUNTY

BATESVILLE

Adler House, 292 Boswell St. Circa-1915 Charles L. Thompson Craftsman design. 12/22/82.

Bartlett-Kirk House, 910 College St. 1890 Queen Anne Revival–style structure. 08/16/94.

Batesville Commercial Historic District (as amended), Main and Central Sts. Historic commercial and public structures erected between 1877 and 1940. Originally listed: 10/07/82. Amended: 10/05/90.

Batesville Confederate Monument, corner of S. Broad and W. Main. 1907 commemorative monument. 05/03/96.

Batesville East Main Historic District (as amended), Main St. between 7th and 11th Sts. Residences built between 1870 and 1930 in Plain Traditional, Craftsman, Colonial Revival, Queen Anne, and Italianate styles. Originally listed: 12/22/83. Amended: 12/27/96.

Bethel African Methodist Episcopal Church, 895 Oak St. 1882 church with 1910 addition housed city's first black congregation. 10/16/86.

Capt. John T. Warner House, 822 E. College St. 1879 home of prominent river captain, lawyer, and mayor. 09/02/82.

Charles R. Handford House, 658 E. Boswell St. 1888 Folk Victorian house. 05/02/75.

Cook-Morrow House, 875 Main St. 1909 home of wealthy planter and merchant. 07/29/77.

Dowdy Building, 154 S. 3rd St. Circa-1918 design by architect Theo Sanders. 12/22/82.

Edward Dickinson House, 672 E. Boswell St. Circa-1875 Gothic Revival residence. 11/26/86.

Garrott House, 561 E. Main St. 1842 residence. 06/24/71.

Glenn House, 653 Water St. Circa-1850 structure altered over decades with Greek Revival and Victorian details. 05/02/75.

James S. Handford House, 659 E. Boswell St. 1888 Folk Victorian house; mirror image of 658 E. Boswell St. 05/02/75.

Batesville Commercial Historic District, Batesville, Independence County.

Luster Urban Farmstead, 487 N. Central Ave. 1885 wood-frame I-house with outbuildings. 09/16/83.

Mitchell House, 1138 Main St. 1917 Charles L. Thompson Craftsman design. 12/22/82.

Morrow Hall, 7th and Boswell Sts. 1872 structure originally housed Arkansas College. 10/18/72.

National Guard Armory, 380 S. 9th St. 1936 Ozark sandstone structure designed with Art Deco and Gothic Revival influences by architect Peter Blaauw. 05/29/98.

Saint Paul's Parish Church, 5th and Main Sts. 1916 Thompson Gothic Revival design. 12/22/82.

Spring Mill, five miles north of Batesville on Hwy. 69. Circa-1869 grist mill. 03/01/74.

Wheel Store, River and Broad Sts. 1887 commercial structure linked to agrarian reform organization formed in Arkansas. 12/08/88.

Wycough-Jones House, 683 Water St. Circa-1878 residence with Victorian-era features. 05/02/75.

DESHA

Wyatt House, Hwy. 25 and Gainer Ferry Rd. Circa-1870 dogtrot expanded to I-house configuration around 1900. 03/05/99.

JAMESTOWN

Jamestown School, Hwy. 230. 1926 Plain Traditional building with Craftsman details. 09/04/92.

LOCUST GROVE

Locust Grove School, Hwy. 230. Circa-1935 educational structure. 09/04/92.

MOOREFIELD

Moorefield School, north side of Ham St. 1936–37 National Youth Administration–built structure. 09/04/92.

NEWARK

Dearing House, Hwy. 122. Circa-1890 frame house that received second story in 1914. 05/03/76.

OIL TROUGH

Hulsey Bend School, east of junction of Hwys. 122 and 14 on Freeze Bend Rd. Circa-1900 one-room schoolhouse. 02/12/99.

PFEIFFER

Pfeiffer House, Hwy. 167. 1924 vernacular Craftsman house. 05/01/89.

A. C. Jeffery Farmstead, Mount Olive vicinity, Izard County.

ROSIE

Cedar Creek Bridge, County Rd. 235 over Cedar Creek, one and one-half miles south of Hwy. 14. 1941 closed-spandrel deck-arch bridge. 05/18/95.

THIDA

Thida Grove School, County Rd. 20. Circa-1920 school building. 09/04/92.

ADDRESS RESTRICTED

Franklin Desha House. Circa-1847 weatherboarded dogtrot house linked to important Arkansas families. 10/09/86.

Goff Petroglyph Site. Circa-1500 rock art site. 05/04/75.

Wyatt Petroglyphs Site. Circa-1500 rock art site. 05/04/82.

IZARD COUNTY

BOSWELL

Boswell School, County Rd. 196. 1934 Works Progress Administration–built school. 09/18/92.

Sylvester Smith Farmstead, County Rd. 10. 1922–23 structures built by rural entrepreneur. 09/08/92.

BROCKWELL

Pine Ridge School Building, County Rd. 237. Circa-1920 stone school building. 03/07/94.

CALICO ROCK

Calico Rock Historic District (as amended), Main St. Commercial structures from 1903 to 1935. Originally listed: 11/19/85. Amended: 10/26/89.

Calico Rock Home Economics Building, 2nd St. 1940 National Youth Administration–built structure. 09/10/92.

MELBOURNE

Izard County Courthouse, Hwy. 69 at Courthouse Square. Art Deco structure built between 1938 and 1940 by National Youth Administration. 09/30/93.

Jumbo Church of Christ, four miles northwest of intersection of Sylamore and Jumbo Rds. 1927–8 vernacular church building. 02/18/99.

Philadelphia Methodist Church, County Rd. 1796 north of Melbourne. 1858 frame church. 09/29/76.

Rector Log Barn, County Rd. 218 northwest of State Hwy. 9. Circa-1855 log-and-frame barn. 06/03/93.

MOUNT OLIVE

A. C. Jeffery Farmstead, County Rd. 18 north of Mount Olive. Circa-1848 I-house with related out-buildings. 08/11/94.

SAGE

Caney Springs Cumberland Presbyterian Church, northwest of junction of Hwy. 289 and County Rd. 70. 1889 one-room frame structure. 06/09/95.

JACKSON COUNTY

JACKSONPORT

Jackson Guards Memorial, Jacksonport State Park. 1914 commemorative sculpture. 04/26/96.

Jacksonport State Park, between Dillard St. and White River. Circa-1833 river port containing old courthouse; site of surrender of Confederate Army of northern Arkansas. 01/21/70.

NEWPORT

Arkansas Bank and Trust Co., 103 Newport. 1916 Neoclassical building. 10/16/86.

Empie–Van Dyke House, 403 Laurel St. 1891 Queen Anne house. 12/28/77.

First Presbyterian Church, 4th and Main Sts. 1910 Classical Revival Church designed by Charles L. Thompson. 12/22/82.

Jackson County Courthouse, 3rd and Main Sts. 1892 Richardsonian Romanesque structure. 11/18/76.

Jackson County Jail, 503 3rd St. 1905 Romanesque-inspired stone building. 08/10/79.

Missouri-Pacific Depot, Walnut and Front Sts. Circa-1910 brick-and-stucco depot. 06/11/92.

Newport American Legion Community Hut, Remmel Park north of Remmel Ave. 1934 Rustic-style building. 12/10/92.

Newport Bridge, U.S. 67 over White River. 1929–30 cantilevered steel-truss bridge. 04/09/90.

Newport Junior and Senior High School, Remmel Park. 1930 Charles L. Thompson Art Deco design. 12/22/82.

T. J. Gregg House, 412 Pine St. Circa-1920 Colonial Revival design by Thompson. 12/22/82.

SWIFTON

New Home School, County Rd. 96. Circa-1915 Plain Traditional–style building. 10/08/92.

Newport Bridge, Newport, Jackson County.

Dollarway Road, Redfield, Jefferson County.

WELDON

Rock Island Depot, Hwy. 17. Circa-1913 frame Craftsman-style structure. 06/11/92.

JEFFERSON COUNTY

ALTHEIMER

The Elms, south of Altheimer. 1866 raised cottage. 07/07/78.

Lake Dick, four miles south of Altheimer and one mile west of Hwy. 88. 1936–38 Farm Security Administration site. 07/30/75.

Roselawn, Collier Lee Rd. south of Hwy. 88. Wood-frame plantation house built between 1870 and 1888. 05/23/78.

NEW GASCONY

Gracie House, off Hwy. 88. Circa-1915 Charles L. Thompson Craftsman design. 12/22/82.

PINE BLUFF

Austin House, 704 W. 5th Ave. 1904 Charles L. Thompson Colonial Revival design. 12/22/82.

Boone-Murphy-Moore House, 714 W. 4th Ave. Pre-1861 frame house used as Union headquarters during Civil War. 02/14/79.

Caldwell Hall, University Dr., UAPB campus. 1928 Thompson Gothic Revival design. 12/22/82.

Collier House, 1227 W. 5th Ave. 1913 Thompson Craftsman design. 12/22/82.

Dilley House, 656 Laurel St. 1902 home of early Arkansas industrialist. 08/03/77.

Du Bocage, 1115 W. 4th Ave. 1866 Greek Revival house. 06/24/74.

Ferguson House, 902 E. 4th Ave. Circa-1896 house with Queen Anne details; home of Martha Mitchell. 01/18/78.

Fifth Avenue Historic District, 5th Ave. Historic residential area with buildings dating from 1880 to 1915. 10/29/80.

Fox House, 1303 S. Olive St. Circa-1910 Charles L. Thompson Craftsman design. 12/22/82.

Gibson-Burnham House, 1326 Cherry St. 1904 Colonial Revival structure. 05/06/91.

Hospital and Benevolent Association, 11th Ave. and Cherry. 1908 Thompson Colonial Revival design. 12/22/82.

The Hotel Pines, Main St. and W. 5th Ave. 1910–13 hotel with Classical influences. 08/10/79.

Howson House, 1700 S. Olive St. 1918 Thompson Craftsman/Tudor Revival design. 12/22/82.

Hudson-Grace-Borreson House, 719 W. Barraque St. Circa-1830 one-story cabin altered over years into two-story house with Greek Revival and Victorian features. 06/24/71.

Hudson House, 304 W. 15th Ave. 1911 Thompson Craftsman design. 12/22/82.

Johnson House, 315 Martin St. 1912 Thompson Craftsman design. 12/22/82.

Katzenstein House, 902 W. 5th Ave. 1913 Thompson Craftsman design. 12/22/82.

MacMillan-Wilkins-Dilley-Irwin House, 407 Martin Ave. 1903 Prairie-style house. 12/12/76.

Masonic Temple, E. 4th Ave. and State St. 1902–4 Neoclassical home of Arkansas black Masonic order. 11/30/78.

Merchants and Planters Bank Building, 100 Main St. 1892 Romanesque Revival bank building. 08/01/78.

Mills House, 715 W. Barraque St. 1902 frame structure with Folk Victorian–style details. 05/29/98.

Nichol House, 205 Park Place. 1916 Charles L. Thompson Craftsman design with Prairie influence. 11/12/93.

Parkview Apartments, 300 W. 13th Ave. Circa-1925 Mediterranean Revival structure. 05/01/89.

Pine Bluff Confederate Monument, Jefferson County Courthouse. 1910 commemorative sculpture. 04/26/96.

Plum Bayou Homesteads, thirty miles north of Pine Bluff and east of the Arkansas River. 1935 Farm Security Administration site. 06/05/75.

Prigmore House, 1104 W. 5th Ave. Circa-1873 Midwestern I-house plan. 04/10/86.

Puddephatt House, 1820 S. Olive St. Circa-1911 Thompson Craftsman design. 12/22/82.

R. E. Lee House, 1302 W. 2nd Ave. 1893 Queen Anne residence. 06/08/82.

R. M. Knox House, 1504 W. 6th Ave. 1885 house in Eastlake style. 06/05/75.

Roth-Rosenzweig-Lambert House, 717 W. 2nd Ave. 1894 Queen Anne house. 12/12/76.

Russell House, 1617 S. Olive St. 1912 Thompson Craftsman design. 12/22/82.

Saenger Theater, southeast corner of W. 2nd Ave. and Pine St. 1924 Classical/Colonial Revival–style movie house, 03/23/95.

Temple House, 1702 S. Oak St. Circa-1910 Charles L. Thompson Prairie-style design. 12/22/82.

Trinity Episcopal Church, 3rd Ave. and Oak Sts. 1866–1870 Gothic-style church. 07/30/74.

Trulock-Cook House, 703 W. 2nd Ave. Circa-1903 mix of Shingle and Colonial Revival styles. 02/23/79.

Trulock-Gould-Mullins House, 704 W. Barraque St. 1876 vernacular Italianate residence. 01/03/78.

Union Station, E. 4th Ave. and State St. 1906 railroad depot. 12/14/78.

Walter B. Sorrells Cottage, off Hwy. 104. 1920 boys industrial school designed with Craftsman and English Revival details by Pine Bluff architect Mitchell Selligman. 12/22/82.

W. E. O'Bryant Bell Tower, center of University of Arkansas at Pine Bluff quadrangle at 1200 N. University Dr. Brick structure erected between 1943 and 1947. 06/03/98.

Yauch-Ragar House, 625 State St. 1907 vernacular Colonial Revival house. 01/20/78.

REDFIELD

Dollarway Road, south of Hwy. 65 near Redfield. Longest continuously paved concrete road in U.S. when built in 1913 and 1914. 05/17/74.

West James Street Overpass, W. James St. over Missouri-Pacific tracks two blocks east of Hwy. 365. 1924 wooden-trestle bridge. 05/18/95.

WHITE HALL

Bellingrath House, 7520 Dollarway Rd. 1932–35 English Revival–style structure. 12/09/94.

Munger House, Lutherville, Johnson County.

JOHNSON COUNTY

CLARKSVILLE

Capt. Archibald S. McKennon House, 215 N. Central. 1868 Adam-style residence. 01/02/76.

Clarksville High School Building Number One, Main St. Elaborate 1936 Craftsman structure. 09/10/92.

Davis House, 212 Fulton St. Circa-1905 Charles L. Thompson Colonial Revival design. 12/22/82.

Dunlap House, 101 Grandview. Circa-1910 Thompson Colonial Revival design. 12/22/82.

First Presbyterian Church, 212 College Ave. 1919 Classical Revival design by Rogers architect A. O. Clark. 05/13/91.

Johnson County Courthouse, Main St. 1938 Classical Revival structure with Colonial Revival influences. 06/14/91.

McKennon House, 115 Grandview. 1907 Thompson Colonial Revival design. 12/22/82.

Missouri-Pacific Depot, Cherry and Main Sts. Circa-1910 Mediterranean-style building. 06/11/92.

Pennington House, 317 Johnson St. 1888–91 structure blending Folk Victorian and Italianate styles. 12/01/94.

Pioneer House, south of Hwy. 123 and west of Johnson County Hospital. Circa-1850 log house expanded in mid-1870s. 03/31/95.

Raymond Munger Memorial Chapel, University of the Ozarks, west of Hwy. 103 on campus. 1932 Collegiate Gothic design by A. O. Clark. 06/08/93.

University of the Ozarks Science Hall, west of Hwy. 103 on campus. 1924 Classical Revival design by Clark. 01/21/93.

HAGARVILLE

Big Piney Creek Bridge, Hwy. 123 over Big Piney Creek. 1930s steel Warren-truss bridge. 04/09/90.

HARMONY

Harmony Presbyterian Church, Hwy. 103 eight miles north of Clarksville. 1915–17 Gothic Revival–style building. 12/01/94.

HUNT

Tankersley-Stewart House, east of County Rd. 27 and north of Hwy. 352 near Hunt. Circa-1895 double-pen box-constructed residence. 05/19/94.

LUTHERVILLE

Lutherville School, nine miles east of Lamar on County Rd. 418. Circa-1904 one-room schoolhouse from German immigrant community. 03/05/99.

Munger House, west of County Rd. 416 about three-quarters of a mile north of Johnson-Pope County line. 1934 Dutch Colonial Revival–style residence. 11/08/96.

OARK

N. E. Dickerson Store, east of Hwy. 215. 1902 box-constructed mercantile store. 09/22/95.

Oark School/Methodist Church, northeast of junction of Hwy. 215 and County Rd. 34. Circa-1923 Craftsman-style structure. 09/29/95.

ADDRESS RESTRICTED

King's Canyon Petroglyphs Site. Circa-1500 rock art site. 05/04/82.

First Presbyterian Church, Stamps, Lafayette County.

Serpent Cave Site. Circa-1500 rock art site. 05/04/82.

LAFAYETTE COUNTY

BRADLEY

Conway Cemetery, south of Hwy. 160 two miles west of Bradley. Graves date from 1855 to the 1920s; contains grave of James Sevier Conway, state's first governor. 11/23/77.

LEWISVILLE

First Methodist Church, northwest corner of 4th and Chestnut Sts. 1913 Classical Revival–style building. 06/20/96.

King-Whatley Building, 2nd and Maple Sts. Circa-1902 bank and office building. 03/30/78.

Lafayette County Courthouse, Courthouse Square. 1940–42 Art Deco–style structure. 02/25/93.

P. D. Burton House, 305 Chestnut St. 1916 Craftsman-style structure. 06/03/98.

Peoples Bank and Loan Building, southwest corner of Spruce and 3rd Sts. 1915 Classical Revival design. 06/20/96.

Triplett Company Building, 2nd St. west of Spruce St. Circa-1915 brick commercial structure. 06/20/96.

STAMPS

First Presbyterian Church, southwest corner of Market and Church. 1905 wood-frame, Gothic Revival–style structure. 06/20/96.

LAWRENCE COUNTY

CLOVER BEND

Clover Bend Historic District, Hwy. 228. Contains high school and other buildings erected between 1937 and 1942 in Farm Security Administration project. 09/17/90. Clover Bend High School individually listed 08/17/83.

W. S. McClintock House, Marianna, Lee County.

IMBODEN

Saint Louis–San Francisco Overpass, Hwy. 62 over Spring River. 1937 steel Pratt deck-truss bridge. 04/09/90.

Dr. John Octavius Hatcher House, 210 W. 3rd St. 1902–3 transitional Queen Anne/Colonial Revival design. 10/23/92.

PORTIA

Dr. F. W. Buercklin House, 104 Main St. Late 1880s structure that served as grocery store and doctor's office. 07/24/98.

Home Economics/FFA Building, City Park Dr. 1938 community/school building erected by Works Progress Administration. 06/14/90.

Portia School, Portia City Park. 1914 red-brick schoolhouse. 12/13/78.

POWHATAN

Ficklin-Imboden House, 3rd and Main Sts. Circa-1850 log home of Lawrence County pioneers. 10/16/89.

Powhatan Courthouse, overlooking Black River. Beaux Arts–style 1888 courthouse. 02/16/70.

Powhatan Jail, Hwy. 25. 1873 vernacular stone jail. 10/16/89.

Powhatan Methodist Church, Hwy. 25. 1872 Greek Revival frame church. 11/23/77.

Powhatan School House, Hwy. 25. Circa-1880 wood-frame school building. 07/31/78.

Telephone Exchange Building, 1st and Main Sts. 1887 vernacular panel-brick structure. 10/16/89.

RURAL LAWRENCE COUNTY

Cache River Bridge, Hwy. 412 spanning Cache River. 1934 Parker pony-truss bridge. 04/09/90.

SMITHVILLE

Smithville Public School Building, Hwy. 117. 1936 fieldstone structure built by Works Progress Administration. 01/14/93.

WALNUT RIDGE

Missouri-Pacific Depot, 1st St. Circa-1910 Mediterranean-style structure. 06/11/92.

Old Walnut Ridge Post Office, 225 W. Main St. 1935 Colonial Revival building. 05/20/94.

LEE COUNTY

BLACKTON

Louisiana Purchase Initial Survey Point, southeast of Blackton at junction with Monroe and Phillips Counties. Site in 1815 from which all surveys of Louisiana Purchase were determined. The Louisiana Purchase Initial Survey Point is a National Historic Landmark. NHL: 04/19/93. NR: 02/23/72.

MARIANNA

Elks Club, 67 W. Main St. 1911 Mediterranean Revival meeting hall. 07/27/79.

General Robert E. Lee Monument, Marianna City Park. 1910 commemorative sculpture. 05/10/96.

J. M. McClintock House, 43 Magnolia St. Circa-1912 Charles L. Thompson Bungalow design. 12/22/82.

John A. Plummer House, 269 Pearl St. Circa-1900 Queen Anne/Colonial Revival house. 06/16/98.

Lee County Courthouse, 15 Chestnut St. 1936 Classical Revival structure with accompanying jails built in 1890 and 1936. 09/07/95.

Marianna Missouri-Pacific Depot, Carolina St. S. Circa-1915 Mediterranean-style structure. 08/05/94.

W. S. McClintock House, 82 W. Main St. 1912 Thompson Classical Revival design. 12/28/77.

LINCOLN COUNTY

RELFS BLUFF

Mount Zion Presbyterian Church, Hwy. 81. 1925 Craftsman church. 01/21/88.

STAR CITY

Crow House, seven miles southeast of Star City. Circa-1873 dogtrot house altered over years to current appearance. 06/29/76.

Lincoln County Courthouse, 300 S. Drew. 1943 Art Deco–style government building. 03/07/94.

Oscar Crow House, 404 Washington St. 1929 Craftsman-style house. 10/08/92.

Star City Commercial Historic District, Jefferson and Bradley Sts. Circa-1916 to circa-1928 commercial architecture. 02/26/99.

Star City Confederate Memorial, Star City Town Square. 1928 commemorative sculpture. 04/26/96.

S. S. P. Mills and Son Building, Wilton, Little River County.

LITTLE RIVER COUNTY

ALLEENE

Will Reed Farm House, Main St. 1895 log house. 07/14/78.

ASHDOWN

Hunter-Coulter House, northwest corner of 2nd and Commerce. 1918 Craftsman-style building. 06/20/96.

Judge Jefferson Thomas Cowling House, 611 Willow St. 1910 house reflecting transition from Queen Anne to Colonial Revival styles. 12/08/88.

Little River County Courthouse, Main and 2nd Sts. 1907 Classical Revival structure. 09/29/76.

Memphis, Paris and Gulf Railroad Depot, north corner of Whitaker Ave. and Frisco St. 1908 depot with Folk Victorian–style details. 03/17/94.

FOREMAN

Anderson-Hobson Mercantile Store, 201 Schuman St. 1910 Italianate-style commercial building. 06/20/96.

Hawkins House, northwest corner of 3rd Ave. and 3rd St. 1912 American Foursquare–style structure. 06/20/96.

New Rocky Comfort Jail, southeast corner of junction of 3rd and Schuman Sts. 1902 Plain Traditional–style structure. 12/09/94.

Saint Barnabas Episcopal Church, northeast corner of Tracy Lawrence Ave. and Bell St. 1898 structure with simple Gothic Revival design. 07/23/98.

WILTON

S. S. P. Mills and Son Building, northwest corner of Texarkana Ave. and Main St. 1912 brick commercial structure. 06/20/96.

LOGAN COUNTY

BOONEVILLE

Bank of Booneville Building, 1 W. Main. 1902 commercial structure. 04/26/78.

Dr. Stephen N. Chism House, east side of Hwy. 23, south of junction with Hwy. 217. Two-story dogtrot log structure built circa 1844–45. 08/16/94.

Farmers and Merchants Bank/Masonic Lodge, 288 N. Broadway. 1906 commercial structure. 11/19/93.

Logan County Courthouse, Southern Judicial District, southeast corner of 4th and N. Broadway. 1928–29 public building designed in Italian Renaissance Revival style. 03/08/97.

Rock Island Railroad Depot, north end of Rhyne Ave. Circa-1900 Spanish Mission–style building. 06/11/92.

CORLEY

Burnett Springs, end of County Rd. 704 east of Corley. Site of late nineteenth-century resort community. 09/22/95.

Cove Creek Bridge, Hwy. 309 over Cove Creek. 1936 closed-spandrel arch bridge. 05/26/95.

Cove Creek Tributary Bridge, Hwy. 309 over Cove Creek tributary. Stone-arch bridge built in 1936. 05/26/95.

Cove Lake Bathhouse, Forest Service Rd. 1608A. 1937 Rustic-style structure. 09/11/95.

Cove Lake Spillway Dam/Bridge, Hwy. 309 nine miles south of Paris. 1937 masonry-arch bridge. 09/11/95.

DRIGGS

John Gabriel Fort House, Reveille Valley Rd. southeast of Driggs. Circa-1848 double-pen log house. 03/28/96.

LIBERTY

New Liberty School, off Hwy. 22. 1922 Plain Traditional–style stone building with Craftsman details. 09/10/92.

Evelyn Gill Walker House
detail, Paris, Logan County.

MAGAZINE

Magazine City Hall/Jail, northwest of intersection of Garland and Priddy Sts. 1934–35 concrete-block and fieldstone structure. 06/08/93.

NEW BLAINE

Anhalt Barn, County Rd. 68. 1878 stone and wood-frame barn. 02/25/93.

Elizabeth Lodge 215 F. & A. M., off Hwy. 22. 1867 frame structure that still serves local Masons. 05/04/76.

New Blaine School, junction of Hwy. 22 and Spring Rd. 1925 cut-stone structure; early example of style later used by Works Progress Administration. 08/18/92.

PARIS

American Legion Post Number 121, Legion Hut Rd. off Hwy. 107. WPA-built Rustic-style structure erected in 1934. 06/20/95.

Evelyn Gill Walker House, 18 S. Spruce St. Unusual variation of Rustic style; built between 1938 and 1943. 09/16/93.

First Christian Church, 120 E. Walnut St. 1930–36 stone structure combining Collegiate Gothic and Romanesque Revival styles. 06/30/95.

Logan County Courthouse, Eastern District, Courthouse Square. 1908 Neoclassical structure. 07/30/76.

Methodist Episcopal Church, South, 205 N. Elm St. 1917–25 Collegiate Gothic–style building. 06/20/95.

Old Logan County Jail, 204 N. Vine St. 1903 building in restrained Italianate style. 11/19/93.

Paris Post Office, 206 N. Elm St. 1938 structure featuring Depression-era mural. 08/14/98.

Smith Hospital, north end of Express St. 1913 structure with 1923 addition; first hospital in Logan County. 04/11/94.

Tolbert E. Gill House, Hwy. 22. Elaborate stonework and outdoor sculptures constructed between 1920 and 1935. 09/30/93.

RATCLIFF

Saint Anthony's Catholic Church, north of Hwy. 22. 1903 church of German immigrants. 08/21/86.

SUBIACO

Schriver House, Leo Ave. north of junction with Hwy. 22. Circa-1885 frame residence with Queen Anne Revival details. 09/22/95.

First Christian Church, Lonoke, Lonoke County.

SUGAR GROVE

Jack Creek Bathhouse, Forest Service Rd. 141 southwest of Sugar Grove. Circa-1936 fieldstone and log structure built by Civilian Conservation Corps. 10/21/93.

Petit Jean River Bridge, Hwy. 109 over Petit Jean River. 1938 Pratt through-truss steel bridge. 05/26/95.

LONOKE COUNTY

CABOT

Camp Nelson Confederate Cemetery, Rye. St. approximately one mile northwest of junction of Hwys. 321 and 319. Cemetery established in 1897. 05/03/96.

Dr. E. F. Utley House, 401 W. Pine. Colonial Revival–style structure built between 1914 and 1922. 06/03/98.

CARLISLE

Carlisle Rock Island Depot, Main St. and Court Ave. Circa-1920 Tudor Revival depot. 06/14/90.

LONOKE

Eagle House, 217 Ash St. Circa-1915 Charles L. Thompson Craftsman design. 12/22/82.

First Christian Church, northwest corner of 2nd and Depot Sts. 1916 Craftsman-style structure with Tudor Revival–style details. 07/09/97.

Joe P. Eagle/D. R. Boone Building, 105–107 Front St. 1905 Thompson design. 12/09/94.

Lonoke Confederate Monument, courthouse lawn. 1910 commemorative sculpture. 05/03/96.

Lonoke County Courthouse, N. Center St. 1928 Neoclassical design by Little Rock architect H. Ray Burks. 06/08/82.

Lonoke Downtown Historic District, junction of Front and Center Sts. Collection of commercial buildings constructed between 1900 and 1945. 05/10/96.

Rock Island Depot, Hwy. 70 and Center St. 1912 Mediterranean-style depot. 10/04/84.

Shull House, 418 Park Ave. 1917 Thompson Craftsman design. 12/22/82.

Thomas Sloan Boyd House, 220 Park Ave. Circa-1875 vernacular brick Greek Revival house. 01/01/76.

Trimble House, 518 Center St. 1916 Thompson Craftsman design. 12/22/82.

Walls-McCrary House, 406 Jefferson St. 1913 Thompson Colonial Revival design. 12/22/82.

Wheat House, 604 Center St. Thompson Colonial Revival design built circa 1900–1910. 12/22/82.

W. P. Fletcher House, 604 W. 4th St. Circa-1880 house with 1903–4 Colonial Revival addition; home of pioneer in rice industry. 09/05/90.

OLD AUSTIN

Sears House, junction of Hwys. 38 and 319. Circa-1860 Greek Revival house with Italianate details. 08/05/92.

SCOTT

Ashley-Alexander House, north of Scott. Circa-1835 log-and-clapboard house. 06/18/76.

Dortch Plantation, northeast of Scott off Hwy. 130. Circa-1904 farm complex with outbuildings, fields, and lake. 03/21/79.

Marlsgate, northeast of Scott off Hwy. 130. 1904 Charles L. Thompson–designed main house on Dortch Plantation. 12/06/75.

Toltec Indian Mounds, five miles southeast of Scott on Hwy. 130. State archeological park at site of Native American activity from 700 to 1800 A.D. The Toltec Mounds are a National Historic Landmark. NHL: 06/02/78. NR: 01/12/73.

TOMBERLIN

Walls Farm Barn and Corn Crib, Hwy. 31 near Tomberlin. 1907–8 wood-frame structures reflecting traditional farm outbuilding construction techniques. 11/29/95.

WOODLAWN

Woodlawn School, Bizzell Rd. at State Rt. 31. 1921 Craftsman-style building. 02/25/93.

ADDRESS RESTRICTED

Coy Mound Site. 600–1000 A.D. Plum Bayou culture archeological site. 09/22/95.

MADISON COUNTY

HUNTSVILLE

Madison County Courthouse, 1 Main St. 1939 structure with restrained Art Deco design. 11/19/93.

KINGSTON

Bank of Kingston, 101 Public Square. Imposing 1911 bank building. 03/25/82.

Madison County Courthouse, Huntsville, Madison County.

Cowdrey House, Yellville,
Marion County.

PETTIGREW

Pettigrew School, north of Hwy. 16. Traditional wood-frame schoolhouse built circa 1915. 03/23/95.

THORNEY

Enterprise School, County Rds. 8 and 192. Circa-1935 structure showing Craftsman and Colonial Revival details. 09/10/92.

MARION COUNTY

BIG FLAT

Cold Springs School, east of Buffalo National River near Big Flat. Circa-1935 Craftsman-style structure. 10/20/92.

BRUNO

Aggie Hall, County Rd. 9. 1926 building was home of Lincoln Aggie Club; believed to be nation's first Future Farmers' organization. 09/04/92.

Aggie Workshop, Hwy. 235 Spur. 1935 educational structure. 09/04/92.

Bruno School Building, County Rd. 9. Circa-1920 Plain Traditional–style structure with Craftsman details. 09/04/92.

Hirst-Mathew Hall, Hwy. 235 Spur. 1929 home economics building in school complex. 09/04/92.

Pea Ridge School Building, County Rd. 6 four miles south of Bruno. Circa-1899 one-room schoolhouse. 06/08/93.

EROS

Eros School Building, County Rd. 9. Circa-1935 structure built as Depression-era federal relief project. 09/04/92.

FAIRVIEW

Fairview School Building, County Rd. 203. 1927 school built by local volunteers. 09/04/92.

PYATT

Pyatt School, County Rd. 12. Circa-1925 Plain Traditional–style building with Colonial Revival–style influences. 09/04/92.

YELLVILLE

Buffalo Point, Buffalo National River near Yellville. 1939–41 Civilian Conservation Corps–built structures. 10/20/88.

Carter-Jones House, 30 Carter St. Circa-1847 structure altered to Queen Anne–influenced appearance in 1901. 07/21/87.

Cowdrey House. 1 Valley St. 1904 house with Victorian detailing. 07/20/78.

Layton Building, 1110 Mill St. 1906 Italianate-influenced commercial building. 04/26/78.

Marion County Courthouse, Courthouse Square. 1943–44 structure erected in shell of burned-out 1905 courthouse. 05/19/94.

Rush Historic District, Rush Rd. near Yellville. Remains of 1880 to 1940 zinc mining community. 02/27/87.

ADDRESS RESTRICTED

Sunburst Shelter. Circa-1500 rock art site. 05/04/82.

MILLER COUNTY

DODDRIDGE

Kiblah School, County Rd. 192 near Doddridge. 1927 Craftsman–Greek Revival school for historic black community. 11/20/89.

GARLAND

Wynn-Price House, Price St. west of Hwy. 82. Circa-1844 Greek Revival plantation house. 01/23/92.

MOUNT PLEASANT

Averitt House, west of Mount Pleasant off Hwy. 71 six miles south of Texarkana. 1931–33 log house designed in Rustic style. 07/24/92.

TEXARKANA

Alvah Horace Whitmarsh House, 711 Pecan St. 1894 Queen Anne residence. 08/29/80.

Augustus M. Garrison House, 600 Pecan St. 1895 Queen Anne house. 03/25/82.

Bottoms House, 500 Hickory St. 1910 house with Prairie and Craftsman influences. 06/08/82.

Canaan Baptist Church, Laurel and 10th Sts. 1929 church of black congregation; shows Colonial and Gothic Revival influences. 06/14/90.

Charles J. Neif House, 1410 Pecan St. Structure converted to Craftsman-style bungalow around 1914. 08/04/94.

Claude Foulke House, 501 Pecan St. 1903 Neoclassical structure. 04/22/82.

Dean House, 1520 Beech St. 1911 Colonial Revival house. 12/12/76.

First Methodist Church, 400 E. 6th St. Charles L. Thompson Gothic Revival design built circa 1900 to 1910. 12/22/82.

Averitt House interior, Mount Pleasant vicinity, Miller County.

J. K. Wadley House, 618 Pecan St. 1895 building designed in "Free Classic" subtype of Queen Anne style. 02/12/99.

Kittrell House, 1103 Hickory St. Thompson Colonial Revival design built circa 1900 to 1910. 12/22/82.

Miller County Courthouse, 400 Laurel St. 1939 Works Progress Administration Moderne-style design by architect E. C. Siebert. 05/29/98.

Orr School, 831 Laurel St. Circa-1880 school attended by black ragtime composer Scott Joplin. 07/30/76.

Ritchie Grocery Building, Front and Olive Sts. 1905 Romanesque Revival commercial structure. 06/14/90.

Texarkana Union Station, State Line and Front St. Classical structure erected between 1928 and 1930. 11/19/78.

ADDRESS RESTRICTED

Crenshaw Site. 700–1200 A.D. site with evidence of Fourche Maline through Early Caddo occupation. 01/26/94.

MISSISSIPPI COUNTY

BLYTHEVILLE

Blytheville Greyhound Bus Station, 109 N. 5th St. Circa-1937 Art Moderne bus station. 08/17/87.

Kress Building, 210 W. Main St. 1938 Art Deco–style commercial building. 06/13/97.

Mississippi County Courthouse, Chickasawba District, 200 W. Walnut St. 1919–21 Colonial Revival–style structure. 12/06/96.

DYESS

Dyess Colony Center, Hwy. 297. Administrative center of 1934 planned agricultural community. 01/01/76.

KEISER

Keiser School, Main and School Sts. 1929 Collegiate Gothic–style structure. 10/08/92.

Herman Davis Memorial, Manila, Mississippi County.

LEACHVILLE

Blytheville, Leachville and Arkansas Southern Railroad Depot, 2nd and McNamee Sts. Circa-1910 Plain Traditional–style structure. 06/11/92.

MANILA

Herman Davis Memorial, northeast corner of Baltimore Ave. and Hwy. 18. 1920s park and monument honoring Arkansas's greatest World War I hero. 04/07/95.

Jonesboro, Lake City and Eastern Railroad Depot, northwest corner of S. Dewey and Baltimore. Circa-1910 wood-frame structure. 03/08/97.

OSCEOLA

Bank of Osceola, 207 E. Hale Ave. 1909 commercial building. 08/06/87.

City Hall, 316 W. Hale Ave. 1936 Works Progress Administration–built municipal structure. 08/06/87.

First Baptist Church, 513 Pecan St. 1915 Classical Revival–style structure. 09/07/95.

Florida Brothers Building, 319 W. Hale Ave. 1936 Art Deco–influenced structure. 08/06/87.

Hale Avenue Historic District, south side of Hale Ave. across from courthouse. Historic commercial buildings erected between 1902 and 1917. 09/14/87.

Mississippi County Courthouse, Hale Ave. and Poplar St. 1912 Neoclassical structure. 12/13/78.

Mississippi County Jail, 300 S. Poplar St. Vernacular 1926 public building. 08/06/87.

Old Telephone Building, 100 block of Ash St. 1911 communications center. 08/06/87.

Osceola Times Building, 112 N. Poplar St. 1901 newspaper office. 08/06/87.

Planters Bank Building, 200 E. Hale Ave. Circa-1920 Neoclassical design by architect Uzell Branson. 08/06/87.

ADDRESS RESTRICTED

Chickasawba Mound. 1500–1850 A.D. Mississippian and Euroamerican site. 11/16/84.

Eaker Site. 600–1450 A.D. Mississippian, Nodena, and Late Woodland site. The Eaker Site is a National Historic Landmark. NHL: 06/19/96. NR: 11/25/92.

Nodena Site. 1400–1700 A.D. Mississippian site. The Nodena Site is a National Historic Landmark. NHL: 07/19/64. NR: 10/15/66.

Zebree Homesteads. 900–1500 A.D. Mississippian site. 05/02/75.

MONROE COUNTY

BLACKTON

Palmer House, four miles southeast of Blackton off Hwy. 49. 1873 Italianate brick home of prominent lawyer. 05/04/76.

BRINKLEY

Gazzola and Vaccaro Building, 131–133 W. Cypress St. 1916 Charles L. Thompson Prairie-style design. 12/22/82.

Union Station, Lick Skillet Railroad Work Station Historic District, Brinkley, Monroe County.

Gould Jones Reservoir, Jasper, Newton County.

NEVADA COUNTY

OAK GROVE

Wortham Gymnasium, Hwy. 200. 1935 Works Progress Administration–built structure serving black community. 04/19/90.

PRESCOTT

D. L. McRae House, 424 E. Main. Circa-1912 Charles L. Thompson Craftsman design. 12/22/82.

Elkins' Ferry Battlefield, ten miles north of Prescott on Little Missouri River. Site of April 3–4, 1864, Civil War action. The Elkins' Ferry Battlefield is part of the Camden Expedition National Historic Landmark. NHL: 04/19/94. NR: 04/19/94.

Henry McKenzie House, 324 E. Main. 1902 structure reflecting transition between Queen Anne and Colonial Revival styles. 09/03/98.

Missouri-Pacific Depot, 300 W. 1st St. N. 1912 railroad depot. 11/17/78.

Prairie DeAnn Battlefield, north and south of Hwy. 24 and southwest of Prescott. Site of April 9–12, 1864, skirmishes during Union Red River Campaign. The Prairie DeAnn Battlefield is part of the Camden Expedition National Historic Landmark. NHL: 04/19/94. NR: 03/22/74.

T. C. McRae House, 506 E. Main. 1919 Thompson Craftsman design. 12/22/82.

ROSSTON

Carolina Methodist Church, off Hwy. 4 near Rosston. Circa-1871 vernacular Greek Revival church. 01/03/91.

NEWTON COUNTY

BOXLEY

Villines Mill, one mile north of Boxley on Hwy. 43. Circa-1870 frame structure with equipment for flour and grist milling. 07/31/74.

ERBIE

Parker-Hickman Farm Historic District, Buffalo National River at Erbie. 1850s pioneers' house with associated outbuildings and site features. 08/11/87.

JASPER

Dr. Hudson Sanitarium Agricultural Building Historic District, Hwy. 327. 1936–39 barn and residences linked to planned rural tuberculosis sanitarium. 10/08/92.

Gould Jones Reservoir, Hwy. 7 at Newton County Library. 1946 water supply structure. 08/24/98.

Newton County Courthouse, Courthouse Square. 1939 native-stone Art Deco structure built by Works Progress Administration. 12/01/94.

Newton County Jail, junction of Spring and Elm Sts. 1902–3 stone structure with Italianate-style details. 12/01/94.

Fort Lookout, Camden, Ouachita County.

PARTHENON

Little Buffalo River Bridge, Hwy. 327 over Little Buffalo River. 1939 concrete tee-beam bridge built by Works Progress Administration. 05/26/95.

PONCA

Big Buffalo Valley Historic District (as amended), Buffalo National River near Ponca. Pioneer structures and site features dating to the 1850s. Originally listed: 07/29/87. Amended: 11/07/90.

PRUITT

Buffalo River Bridge, Hwy. 7 over Buffalo River. 1931 Pennsylvania-truss bridge. 04/09/90.

RURAL NEWTON COUNTY

Harp Creek Bridge, Hwy. 7 over Harp Creek about ten miles south of Harrison. 1928 open-spandrel, concrete deck-arch bridge. 04/09/90.

OUACHITA COUNTY

CAMDEN

Benjamin T. Powell House, 305 California Ave. Circa-1859 cotton grower's house with Classical details. 01/21/74.

Bragg House, four miles west of Camden on Hwy. 4. 1852 frame house of sawmill operator. 03/01/74.

Camden Confederate Monument, courthouse lawn. 1914 commemorative sculpture. 05/07/96.

Clifton and Greening Streets Historic District, bounded by Dallas Ave., Cleveland Ave., Clifton St., and Greening St. Structures from 1890 to 1948 exhibiting Queen Anne, Colonial Revival, Craftsman, and other styles. 08/14/98.

Elliott-Meek House, 761 Washington St. 1857 Greek Revival structure. 03/01/74.

Fort Lookout, Van Buren Rd. Earthen redoubt used in defending Camden in 1864. Fort Lookout is part of the Camden Expedition National Historic Landmark, NHL: 04/19/94. NR: 04/19/94.

Houston Methodist
Episcopal Church, South,
Houston, Perry County.

Fort Southerland. Bradley Ferry Rd. Earthen fortification used in 1864 defense of Camden. Fort
Southerland is part of the Camden Expedition
National Historic Landmark. NHL: 04/19/94. NR:
04/19/94.

Graham-Gaughan-Betts House, 710 Washington
St. N.W. 1858 frame house with ornate porch.
10/18/74.

Leake-Ingham Building, 926 Washington St. N.W.
Circa-1850 Greek Revival structure has served as law
office, Freedmen's Bureau office, and library.
05/02/75.

McCollum-Chidester House, 926 Washington St.
N.W. Circa-1847 plantation house. 06/24/71.

Missouri-Pacific Railroad Depot, Main and 1st Sts.
Circa-1917 Mediterranean-style building. 06/11/92.

Oakland Cemetery, Confederate Section, north of
Pearl St. between Adams and Young Sts. Circa-1865
burial plot with 1886 monument. 12/12/96.

Oakland Farm, Tate and Oakland Sts., south of
Camden. 1886 cypress house. 03/24/78.

Old Camden Post Office, 133 Washington St. S.W.
1895–96 stone and pressed-brick public building.
05/02/77.

Ouachita County Courthouse, 145 Jefferson Ave.
1933 Art Deco/Colonial Revival building. 11/13/89.

Richmond-Tufts House, Hwy. 24 northwest of
Camden. 1853 house later owned by prominent
"carpetbagger." 12/02/77.

Rowland B. Smith House, 234 Agee. Simple circa-
1856 frame house. 01/21/74.

Sidney A. Umsted House, 404 Washington St.
N.W. 1923–24 Mediterranean-style home of oil-boom
pioneer. 06/30/95.

Tate's Barn, 902 Tate St. Elaborate circa-1880 farm
structure. 11/09/72.

Two Bayou Methodist Church and Cemetery,
County Rd. 125. Circa-1875 vernacular church building with associated cemetery. 07/09/98.

Tyson Family Commercial Building, 151 Adams
St. Circa-1920 vernacular commercial structure.
11/21/94.

CHIDESTER

Poison Spring State Park, Hwy. 76 near Chidester.
Site of April 18, 1864, battle, in which Confederates
decimated Union supply train. The Poison Spring
battlefield is part of the Camden Expedition National
Historic Landmark. NHL: 04/19/94. NR: 12/03/69.

FRENCHPORT

Capt. John T. Burkett House, 607 Ouachita County Rd. 65. Circa-1900 Folk Victorian–style home of riverboat captain. 06/03/98.

OGEMAW

Holt-Poindexter Store Building, County Rd. 101 near Ogemaw. 1904 country store. 10/23/86.

STEPHENS

Lester and Haltom Number One Well Site, northeast of Stephens on Old Wire Rd. Site of first oil discovery in Arkansas on April 14, 1920. 04/03/76.

PERRY COUNTY

BIGELOW

Bigelow Methodist Episcopal Church, South, west of junction of Volman and Emma Sts. Circa-1908 Plain Traditional–style religious building. 04/04/96.

C. L. Sailor House, Wilson and Wiley Sts. 1917 Colonial Revival/Craftsman–style home of local business leader. 07/23/98.

HOLLIS

Fourche LaFave River Bridge, Hwy. 7 over Fourche LaFave River. 1941 open-spandrel, concrete-arch bridge. 05/26/95.

HOUSTON

Houston Methodist Episcopal Church, South, southwest side of Hwy. 69 near junction with Hwy. 216. 1912 Colonial Revival–style structure. 05/20/94.

LAKE SYLVIA

Camp Ouachita Girl Scout Camp Historic District, south of Hwy. 9 on Hwy. 324 near Thornburg. Civilian Conservation Corps–built camp area and lake dating from 1936 to 1938. 01/02/92.

PERRYVILLE

Perry County Courthouse, Main and Pine Sts. 1888 brick public building. 07/06/76.

Perryville American Legion Building, Plum and Main Sts. Circa-1935 Rustic-style structure. 09/05/90.

Centennial Baptist Church, Helena, Phillips County.

PHILLIPS COUNTY

HELENA

Allin Home, 515 Columbia St. Circa-1870 Italianate structure. 06/04/73.

Almer Store, 824 Columbia St. Circa-1875 frame structure with Greek Revival and Victorian details. 10/18/74.

Altman House, 1202 Perry St. 1914 structure blending Classical Revival and Arts and Crafts movement details. 01/21/88.

Battery A Site, Battle of Helena, near Adams and Columbia Sts. A Union hilltop fortification during July 4, 1863, Battle of Helena. 08/18/92.

Battery B Site, Battle of Helena, near Liberty St. and Summit Rd. Remains of Union hilltop fortification. 08/18/92.

Battery C, near Clark and York Sts. Scene of heavy fighting during Battle of Helena. 12/01/78.

Battery D, Military Rd. Another hotly contested site during Battle of Helena. 09/17/74.

Beech Street Historic District, bounded by McDonough, Columbia, Beech, Elm, Perry, and College Sts. Residential and commercial structures built between 1858 and 1935. 01/30/87.

Centennial Baptist Church, York and Columbia Sts. 1905 Gothic Revival structure linked to black leader Dr. Elias Camp Morris. 03/26/87.

Cherry Street Historic District, Cherry St. between Porter and Elm Sts. Commercial buildings erected between 1879 and 1935. 08/17/87.

Coolidge House, 820 Perry St. 1880 Queen Anne cottage. 09/08/83.

E. S. Ready House, 929 Beech St. 1910 Charles L. Thompson design. 01/01/76.

Estevan Hall, 653 S. Biscoe St. Circa-1820 structure altered in 1870s to present appearance. 10/22/74.

Helena Confederate Cemetery, southwest corner of Maple Hill Cemetery. 1869 cemetery containing grave of Gen. Patrick Cleburne. 05/03/96.

Helena Depot (Delta Cultural Center), Natchez and Missouri Sts. Circa-1915 Craftsman depot with Classical Revival influences. 11/05/87.

Helena Library and Museum, 623 Pecan St. 1891 Second Empire–style library with 1929 museum addition. 12/06/75.

Horner-Gladin House, 626 Porter St. 1881 Classically influenced home of prominent Helena family. 12/04/75.

James C. Tappan House, 717 Poplar St. Circa-1858 Greek Revival structure with Italianate details. 06/04/73.

Jerome Bonaparte Pillow House, 718 Perry St. Circa-1897 Queen Anne structure. 05/07/73.

Keesee House, 723 Arkansas St. 1901 structure blending Queen Anne and Colonial Revival styles. 09/08/83.

Maj. James Alexander Tappan House, 727 Columbia St. 1892 Queen Anne house. 09/09/74.

Moore-Hornor House, 323 Beech St. 1858 brick Greek Revival structure with Italianate details. 06/04/73.

New Light Missionary Baptist Church, 522 Arkansas St. 1917 African-American church designed in free interpretation of Gothic Revival style. 12/07/95.

Perry Street Historic District, Perry St. between Pecan and Franklin and including Pecan from Porter to Perry. Houses and public buildings erected between 1891 and 1925. 11/26/86.

Phillips County Courthouse, 622 Cherry St. 1914 Classical design by Little Rock architect Frank W. Gibb. 07/15/77.

Richard L. Kitchens Post Number Forty-One, 409 Porter St. 1922 American Legion Post built largely of cypress logs. 09/08/83.

Short-Diesch House, 409 Biscoe St. 1901 house mixing Classical and Colonial elements. 10/18/74.

Spirit of the American Doughboy Monument, center of intersection of Cherry and Perry Sts. 1927 World War I monument. 05/23/97.

William A. Short House, 317 Biscoe St. 1904 Colonial Revival structure. 04/18/85.

William Nicholas Straub House, 531 Perry St. 1900 structure mixing Colonial Revival and Shingle styles. 04/18/85.

Rosenwald School, Delight, Pike County.

West House, 229 Beech St. 1900 mix of Colonial Revival and Queen Anne styles. 09/08/83.

White House, 1015 Perry St. Circa-1910 Charles L. Thompson Colonial Revival design. 12/22/82.

LAMBROOK

Warrens Bridge, County Rd. 141 over Lambrook Levee Ditch. 1930 timber-trestle bridge. 05/18/95.

LEXA

Richardson–Turner House, 1469 Hwy. 1 N. 1894 Queen Anne–style farmhouse. 05/29/98.

MARVELL

First Baptist Church, Pine and Carruth. 1925 Collegiate Gothic church. 05/13/91.

Mayo House, 302 Elm St. Colonial Revival–style house built between 1917 and 1919. 12/19/97.

POSTELLE

Little Cypress Creek Bridge, County Rd. 66G over Little Cypress Creek. 1940 aluminum multi-beam bridge. 05/18/95.

WEST HELENA

Chicago Mill Co. Office Building, 129 W. Washington St. Circa-1920 lumber company head-quarters. 10/31/96.

Denison House, 427 Garland Ave. Circa-1910 Colonial Revival–style structure. 10/31/96.

Faust House, 114 Richmond Hill. Spanish Revival–style house built in 1924. 10/31/96.

Gemmill-Faust House, 321 Saint Andrew's Terrace. Circa-1920 Prairie-style home. 10/31/96.

Myers House, 221 Saint Andrew's Terrace. Circa-1920 residence synthesizing Prairie and Craftsman styles. 10/31/96.

Nelson House, 303 Saint Andrew's Terrace. Circa-1915 American Foursquare–type house. 10/31/96.

PIKE COUNTY

DELIGHT

Rosenwald School, Hwy. 26 near Delight. Works Progress Administration–built 1938 frame school linked to philanthropist Julius Rosenwald. 09/17/90.

GLENWOOD

Glenwood Iron Mountain Railroad Depot, west of junction of railroad tracks with Hwy. 70. Circa-1910 wood-frame railroad structure. 06/28/96.

Bacon Hotel, Whitehall,
Poinsett County.

MURFREESBORO

Conway Hotel, 108 Courthouse Square. 1913
Craftsman hotel. 03/06/86.

Crater of Diamonds State Park, Hwy. 301 near
Murfreesboro. Only diamond mine in North America;
diamonds discovered here in 1906. 06/18/73.

Pike County Courthouse, Courthouse Square. 1932
Art Deco design by Texarkana architects Witt, Siebert
and Halsey. 10/16/86.

POINSETT COUNTY

HARRISBURG

Modern News Building, 216 N. Main. Home of
Harrisburg *Modern News* newspaper from 1880 to the
present. 06/18/76.

Poinsett County Courthouse, Court Square. 1917
Classical Revival design by Pine Bluff architect
Mitchell Selligman. 11/03/89.

MARKED TREE

Marked Tree Lock and Siphons, on the Saint
Francis River. Unique 1939 flood-control project.
05/02/88.

RIVERVALE

Rivervale Inverted Siphons, Hwy. 35. 1926 structure draining Saint Francis and Little River basins.
03/22/91.

TRUMANN

Poinsett Community Club, Main and Poinsett Sts.
1927 Craftsman-style public building. 10/09/86.

WHITEHALL

Bacon Hotel, southeast of junction of Homestead Rd.
and railroad tracks. 1912 Folk Victorian–style rooming
house. 12/13/95.

POLK COUNTY

ATHENS

Bard Springs Bathhouse, Forest Service Rd. 106
northwest of Athens. Circa-1936 fieldstone structure
built by Civilian Conservation Corps. 10/20/93.

Bard Springs Dam Number One, Forest Service
Rd. 106 northwest of Athens. Circa-1936 fieldstone
dam built by CCC. 10/21/93.

Bard Springs Dam Number Two, Forest Service Rd. 106 northwest of Athens. CCC-built circa-1936 fieldstone structure. 10/21/93.

Bard Springs Picnic Shelter, Forest Service Rd. 106 northwest of Athens. Circa-1936 log structure erected by CCC. 10/20/93.

Shady Lake Bathhouse, County Rd. 64. Circa-1940 log and novelty-siding structure built by CCC. 10/20/93.

Shady Lake Caretaker's House, Forest Service Rd. 38. Frame residence built circa 1940 by CCC. 10/20/93.

Shady Lake Dam, County Rd. 64. Circa-1940 CCC-built cast-concrete structure. 10/20/93.

Shady Lake Picnic Pavilion, Forest Service Rd. 38. CCC-built circa-1940 log building. 10/20/93.

Tall Peak Fire Tower, Forest Service Rd. 38A northwest of Athens. Wood and fieldstone structure built circa 1938 by CCC. 10/20/93.

BOGG SPRINGS

Bogg Springs Hotel, Hwy. 84. Resort complex structure built between 1904 and 1907. 09/30/93.

CAMP PIONEER

Mountain Fork Bridge, County Rd. 38 west of Camp Pioneer. Turn-of-the-century Pratt steel pony-truss bridge. 04/09/90.

MENA

C. E. Foster House, Queen Wilhelmina State Park. Circa-1931 two-section stone building designed in Rustic style. 02/25/93.

Ebenezer Monument, behind First Baptist Church at 811 Port Arthur St. 1936 stone-and-concrete monument linked to anti-communist sentiment against nearby Commonwealth College. 01/30/92.

Elks Lodge, 500 Mena St. 1908 Colonial Revival–style structure. 06/04/98.

Janssen Park, off Hwy. 8. City park featuring 1851 log cabin. 12/13/79.

Judge Benjamin Shaver House, 501 12th St. 1896 Colonial Revival house. 12/06/79.

Mena Kansas City–Southern Depot, Mena and Pickering. 1920 Mediterranean-style depot. 06/05/91.

National Guard Armory, DeQueen and Maple Sts. 1930–31 fieldstone and masonry armory. 06/05/91.

Saint Agnes Catholic Church, Mena, Polk County.

John W. White House,
Russellville, Pope County.

Old Post Office (City Hall), 520 Mena St, 1917 post office with Colonial and Classical influences. 06/05/91.

Polk County Courthouse, Church Ave. and DeQueen St. Restrained 1939 Art Deco design. 11/20/92.

Saint Agnes Catholic Church, 8th and Walnut Sts. 1921–22 Spanish Mission–style church. 06/05/91.

State Line Marker, seventeen miles northwest of Mena on Hwy. 88. 1877 marker separating Arkansas from Choctaw lands. 11/18/76.

VANDERVOORT

Bee Mountain Fire Tower, Forest Service Rd. 30 northeast of Vandervoort. Fieldstone and wood building erected by CCC circa 1938. 10/20/93.

POPE COUNTY

ATKINS

Missouri-Pacific Depot, State Hwy. 64. Circa-1910 Mediterranean-style depot. 06/11/92.

CENTER VALLEY

Center Valley Well House, Hwy. 124. 1940 stone-masonry open-well house. 09/10/92.

POTTSVILLE

Potts Inn, Main and Center Sts. 1858 stagecoach inn. 06/22/70.

RUSSELLVILLE

Caraway Hall, N. Arkansas St. at Arkansas Tech University. 1934 Colonial Revival–style dormitory. 09/10/92.

Confederate Mothers Memorial Park, junction of Hwy. 326 and S. Glenwood Ave. Commemorative park established between 1921 and 1924. 05/03/96.

Girls' Domestic Science and Arts Building, east of N. El Paso St. at Arkansas Tech University. 1913 structure altered to present appearance in 1935. 09/18/92.

Henry R. Koen Forest Service Building, 605 W. Main St. Rustic-style 1939 Civilian Conservation Corps–built structure. 12/21/89.

Hughes Hall, W. "M" St. at Arkansas Tech University. 1940 Plain Traditional–style structure. 09/18/92.

John W. White House, 1509 W. Main St. 1916 mixture of Prairie and Craftsman styles. 05/05/88.

Missouri-Pacific Depot, near "C" St. and Denver Ave. 1910 Mediterranean-style structure. 06/11/92.

Mountain View School, Hwy. 326. 1926 Craftsman-style building. 09/10/92.

Norristown Cemetery, Lock and Dam Rd. off Hwy. 78 near Russellville. Features graves dated from 1852 to 1934; last vestige of historic river community. 04/14/95.

Physical Education Building, N. El Paso St. and W. "O" St. at Arkansas Tech University. 1937 Classical Revival–style building. 09/10/92.

Riggs-Hamilton American Legion Post Number Twenty, 215 N. Denver Ave. Circa-1935 stone structure built by the Works Progress Administration. 08/15/94.

Russellville Downtown Historic District, bounded by W. 2nd St., Arkansas Ave., El Paso St., and the Missouri-Pacific railroad tracks. Collection of historic commercial structures built between 1875 and the 1940s. 09/03/96.

Williamson Hall, N. El Paso St. at Arkansas Tech University. 1940 Classical Revival building. 09/18/92.

Wilson Hall, N. El Paso St. on campus of Arkansas Tech University. 1925 Colonial Revivial–style structure. 09/18/92.

Wilson House, 214 E. 5th St. 1902–3 Classical Revival house. 03/29/78.

W. J. White House, 1412 W. Main St. 1908 structure blending Craftsman and Victorian details. 12/13/78.

ADDRESS RESTRICTED

Crow Mountain Petroglyph Site. Circa-1500 rock art site. 05/04/82.

PRAIRIE COUNTY

DES ARC

American Legion Hut, Des Arc, 206 Erwin St. 1934 Rustic-style log structure built by Works Progress Administration. 06/09/95.

Bedford Brown Bethell House, 2nd and Curran Sts. 1912–13 Colonial Revival architecture. 12/04/78.

White River Bridge, DeValls Bluff, Prairie County.

Bethel House, Erwin and 2nd Sts. 1918 Charles L. Thompson Craftsman design. 12/22/82.

First Presbyterian Church, Hwy. 38. 1912 Colonial Revival church. 06/14/90.

Frith-Plunkett House, 8th and Main Sts. 1858 Greek Revival house. 06/10/82.

Prairie County Courthouse, Main St. 1913 Classical Revival public building. 04/18/77.

DEVALLS BLUFF

Prairie County Courthouse, Magnolia and Pine Sts. 1939 structure built by Works Progress Administration using materials salvaged from 1910 courthouse. 04/20/95.

White River Bridge at DeValls Bluff, Hwy. 70 over White River. 1923–24 vertical-lift bridge. 04/09/90.

HAZEN

Barrett-Rogers Building, 100 N. Hazen Ave. 1906 wood-frame, false-front commercial building. 07/23/98.

Rock Island Depot, Hwy. 70. 1915 depot with Craftsman and Tudor Revival influences. 12/22/87.

PULASKI COUNTY

CATO

Frenchmen's Mountain Methodist Episcopal Church, South, and Cemetery, Cato Rd. west of Cato. 1880 wood-frame church. 10/22/76.

HENSLEY

Harris House, southeast of Hensley off Hwy. 365. 1856 frame cypress house. 01/01/76.

JACKSONVILLE

Pulaski County Road 71D Bridge, over Bayou Meto. Works Progress Administration–built 1939 open-masonry substructure bridge. 05/26/95.

Choctaw Route Station detail, Little Rock, Pulaski County.

LITTLE ROCK

Abrams House, 300 S. Pulaski St. 1904 transitional Queen Anne/Colonial Revival residence. 02/18/99.

Absalom Fowler House, 502 E. 7th St. Circa-1840 late Federal-style building. 06/04/73.

Ada Thompson Memorial Home, 2021 S. Main St. 1909 Colonial Revival structure. 08/03/77.

Albert Pike Hotel, 7th and Scott. 1929 Spanish Revival design. 11/21/78.

Albert Pike Memorial Temple, 700–724 Scott St. 1924 Classical Revival building. 11/13/86.

Albert Retan House, 506 N. Elm. 1893 Queen Anne/Colonial Revival mix. 12/03/80.

Angelo Marre House (Villa Marre), 1321 Scott St. Circa-1882 Second Empire–style house. 06/15/70.

Arkansas Power and Light Building, 9th and Louisiana Sts. 1953–59 International-style office building. 09/14/92.

Arkansas State Capitol, 7th, Woodlane, and Markham Sts. Classical Revival structure built between 1899 and 1911. 06/28/74.

Arthur J. Jones House, 814 Scott St. Circa-1861 "carpenter Gothic" house. 01/01/76.

Associated Reformed Presbyterian Church, 3323 W. 12th St. Circa-1925 Charles L. Thompson Classical Revival design. 12/22/82.

Augustus Garland House, 1404 Scott St. 1873 Italianate home of prominent politician. 06/10/75.

Baer House, 1010 Rock St. Circa-1915 Thompson Craftsman design. 12/22/82.

Barlow Apartments, 2115 Scott St. 1921 Craftsman-style structure. 04/07/95.

Beal-Burrow Dry Goods Building, 107 E. Markham St. 1920 Thompson design incorporating Prairie-style elements. 06/26/95.

Bechle Apartment Building, 1000 E. 9th St. 1909 Thompson Colonial Revival design. 10/02/78.

Bechle House, 1004 E. 9th St. Turn-of-the-century home of German immigrants. 02/08/79.

Beyerlein House, 412 W. 14th St. Circa-1917 Thompson Craftsman design. 12/22/82.

Bishop Hiram A. Boaz House, 22 Armistead Rd. 1926 Tudor Revival–style home of first Methodist bishop to reside in Arkansas. 03/07/94.

Boone House, 4014 Lookout Rd. 1927 Thompson Tudor Revival design. 12/22/82.

Boyle Park, bounded by 38th St., Dorchester Dr., Covewood Circle, Glenmere Dr., Kanis Rd., and W. 12th St. Contains structures built between 1935 and 1937 by Civilian Conservation Corps. 09/22/95.

B.P.O.E. Elks Club, 4th and Scott. 1908 Second Renaissance Revival design by architect Theo Sanders. 12/22/82.

Bruner House, 1415 Cantrell Rd. Circa-1891 American Queen Anne house. 04/11/77.

Buhler House, 1820 Fair Park. 1930–31 steel-frame construction residence. 04/25/88.

Bush House, 1516 Ringo St. Circa-1919 Thompson Craftsman design. 11/22/82.

Capital Hotel, 117 W. Markham St. 1877 Italianate hotel with cast-iron façade. 07/30/74.

Central High School Neighborhood Historic District (as amended), bounded roughly by Martin Luther King Dr., Thayer Ave., W. 12th St., and Roosevelt Rd. Structures built between 1900 and 1930 reflecting a variety of architectural styles. Originally listed: 08/16/96. Amended: 01/17/97.

Central Presbyterian Church, 1921 Arch St. 1921 Thompson Gothic Revival and Craftsman design. 12/22/82.

Charles Clary Waters House, 2004 W. 22nd St. 1906 Classical Revival structure. 08/10/79.

Chisum House, 1320 Cumberland St. 1894 Queen Anne house. 12/04/75.

Choctaw Route Station, 1010 E. 3rd St. Circa-1899 railroad station with elaborate terra cotta detail. 05/06/75.

Compton-Wood House. 800 S. Dr. M. L. King Jr. Dr. 1902 house in late Queen Anne style. 05/07/80.

Confederate Soldiers Monument, State Capitol. 1905 commemorative sculpture. 04/26/96.

Cornish House, 1800 Arch St. 1917 Theo Sanders Craftsman/Tudor Revival design. 12/22/82.

Croxson House, 1901 Gaines St. 1908 Thompson Dutch Colonial design. 12/22/82.

Curran Hall, 615 E. Capitol St. 1842 Greek Revival structure reputedly designed by architect Gideon Shryock. 01/01/76.

Darragh House, 2412 Broadway. Circa-1916 Thompson Dutch Colonial design. 12/22/82.

David O. Dodd Memorial, 300 W. Markham St. 1923 commemorative sculpture. 04/26/96.

Deane House, 1801 Arch St. Circa-1888 mixture of Queen Anne and Colonial Revival styles. 09/05/75.

Democrat Printing and Lithograph Co. Building, northwest corner of 2nd and Scott. 1924 Sanders and Ginnocchio design. 12/17/98.

Dunaway House, 2022 Battery. 1915 Thompson Craftsman design. 12/22/82.

Dunbar Junior and Senior High School, Wright and Ringo. 1929 black vocational education school. 08/06/80.

Hornibrook House, Little Rock, Pulaski County.

East Markham Street Historic District, 301–323 Markham St. Commercial buildings from the 1870s to 1905. 05/05/99.

England House, 2121 Arch St. Circa-1917 Thompson Prairie and Colonial Revival design. 12/22/82.

Exchange Bank Building, 423 Main St. 1921 Thompson Classical Revival design. 10/23/86.

Farrell House, 2109 Louisiana St. 1914 Thompson Craftsman design. 10/11/84.

Farrell House, 2111 Louisiana St. 1914 Thompson Craftsman design. 12/22/82.

Farrell House, 2115 Louisiana St. 1914 Thompson Craftsman design. 12/22/82.

Farrell House, 2121 Louisiana St. 1914 Thompson Craftsman design. 12/22/82.

Federal Reserve Bank Building, 123 W. 3rd St. 1924 Thompson Neoclassical design. 10/23/86.

First Baptist Church, junction of 12th and Louisiana Sts. 1941 single-story cut-stone Collegiate Gothic–style church. 08/09/94.

First Church of Christ, Scientist, 20th and Louisiana Sts. 1919 John Parks Almand Mission-style design. 10/04/84.

First Missionary Baptist Church, 701 S. Gaines St. 1882 Gothic Revival church of one of state's oldest black congregations. 09/29/83.

First Presbyterian Church, 123 E. 8th St. 1921 Gothic design. 10/09/86.

First United Methodist Church, 723 Center St. 1900 Romanesque Revival church. 10/09/86.

Fletcher House, 909 Cumberland St. Circa-1900 Thompson Colonial Revival design. 12/22/82.

Florence Crittenton Home, 3600 W. 11th St. 1917 Thompson Colonial Revival design. 12/22/82.

Fones House, 902 W. 2nd St. 1878 Italianate architecture. 08/19/75.

Fordyce House, 2115 S. Broadway. 1904 Egyptian Revival design by Thompson. 08/06/75.

Frauenthal House, 2008 Arch St. 1919 Thompson Mediterranean and Colonial Revival design. 12/22/82.

Frederick Hanger House, 1010 Scott St. 1889 Queen Anne residence. 03/15/74.

French-England House, 1700 Broadway. Circa-1900 Thompson Colonial Revival design. 12/22/82.

Fulk Building, 300 Main St. 1900 structure with Romanesque Revival details. 11/13/86.

Gazette Building, 112 W. 3rd St. 1908 Beaux Arts design. 10/22/76.

George R. Mann Building, 115 E. 5th St. Circa-1910 Classical Revival building. 12/29/83.

Governor's Mansion Historic District (as amended), bounded roughly by Roosevelt, Chester, 13th, and Louisiana Sts. Primarily residential structures built between 1880 and 1930 and featuring 1948–50 Jeffersonian-style Governor's Mansion. Originally listed: 09/13/78. Amended: 09/15/88, 11/22/93, and 12/05/96.

Gus Blass Department Store, 324 Main St. 1912 Sullivanesque structure was one of Little Rock's first "skyscrapers"; George R. Mann design. 11/13/86.

Hall House, 32 Edgehill. 1928 Tudor Revival residence. 12/22/82.

Halliburton Townhouses, 1601 and 1605 Center St. Identical 1905–6 Classical Revival structures. 12/12/76.

Hardy House, 2400 Broadway. 1921 Thompson English Country House design. 12/22/82.

Harris House, 6507 Fourche Dam Pike. 1924 Spanish Eclectic–style building. 06/03/98.

Harry Pettefer House, 105 E. 24th St. Circa-1888 frame home of prominent contractor. 10/19/78.

Healey and Roth Mortuary, 815 Main St. 1925 Thompson Second Renaissance Revival style. 12/22/82.

Hemmingway House, 1720 Arch St. Circa-1894 Thompson Queen Anne design. 12/22/82.

Herschell-Spillman Carousel, War Memorial Park. 1920s hand-carved carousel horses. 12/01/89.

Hillcrest Historic District, bounded by Woodrow, Jackson, Markham, and N. Lookout Rd. Houses, commercial structures, and institutional buildings erected between 1890 and 1940. 12/18/90.

Hillcrest Historic District Amendment, bounded by Evergreen, Harrison, Lee, and Jackson Sts. Mainly residential structures dating from 1920 to 1940. 10/08/92.

Holcomb Court Apartments, 2201 Main St. 1925 Craftsman-style structure. 04/07/95.

Hornibrook House, 2120 S. Louisiana St. 1888 Queen Anne house. 07/30/74.

Hotze House, 1614 Louisiana St. 1900 Thompson design linking Colonial Revival and Beaux Arts styles. 08/11/75.

Ish House, 1600 Scott St. 1880 home of black educator and his son, a doctor. 01/03/78.

Jesse Hinderliter House, Arkansas Territorial Restoration, 214 E. 3rd St. Circa-1830 frontier tavern. 03/05/70.

Johnson House, 514 E. 8th St. Circa-1900 Thompson Colonial Revival design. 12/22/82.

Johnson House, 516 E. 8th St. Circa-1900 Thompson Colonial Revival design. 12/22/82.

Johnson House, 518 E. 8th St. Circa-1900 Thompson Colonial Revival design. 12/22/82.

Johnswood, 10314 Cantrell Rd. 1941 home of writers John Gould Fletcher and Charlie May Simon. 05/20/94.

Joseph M. Frank House, 912 W. 4th St. 1900 house using Queen Anne and Classical Revival details. 10/03/85.

Joseph Taylor Robinson House, 2122 Broadway. 1904 Stick-style/early Craftsman home of famous Arkansas politician. The Joseph Taylor Robinson House is a National Historic Landmark. NHL: 10/12/94. NR: 03/28/75.

J. P. Runyan House, 1514 S. Schiller. 1901 Neoclassical house occupied by Gov. John Sebastian Little in 1907. 08/18/92.

Kahn-Jennings House, 5300 Sherwood. 1927 English Revival design by architect Max Mayer. 09/08/92.

Keith House, 2200 Broadway. 1912 Thompson Craftsman/Prairie design. 12/22/82.

Lafayette Hotel, 525 S. Louisiana St. 1925 design by Saint Louis architect George D. Barnett. 09/30/82.

Lamar Porter Athletic Field, 7th and Johnson. 1936 Works Progress Administration–built baseball field. 12/06/90.

Lamb-McSwain House, 2124 Rice St. 1926 Craftsman bungalow. 06/04/98.

Leiper-Scott House, 312 S. Pulaski St. 1902 house with Queen Anne and Colonial Revival features. 05/01/80.

Zeb Ward Building, Little Rock, Pulaski County.

Lincoln Avenue Viaduct, Cantrell Rd. over Missouri-Pacific tracks. 1928 through rainbow-arch bridge. 04/09/90.

Lincoln Building, 1423–1425 S. Main St. Circa-1905 restrained Neoclassical design. 08/05/94.

The Little Rock, south bank of Arkansas River at Rock St. Landmark that served as starting point for land surveys south of the Arkansas River. 10/06/70.

Little Rock Boys Club, 8th and Scott. 1930 Thompson Colonial Revival design. 12/22/82.

Little Rock Central Fire Station, 520 W. Markham St. 1913 Thompson Neoclassical design. 10/18/79.

Little Rock City Hall, 500 W. Markham St. 1907 Thompson design blending Classical Roman and Italian Renaissance elements. 10/18/79.

Little Rock Confederate Memorial, Little Rock National Cemetery. 1913 commemorative monument. 05/03/96.

Little Rock High School, 14th and Park St. 1927 structure was focus of national attention during 1957 desegregation crisis. Little Rock Central High School is a National Historic Landmark. NHL: 05/20/82. NR: 08/19/77.

Little Rock National Cemetery, 2523 Confederate Blvd. Civil War–era burial ground for Union soldiers. 12/20/96.

Little Rock YMCA, 524 Broadway. 1928 Spanish Revival design. 07/22/79.

Luxor Apartments, 1923 Main St. 1924 Craftsman-style building. 04/07/95.

MacArthur Park Historic District (as amended), bounded by Capitol, Scott, E. 9th, and I-30. Contains structures built between 1870 and 1935. Originally listed: 07/25/77. Amended: 05/22/86.

Main Building, Arkansas Baptist College, 1600 High St. 1893 school for black theologians. 04/30/76.

Marshall House, 2009 Arch St. 1908 Thompson Georgian Revival design. 12/22/82.

Marshall Square Historic District, bounded by 17th, McAlmont, 18th, and Vance Sts. Solid block of vernacular 1918 rental houses. 08/10/79.

Maxwell F. Mayer House, 2016 Battery. 1922–25 Tudor Revival–style residence. 12/09/94.

McDonald-Wait-Newton House, 1406 Cantrell Rd. 1869 Second Empire design. 07/14/78.

McLean House, 470 Ridgeway. 1920 Thompson Colonial Revival design. 12/22/82.

Mehaffey House, 2101 Louisiana St. Circa-1905 Thompson transitional Colonial Revival design. 12/22/82.

Memorial to Company A, Capitol Guards, MacArthur Park. 1911 commemorative sculpture. 04/26/96.

Mims-Breedlove-Priest-Weatherton House, 2108 Beechwood Ave. Circa-1910 Craftsman bungalow. 12/03/98.

Minnesota Monument, Little Rock National Cemetery. 1916 memorial to Union Civil War casualties. 05/03/96.

Mitchell House, 1415 Spring St. 1911 Thompson Colonial Revival design. 12/22/82.

Monument to Confederate Women, State Capitol. 1913 commemorative sculpture. 04/26/96.

Moore Building, 519–523 Center St. 1929 Spanish Revival design. 10/23/86.

Moore House, 20 Armistead Rd. 1929 Tudor Revival design. 12/22/82.

MoPac Station (Union Station), Markham and Victory. Sprawling 1921 train station. 06/17/77.

Mosaic Templars of America Headquarters Building, 900 Broadway. 1911 headquarters of black fraternal organization. 04/19/90.

Mount Holly Cemetery, 12th St. and Broadway. Graves dating to 1843 include those of governors, senators, publishers, a Pulitzer Prize winner, and a Confederate spy. 03/05/70.

Mount Holly Mausoleum, 12th St. and Broadway. 1917 Thompson Greek Revival design. 12/22/82.

Mount Zion Baptist Church, 900 Cross St. 1926 church of black congregation features Prairie styling. 03/27/87.

Nash House, 409 E. 6th St. Circa-1907 Thompson Colonial Revival design. 12/22/82.

Nash House, 601 Rock St. 1907 Thompson Colonial Revival design. 12/22/82.

Old Post Office and Customs House, 2nd and Spring. 1881 Italianate sandstone building. 05/07/73.

Old State House, 300 W. Markham St. 1836 Gideon Shryock Greek Revival design for state's first Capitol building. The Old State House is a National Historic Landmark. NHL: 12/09/97. NR: 12/03/69.

Pearson-Robinson House, 1900 Marshall. 1900 home of Sen. Joe T. Robinson. 07/24/78.

Peoples Building and Loan Building, 213–217 W. 2nd St. 1903 Classically influenced building. 09/02/82.

Pike-Fletcher-Terry House, 411 E. 7th St. 1840 Greek Revival building; home to generations of famous Arkansans. 08/21/72.

Pulaski County Courthouse, 405 W. Markham St. 1889 Max A. Orlopp Romanesque Revival structure with 1914 Classical Revival addition. 10/18/79.

Ragland House, 1617 Center. 1891–92 Queen Anne design by Thompson. 06/17/77.

Railroad Call Historic District, 108–114 S. Pulaski St. 1906 transitional Colonial Revival–style railroad worker housing. 07/09/97.

Reichardt House, 1201 Welch St. Circa-1870 I-house with Folk Victorian additions. 05/02/75.

Reid House, 1425 Kavanaugh. 1911 Thompson Dutch Colonial design. 12/22/82.

Remmel Apartments, 409–411 W. 17th St. 1917 Thompson Craftsman design. 12/22/82.

Remmel Apartments, 1704–1706 Spring St. 1917 Thompson Craftsman design. 12/22/82.

Remmel Apartments, 1708–1710 Spring St. 1917 Thompson Craftsman design. 12/22/82.

Remmel Flats, 1700–1702 Spring St. 1906 Thompson Colonial Revival design. 12/22/82.

Retan House, 2510 Broadway. Circa-1915 Thompson Prairie-style design. 12/22/82.

Rogers House, 400 W. 18th St. 1914 Thompson Colonial Revival design. 12/22/82.

Rose Building, 307 Main St. 1900 Classical Revival design by George R. Mann. 11/13/86.

Roselawn Memorial Park Gatehouse, 2801 Asher. 1924 Thompson Spanish Colonial Revival design. 12/22/82.

Safferstone House, 2205 Arch St. Circa-1920 Spanish Mission design. 12/22/82.

Saint Andrew's Catholic Cathedral, 617 Louisiana St. 1878 Gothic Revival building. 11/13/86.

Saint Edward's Church, 823 Sherman. 1901 Thompson Gothic design. 12/22/82.

T. R. Pugh Memorial
Park, North Little
Rock, Pulaski County.

Sanders House, 2100 Gaines St. 1917 Theo Sanders
Colonial Revival design. 12/22/82.

Schaer House, 1862 Arch St. 1923 Thompson
Craftsman design. 12/22/82.

Skillern House, 2522 Arch St. 1915 Thompson
Craftsman design. 12/22/82.

Snyder House, 4004 S. Lookout Rd. 1925
Craftsman/Colonial Revival design. 12/22/82.

Solomon Gans House, 1010 W. 3rd St. 1896
Richardsonian Romanesque–style house. 03/29/84.

South Main Street Apartments Historic District,
2209–2214 Main St. Pair of 1941 Colonial
Revival–style structures. 04/07/95.

Stewart House, 1406 Summit St. Circa-1900
Thompson Colonial Revival design. 12/22/82.

Taborian Hall, 9th and State Sts. 1916 headquarters
of black fraternal group; features ballroom. 04/29/82.

Taylor Building, 304 Main St. Circa-1900
Romanesque Revival design. 11/13/86.

Ten-Mile House, Hwy. 5 west of Little Rock.
Federal-style stagecoach stop built circa 1822–35.
06/22/70.

Terminal Hotel, Victory at Markham. 1905 Colonial
Revival building. 11/17/78.

Terminal Warehouse Building, 500 E. Markham
St. 1926 Venetian Gothic design by Eugene Stern.
04/29/82.

Thomas R. McGuire House, 114 Rice St. 1904 cast-
concrete block Colonial Revival residence. 12/19/91.

Thurston House, 923 Cumberland St. Circa-1900
Thompson design blending Queen Anne and Colonial
Revival styles. 12/22/82.

Trapnall Hall, 423 E. Capitol St. 1843 Greek Revival
house. 04/13/73.

Trinity Episcopal Church, 310 W. 17th St. 1892
Gothic-style church. 05/13/76.

Trinity Hospital, southwest corner of Main and 20th.
1924 Max Mayer design of pioneer HMO clinic.
11/18/98.

Turner House, 1701 Center St. 1904–5 Thompson
Colonial Revival design. 12/22/82.

Turner-Ledbetter House, 1700 S. Louisiana St.
1891–92 Queen Anne house with later Colonial
Revival and Craftsman additions. 06/18/87.

U. M. Rose School, Izard and W. 13th. 1915 John Parks Almand Colonial Revival design. 12/08/88.

Union Life Building, 212 Center St. 1911–17 structure in Chicago style of commercial architecture. 09/25/81.

U.S. Arsenal Building, MacArthur Park, 9th at Commerce. 1840 military arsenal; reputed birthplace of Douglas MacArthur. The U.S. Arsenal Building is part of the Camden Expedition National Historic Landmark. NHL: 04/19/94. NR: 07/28/70.

Vanetten House, 1012 Cumberland St. Circa-1900 Thompson Colonial Revival design. 12/22/82.

Van Frank Cottages, 515, 517, and 519 E. 15th St. and 1510 Park Ln. 1908 Colonial Revival cottages. 10/21/85.

Vaughan House, 2201 Broadway. Circa-1910 Thompson Colonial Revival design. 12/22/82.

Vaughn House, 104 Rosetta. 1914 Craftsman-style residence. 02/19/99.

Vinson House, 2123 Broadway. Circa-1905 Thompson Classical Revival design. 05/06/76.

Wallace Building, 101–111 Main St. 1928 Art Deco structure. 02/18/99.

Walnut Grove Methodist Church, west of Little Rock on Walnut Grove Rd. Circa-1886 vernacular Greek Revival church. 09/28/77.

Ward-Hays House, 1008 W. 2nd St. Circa-1886 home of state prison system leader and Missouri-Pacific Railroad official. 08/11/75.

Werner Knoop House, 6 Ozark Point. 1936–37 Art Moderne residence. 08/03/90.

White-Baucum House, 201 S. Izard St. 1869–70 Italianate house. 02/29/80.

William L. Terry House, 1422 Scott St. Circa-1880 restrained Queen Anne building. 01/01/76.

Williamson House, 325 Fairfax. Circa-1911 Thompson Craftsman design. 11/15/84.

William Woodruff House, 1017 E. 8th St. 1853 home of *Arkansas Gazette* publisher. 03/21/89.

Winfield Methodist Church, 1601 Louisiana St. 1921 Thompson Gothic Revival design. 12/22/82.

Worthen Bank Building, 401 Main St. 1928 Neoclassical structure with Art Deco details. 11/13/86.

YMCA-Democrat Building, Capitol and Scott Sts. 1904 Thompson Renaissance Revival design for Arkansas's first YMCA building; used since 1930 by the *Arkansas Democrat* (now the *Arkansas Democrat-Gazette*). 06/11/92.

Zeb Ward Building, 1001–1003 W. Markham St. 1881 brick commercial building. 04/19/78.

MARCHE COMMUNITY

Immaculate Heart of Mary Church, north of North Little Rock off Hwy. 365. 1932 Charles L. Thompson Gothic Revival design. 12/22/82.

Immaculate Heart of Mary School, off Hwy. 365 north of Blue Hill Rd. 1925 Craftsman-style building. 09/16/93.

MAUMELLE

Pyeatte-Mason Cemetery, southwest corner of Waterside and Lily. Graveyard for Crystal Hill settlement with graves dating to 1818. 11/07/96.

NORTH LITTLE ROCK

Amboy Overpass, Hwy. 365 over Union-Pacific tracks north of Hwy. 176. 1941 open-masonry substructure bridge. 05/18/95.

Argenta Historic District, residential area between Melrose Circle, Willow St., and 4th St. and commercial area on Main St. between W. 6th St. and W. 3rd St. Structures built between 1890 and 1940 from earliest period of North Little Rock's development. 03/15/93.

Arkansas II Riverboat, south end of Locust St. on Arkansas River. Corps of Engineers snagboat built in 1939 and 1940. 06/14/90.

Baker House, 109 5th St. 1898–99 Queen Anne house. 12/06/78.

Barth-Hempfling House, 507 Main St. 1886 Queen Anne cottage. 10/16/86.

Cherry House, 217 Dooley Rd. 1930 Colonial Revival building. 06/01/92.

Cherry-Luter Estate, 521 W. Scenic Dr. Circa-1923 French Eclectic–style house with associated outbuildings. 09/04/92.

Cook House, 116 W. 7th St. 1914 vernacular frame residence. 11/19/93.

Crestview Park, off Crestview Blvd. Circa-1922 concrete sculptures by Dionicio Rodriguez. 12/04/86.

Edgemere Street Bridge, Edgemere St. 1920s masonry deck arch bridge. 04/09/90.

Engleberger House, 2105 N. Maple St. 1895 Queen Anne Revival house. 06/14/90.

E. O. Manees House, 216 W. 4th St. 1895 house combining Classical and Colonial Revival styles. 08/06/75.

Faucette Building, 4th and Main Sts. 1891 building linked to developers of North Little Rock. 12/06/78.

First Presbyterian Church Manse, 415 N. Maple St. Structure with unusual Craftsman design built in 1927. 11/19/93.

Fort Logan H. Roots Military Post Historic District, Scenic Hill Dr. 1893 military post. 09/04/74.

Hodge-Cook House, 620 N. Maple St. Circa-1898 vernacular Colonial Revival design. 11/19/93.

Howell-Garner-Monfee House, 300 W. 4th St. 1906 Colonial Revival house. 12/22/82.

James Peter Faucette House, 316 W. 4th St. Circa-1912 Colonial Revival house. 01/04/78.

Jeffries House, 415 Skyline Dr. 1931 Colonial Revival building. 06/01/92.

Joseph E. England Jr. House, 313 Skyline Dr. Circa-1928 English Revival house. 06/01/92.

Justin Matthews Jr. House, 257 Skyline Dr. 1928 Spanish Colonial Revival building. 12/18/90.

Kleiber House, 637 Skyline Dr. 1929 house with elements of Monterey style. 06/01/92.

Lake Number One Bridge, Avondale Rd. 1930s masonry deck arch bridge. 04/09/90.

Lakeshore Drive Bridge, Lakeshore Dr. 1930s masonry deck arch bridge. 04/09/90.

Lakewood Park, off Lakewood and Edgemere Drs. Seven circa-1933 concrete sculptures by Dionicio Rodriguez. 12/04/86.

Lloyd England Hall, northwest corner of Missouri Ave. and 6th St. in Camp Robinson. 1931 Spanish Colonial Revival–style structure. 05/09/97.

Matthews-Bradshaw House, 524 Skyline Dr. 1929 French Eclectic–style structure. 06/01/92.

Matthews-Bryan House, 320 Dooley Rd. 1930 English Revival–style building. 06/01/92.

Matthews-Dillon House, 701 Skyline Dr. 1928 English Revival building. 06/01/92.

Matthews-Godt House, 248 Skyline Dr. 1928 English Revival structure in Edgemont neighborhood. 06/01/92.

Matthews House, 406 Goshen. "Modernistic" 1928 Frank R. Carmean design blends International and Art Deco styles. 09/29/83.

Matthews-MacFayden House, 206 Dooley Rd. 1930 English Revival house. 06/01/92.

North Little Rock City Hall, 3rd and Main Sts. 1914 Neoclassical design. 08/06/75.

North Little Rock High School, 101 W. 22nd St. 1928–30 structure reflecting "zigzag moderne" trend of Art Deco style. 02/25/93.

North Little Rock Post Office, 420 N. Main St. 1931 Charles L. Thompson Georgian Revival design. 12/22/82.

Old Central Fire Station, 506 Main St. 1904 building is one of city's oldest. 12/22/77.

Owings House, 563 Skyline Dr. 1927–28 Spanish Colonial Revival building. 06/01/92.

Park Hill Fire Station and Water Company Complex, 3417–3421 Magnolia St. Six 1938 structures built by water company and Works Progress Administration. 11/19/93.

Pruniski House, 345 Goshen. 1937 Monterey-style house. 02/09/90.

Rapillard House, 123 W. 7th St. 1927 English Revival–style residence. 11/19/93.

Rock Island–Argenta Depot, 4th and Hazel. 1913 Mediterranean-style depot. 09/21/89.

Saint Joseph's Home, Camp Robinson Rd. 1910 Roman Catholic orphanage. 05/04/76.

T. R. Pugh Memorial Park, off Fairway Ave. Extensive collection of Dionicio Rodriguez's 1933 sculptures, including Carmean-designed "Old Mill." 12/04/86.

Waterside Street Bridge, Waterside St. Circa-1935 closed-spandrel masonry-deck bridge. 06/14/90.

Young House, 436 Skyline Dr. 1929 Craftsman Bungalow. 06/01/92.

SCOTT

All Souls Church, off Hwy. 130. 1906 Gothic Revival church. 08/12/77.

Land's End Plantation, Hwy. 161. 1925–27 Tudor Revival–style house with associated outbuildings and site features. 01/27/99.

McKenzie House, Hwy. 161. 1867–75 Plain Traditional house with Italianate details. 03/05/92.

SWEET HOME

Hanger Cotton Gin, Harper Rd. and Gates Lane. Circa-1876 steam-powered cotton gin. 10/08/76.

RANDOLPH COUNTY

BIRDELL

Old Union School, 504 Old Union Rd. 1913 Plain Traditional–style school structure. 11/12/93.

BLACK ROCK

Old Davidsonville Historic Site, northeast of Black Rock on Black River. Site of river town that existed circa 1800–1829. 01/18/74.

POCAHONTAS

Black River Bridge, Hwy. 67 over Black River. 1934 swing bridge. 04/09/90.

Daniel V. Bates House, Hwy. 67 west of Broadway. 1905 mixture of Queen Anne details and rustic stone elements. 12/27/79.

Old Randolph County Courthouse, Broadway and Vance. 1875 Italianate structure. 04/24/73.

Old Randolph County Courthouse, Pocahontas, Randolph County.

Forrest City High School, Forrest City, Saint Francis County.

Randolph County Courthouse, junction of Broadway and N. Marr. 1940 Art Deco structure erected by Works Progress Administration. 08/22/96.

WARM SPRINGS

Hillyard Cabin, Old Burr Rd. Circa-1934 single-pen vacation cabin. 08/16/94.

SAINT FRANCIS COUNTY

COLT

William Stone House, junction of Hwy. 306 and Ellis Lane. 1900 home with Colonial Revival and Folk Victorian details. 10/08/92.

FORREST CITY

First United Methodist Church, 101 S. Izard. 1917 Classical Revival–style structure. 05/19/94.

Forrest City High School, Rosser St. 1915 Classical Revival school building. 10/08/92.

Mann House, 422 Forest St. 1913 Charles L. Thompson Colonial Revival design. 12/22/82.

Stuart Springs, Stuart St. 1905 park surrounds three springs that once provided town's water. 08/03/77.

MADISON

Saint Francis River Bridge, Hwy. 70 over Saint Francis River. 1933 swing bridge. 04/09/90.

WHEATLEY

Smith House, Memphis Ave. 1919 Charles L. Thompson Craftsman design. 12/22/82.

SALINE COUNTY

BAUXITE

Rucker House, Hwy. 183 and Gibbons Rd. 1905 home of Alcoa supervisor. 06/16/88.

BENTON

Dr. James Wyatt Walton House, 301 W. Sevier. 1903 Thompson design for prominent doctor. 12/22/77.

Gann Building, 218 S. Market St. 1893 doctor's office built of bauxite. 10/21/75.

Gann House, 224 S. Market St. Circa-1895 Queen Anne house. 01/02/76.

Gann Row Historic District, bordered by Pine, Market, Maple, and S. Main Sts. Working-class district of Craftsman and Folk Victorian–style structures. 02/05/99.

J. W. & Ann Lowe Clary House, 305 N. East St. Circa-1926 transitional Craftsman/Tudor Revival building. 02/19/93.

Old River Bridge, southwest of Benton spanning Saline River on River Rd. 1899 iron bridge. 09/15/77.

Saline County Courthouse, Courthouse Square. 1900 Charles L. Thompson–designed Romanesque Revival structure. 11/22/76.

Saline River Bridge, County Rd. 365. 1928 open-spandrel, deck-arch bridge. 04/09/90.

Shoppach House, 508 N. Main. 1852 structure is county's first brick house. 10/10/75.

BRYANT

Andrew Hunter House, west of Bryant on Hwy. 5. Circa-1870 frame house of Methodist Church pioneer. 12/12/76.

PLEASANT HILL

Pleasant Hill Methodist Church, Lawson and Lake Norrell Rds. 1894 vernacular Greek Revival church. 06/05/91.

ADDRESS RESTRICTED

Hughes Mound Site. 1500–1700 A.D. Caddoan site. 10/10/85.

SCOTT COUNTY

BLUE BALL

Powder Magazine, County Rd. 96 north of Blue Ball. Circa-1935 cut-stone and concrete structure built by Civilian Conservation Corps. 10/20/93.

WALDRON

C. E. Forrester House, 140 Danville Rd. 1896 I-house with circa-1904 addition. 09/03/98.

Cold Spring, County Rd. 93 northeast of Waldron. Circa-1936 concrete structure built by CCC. 10/21/93.

Mount Pleasant Methodist Church, Hwy. 248. 1891 frame church. 06/05/86.

Gann Building, Benton, Saline County.

Scott County Courthouse, Waldron, Scott County.

Poteau Work Center, off Hwy. 80. Circa-1939 CCC-built wood-frame building. 10/20/93.

Poteau Work Center Residence Number Two, off Hwy. 80. Wood-frame structure built circa 1939 by CCC. 10/20/93.

Scott County Courthouse, Courthouse Square. 1933–34 Art Deco structure. 11/13/89.

SEARCY COUNTY

BAKER

Jasper E. Treece Building, west of County Rd. 55 one-half mile south of intersection with State Rd. 74. 1878 stone vegetable- and grain-storage structure. 08/18/93.

GILBERT

Mays General Store, Front St. 1901 commercial structure with 1906 addition. 09/01/83.

LESLIE

American Legion Post Number 131, northeast side of Center St. Circa-1935 Rustic-style building erected by Works Progress Administration. 12/02/93.

Columbus Hatchett House, north corner of Main and Hazel. Circa-1910 vernacular Colonial Revival house. 08/18/93.

Dr. Clay House, Hwy. 66. 1907 Folk Victorian residence. 12/02/93.

Dr. Cleveland Hollabaugh House, Oak St. 1907 structure with Folk Victorian and Craftsman influences. 12/02/93.

Dr. J. O. Cotton House, southeast corner of Hwy. 66 and High St. 1915 Craftsman-style design. 12/02/93.

Dr. Robinson House, Hwy. 66. 1917–18 building reflecting Colonial Revival and Folk Victorian influences. 12/02/93.

Farmers Bank Building, corner of Main and Walnut. Circa-1910 vernacular Richardsonian Romanesque building. 08/18/93.

Greene Thomas Farm, west of County Rd. 55 one-quarter mile south of intersection with County Rd. 74. Features 1930 Craftsman residence, circa-1937 barn, and circa-1920 stone outbuilding. 08/18/93.

Guy Bartley House, northeast corner of Elm and 5th Sts. Circa-1906 Colonial Revival–style building. 12/02/93.

J. C. Miller House, northwest corner of Oak and High Sts. Circa-1905 American Foursquare–style house. 12/02/93.

Leslie–Rolen House, east corner of Cherry and High. 1907 Plain Traditional–style frame residence. 08/18/93.

Missouri and North Arkansas Depot, Hwy. 66. Circa-1925 stone-masonry depot. 06/11/92.

Treat Commercial Building, northwest side of Oak St. between High and 4th Sts. 1910 commercial structure. 08/18/93.

MARSHALL

Aday–Stephenson House, west side of Pine St. Vernacular wood-frame residence erected between 1903 and 1905. 12/02/93.

Anthony Luna House, southwest corner of Main and Spring Sts. 1891 Plain Traditional building with Folk Victorian influences. 10/04/93.

Bank of Marshall Building, southeast corner of Main and Center Sts. Colonial Revival–style commercial building erected in 1913 and 1914. 10/04/93.

Bates Tourist Court, south side of Fair St. Features three 1935 stone-veneer rental cabins. 10/04/93.

Bromley–Mills–Treece House, north side of Main St. Circa-1900 Plain Traditional house with Colonial Revival–style porch. 10/04/93.

Bud Fendley House, 201 Spring St. 1928 Craftsman-style house. 08/18/93.

Charley Passmore House, south side of Campus St. 1938 Craftsman-style structure. 10/04/93.

Dr. Sam G. Daniel House, north side of Nome St. one block west of courthouse square. 1902–3 Queen Anne Revival residence. 08/18/93.

Dugger and Schultz Millinery Store Building, southwest corner of Glade and Nome. 1905 stone structure with Romanesque Revival influences. 10/04/93.

Ferguson Gas Station, northeast corner of Center St. and Hwy. 65. Circa-1927 English Cottage–type commercial building. 10/04/93.

J. M. McCall House, east side of Spring St. Circa-1910 Craftsman-style structure. 10/04/93.

Noah Bryan Store, southwest corner of Glade and Main Sts. 1926 native-stone commercial structure. 08/18/93.

Oscar Redman Building, 119 E. Main St. Circa-1920 concrete-block commercial building. 08/18/93.

S. A. Lay House, corner of Glade St. and Hwy. 65. 1921 Craftsman residence. 10/04/93.

Bank of Marshall Building, Marshall, Searcy County.

Sanders-Hollabaugh House, east side of Church St. 1903 vernacular "prow" house, 10/04/93.

Searcy County Courthouse, Courthouse Square. 1889 native-stone public building. 10/21/76.

T. M. Ferguson House, west side of Canaan St. Plain Traditional–style residence built between 1900 and 1903. 10/04/93.

Vinie McCall House, east side of Spring St. Circa-1895 Plain Traditional house with Folk Victorian details. 10/04/93.

W. F. Reeves House, north side of Short St. 1903–4 Folk Victorian–style residence. 10/04/93.

Zeb Ferguson House, Hwy. 65. Circa-1928 residence featuring decorative stone details. 10/04/93.

MORNING STAR

Sam Marshall House, County Rd. 163 near Morning Star. Traditional log cabin built in 1929. 10/04/93.

Thomas Lynch House, two and one-half miles north of Morning Star on County Rd. 52. Circa-1900 log dogtrot building. 08/18/93.

OXLEY

Campbell Post Office/Kuykendall General Store, County Rd. 73 northwest of Oxley. Circa-1900 wood-frame building with subtle Greek Revival–style influences. 12/02/93.

SAINT JOE

Benjamin Franklin Henley House, off Hwy. 65. Circa-1870 frame house with circa-1876 additions. 12/05/85.

Saint Joe, Missouri, and North Arkansas Railroad Depot, Hwy. 65. 1913 wood-frame railroad structure. 09/16/93.

SNOWBALL

Gates-Helm Farm, County Rd. 13 one mile north of intersection with County Rd. 250. Features circa-1870 log house and barn and circa-1900 wood-frame residence. 08/18/93.

ADDRESS RESTRICTED

Calf Creek Site. 1000 B.C.–1500 A.D. Late Archaic, Woodland, and Mississippian site. 06/29/76.

Cooper's Bluff Site. Circa-1500 rock art site. 05/04/82.

SEBASTIAN COUNTY

FORT SMITH

Angus McLeod House, 912 N. 13th St. 1905 Neoclassical residence. 12/08/78.

Atkinson-Williams Warehouse, 320 Rogers Ave. 1906 commercial structure. 12/12/79.

Belle Grove Historic District, bounded by N. 4th, N. 9th, N. "B", and N. "H" Sts. Residential district with buildings dating from 1865 to 1920. 07/16/73.

Birney Safety Streetcar Number 224, housed at 100 S. 4th St. Restored 1926 trolley car. 05/19/94.

Bonneville House, 318 N. 7th St. 1880 Italianate house. 09/22/71.

Christ the King Church, Greenwood and S. "S" St. 1930 Charles L. Thompson Spanish Mission design. 12/22/82.

Commercial Hotel, 123 N. 1st St. 1899 hotel. 05/07/73.

C. R. Breckenridge House, 504 N. 16th St. 1903 home of Arkansas politician and minister to Russia. 08/07/79.

Ferguson-Calderara House, 214 N. 14th St. Classically detailed 1904 home of lumberman. 12/11/79.

Fort Smith Confederate Monument, 6th St. and Rogers Ave. 1903 commemorative sculpture. 04/26/96.

Fort Smith Masonic Temple, 200 N. 11th St. 1927 Art Deco structure with Egyptian Revival interior. 11/20/92.

Fort Smith National Cemetery, 522 Garland Ave. 1867 military cemetery. 05/22/99.

Birney Safety Streetcar Number 224, Fort Smith, Sebastian County.

Fort Smith National Historic Site, 3rd St. and Rogers Ave. 1817–24 frontier fort established to keep peace among Indian tribes; site of "hanging judge" Isaac C. Parker's court. Fort Smith National Historic Site is a National Historic Landmark. NHL: 12/19/60. NR: 03/07/86.

Horace Franklin Rogers House, 2900 Rogers Ave. 1904 home of prominent citizen. 05/02/79.

James Sparks House, 206 N. 14th St. Circa-1887 Romanesque architecture. 09/14/72.

Joseph Knoble Brewery, N. 3rd and "E" Sts. 1851 brewery building. 03/24/72.

Josiah Foster Building, 222 Garrison Ave. 1897 commercial building. 01/20/78.

Karl Edward Bracht House, 315 N. 13th St. Circa-1866 house with Italianate details. 05/02/79.

Oak Cemetery, southeast of intersection of Greenwood and Dodson. City cemetery with graves dating to 1853. 06/02/95.

Sebastian County Courthouse/Fort Smith City Hall, 100 S. 6th St. 1937 structure designed in Art Deco variation. 06/08/93.

Spirit of the American Doughboy Monument, 4901 Midland. 1930 World War I commemorative sculpture. 05/23/97.

Tillman Shaw House, 500 S. 19th St. 1909 house with Spanish Colonial, Prairie, and Colonial Revival details. 05/16/88.

West Garrison Avenue Historic District, 100–525 Garrison Ave. Commercial district with structures built between 1870 and 1920. 04/26/79.

W. H. H. Clayton House, 514 N. 6th St. Circa-1880 home of frontier prosecutor. 09/04/70.

William J. Murphy House, 923 N. 13th St. Circa-1895 Colonial Revival house. 08/07/79.

GREENWOOD

Old Sebastian County Jail, Hwy. 10 east of the courthouse. 1889–92 stone structure. 12/01/94.

State Highway 96 Bridge, over tributary of Vache Grasse Creek. 1938 steel pony-truss bridge. 05/05/95.

HACKETT

Hackett Creek Bridge, Hwy. 45 at Hackett Creek crossing. 1941 open-masonry substructure bridge. 05/05/95.

HARTFORD

Sebastian County Road 5G Bridge, over West Creek tributary. 1943 open-masonry substructure bridge built by Works Progress Administration. 05/05/95.

JENNY LIND

Jenny Lind Bridge, County Rd. 8 over Vache Grasse Creek tributary near Jenny Lind. Late 1930s masonry-arch bridge. 04/06/90.

MANSFIELD

Coop Creek Bridge, County Rd. 236 at Coop Creek crossing. 1940 open-masonry substructure bridge. 05/05/95.

MILLTOWN

Milltown Bridge, County Rd. 77 one and one-half miles west of Milltown. 1930s masonry-arch bridge. 04/06/90.

Vache Grasse Creek Bridge, County Rd. 75A over Vache Grasse Creek. 1940 closed-spandrel arch bridge. 05/05/95.

WEST HARTFORD

Sebastian County Road 4G Bridge, over tributary of Sugar Loaf Creek. 1940 open-masonry substructure bridge. 05/05/95.

SEVIER COUNTY

DEQUEEN

DeQueen and Eastern Railroad Machine Shop, northwest corner of D & E rail yard, next to Hwy. 329. 1905 Italianate-style building. 06/20/96.

First Presbyterian Church, junction of Vandervoort and N. 5th Sts. 1898 Gothic Revival–style structure. 12/01/94.

Hayes Hardware Store, 314 DeQueen. Circa-1900 vernacular commercial design. 12/03/80.

Hotel Dee Swift, 123 N. Port Arthur St. Railroad hotel built in 1900. 06/20/96.

GILLHAM

Goff and Gamble Merchandise Store, one block north of railroad tracks in center of Gillham. Sprawling commercial building erected in three phases between 1900 and 1911. 06/20/96.

KING

King Schoolhouse, one mile east of Hwy. 71. 1915 structure with Colonial Revival–style details. 06/20/96.

LOCKESBURG

First United Methodist Church, east of junction of 2nd and 5th Sts. 1926 structure designed in free interpretation of Gothic Revival style. 05/19/94.

Little Cossatot River Bridge, County Rd. 139 H over Little Cossatot River. 1908 Warren pony-truss bridge. 04/06/90.

Locke-Nall House, off Hwy. 59/71 north of Lockesburg. Circa-1870 frame Greek Revival residence. 05/01/89.

SHARP COUNTY

CAVE CITY

Crystal River Tourist Camp Historic District, Hwy. 167. 1934 automobile tourist camp in "Mannerist" interpretation of Rustic style. 06/06/91.

EVENING SHADE

Charles W. Shaver House, east side of Court St. Greek Revival–influenced 1874 structure. 09/30/82.

Coger House, south side of Main St. Circa-1870 Greek Revival structure with Victorian details. 06/02/82.

John McCaleb House, southeast corner of Main St. and Sidney Rd. Circa-1900 Queen Anne design. 06/02/82.

John W. Shaver House, northwest corner of Main and Cammack Sts. 1854 home of pioneer fur trader. 06/02/82.

Lee Weaver House, Hardy, Sharp County.

Metcalf House, south side of Gin Dr. Circa-1880 I-house with Greek Revival details. 06/02/82.

Sam Davidson House, west side of Cammack St. Circa-1880 structure with Bungalow-style porch. 06/02/82.

Stokes House, east side of Cammack St. 1882 structure with vernacular Queen Anne details. 06/02/82.

W. A. Edwards House, south side of Main St. Circa-1890 house with Folk Victorian and Colonial Revival influences. 06/02/82.

Wilkerson House, west side of Sidney Rd. Circa-1900 Greek Revival house. 06/02/82.

HARDY

Carrie Tucker House, Hwy. 62 east of Echo Lane. Circa-1928 vernacular English Revival design. 02/12/99.

Ernest Daugherty House, 3rd St. west of Kelly Ave. Craftsman-style structure built in 1932. 12/17/98.

Esther Locke House, southeast corner of Spring and 3rd Sts. Built in 1936 and 1937 as a combination residence and boarding house. 12/17/98.

Floyd Jackson House, east side of Jackson St. Built in 1929 in a Craftsman design accentuated with beaded mortar. 12/17/98.

Fred Carter House, School Ave. north of 4th St. Flagstone structure with attached garage built circa 1947. 12/17/98.

Fred Graham House, Hwy. 62 west of Springwood Rd. 1931 Tudor Revival–style structure. 02/12/99.

Hardy Downtown Historic District, bounded by Kelly, Front, Church, and 3rd Sts. Collection of commercial, residential, and institutional structures dated from 1880 to 1945. 09/22/95.

Lee Weaver House, Main and Cope Sts. 1924 raised bungalow built of native stone. 12/17/98.

Sherman Bates House, Hwy. 63 and Echo Lane. 1940 structure designed in a vernacular interpretation of the Tudor Revival style. 12/17/98.

Silas Sherrill House, 4th and Spring Sts. Built in 1927 and 1928 in the Craftsman style of architecture. 12/17/98.

Web Long House and Motel, Hwy. 63 east of Springwood Rd. 1943 house representing transition from Minimalist Traditional building style to Ranch style; coupled with one of the first true motels—as opposed to individual tourist courts—in the area. 12/17/98.

William Shaver House, School Ave. north of 4th St. 1947 flagstone structure. 12/17/98.

John Avey Barn, Big Springs, Stone County.

Woodland Courts, near junction of Dawson and Old CCC Rds. Ten circa-1938 Plain Traditional–style cabins. 11/27/92.

POUGHKEEPSIE

Poughkeepsie School Building, Hwy. 58. 1929 Plain Traditional–style building. 09/10/92.

WILLIFORD

Williford Methodist Church, near Ferguson and Hail Sts. Circa-1910 vernacular Gothic Revival building. 11/27/92.

STONE COUNTY

ALCO

Alco School, off Hwy. 66. 1938 National Youth Administration–built structure. 09/04/92.

BIG SPRINGS

George Anderson House, west of Big Springs. Circa-1890 log dogtrot house. 09/17/85.

John Avey Barn, off Hwy. 66. 1906 gambrel-roof barn partially built into hillside. 09/17/85.

Orvall Gammill Barn, northwest of Big Springs. Circa-1922 log-and-lumber, transverse-crib barn. 09/17/85.

CALICO ROCK VICINITY

Sugarloaf Fire Tower Historic District, end of Forest Service Rd. 1123. Collection of 1937 structures built by Civilian Conservation Corps. 09/11/85.

EAST RICHWOODS

H. S. Mabry Barn, near Johnson Creek. Unusually large circa-1922 transverse-crib barn. 09/17/85.

FIFTY-SIX

Mirror Lake Historic District, Forest Service Rd. 1110E. Contains dam, bridge, observation tower, and lake built by CCC in 1940. 09/11/95.

FOX

Bonds House, County Rd. 2 near Fox. Circa-1900 dogtrot house. 02/03/92.

LUBER

Luber School, County Rd. 214. Circa-1930 Plain Traditional–style structure. 09/04/92.

MARCELLA

Binks Hess House and Barn, off Hwy. 14. Circa-1871 Greek Revival dogtrot house with transverse-crib barn. 09/17/85.

H. J. Dougherty House, Hwy. 14. Circa-1905 dogtrot house. 09/17/85.

Jessie Abernathy House, off Hwy. 14. 1884 central-hall plan house. 09/17/85.

Marcella Church and School, Hwy. 14. Circa-1900 vernacular Greek Revival structure. 09/17/85.

Owen Martin House, Hwy. 14. Circa-1920 double-pen house. 10/25/85.

Taylor-Stokes House, off Hwy. 14 near Marcella. Circa-1876 log house. 09/17/85.

Thomas E. Hess House, Hwy. 14. 1900 I-house. 12/27/83.

Thomas M. Hess House, off Hwy. 14. Circa-1868 central-hall house with Queen Anne porch. 09/17/85.

MELROSE

Walter Gray House, Hwy. 14. Circa-1910 dogtrot house. 09/17/85.

MOUNTAIN VIEW

A. B. Brewer Building, Hwy. 66. 1929 stone commercial building. 10/25/85.

Brewer's Mill, Hwy. 66. 1914 industrial structure. 09/17/85.

C. B. Case Motor Company Building, Hwy. 66. 1928 office of county's first automobile dealership. 09/17/85.

Clark-King House, northeast of Mountain View. Circa-1885 double-pen log house. 09/17/85.

C. L. Smith and Son General Store, Hwy. 66. 1905 Romanesque-inspired structure. 09/17/85.

Commercial Hotel, off Hwy. 66. 1925 Craftsman hotel. 09/17/85.

Dew Drop Inn, off Hwy. 66. Circa-1920 Craftsman hotel. 09/17/85.

Farmers and Merchants Bank, Hwy. 66. 1910 vernacular Romanesque-style stone building. 09/17/85.

George W. Lackey House, 124 Washington St. 1915 home of Mountain View businessman and civic leader. 10/01/90.

John F. Brewer House, west side of Peabody St., one block south of Courthouse Square. Circa-1924 Craftsman Bungalow. 10/25/85.

John L. Lancaster House, Courthouse Square. Circa-1899 frame house with high-style elements. 09/17/85.

Lackey General Merchandise and Warehouse, Courthouse Square. 1924 stone commercial building. 09/17/85.

Noah McCarn House, Hwy. 5. 1920 dogtrot house. 09/17/85.

Noricks Chapel School, County Rd. 28. 1907 wood-frame school building. 06/04/98.

Stegall General Store, Hwy. 66. 1926 stone commercial building. 09/17/85.

Stone County Courthouse, Courthouse Square. 1922 stone building designed by architect C. A. Ferrell. 09/17/85.

Stone County Recorder Building, Courthouse Square. Circa-1907 frame commercial building. 09/17/85.

NEWNATA

Clarence Anderson Barn, Hwy. 66. Circa-1925 transverse-crib barn with dormers. 09/17/85.

OLD LEXINGTON

Joe Guffey House, Hwy. 110. Circa-1900 house on T-shaped plan. 09/17/85.

ONIA

Bluff Springs Church and School, three and one-half miles west of Onia. 1900 box-constructed building. 09/17/85.

Roasting Ear Church and School, on Roasting Ear Creek northeast of Onia. Circa-1918 vernacular Greek Revival structure. 09/17/85.

OPTIMUS

Miles Jeffery Barn, off Hwy. 5. Circa-1858 single-crib barn altered over years into triple-crib barn. 09/17/85.

C. B. Case Motor Company Building, Mountain View, Stone County.

PLEASANT GROVE

Davis Barn, west of Pleasant Grove. Circa-1915 double-crib frame barn. 09/17/85.

Henry Copeland House, Hwy, 14. Circa-1900 double-pen frame house. 09/17/85.

John Bettis House, Hwy. 14. Circa-1929 Craftsman farmhouse. 09/17/85.

Zachariah Ford House, near the White River. Circa-1856 log house converted to dogtrot around 1885. 09/17/85.

ROUND BOTTOM

Fred Lancaster Barn, near White River. Circa-1918 log four-crib barn. 09/17/85.

William Dillard Homestead, near White River. Circa-1837 log cabin and double-crib log barn. 09/17/85.

SAINT JAMES

Pinky Pruitt Barn, Hwy. 14. Circa-1890 single-crib plan barn. 09/17/85.

TIMBO

Jim Morris Barn, Hwy. 66. Circa-1900 transverse-crib barn. 09/17/85.

Wesley Copeland House, southeast of Timbo. Circa-1858 dogtrot house. 09/17/85.

TURKEY CREEK

Turkey Creek School, Hwy. 9. 1925 traditional frame school building. 10/25/85.

WEST RICHWOODS

Samuel Brown House, off Hwy. 66. Circa-1848 weatherboard-covered dogtrot house. 09/17/85.

West Richwoods Church and School, Hwy. 9. Circa-1921 early twentieth-century public school. 09/17/85.

ADDRESS RESTRICTED

Fox Pictograph. Circa-1500 rock art site. 05/04/82.

Pictograph Cave. Circa-1500 rock art site. 05/04/82.

UNION COUNTY

EL DORADO

Bank of Commerce, 200 N. Washington St. 1919–20 Classical Revival structure. 03/25/82.

Charles H. Murphy Sr. House, 900 N. Madison St. 1925–26 Charles L. Thompson Tudor Revival design. 09/08/83.

El Dorado Apartments, 420 Wilson Place. 1926 structure built following oil boom. 12/01/83.

El Dorado Confederate Monument, Union County Courthouse. 1910 commemorative sculpture. 04/26/96.

El Dorado Junior College Building, 300 S. West Ave. 1905 Neoclassical school. 09/13/78.

Exchange Bank, Washington and Oak Sts. 1926–27 Venetian Gothic design. 12/16/86.

First Presbyterian Church, 300 E. Main. 1926 Collegiate Gothic structure. 05/14/91.

Henry Crawford McKinney House, 510 E. Faulkner. 1925 Thompson Classical Revival design. 09/01/83.

Joel Smith House, Hwy. 167. Circa-1840 structure is rare Arkansas example of vernacular late Colonial style. 08/24/90.

John Newton House, 510 N. Jackson St. Circa-1853 Greek Revival residence. 11/06/74.

Municipal Building, 204 N. West Ave. 1927 Eugene John Stern design features Art Deco and Classical details. 06/30/83.

Rialto Theater 117 E. Cedar St. 1929 Classical Revival movie house. 08/21/86.

Smith-McCurry House, Hwy. 15 three and one-half miles east of El Dorado. 1867 dogtrot home of Mamie Smith McCurry, a pioneer in the Arkansas oil business. 10/15/92.

Union County Courthouse, Union Square. 1927–28 Classical Revival design. 06/30/83.

LISBON

Mount Moriah Masonic Lodge Number Eighteen, off Hwy. 172. 1858 structure is oldest Masonic lodge in Arkansas. 03/13/87.

Willett House, 6563 Mount Holly Rd. 1926 Craftsman-style farmhouse with associated outbuildings. 09/14/95.

SMACKOVER

D. McDonald House, 8th and Broadway. 1928–29 Mediterranean villa design. 12/27/90.

Smackover Historic Commercial District, 601–628 Broadway. Vernacular commercial and public buildings from 1925 to 1940. 06/14/90.

John Newton House, El Dorado, Union County.

VAN BUREN COUNTY

BEE BRANCH

Collums–Baker House, Hwy. 65 south of Bee Branch. 1907 Folk Victorian–style residence. 11/24/92.

CLINTON

Van Buren County Courthouse, Courthouse Square. 1934 Works Progress Administration–built Rustic-style structure with Art Deco influences. 05/13/91.

DAMASCUS

Damascus Gymnasium, Hwy. 285. 1933 WPA-built Craftsman-style building. 09/04/92.

SCOTLAND

Van Buren County Road 2E Bridge, over tributary of Driver's Creek. 1940 open-masonry substructure bridge built by WPA. 05/05/95.

ADDRESS RESTRICTED

Edgemont Shelter. Circa-1500 rock art site. 05/04/82.

Lynn Creek Shelter. 8000 B.C.–1500 A.D. Archaic through Mississippian site with evidence of historic activity. 03/21/78.

WASHINGTON COUNTY

CANE HILL

A. R. Carroll Building, northwest corner of Main St. and County Rd. 764. 1900 commercial building with pressed-tin façade. 11/17/82.

Blackburn House, Main and College Sts. 1898 house mixing Queen Anne and Colonial Revival styles. 11/17/82.

Cane Hill Battlefield, following Hwy. 45 and County Rds. 291, 8, 184, and 285. Scene of November 28, 1862, Civil War battle. 03/07/94.

Lynn Creek Shelter, Address Restricted, Van Buren County.

Cane Hill Cemetery, south of County Rd. 13. Cemetery with graves dating to the 1830s. 11/17/82.

Cane Hill College Building, McClellen and College Sts. 1887 brick college structure. 11/17/82.

D. N. Edmiston House, northwest corner of Main St. and County Rd. 763. 1886 Italianate house. 11/17/82.

Earle House, east of Hwy. 45. 1859 Greek Revival home of college president. 11/17/82.

E. W. McClellan House, southwest of Cane Hill off Hwy. 45. Circa-1866 frame Greek Revival house. 11/17/82.

Henry Pyeatt House, west of Hwy. 45. Circa-1866 I-house with Greek Revival details. 11/17/82.

John Edmiston House, west of Hwy. 45. 1896 house with Queen Anne and Eastlake details. 11/17/82.

Methodist Manse, Main and Spring Sts. 1834 brick house resembles Federal style. 11/17/82.

Moore House, northwest of Cane Hill on County Rd. 13. 1856 frame house with additions from 1893 and 1896 and a log granary. 11/17/82.

Pyeatte Mill Site, Hwy. 45. 1902 site features massive water wheel. 11/17/82.

United Presbyterian Church of Cane Hill, west side of Main St. 1891 vernacular Gothic Revival building. 11/17/82.

William Welch House, east side of Main St. Circa-1855 vernacular Greek Revival structure. 11/17/82.

Zeb Edmiston House, east side of Main St. 1872 vernacular Greek Revival residence. 11/17/82.

DURHAM

Durham School, County Rd. 183. 1929 Craftsman-style structure. 09/04/92.

ELKINS

Maguire-Williams House, Hwy. 74. Log-and-frame structure built in three stages between 1838 and 1877. 09/07/95.

Tom Smith House, Hwy. 74. Circa-1834 brick structure designed in late Georgian style. 10/08/92.

FARMINGTON

Walnut Grove Presbyterian Church, Hwy. 170. 1903 structure designed in synthesis of Romanesque Revival and Classical Revival styles. 12/07/95.

FAYETTEVILLE

Agricultural Building, Campus Dr. at the University of Arkansas. 1936 Collegiate Gothic–style building. 09/04/92.

Business Administration Building, Campus Dr. at the University of Arkansas. 1939 Collegiate Gothic structure. 09/04/92.

Chemistry Building, Campus Dr. at the University of Arkansas. 1934 Collegiate Gothic building. 09/04/92.

Chi Omega Chapter House, 940 Maple St. 1928 Colonial Revival–style structure with Classical Revival details. 04/20/95.

Chi Omega Greek Theater, Dickson St. at the University of Arkansas. Circa-1927 outdoor amphitheater. 09/04/92.

Old Main,
Fayetteville,
Washington County.

Ella Carnell Hall, University of Arkansas. Circa-1900 Charles L. Thompson Colonial Revival dormitory. 12/22/82.

Evergreen Cemetery, corner of University and Williams Sts. Early Fayetteville burial ground with graves dating to 1840s. 10/30/97.

Fayetteville Confederate Cemetery, Rock St. Cemetery started in 1872 by Southern Memorial Association of Washington County with site improvements added through the 1920s. 06/03/93.

Frisco Depot, 550 W. Dickson St. 1925 depot in Mission/Spanish Colonial Revival style. 12/08/88.

Gregg House, 339 N. Gregg St. 1871 Italianate house. 09/17/74.

Guisinger Building, E. Mountain St. at southeast corner of town square. 1886 Italianate commercial building. 09/20/84.

Happy Hollow Farm, County Rd. 10. 1908 home of writer William Rheem Lighton. 08/06/86.

Headquarters House, 118 E. Dickson St. 1853 structure that served as Union Army headquarters during Battle of Fayetteville. 06/24/71.

Hemingway House and Barn, 3310 Old Missouri Rd. 1907 Thompson-designed Dutch Colonial house and gambrel-roofed barn. 08/12/82.

Home Economics Building, off Campus Dr. at the University of Arkansas. 1939 Collegiate Gothic structure. 09/04/92.

Jackson House, 1500 Mission Hwy. (Hwy. 45). 1874 brick house with Classical influences. 08/17/82.

Johnson Barn, Cato Springs Rd. 1933 barn designed by Johnson brothers using best design features of other local barns. 06/21/90.

John S. Vest House, 21 N. West St. 1870 house with Italianate and Gothic details. 11/27/79.

Lafayette Street Overpass, over Frisco Railroad lines. 1938 Art Deco–style bridge. 05/26/95.

Lewis Brothers Building, 1 S. Block. 1908 Queen Anne–Classical Revival mix. 08/17/87.

Lynn Shelton American Legion Post Number Twenty-Seven, 28 S. College Ave. 1939–40 stone meeting house. 01/04/96.

Bean Cemetery, Lincoln, Washington County.

Magnolia Company Filling Station, 429 W. Lafayette. 1925 Craftsman gas station. 11/15/78.

Maple Street Overpass, over Frisco Railroad lines. 1936 concrete bridge designed by Frederick Lutt Johann. 05/26/95.

Men's Gymnasium, Garland Ave. at the University of Arkansas. 1936 Plain Traditional–style building with Collegiate Gothic details. 09/04/92.

Mount Nord Historic District, Mount Nord Ave. Residential area with buildings ranging from 1901 to 1925. 09/16/82.

Old Bank of Fayetteville Building, 100 W. Center St. 1889 structure features Queen Anne and Romanesque Revival influences. 03/07/94.

Old Main, University of Arkansas, Arkansas Ave. 1879 Second Empire structure. 06/15/70.

The Old Post Office, the Square. 1911 Classical Revival building. 08/27/74.

Ridge House, 230 W. Center. Circa-1840 Salt Box–type house; home of family of slain Cherokee Chief John Ridge. 11/02/72.

Routh-Bailey House, three miles east of Fayetteville on Old Wire Rd. Circa-1850 I-house. 09/28/89.

Student Union Building, Campus Dr. and Maple St. at the University of Arkansas. 1939 Collegiate Gothic/Classical Revival building. 09/04/92.

Troy Gordon House, 9 E. Township Rd. Circa-1851 Greek Revival house. 12/01/78.

Villa Rosa, 617 W. Lafayette. 1932 Italian Renaissance home of Arkansas poet laureate, Rosa Marinoni. 12/27/90.

Vol Walker Library, Campus Dr. at the University of Arkansas. 1935 Classical Revival building. 09/04/92.

Wade-Heerwagen House, 338 Washington Ave. N. 1873 frame vernacular residence. 06/15/78.

Walker-Knerr-Williams House, Knerr Rd. 1878 house with Georgian and Victorian elements. 06/10/75.

Walker-Stone House, 207 Center St. 1845 home of merchant. 09/04/70.

Washington County Courthouse, College Ave. and E. Center St. 1905 Richardsonian Romanesque structure. 02/23/72.

Washington County Jail, College and County Aves. 1896 Richardsonian Romanesque design. 12/01/78.

Washington-Willow Historic District (as amended), bounded by College and Olive Aves. and Prospect and Spring Sts. Residential area with structures built between 1828 and 1945. Originally listed: 05/23/80. Amended: 03/28/95.

Waters-Pierce Oil Co. Building, West St. 1912 Thompson commercial Colonial Revival design. 12/08/88.

Wilson Park (Rock House) Historic District, bounded by College and Wilson Aves. and Maple and Louise Sts. Historic residential area with buildings dating from 1900 to 1945. 03/31/95.

Wilson-Pittman-Campbell-Gregory House, 405 E. Dickson St. 1866 structure with 1870–71 Italianate addition. 05/06/80.

Wyman Bridge, County Rd. 48 over West Fork of White River. 1908 Parker through-truss bridge. 04/09/90.

Old Springdale High School, Springdale, Washington County.

GREENLAND

Black Oak Cemetery, County Rd. 243. Cemetery with graves dating from circa 1843 to mid-1930s. 06/03/98.

JOHNSON

Johnson House and Mill, west of Johnson on Johnson Rd. 1882 brick farmhouse and two-story frame mill with outbuildings. 12/12/76.

Johnson Switch Building, 3201 Main St. 1904 commercial building with pressed-tin siding. 02/26/99.

LINCOLN

Bean Cemetery, north of Hwy. 62. African-American cemetery with graves dating to 1874. 03/07/94.

MORROW

Twin Bridges Historic District, County Rds. 11 and 3412. Pair of 1922 closed-spandrel, concrete-deck bridges. 03/07/94.

PRAIRIE GROVE

Borden House, northeast of Prairie Grove on Hwy. 62. Circa-1870 frame house on Prairie Grove battlefield. 03/17/77.

John Tilley House, Rhea's Mill Rd. west of Prairie Grove. 1855 brick residence. 11/03/78.

Lake-Bell House, north of Prairie Grove. Circa-1870 brick house with Greek Revival detailing. 11/08/74.

Prairie Grove Battlefield Park (as amended), Hwy. 62. Site of December 7, 1862, Civil War battle. Originally listed: 09/04/70. Amended: 11/09/92.

Southern Mercantile Building, 107 E. Buchanan. 1920 vernacular commercial building. 06/14/90.

SAVOY

Lake Wedington Historic District, junction of Hwy. 16 and Forest Service Rd. 1750. Collection of recreational structures built in 1936 and 1937 through Soil Conservation Service and Works Progress Administration. 09/11/95.

SPRINGDALE

Dodson Memorial Building, Pleasant St. and Emma Ave. 1931 structure combines Craftsman and English Revival styles. 09/04/92.

Fishback School, Hwy. 68N. 1925 Plain Traditional building with Colonial Revival influences. 09/04/92.

House at 712 North Mill Street, 712 M. Mill St. Circa-1914 Craftsman Bungalow. 09/04/92.

Old Springdale High School, Johnson St. 1909–10 Romanesque Revival design by A. O. Clark. 05/19/94.

Rabbit's Foot Lodge, 3600 Silent Grove Rd. 1908 log structure owned by Sen. J. William Fulbright. 09/11/86.

Shiloh Church, Huntsville and Main Sts. 1870 meeting hall. 06/05/75.

Shiloh Historic District, bounded by Spring Creek, Shiloh, Main, Johnson, and Mill Sts. Sites and structures dating from 1830 to 1930. 08/31/78.

SPRING VALLEY

Spring Valley School District 120 Building, County Rd. 379. 1934 Plain Traditional–style structure. 09/04/92.

TONTITOWN

Bariola House, 329 Ardemagni Rd. 1910–15 stone structure built to house families of three brothers. 03/05/92.

Tontitown School Building, Hwy. 412. Circa-1920 Plain Traditional–style building with Classical details. 09/04/92.

VINEY GROVE

Washington County Road 80F Bridge, County Rd. 80F over Muddy Fork of Illinois River. 1940 steel through-truss bridge erected by Works Progress Administration. 05/05/95.

WEST FORK

Mineral Springs Community Building, County Rd. 34. Simple 1915 school, church, and meeting hall. 05/29/98.

S. A. Kimbrough House
detail, Beebe, White County.

WINSLOW

Devil's Den State Park Historic District, Hwy. 74 near Winslow. Cabins and other site features built around 1936 by Civilian Conservation Corps. 06/24/94.

ADDRESS RESTRICTED

Bluff Point. Circa-1500 rock art site. 05/04/82.

Brown Bluff. 100–1600 A. D. Mississippian site. 06/24/87.

Nathan Combs House. Circa-1868 brick farmhouse. 12/12/76.

WHITE COUNTY

BALD KNOB

Brown House, east side of Elm St. Circa-1925 Craftsman house. 09/13/91.

Campbell-Chrisp House, 102 Elm St. Circa-1899 mixture of Romanesque Revival and Colonial Revival styles. 09/05/91.

Elm Street House, south side of Elm St. Circa-1925 Craftsman house. 09/13/91.

Fox Motel House, Hwy. 367. Circa-1925 Craftsman structure. 07/12/92.

Jameson-Richards Cafe, Hwy. 367. Circa-1931 vernacular English Revival design. 09/05/91.

Jameson-Richards Gas Station, Hwy. 367 and Vine St. Circa-1931 vernacular English Revival structure. 09/05/91.

Jim Wright Farmstead Historic District, State Hwy. 258. Eight structures and site features dating from 1890 to 1939. 09/05/91.

Luke Bone Grocery–Boarding House, Main and Market Sts. Circa-1915 vernacular commercial structure. 09/13/91.

Methodist Episcopal Church, South, Main and Center Sts. 1927 mixture of English Revival and Gothic Revival styles. 07/20/92.

Milt Gooden House, County Rd. 83. Circa-1921 double-pen vernacular house. 07/13/92.

Missouri-Pacific Railroad Depot, Market and Ramey Sts. 1915 Colonial Revival depot. 07/20/92.

Moody House, 104 Market St. Circa-1914 gable-entry structure. 07/20/92.

Saint Richard's Catholic Church, Hickory and Cleveland Sts. 1939 Rustic-style church. 07/20/92.

Sam Cooley Barn, County Rd. 96. Circa-1920 barn with gable-roof vents. 07/11/92.

BEEBE

Beebe Jail, east of junction of N. Main and Illionis Sts. 1935 Works Progress Administration–built jail. 09/13/91.

Beebe Theater, Center St. Circa-1930 vernacular brick structure. 09/05/91.

Berry House, 208 Hickory St. Circa-1930 Craftsman house. 09/05/91.

Col. Ralph Andrews House, 517 W. Center St. 1885 vernacular frame house. 09/05/91.

Cross House, 410 S. Main St. Circa-1900 vernacular frame house. 07/10/92.

Hill Farm, north of Hwy. 67 southwest of Beebe. 1928 Craftsman house. 07/21/92.

Laws-Jarvis House, 409 N. Main St. Circa-1880 vernacular Greek Revival design. 07/22/92.

Lemay House, 305 S. Cypress St. Circa-1890 vernacular frame house. 07/20/92.

Lizzie Garrard House, 221 N. Cypress St. Circa-1906 Folk Victorian house. 09/05/91.

Missouri-Pacific Depot, Center St. 1910 railroad structure. 04/24/79.

Plummer House, 314 Alabama St. Circa-1915 vernacular frame house. 07/22/92.

Powell Clothing Building, 201 N. Main St. Circa-1885 vernacular commercial design. 09/05/91.

S. A. Kimbrough House, 302 E. Illinois St. Circa-1870 vernacular frame house. 09/05/91.

Sellers House, 702 W. Center St. Circa-1925 Craftsman house. 09/05/91.

Shue House, 108 Holly St. 1935 Craftsman house. 09/05/91.

Smith-Moore House, 901 N. Main St. Circa-1880 vernacular frame house. 07/20/92.

Staggs-Huffaker Building, N. Main and W. Illinois Sts. Circa-1880 brick commercial building. 09/05/91.

Stipe Cotton Gin, Florida and Cypress Sts. Circa-1930 cotton gin. 07/20/92.

William Thomas Abington House, Center St. southwest of Hwy. 367. 1880 central-hall-plan home of doctor. 07/11/92.

BRADFORD

Arthur Williams Homestead Feed Storage Shed, Falwell Rd. Circa-1915 box and wood-frame structure. 07/23/92.

Cremane House, County Rd. 95. Circa-1910 two-story, double-pile residence. 07/10/92.

Dr. Frizell House, Hwy. 67 and Elm St. 1929 Craftsman house. 07/12/92.

Dr. Lovell House, Walnut St. east of Main St. Circa-1900 double-pen I-house. 07/20/92.

Jim Little House, north side of Walnut St. Circa-1895 vernacular frame structure. 09/05/91.

Marshall Hickmon Homestead, Hwy. 87. 1933 Craftsman house. 07/21/92.

Mason House, W. Main St. west of Walnut St. 1935 Craftsman house. 07/20/92.

Morris House, Rt. 1. 1860 vernacular house with Greek Revival elements. 12/04/78.

U. L. Hickmon Hardware Store, Main and 2nd Sts. 1925 stucco-covered commercial structure. 09/05/91.

Ward-Stout House, Front and Walnut Sts. 1932 Craftsman house. 09/05/91.

CENTER HILL

Col. John Critz Farm Springhouse, County Rd. 818. 1858 stone springhouse. 07/10/92.

Smyrna Methodist Church, Hwy. 36 east of Center Hill. Circa-1854 vernacular Greek Revival church. 07/20/92.

CLAY

Sam Ray House, State Rd. 305. Circa-1915 house with Creole floor plan. 07/23/92.

William Howell House Storm Cellar, County Rd. 47. Circa-1930 stone storm cellar. 07/20/92.

Judsonia Community Building Historic District, Judsonia, White County.

CROSBY

Gray House, County Rds. 758 and 46. Circa-1875 frame dogtrot house. 07/21/92.

Gray-Kincaid House, County Rds. 46 and 759. Circa-1910 central-hall residence. 07/21/92.

Morris Institute Dairy Barn, County Rd. 41. Circa-1930 two-story dairy barn. 07/20/92.

DENMARK

Brady Hays Homestead, Hwy. 167. Circa-1885 double-pen farmhouse with barn. 09/13/91.

William Henry Watson Homestead, County Rd. 68. Circa-1890 dogtrot residence. 07/20/92.

DONIPHAN

Doniphan Lumber Mill Historic District, Hwy. 167. Circa-1905 lumber-mill complex. 09/13/91.

EL PASO

David Doyle House Number Two, County Rd. 953 and State Rd. 5. Circa-1904 vernacular frame house. 09/05/91.

El Paso Bank, County Rd. 3. 1912 vernacular commercial structure. 09/05/91.

FLOYD

Ackins House, State Rds. 31 and 305. Circa-1880 vernacular frame structure. 01/11/92.

Floyd Cotton Gin, Hwys. 31 and 305. Circa-1930 gin from heyday of cotton farming. 07/12/92.

L. D. Hutchinson House, State Rd. 31. 1914 vernacular home of prominent citizen. 07/22/92.

FOURMILE HILL

Thomas House, County Rd. 751. Circa-1905 vernacular frame house. 07/23/92.

GARNER

Walker Homestead Historic District, County Rd. 56. Six historic structures built between 1850 to 1930. 07/20/92.

GRAVEL HILL

Gravel Hill Baptist Church, Gravel Hill Rd. 1935 Rustic-style structure. 07/21/92.

GRIFFITHVILLE

A. J. Smith House, State Rd. 385. Circa-1887 vernacular frame house. 09/05/91.

Griffithville School, Hwy. 11. 1939 Works Progress Administration Craftsman design. 07/13/92.

J. A. Neaville House, Hwy. 385 north of junction with Hwy. 11. 1917 Craftsman house. 07/22/92.

HOLLY SPRINGS

Joe Emmer House, County Rd. 47. Circa-1890 single-pen log house. 07/12/92.

HOPEWELL

Hopewell District Number Forty-Five School, Hwy. 258 west of Lake Bald Knob. Circa-1939 WPA structure. 07/13/92.

JUDSONIA

Alfred W. Henson House, 111 Main St. 1884 Neoclassical structure. 10/23/86.

Captain Larned House, Hwy. 157. Circa-1905 Folk Victorian design. 07/22/92.

C. D. Kelly House, Main and Adams. Circa-1925 Craftsman house. 09/05/91.

Grand Army of the Republic Memorial, Evergreen Cemetery. 1894 commemorative monument and burial plot. 05/03/96.

Hoag House, State Rds. 157 and 367. Circa-1900 box house with Folk Victorian details. 07/21/92.

Jack Wood House, east side of Judson Ave. One-and-one-half story box-construction residence built in 1890. 11/02/89.

James W. Edie House, Jackson and Washington Sts. Circa-1883 frame vernacular house. 09/05/91.

Judsonia Bridge, County Rd. 66 over Little Red River. 1924 cantilevered swing bridge. 04/09/90.

Judsonia Community Building Historic District, Judson and 6th. 1939 Works Progress Administration–built community center. 09/05/91.

Judsonia High School Gymnasium, west side of Broadman Ave. 1937 WPA-built frame gym. 09/13/91.

KENSETT

Fred Hall House, 2nd and W. Searcy. Circa-1930 Craftsman house. 09/05/91.

Mills House, 200 W. Searcy. 1921 Craftsman house. 09/05/91.

Robertson House, 2nd and Dandridge. Circa-1910 vernacular frame house. 09/05/91.

LETONA

Letona Hotel, Letona. Circa-1910 vernacular frame structure. 09/13/91.

Martindale Corn Crib, State Hwy. 310. 1924 wood-frame storage building. 07/20/92.

Wesley Marsh House, State Rds. 16 and 305. Circa-1900 vernacular residence. 07/20/92.

LITTLE RED

Joe Brown House and Farmstead, County Rd. 529. Circa-1890 frame double-pen house. 09/13/91.

Leggett House, State Rd. 124. Circa-1870 house with circa-1905 additions. 07/13/92.

LONE STAR

Lone Star School, east of Big Mingo Creek near Lone Star. Circa-1920 frame school building. 07/20/92.

MCRAE

Booth-Weir House, W. 1st St. 1911 home of businessman and doctor. 09/05/91.

Caldwell House, E. 2nd and Smith Sts. Circa-1925 Craftsman bungalow. 09/05/91.

Childers Farmstead, east of Hwy. 367 south of McRae. Circa-1925 Greek Revival farmhouse with outbuildings. 07/11/92.

Emmett McDonald House, County Rd. 443. Circa-1935 gable-entry house. 07/20/92.

McRae Jail, east of 1st St. 1934 jail built by Works Progress Administration. 07/20/92.

MIDWAY

Blunt House, Livestock Barn, County Rd. 357. Circa-1920 gambrel-roof barn. 07/10/92.

Edward Ransom Farmstead, Livestock and Equipment Barn, County Rd. 359. Circa-1915 frame barn with unusual log cribs. 07/22/92.

First Wood Freeman House, Searcy, White County.

John Thrasher Farmstead, off County Rd. 359 west of Hwy. 167. Circa-1885 double-pen, saddlebag design. 07/23/92.

MOUNTAIN HOME

Albert Whisinant House, State Rd. 16. Circa-1920 vernacular frame house. 07/23/92.

NEW MOUNT PISGAH

New Mount Pisgah School, between Mount Pisgah and Little Creek. 1938 fieldstone school. 07/20/92.

NIMMO

Nimmo Clubhouse, County Rd. 65. Circa-1930 box construction structure. 07/22/92.

PANGBURN

Austin Pangburn House, Main and Austin. Circa-1908 vernacular Colonial Revival house. 09/05/91.

Avanell Wright House, Main and Pine. Circa-1910 vernacular Colonial Revival design. 09/05/91.

Cary House, Searcy and Short. Circa-1910 vernacular frame house. 07/10/92.

Churchill-Hilger House, Main and Searcy. 1914 Craftsman home of prominent early Pangburn resident. 09/05/91.

Dr. McAdams House, Main and Searcy. Circa-1910 vernacular frame house. 09/13/91.

Glenn Homestead, Livestock and Equipment Barn, State Hwy. 124. Circa-1939 round-roofed barn. 07/20/92.

James William Boggs House, north side of Austin St. 1908 vernacular frame house. 09/05/91.

John Shutter House, Austin and Main. 1908 frame double-pile house. 09/05/91.

McAdams House, Maple and South. Circa-1915 vernacular frame house. 09/05/91.

Patman House, Mountain and Jackson. Circa-1920 vernacular double-pen house. 09/05/91.

Rufus Gray House, Austin and South. 1912 vernacular frame house. 09/05/91.

Walter Marsh House, Maple and Torrence. Circa-1920 vernacular double-pile house. 09/05/91.

PLAINVIEW

Emmett Miller House, Hwy. 371 east of Plainview. 1938 Craftsman house. 07/20/92.

Louis Gray Homestead, Barn, State Hwy. 127. Circa-1932 frame gambrel-roof barn. 07/21/92.

Rock Building, County Rd. 370. Circa-1915 vernacular fieldstone structure. 07/23/92.

Thomas Hunt House, State Rd. 157. Circa-1885 frame double-pen house. 07/22/92.

PROVIDENCE

Big Four School Building, County Rd. 383. 1930s Works Progress Administration redesign of 1915 school. 07/10/92.

J. C. Rhew Company Packing Shed, County Rd. 376. Circa-1940 strawberry-crating shed and picker residence. 07/23/92.

Louis N. Hilger Homestead Livestock/Equipment Barn, County Rd. 374. Circa-1939 braced-frame barn. 07/21/92.

Stanley Simpson Farmstead and Picking Shed, County Rd. 390. Circa-1930 mobile wood strawberry-storage structure. 09/13/91.

Tobe Hoofman Farmstead, County Rd. 67. Four circa-1910 buildings on subsistence farm. 07/22/92.

ROMANCE

Pence-Carmichael Farm Barn and Root Cellar, off Hwy. 31 east of Romance. 1910 barn with unusual floor plan and 1935 stone root cellar. 07/20/92.

Roy Harper House, County Rd. 16. Circa-1912 box-construction house. 07/21/92.

Scott-Davis House, County Rd. 15. Circa-1905 central-hall adaptation of circa-1869 log dogtrot. 07/20/92.

ROSEBUD

E. D. Maddox Farm and Chicken House, County Rd. 36. 1938 structure with open, diagonal framing. 07/20/92.

RUSSELL

Harvey Lea House, County Rd. 70. 1925 Craftsman house. 07/13/92.

Henry Klotz Sr. House, 1st St. 1921 house ordered from Sears, Roebuck and Co. catalogue. 07/22/92.

Henry W. Klotz Service Station, W. 1st St. 1938 fieldstone commercial structure. 09/13/91.

Howard O'Neal Barn, County Rd. 73. Circa-1938 transverse-crib barn. 07/20/92.

Russell Jail, off Elm St. Circa-1935 Works Progress Administration–built jail. 07/23/92.

Weber House, north side of Elm St. 1933 Craftsman house. 09/05/91.

SEARCY

American Legion Hall, north side of Race St. 1939 fieldstone structure. 09/13/91.

Arnold Farmstead, north side of McRae Ave. Six 1925 structures from suburban farmstead. 09/13/91.

Arthur W. Hoofman House, E. Race and N. Cross. Circa-1931 English Revival design. 07/22/92.

Arthur W. Woodson House, 1005 W. Arch Ave. 1923 Craftsman bungalow. 09/05/91.

Baldock House, S. Elm and Woodruff. 1910 vernacular brick house. 09/05/91.

Bank of Searcy, 301 N. Spruce St. Circa-1905 Classical Revival structure. 09/05/91.

Bell House, 302 W. Woodruff Ave. 1925 Craftsman house. 09/05/91.

Benjamin Clayton Black House, 300 E. Race St. 1874 Italianate residence. 11/20/74.

Ben Lightle House, N. Locust and E. Market. 1898 Folk Victorian house. 09/05/91.

Bloom House, N. Maple and Academy. Circa-1930 Craftsman house. 09/05/91.

Bob Rogers House, S. Spring and W. Woodruff. Circa-1870 Greek Revival I-house. 09/13/91.

Brooks House, 704 E. Market. Circa-1935 English Revival design. 07/10/92.

Burnett House, County Rd. 766. Circa-1870 vernacular frame house. 07/11/92.

Coward House, 1105 N. Maple St. Circa-1915 vernacular brick house. 07/10/92.

Cumberland Presbyterian Church, north side of E. Race St. 1903 Romanesque Revival/Classical Revival structure. 07/10/92.

Dalton Woodson House, 1007 W. Arch Ave. 1929 English Revival design. 09/05/91.

Dean L. C. Sears House, 805 E. Center. 1935 English Revival house with Rustic details. 07/20/92.

Deener House, 310 E. Center. Circa-1912 Charles L. Thompson Craftsman design. 12/22/82.

Dr. Emmett Snipes House, S. Market and N. Locust. Circa-1900 Folk Victorian house with Colonial Revival elements. 09/05/91.

First Christian Church, N. Main and E. Market. 1925 Classical Revival design. 07/12/92.

First United Methodist Church, Main and Market. 1877 English Gothic Revival design. 07/12/92.

First Wood Freeman House, 702 Arch Ave. Circa-1934 English Revival design. 09/05/91.

Greene Booth House, S. Pecan and W. Center. Circa-1925 Craftsman house. 09/05/91.

Hassell House, S. Elm and W. Woodruff. Circa-1910 vernacular brick house. 09/05/91.

Hicks-Dugan-Deener House, 306 E. Center. Circa-1855 Greek Revival house. 04/18/85.

Honey Hill Christian Union Church, County Rd. 54. 1925 Craftsman church. 07/21/92.

Hoofman Farmstead Barn, between Plainview and the Little Red River near Searcy. Circa-1920 stone outbuilding. 07/22/92.

Hunt House, 707 W. Center. Circa-1935 English Revival design. 09/13/91.

Ida Hicks House, 410 W. Arch Ave. 1913 Craftsman house. 09/05/91.

Jesse N. Cypert Law Office, 104 E. Race St. Circa-1880 vernacular brick commercial structure. 07/12/92.

Joiner House, 708 E. Market. 1928 English Revival house. 07/22/92.

Lattimer House, Oak and Market. Circa-1895 Queen Anne Revival house. 09/05/91.

Lightle House, 107 N. Elm St. 1918 Colonial Revival design with Craftsman elements. 09/05/91.

Lightle House, 605 E. Race St. 1923 Thompson Colonial Revival design. 12/22/82.

Lightle House, County Rd. 76. Circa-1920 vernacular saddlebag structure. 07/20/92.

Mark P. Jones House, Center and Fir. Circa-1928 English Revival design. 09/05/91.

Mary Alice Hammond House, County Rd. 839. Circa-1870 vernacular wood-frame house. 07/21/92.

Mayfair Hotel, Spring and Center. 1924 Spanish Revival design. 09/05/91.

Moore House, 405 Center. Circa-1925 Folk Victorian/Craftsman house. 09/13/91.

National Guard Armory Building, Race and Locust Sts. 1930 Art Deco design. 09/13/91.

Paschall House, N. Oak and E. Center. Circa-1890 brick I-house. 09/05/91.

Pattie Cobb Hall, Harding University, 900 E. Center. 1919 Colonial Revival structure. 09/05/91.

Porter Rodgers Sr. House, N. Oak and E. Race Sts. Circa-1925 Colonial Revival house. 09/05/91.

Rascoe House, 702 Main St. Circa-1915 vernacular residence. 07/23/92.

Rialto Theater, Race and Spring. 1940 Art Deco design. 09/13/91.

Robertson Drugstore, Spring and Arch. Circa-1860 commercial building. 09/13/91.

Searcy City Hall, Gum and Race. 1939 Works Progress Administration project. 09/05/91.

Searcy Confederate Monument, W. Arch Ave. and Spring St. 1917 commemorative sculpture. 04/26/96.

Searcy Post Office, Gum and Arch. 1914 Italian Renaissance design. 07/20/92.

Second Wood Freeman House, 703 W. Race St. Circa-1935 English Revival house. 09/05/91.

Smith House, 607 W. Arch Ave. Circa-1920 Sears, Roebuck and Co. house model #264P202. 09/05/91.

Titus House, 406 E. Center. Circa-1925 Craftsman house. 09/05/91.

Tom Watkins House, Oak and Race Sts. Circa-1920 Thompson Craftsman design. 09/05/91.

Trinity Episcopal Church, east side of N. Elm St. Circa-1902 English parish church design. 07/23/92.

Watkins House, 1208 E. Race St. 1919–20 Colonial Revival design with Craftsman elements. 09/05/91.

White County Courthouse, Court Square. Classical 1870 courthouse with 1912 additions. 08/03/77.

Wilburn House, 707 E. Race St. Circa-1875 Greek Revival design. 09/05/91.

William H. Lightle House, 601 E. Race St. 1881 house with Italianate details. 09/05/91.

Williams House, County Rd. 54 and State Rd. 267. Circa-1910 vernacular frame house. 07/23/92.

STEPROCK

Morris Hartsell Farmstead, Hwy 157. Circa-1880 farmstead with double-pen, log-and-frame house and outbuildings. 09/13/91.

STEVENS CREEK

Chandler House, County Rds. 327 and 379. Circa-1885 vernacular frame house. 07/10/92.

Holly Grove School, County Rd. 379. 1939 National Youth Administration design. 07/13/92.

Thompson House, Holly Grove Cemetery and County Rd. 328. Circa-1890 vernacular frame residence. 07/23/92.

TWENTYTHREE

Leonard Gordon Homestead Hexagonal Grain Crib, County Rd. 69. Circa-1920 hexagonal structure. 07/21/92.

VELVET RIDGE

Prince House, County Rd. 68. Circa-1920 double-pen box house. 07/22/92.

VINITY CORNER

Thomas Jefferson Hale General Merchandise Store, County Rds. 62 and 433. 1925 sheet-metal-sided commercial structure. 07/21/92.

WEST POINT

Otha Walker Homestead, State Rd. 36. Circa-1915 central-hall house. 07/23/92.

ADDRESS RESTRICTED

Darden-Gifford House. 1887 vernacular Queen Anne residence. 01/01/76.

Augusta Presbyterian Church, Augusta, Woodruff County.

WOODRUFF COUNTY

AUGUSTA

Augusta Bridge, Hwy. 64 over White River. 1930 double-cantilevered bridge. 04/09/90.

Augusta Presbyterian Church, 3rd and Walnut. 1871 Gothic Revival church. 10/16/86.

Ferguson House, 416 N. 3rd St. 1861 Greek Revival residence. 12/06/75.

Woodruff County Courthouse, 500 N. 3rd St. 1901 Charles L. Thompson Richardsonian Romanesque design. 12/22/82.

YELL COUNTY

BELLEVILLE VICINITY

Spring Lake Bridge, Hwy. 307 over Bob Barnes Branch. 1936 masonry-arch bridge built by United States Resettlement Administration. 06/21/90.

DARDANELLE

Dardanelle Agriculture and Post Office, 103 N. Front St. 1937 structure featuring Depression-era mural. 08/14/98.

Dardanelle Confederate Monument, Union and Front Sts. 1921 commemorative sculpture. 04/26/96.

First Presbyterian Church, 2nd and Quay. 1912 Neoclassical structure. 07/09/87.

First Presbyterian Church–Berry House, 203 Pecan St. 1872 church remodeled circa 1912 to reflect Craftsman style of architecture. 06/03/98.

John C. Brooks House (Steamboat House), 601 N. Front St. Circa-1889 "Steamboat Gothic" design. 06/05/75.

Kimball House, 715 N. Front St. 1876 Italianate structure. 06/23/82.

Methodist Episcopal Church, South, northwest corner of Locust Dr. and 2nd St. 1891 structure remodeled to Prairie style in 1917. 11/07/96.

Pavilion, north of Hwy. 155 at Mount Nebo State Park. Circa-1935 Civilian Conservation Corps–built recreational facility. 06/01/92.

Yell County Courthouse, 209 Union St. 1914 Classical Revival design by architect Frank W. Gibb. 09/08/92.

PLAINVIEW

Mountain View Farm, County Rd. 218. 1917 American Foursquare house with numerous historic outbuildings. 11/07/96.

STAFFORD

Spring Lake Recreation Area Historic District, Forest Service Rd. 1602. 1937 recreational facility built by Works Progress Administration. 09/11/95.

WALTREAK

Mitchell House, Hwy. 80. Circa-1891 dogtrot house with Greek Revival details. 06/07/90.

John C. Brooks House
(Steamboat House),
Dardanelle, Yell County.

INDEX